ISBN: 9781314187199

Published by:
HardPress Publishing
8345 NW 66TH ST #2561
MIAMI FL 33166-2626

Email: info@hardpress.net
Web: http://www.hardpress.net

IRISH TEXTS SOCIETY

CUMANN NA SGRÍBHEANN GAEDHILGE

VOL. XXIII

[1921]

1926

THE BARDIC POEMS

OF

TADHG DALL Ó HUIGINN

(1550 — 1591)

VOL. II

TRANSLATION, NOTES ETC.

A BHFUIL AGUINN

DÁR CHUM

TADHG DALL Ó HUIGINN

(1550 — 1591)

IDIR

MHOLADH AGUS MARBHNADH
AOIR AGUS ÁBHACHT
IOMARBHÁIGH AGUS IOMCHASAOID

ELEANOR KNOTT

DO CHUIR I N-EAGAR

AGUS

D'AISTRIG GO BÉARLA SAXAN

II

AISTRIÚ, NÓTAÍ 7RL.

LÚNDAIN

SIMPKIN, MARSHALL, HAMILTON, KENT & CO., LTD.
D'FHOILLSIGH
AR SON
CHUMAINN NA SGRÍBHEANN GAEDHILGE
[1921]
1926

CONTENTS OF VOLUME TWO

Page

1

TO CONN O'DONNELL

1　Raise the veil from Ireland; long hath she sought a spouse, finding no mate for her couch after the happiness of the men of *Fál* was blasted.

2　It is long since the Isle of Bregia could discover herself to any; a luckless widow is the wife of *Flann*—land of splendid stone dwellings.

3　She could not but lose her beauty, it is thus with uncared for women; Ireland, land of sparkling, melodious streams, hath the complexion of loneliness.

4　Ushnagh's castle, darling of kings, hath been brought to such a state that it is a sorrowful omen to watch over the fair, modest contours of her bright countenance.

·5　Ireland's capitals have been defiled, one after another; a garment of weeds invests each keep, the white rampart of every castle is become a trench.

6　Her round hills have been stripped, her boundaries plowed over, so that *Té*'s Rampart, with its firm (?) dwellings of white masonry, is not recognized by the guides.

7　Nought remains of them save their traces, they have exchanged comeliness for uncomeliness; the brightly-tapestried castles of Niall's *Banbha*—a cause of sorrow are they.

8　Howbeit, we think the more lightly of this mournful gloom which hangs over Ireland, since for *Té*'s Rampart, which was named of Art, succour hath been foretold.

E. Knott, Tadhg Dall Ó Huiginn.　　　　　　　I

9   It is in store for it that a man shall come to dissolve its enchantments; needs must, then, that he shall one day take possession of the Field of the Gaels.

10   For thee, Conn, son of the Calvach, many a prophet hath truly foretold thee—it is fitting that you should seek one another—Ireland hath been waiting.

11   Alas, thou graceful of form, for him who does not give some thing of her desire to the smooth, yew-timbered, bright rampart, first couch of Conn and *Cobhthach*.

12   Look frequently on her bright countenance, bend thine eye upon her in secret; approach her graceful form, speak covertly with Ireland.

13   Embrace her, go to her couch, thou beautiful yet icy of flesh: take to thee the spouse of *Lugh*, lest Ireland be left unwedded.

14   Press the lips like berry-bloom, and the shining, snow-white teeth, in a kiss to Bregia of the smooth hill, amidst the welcome of the five provinces.

15   Great Niall, son of *Eachaidh*, from whom thou art sprung, O bright-cheeked countenance, bestowed just such a kiss, whereby he united (under his sway) the fair Dwelling of Eber.

16   Another such kiss gave Brian of *Bóroimhe*, by which he gained without dispute, thou white of hand, that stately dwelling place of the Sons of *Míl*.

17   As with other women in manifold enchantments, thou canst procure with a kiss the release of tearful *Banbha*, O white-footed, black-lashed youth.

18   As with women under enchantments, Ireland, land of rippling waterfalls, plain of great fins, of shallow streams, will be the possession of him who rescues her.

19 Long ere her time there was a woman even as
this country of the Sons of *Mil,* in ancient Africa, sandy,
bright, of fertile hills, many-rivered, salmonful.

20 The man of yore who loved the princess of the
wondrous isles changed the white-handed maiden of the
soft, shining hair into a great, forbidding she-dragon.

21 The daughter of Hippocrates, son of *Nil,* spent
a while in dragon's shape, under many and manifold
enchantments, from which it had been difficult to rescue her.

22 Be the reason what it may, for one day in each
year, in order to rekindle her sorrow, the gift of beauty
was granted to her sparkling, youthful countenance.

23 A merchant's son from the land of the west went
to her once upon a time, and found the bright, sweetly-
speaking, womanly beauty in her modest maiden's form.

24 He set the desire of his heart upon the woman,
and prayed that the lovely, shining-haired one might be
a mate for his own bright figure, though to seek her
was a cause of remorse.

25 The bright-eyed queen replied, "I would be thine
were it possible, thou wondrous, comely youth, long-handed,
gentle, dark-browed."

26 "By consent or force thou shalt be mine," said the
brown-lashed youth. "I have forsaken the glances of
man, it cannot be," returned the maiden.

27 "At all other times I am in the shape of a fiery
dragon, so that my face (though now) smooth, modestly
blushing, beloved, is horrifying to behold."

28 "Is help in store for thee in days to come?" said
the youth, "thou bright form, with clear countenance,
when dost thou expect thy deliverance?"

29 "It is destined for me that a knight from the
warriors of *Féilim's* Land shall come when I am in
dragon's shape, with a kiss whereby I shall be delivered.

1*

30　The compassionate warrior shall be a husband to me, it is destined for him that he shall be made king over the islands, a thing difficult to accomplish."

31　"It is destined for me", said the youth, "I am from Ireland, to bestow that kiss which shall quench thy rage, thou curly-haired maiden, so young and noble."

32　"How could the thing thou sayest be destined for thee, my heart's fruit?" said the stately maiden, "since thou hast never been a knight."

33　On hearing that, the merchant's son took orders of chivalry; he departed from the rosy maiden of the soft, shining hair to learn a strange calling.

34　At the break of day he came again to visit the maiden; astonishing was the state in which he found the gracious beauty of the fair, soft tresses.

35　He found in the early morn the graceful figure with smooth brows, and the smooth, silky, heavy, luxuriant tresses, transformed into an awesome, fiery dragon.

36　On beholding the terrifying monster he fled in panic; that expedition ended in his death; a case not easy to succour.

37　The daughter of Hippocrates then returned to her chamber, and the heart of the white-footed, sweet-voiced maiden was full of sorrow.

38　She vowed that from that day on she would arise for no man until the coming of the prophesied one who was destined to release her from her bonds.

39　And even yet—long is the suffering—her gray modest-lashed eye, her pleasing form, her rosy countenance await her deliverer.

40　Ireland is that woman, O silky of hair, thou art the man who shall deliver Ireland; and the hideous visage of the dragon is the tormenting host of ruthless foreigners.

41   Draw near to her, thou curly-headed one, do not shrink from the dragonlike aspect which clothes the sweet, beguiling streams of the Boyne; deliver Ireland from her disfigurement.

42   Many say of thee, Conn, descendant of Conn the Hundredfighter, thou heedest not that *Cobhthach's* Plain has been for some time in the custody of foreigners.

43   They are right, O bright countenance, not very thankful are the Sons of *Míl* to thee, Conn, son of the Calvach, as regards the famed land of bright apple-trees.

44   Even though thou mayst not be supreme in the Land of the Gaels, thou thick-haired one, it is in thy power, Conn, to free the country of *Banbha* from its fetters.

45   It is easy for thee to win triumphs, the Sons of *Míl* are eager for war; it needs few forays, thou man of the Inny, to stir up *Banbha.*

46   A house takes fire from the one beside it; if thy intention of battle be heard, from thy head of wavy tresses the rest will take it; it is a ready desire that is ignited.

47   Even as the spreading of a flame, throughout this Plain of *Cobhthach* every territory will have its own reaver, from thy raids upon the foreign soldiery.

48   And the result, O wondrous form, shall be that the people of every territory, together with thee, O face ruddy as the berry, from which the stream is calm, shall storm the dividing boundaries of Gael and foreigner.

49   Take command of them, Conn, and lead them to Frewen; thou bright-handed warrior of Bregia, revivify the soldiery of the Gael.

50   Forsake not for Donegal, or the bay of *Eas Dá Eagann*, or ancient Loch Foyle, of the sparkling wines, the royal rampart of Tara in the east,

51   Alas, if anyone found that for the cocket of Sligo Bay, or for bright Croghan of the fair equipment thou wouldst abandon ancient Tara of *Tuathal Teachtmhar*.

52   The words of soothsayers, the utterances of saints, mate her with thee, O wavy tresses: did they not prophesy of yore the salmon from Frewen's fair harbor?

53   Prophets of thy rule, thou lord of *Bearnas,* are the promise of fruit on the green-leafed bough, the fury of the stream bearing its produce, the wave concealed beneath the washed-up treasure.

54   Abundance of milk from a small number of cattle, abundance of corn stacks before summer, and — soothsayers through whom thou art most clearly recognized — the ruined buildings of the churches repaired.

55   Thou at the service of all, and all submitting to thee; thou above everyone, and everyone above thee; thou at the pleasure of every man, and for all that, the Gaels at thy mercy.

56   The noble Gaels welcome thee to this enterprise, O cheerful heart; as a woman with her unlawful mate, so is Ireland with thy warriors.

2

TO HUGH O'DONNELL

1 Welcome, thou son of Manus, from blue-harbored Tirconell; hasten, bright face, to Croghan's long-speared host.

2 Hasten to us, if thou art coming; to the north a visit is enough; make thy dwelling in Connacht, thou lord of the Ultonian plain.

3 Hasten thee, gentle (?) countenance, to view the province of *Ól nEagmocht;* be not laggard of foot, come hither, admit no hindrance about it.

4 Welcome to thee, come hither, and gather thy noble assembly; make a full hosting, and advance through the fresh, bright-surfaced plain of Connacht.

5 Assemble the warriors of Ulster, it is long since they have been assembled, to check the contest of the tribes of Conn with thy thick, soft, gold-brown locks.

6 Ask of the seed of *Suibhne,* thou chief of Mourne, if they are grieved that the Connachtmen are contending with the powerful striplings of Ulster's land.

7 Say to the clans of noble Niall that they should make a union and alliance; display to them their great ties with us, thou golden king amongst chessmen.

8 Bring to us one after another the seed of *Eóghan,* the race of Conall, around thy bright, modestly-flushing face, to seek the tributes of the province.

9 Gather around thy brightly fringed locks thy battle-allies, thy marriage connections, and the host from *Liathdruim*'s walled castle—Colla's mighty kindred, so smooth of skin.

10 Though we speak thus, we know that on the day of the hosting thou needest only the descendants of noble *Dálach* of Bregia, the many-gifted ones of the five provinces.

11 Those four sections yonder of the race that sprang from Conall—all the armies of Tara would not be capable of fighting against them.

12 *Dálach*'s race, they of the smooth-walled fortresses, the race of *Dochartach*. the host of *Baoigheall*'s seed, and *Gallchobhar*'s bright, haughty stock, from whom the Ulstermen are without rest.

13 Those are the four battalions that follow the high-prince, disturbers of Conn's *Banbha*, valiant raiders of Conall's race.

14 Should the men of Ireland fail thee, the proven warriors of the four battalions, the champions of Tara's hill, will gain for thee the headship of Connacht.

15 Bring with thee the four-hosted seed of Conall in their full strength, that the plain of Croghan, delightful country, of fertile nooks, may be brought under rule.

16 Until thou avenge all that thou hast undergone, make neither peace nor settlement about the rich territory of *Sreang*'s ancient line, thine inherited portion of Ireland.

17 Be not satisfied until thou art here, we know, O bright bosom, that when the race of Conall shall have arisen, it is not yonder they will make peace with us.

18 Thou needst not fear to entrust thyself to them, until the assemblies of that race of Conall be simultaneously laid low thou art not likely to be overthrown in despite of them.

19   It were unfitting for thee to seek other aid, it befits that race of Conall, O shapely of form and white of hand, to do their utmost for thee.

20   Few among them, O modest eye, but are either beloved, worthy fosterers, or goodly fostersons, or sometime fosterbrothers to thee, thou fair-cheeked one.

21   Those who are older than thou are as thy fosterers, while the offspring of the rest are thy goodly fosterchildren, thou prophesied one of the Plain of Cormac.

22   Just such words as these Conall of *Cruacha* uttered long ago on *Magh Léana*, thou star of Sligo's host.

23   It was a day when battle was declared against Conn on *Magh Léana*, at the instigation of foreigners, by fearless *Hugh Nuadhad,* head with a sheltering mane of sleekly waving locks.

24   Around famed *Hugh Nuadhad,* with one accord, gather the pick of the men of Ireland, save only—princely, unconquered troop—the valiant (?) men of Connacht.

25   Conn had with him but the men of Connacht, for his protection in battle against the forces of all the rest of Ireland, warriors with sleek, shapely steeds.   ·

26   "Too few for us are the Connachtmen," said Conn, in converse with Conall, "seeing that all Ireland is opposing us, thou soft, smooth and gentle of countenance."

27   "The men of Ireland, from sea to sea," such were the words of Cònall, "should not make thee to quail whilst thou art amongst the hosts of the plain of Connacht."

28   "Fosterer, fosterchild, or fosterbrother to thee," said Conall, "is everyone in the plain of Croghan, O yellow of hair, O beloved of women."

29   "The elders of Connacht, one and all," continued Conall, "are fosterers to thee, thou gentle, fair, black-lashed youth."

30 "Those of thine own age, O stately eye, are thy foster brethren," said Conall, "since thou wast reared, thou bright of cheek, along with the people of Telton's smooth hills."

31 "To end," said Conall of *Cruacha*, our diffident (?) youths are all fostersons to thee, thou horseman of the Plain of the Champion."

32 "Why, therefore, shouldst thou think thy number too small?" continued the high-king's fosterer, "a host of united friends are here, we shall not stir one foot in thy despite."

33 The battle of the morn is won by Conn, sleek of hair, over *Hugh Nuadhad*; well did Conall fulfil his good pledge to Conn.

34 And thus it is with thee, O'Donnell, thou shalt feel no inferiority in combat, while amongst Conall's warlike stock, O slender, powerful stately-eyed one.

35 O lion of the Erne, there is but one province opposing thee, whilst all Ireland, save Conall, was unitedly attacking Conn.

36 There are many trusty officers as good as Conall around thy dark-lashed cheek; (they are to thee) even as in his day Conn's Conall was to his king.

37 Even as Conn set his trust in the troops of Croghan, and in Conall, set thou thy trust in thy foster-brethren, and in the goodly youth of *Murbhach*.

38 Better these about the warrior of the Plain of the Fair than seven times their number of a summoned and pressed army from the other territories of Ireland.

39 As long as that fierce, watchful host survive, thou wilt fear little vexation, O crimson-bladed champion of *Oileach*.

40 What is it that hinders thee from coming to confront the men of Connacht, continually despoiling the men of Ireland—warriors with lithe, docile steeds?

41 And yet, I understand the reason of thy delay,
thou ruler of fair *Fainn's* plain; it is because the firmly-
dyked plain of Connacht has no means to withstand thee.

42 It oppresses thy mind, Hugh, that Maeve's land,
with fair, noble ramparts, should be spoiled by its own
folk, although you are at variance.

43 Thou wouldst rather it were lost to thee wholly,
O bright countenance, than that it should be destroyed
between you; I think the babe is thine, O sleek-browed,
supple-handed youth.

44 Hast thou heard of the women's dispute, or of the
royal judgment which Solomon pronounced, thou stately
scion from the rippling Moy, about the halving of the babe?

45 One day there came before Solomon two strange
women, a comely, youthful-looking, bright pair, carrying
between them a single infant.

46 Each of the women had come directly to him
to certify that the babe was hers, in order that he might
confirm that.

47 "Since you have no witness in this matter regarding
the babe, I would fain divide it between you." said the
sage of the world.

48 "It is a good decision," said one of the women,
"that great Solomon, son of David, has given us concerning
the rosy, supple-armed offspring: that the child should
be divided between us."

49 "I had rather my own babe were out of harm's
way even shouldst thou have it altogether," replied the
other woman.

50 "Thou art the mother of the boy," said the judge
famed for his awards; "assuredly he has been in thy
womb, thou dost not allow the child to be divided."

51 Even thus, Hugh, son of Manus—where am I
telling it of thee?—thou hast not ravaged the plain of
Connacht on account of wrong or transgression.

52 Since it is thine, thou smooth and soft of skin, thou wouldst not ravage Connacht, O blameless hand; the babe was begot by thee.

53 Thou hast spared Conn's Croghan, thou hast protected the haven of ancient, clear-streamed Sligo against Conall's line, in spite of the impatient men of Ulster.

54 Didst thou follow the counsel of the rest, Telton would be in a blaze, and Croghan dismantled; listen not to their entreaties.

55 Even wert thou thyself attacking them, on account of the Ineen Duv, thou torrential stream from the Bregian Boyne, it would not be possible to devastate them.

56 In any province where that woman is, none dare to talk of strife; the Land of *Fionntan* has shown (?) that she has curbed the race of Conall.

57 Until the daughter of James came to us, and until the land of Bregia became subdued to her will, we would not keep peace with the rest for the twinkling of an eye.

58 From the time that she came across the sea the race of *Dálach*, on account of the queen of *Cobha*'s pure plain, do not remember in their hearts the offences of others.

3

TO HUGH O'DONNELL

1 The race of Conall will praise the children of *Tál,* may hap that these plunderings of Conall's Plain be a token of fortune for the seed of noble *Ros* from the gently-flowing Maigue.

2 For some time past the seed of Brian and that race of Conall have been coupled together; receiving praise and satire.

3 We poets of the North used to compose eulogies for the seed of red-speared Conall in provocation of the tribe of *Cas,* stems from the fair banks of the Fergus.

4 We poets of the seed of Hundred-battling Conn, have, whatever the reason, harmed the repute of the great and ancient race of *Mugh* (*Nuadhad*), valor's inherited capital.

5 We used not to compose a long poem of praise, or even one humorous stanza, without corresponding dispraise of the race of *Corc,* stems most strange to attack.

6 Fearing that we may have to approach them, we are remorseful for what we used to do against the beloved seed of *Cas,* so famed in battle.

7 It was not for the sake of cattle or golden goblets, precious jewels or mantles of red satin, that we found reasons for satirizing the fair warriors of Fermoyle.

8 But that a short time ago—sorrowful indeed—a fine poet from the northern half went yonder to the west to study his art in Munster.

9   And it befell — most harmfully — that the foreign
rulers of *Mac Con's* Munster arrested the poet of Ulster
when he was perfected in his art.

10   The poet of O'Donnell of Donegal, by the dreadful
rule of foreigners — to be brief, he was slain in the south,
which caused the simultaneous ruin of the poets.

11   It was foreign tyranny that caused them to suffer
his murder: the race of *Sadhbh* should not bear the
blame, though it befell them to commit it.

12   However, from arrogance of mind I plied the
edge of my just wrath on the tribe of *Cas*, mischievously
and pridefully.

13   I, like every other man, acted as I should not have
done towards the kindly, generous children of *Tál*, a
proceeding which enhanced my unfairness.

14   It fell out, thereafter, that war arose between the
Ulstermen and the hosts of firmly-walled Croghan; a
cause of deep flushing in bright faces.

15   It was proclaimed by the race of *Dálach* that not
even friends or comrades should be protected throughout
the land of *Oilill*, dry, bright-stoned plain, watered by
melodious streams.

16   Thereupon my kinsfolk, my own friends, oblige
me to go and seek protection and surety from the stern,
powerful kindred of *Dálach*.

17   Despite all they had lavished upon me, this I have
to say of the tribe of Conall, they had no mind to undertake my protection; unhappy the condition of the friends.

18   I do not deny that it is the same to me as if the
seed of Conall were plundering me, for the mighty
champions of *Beanna Boirche* to refuse me in the matter
of protection.

19   Having heard what they recited to me on thy behalf, Hugh O'Donnell, I am filled with wrath and impatience towards thy ruddy, bronzed, bright-cheeked countenance.

20   For thy public proscription of me, thou king of noble Conall's line, the powerfully attended host of *Murbhach* have no sufficing compensation to offer.

21   The hearts of king's children will bound, if I go from thee in enmity; fair faces will flame amongst *Almhu*'s keen-bladed host.

22   Though I am at war with the race of *Dálach* about my cattle, there went not from me into Ulster unjustly even the value of a single cow.

23   Nevertheless, I shall depose against the battalions of the haven of *Duibhlinn* that they plundered me of all that is in my home, O supple-bodied lord of Calry.

24   I shall say, O son of Manus, that thou hast wrought me harm, and requital for the harm thou hast not done me will be given, O lord of *Bearnas*.

25   It was in this fashion, O thick-haired one, that *Maol Miolsgothach* obtained of yore from the race of famous Niall that extraordinary award of goods.

26   One of the nobles of Niall's seed, thus the matter arose, met his death by *Mac Coise;* thereat they became incensed.

27   Upon the kindling of their resentment the road-skilled (?) warriors of Niall's line threaten to go and plunder the poet in return for the unseemly, woeful deed.

28   *Mac Coise* upon hearing this, went to the high-king of *Oileach*—generous hero for whom the sea was calm, helm of sovranty to Ulster.

29   Donnell grandson of Niall, then asked the poet for a story; the best of story-tellers was he, narrator of all Ireland's lore.

30   *Mac Coise* enquired if he had heard a number of entertaining stories; he named them, one after another, to the graceful, white-handed hero of *Bóroimhe*.

31   From the time that *Ceasair* took possession of the plain of Bregia, all the curious stories of the Field of the Gael were known by heart, he found, to the gallant hero of *Maonmhagh*.

32   About the destruction of his own house, then, the poet composed an original fable for his splendid, angelic countenance.

33   *Iorard* said, in short, that some of Donnell's kinsmen had destroyed his dwelling, homestead of bright, glittering stones.

34   *Oileach's* king, with braided locks, Donnell, son of *Muirchcartach*, gave to the elfin, comely countenance requital for the damage he had not wrought.

35   The breadth of his face of pure gold he gave to the poet as an honor-price; and that is but a small part of the various payments he got from the powerful chief of *Gáirighe*.

36   In return for the falsehood he had composed about the kindred of Niall, the slender-handed youths of Bregia thereupon dispensed gifts more than he could reckon to the poet.

37   The choicest of their rings, of their goblets encrusted with precious stones, did *Mac Coise, Maol Miolsgothach*—well did his bluster succeed—get in payment for the hurt they had not wrought.

38   *Mac Coise's* claim against the kindreds of Niall, as I know, O cheery of face, is a sufficing pattern for a claim upon thee, thou lord of the fair Plain of *Conchobhar*.

39   The precious treasures, the gift of cattle, that *Mac Coise* got from *Eoghan's* kin—why should not such be dispensed to me, thou scion from the timbered House of Croghan?

40 It did not become me, thou lord of *Line*, either from affection or from fear of reproach, to be forbearing in the matter, thou wise and righteous of mien.

41 In short, thou man of honorable intention—it is I myself that am patient; a buffet from a red fist in thy bright cheek is the sentence thou deservest from me.

42 Thou hast bidden me, thou smooth of hair, to guard my cattle from thee—my state is nothing but banishment, thou noble king of Frewen.

43 For the love of thine honor, tell me wouldst thou establish thyself there in my place, if I left my native territory?

44 To whom in the world wilt thou guarantee surety or respect, thou protecting shield of Ulster's shore, after thou hast banished me?

45 Hardly should I ever find again, after thy decree, thou slender scion from the Bregian Boyne, one friend with whom it were fitting to live.

46 O supple form, as it is with thee I was reared, thou son of Manus, this increases my depression—that the knee which nursed me should reject me.

47 Amongst them I was brought up, until I had spent the greater part of my life; great was the comradeship with me of every lord of Conall's curly-haired race.

48 Whenever the descendants of *Tál*, or the graceful, vigorous kindred of Niall were mentioned in my presence, thou prince of *Iomghán*, I used not to make (great) people of them.

49 I shall belie myself if I am for any time at odds with thy noble, crimson, melodious countenance; (my) praises of thee will be refuted by my censure.

50 I shall compose a refreshing piece of censure for thee after my lamentation; it shall be as a eulogy of the blood of *Tál*, thou dark-lashed chief of *Iomghán*.

51   It is a piece of fortune for the seed of Brian that I shall become resentful towards the nobles of Conall's line, offspring of a goodly seed from the City of Conn.

52   Wert thou remorseful for the hurt thou hast not done me, I would accept and give an honor-price, O blushing cheek.

53   All the greater is the guilt of *Dálach's* clan in opposing a comrade, since hitherto they have not been wont to plunder any man of letters.

54   From the side of either Corc or Conn—there is no noble connection whom thou owest to resemble, O Hugh O'Donnell, that was not wont to show forbearance towards poets.

4

THE BATTLE OF DRUMLEENE

1   Drumleene is a precinct of vengeance; much evil and injustice hath been committed in contention for that hill, in the valley of conspicuous inlets.

2   Often have its slopes been turned into a crimson, blood-red mass, and every dip of its glowing fields filled with mangled bodies.

3   Many a time ere this has the lake in front of it been turned to blood, and its waves purpled with gore on the brink of the vengeful ridge.

4   The deathful slopes of Drumleene! Never have there been nor ever shall be such evil deeds in any other plain in Ireland as those of this fair fresh-verdured expanse.

5   Since the days of the Children of Nemed, the fresh, brightly-glistening surface of the smooth hill of *Cruachán Lighean* has been bathed in the blood of champions.

6   *Conuing*, son of *Faobhar*, son of *Flath*, it was he who fought the first battle in contest for the land of Bregia, by the calm waters of Drumleene.

7   Nine hundred of the Children of Nemed, of their chieftains, of their soldiery, fell by *Conuing*'s battalions on the brown surface of that field.

8   Then the five sons of mighty *Deala*, son of *Lóch*, gave battle on the hill to the noble warriors of *Fál*, by the ancient dyke of *Cruachán*'s peak.

9   In the same spot, after a space, great *Breas*, son of *Ealatha*, gave battle to the warriors of *Lochlann* for the noble hill of graceful castles.

2*

10 Of the fighting men of *Banbha* there fell by *Breas* upon the ancient, awesome slope one hundred and three worthy to reign, as well as mercenaries of the land.

11 Of three thousand *Fir Bolg* there escaped from the conflict—distress enough was the amount of the spoil— but five.

12 When the mighty race of *Míl* of Spain returned to the land of *Fál*, (such fury as) the fury of these men upon the fair summit of the slopes of Drumleene is untold.

13 In days of conflict the three gallant sons of *Cearmaid* are slain by them, three valiant ones for whom hazels bore fruit-laden branches, pillars of fair *Cathair Chróoinn*.

14 They waged, then, three battles upon the perilous slopes of Drumleene, and they took to themselves the sovranty of Bregia, a step in the Gaelic conquest.

15 The Sons of *Míl*, moreover, and the flower of the *Tuath Dé Danann*, these also perished in the slaughter on the white-knolled green of *Cruachán*.

16 Never on any other hill of *Ughaine*'s Land have there been slain half as many warriors as the number that fell on the glistening mounds of *Cruachán*.

17 Until the stars of heaven be numbered, or the great sands of the sea, it will not be possible to recount the evil deeds wrought on the brightly foliaged hill with its ancient fields.

18 Six royal battles ere now have been waged around the fair hill of Foyle, by the sluggish stream, without recording any petty fray.

19 In short, this is the seventh battle, this mighty conflict of to-morrow, that the champion of Ulster's land will wage upon this mound of which ye have heard.

20 It is he, moreover, who will give battle, Hugh, son of Manus, of Tara's rampart; the cheery and ruddy of countenance, that is most wont to triumph over the foe.

21   This great battle of the morrow is the grievous, destructive plague which has set the four elements trembling throughout the spacious Rampart of *Lughaidh*.

22   That is what has made flaming folds of the hills of the world, and sent the waves through the forest thickets in mighty masses of flame.

23   The spurting fires of heaven, a presage of conflict, have appeared, with the great maned star in a wondrous, warlike array.

24   The sepulchred dead will be struggling and contending, throughout *Fál*'s plain the corpses are quickening, in expectancy of the extraordinary evil.

25   Throughout the delightful expanses of the Field of the Fair the beasts of *Banbha*'s plain are uttering intelligent speech, simultaneously proclaiming the woes of Ireland.

26   Brutes are brought forth in human shape, and men in the form of brutes, many a monster has that created throughout the dyked meadow of *Cobhthach*.

27   The ravenous Fury of battle is inciting the great chief, passing over the isles of Ireland with crimson tresses about her head.

28   Until morn come, the phantom women of faery, the wolves and wild animals, will utter presage of the coming battle to the host of *Macha*.

29   Many this night, throughout both armies, will be the spectres, ghosts and apparitions around the spoiler of *Banbha*'s castles.

30   Many a soldier in the camp of the warrior of Bregia will have had his shield on his wrist since the night before; many the long fingers looped around javelins, hands clasped about swordhilts.

31   In the morn betimes there will be many a meal consumed without comfort, warriors whetting (?) their keen weapons, shrieks of scaldcrows and ravens.

32 Most horrifying, then, will be the clang of the
clashing spears, the whistle of their sharp blades with
dripping points, the harsh calling of their ivory horns.

33 Piteous, at the same time, will be the bellowing of
the gaping brutes, the voices of the wolves from the
heights of *Banbha*, the fluttering of strange banners.

34 Betimes to-morrow morn the blue assembly mound
of *Cruachán*, the woeful ridgepole of all slaughter, will
be a clamorous hillock.

35 The battle of to-morrow morning will be gained,
as is wont, by the keen-eyed host from *Teach Truim* and
the stately race of Conall.

36 Does Hugh pay heed to the complaint of the
creatures in human form, the moaning of the streams,
the clouds in the heavens, the tidings of the soothsayers?

37 Or is it the complaint of Conall's kindred, that the
army of the chieftain of *Fál* is kept parleying about
battle, that afflicts his brown cheek?

38 Long have they been attending him, without returning
to their native lands, the long-handed scion of Bregia is
wearying the Children of *Míl*.

39 Long does it seem to the man from the Moy, and
from the cool brink of *Srúbh Broin,* from the Curlews
and from the lands of Oriel in Ulster, not to return home.

40 Whether it prove his undoing or his advantage,
whether the victory be for or against Hugh, since it
awaits him it is high time to face it.

41 Readily can he go into battle before the mighty
host of the warriors of Tara, few therein that are not
forest-trees of the true family of the race of Conall, towering
above the wood.

42 Gathered about his soft locks are the heroes of the
Tuatha, the warriors of Fanad, the kingly youth of Inishowen, delightful hosts from whom the sea is easy to fish.

43   From the other side he will be joined by the
danger-braving hawks of *Beanna Boghaine* and a fierce
host from the glens of *Bearnas*, a red-speared, blue-bladed
herd.

44   With him moreover, one after another, are his own
kinsmen of the race of Conall, who have no mind to
retreat one step, champions from the castle of *Durlas*.

45   Better these around the warrior of the Plain of
the Fair than seven times their number of a summoned
and pressed army from the other territories of Ireland.

5

LIFFORD CASTLE

1   A beloved dwelling is the castle of Lifford, homestead of a wealth-abounding encampment; forge of hospitality for the men of Ulster, a dwelling it is hard to leave.

2   Beloved are the two who keep that house without excess, without lack; the ward of the stout, even-surfaced tower are the supporting pillars of the province.

3   Short is the day, no matter what its length, in the company of the royal warrior of *Conchobhar's* Plain; fleet are the long days from the lady of bright-walled Tara.

4   The daughter of noble Shane O'Neill, and the son of O'Donnell of *Dún Iomgháin* — they are in the ancient, comely dwelling as entertainers of guests.

5   Dear the hostel in which these are wont to be, dear the folk who dwell in the hostel; the people of the house and the house of that people — happy is any who shall get honor such as theirs.

6   Beloved the delightful, lofty building, its tables, its coverlets, its cupboards; its wondrous, handsome, firm walls, its smooth marble arches.

7   Beloved is the castle in which we used to spend a while at chess-playing, a while with the daughters of the men of Bregia, a while with the fair books of the poets.

8   The fortress of smooth-lawned Lifford — no one in the world can leave it once it is found; that dwelling is the *Durlas* of the north.

9 Or else it is *Eamhain* which used to vary in form, or Croghan of the children of *Mágha*, or Tara of the race of *Cobhthach* —this bright castle, rich in trees and horses.

10 Or it is Naas, the fortress of Leinster, as it was first fashioned; or the fertile, ancient abode of the children of *Corc*, green, conspicuous Cashel.

11 Or it is fair Lifford itself—hardly is any of these castles better—which hath of yore assumed those shapes ye are wont to hold dear.

6

LIOS GRÉINE

1 *Lios Gréine* is the *Eamhain* of Ulster; a dwelling not to be deserted for *Tailte;* a house whose gifts are not excelled, booty taken from the foreigner is bestowed in that bright dwelling.

2 It is the fairy castle of *Ealcmhar* in loveliness, a dwelling which of yore was held by kings; enough is it to set all at variance, a sunny castle like to the *Brugh* of the Boyne.

3 It is akin to *Guaire's Durlas*, it was built by the descendant of the earls; dwelling of feasting, wine-wealthy hosts, royal castle abounding in spears and bridles.

4 *Lios Gréine*, saffron-tinted castle of brave melody, the sight of it will relieve sickness; plenty therein of all kinds of delight, fair stead amidst green-topped hazel-trees.

5 White-lathed, straightly built castle, a habitation beguiling to companies; *Dún Dealgan* — bright fortress similar to the rampart — is such another as this lofty castle.

6 Fort full of booty, of companies, of drinking horns, long shall this dwelling be remembered; much hath the shapely fort laid desolate; a mirthful rampart like to *Lios Luighdheach*.

7 A fort like that of famed Ushnagh, which the Hound of the Feats subdued (?); bring no woman within this tower, similar to Troy is the dwelling.

8 The level green lawn about the sunny castle is like plowed land, from the prancing of vigorous steeds: no one hath tilled the bright sod, but its state is caused by the exercising of young and spirited horses.

9 Horses on the lawn around the bright castle, shining spears being polished: the race of Conn driving round, well-set nails in preparation for exercising their steeds.

10 From the prince who is lord of this house *Banbha* shall know no lack; he is a man whose fame is such as that Hound's—similar to him was the Hound of the Feats.

11 Shane leads us to *Ráth Éanna* ... hostage for the prowess of *Úna's* Land, spouse of Conn ...[1]

12 The darling of Tara hath won great triumph, Shane is proven in combats ...[2] it is right to shun the wrath of a warrior.

13 A keen steed beneath thee, swift as a hawk ...[3]

14 Until thou canst win her will from Tara, thou son of Conn, unflinching in battle—goodly fame is not to be thought little of— thou provest thy worth in conflict.

15 *Lugh* Longhand, lord of Tara, who left no foe unsubdued—many a soothsayer says it of thee—is thy similitude over the Plain of *Connla*.

16 Stretch forth from bright Dungannon, suffer not the land of Niall to be unsubmissive to thee; it is meet to exalt one nut above the cluster, I choose thee for the qualities of *Cú Chulainn*.

17 Sufficing is the agility of thy slender tipped spears-hafts, they will send the foreign hosts across the bright sea; it is no reproach to *Bearchán* to have announced thee— the ancient plain of Niall is well foretold for thee.

18 Not much of other men's wealth does he hoard, bright satin such as is not wont to be in a hostage-cell (?); as he returns triumphant from a territory gentle, sharp and eager are the steeds around the sunny dwelling.

[1] I cannot translate the second line and the third is corrupt.
[2] I do not understand the third line.
[3] See Notes.

TO TURLOGH LUINEACH

1 Many privileges have the seed of Niall, it is long since they, the seed of the forest-tree from the Bregian Boyne, were ordained above the rest of *Mil*'s mighty kin.

2 Even when they are not ruling the Land of the Fair, the high-king of Ireland is not entitled to any increase of homage from the goodly race of *Eóghan*, orchard-stems of *Cobhthach*'s kindred.

3 When any other king rules the Plain of *Ughaine* no exchange of hostages is got from the goodly race of Nine-hostaged Niall.

4 But when one of the O'Neills is made king, then it is no matter of doubt that the keen-bladed race of noble Niall obtains pledges from every Irishman.

5 They, being the most excellent, have given hire to the men of Ireland, but the flower of Bregia's ever-roving host are not bound to accept hire.

6 O'Neill is entitled to the blood-price if any of his people be killed, but he gives no honor-price to any of the strongly fettering host of the Gael.

7 We know, moreover, that in no part of Ireland are their rights withheld, while these hosts so heroic in exploit hold the dues of all Ireland.

8 The descendants of Niall of the Nine Fetters, stems from the Hill of the Fair, there have not been, nor will there ever be any Irishmen such as they.

9   The kings of Ireland who were not of them, and the race of mighty Niall, son of *Eachaidh*—not more numerous in the regal list are kings from other stock than from them.

10   From them are the kings of hilly *Banbha*, from them the choicest of Ireland's noble saints; from the seed of royal Niall of the land of Bregia, the stainless, righteous ones of the Gael.

11   *Mac Coise* estimated the race of Niall, and in no respect did he find in them any traces of wickedness or transgression, any more than in the angels of the haven of paradise.

12   'Whosoever is the worst of Niall's stock, I testify,' said *Mac Coise*, 'that he excels all others besides them, that company from *Tuatha Teamhrach.*'

13   The best of Niall's stock, these, palmtrees from the haven of Derry, he did not speak of as men, but as angels in fleshly body.

14   The judgment of *Mac Coise* of *Cluain* on the seed of Niall of red-weaponed *Oileach* has ever since had wide and enduring repute throughout the host of *Fionntan*'s wine-abounding plain.

15   There are many other reasons whereby the descendants of *Eóghan* especially surpass in nobility the rest of Niall's saintly race, noble stems from a single root.

16   *Eóghan*, son of glorious Niall, branch above the forest of *Macha*'s plain, obtained, beyond the other children of the high-prince, the blessing of the primate Patrick.

17   Patrick of the Haven of the Fair bequeathed to *Eóghan*, rather than to the rest of Niall's seed, and to his vigorous and noble stock, the honor and prowess of Ireland.

18   They ruled the descendants of *Criomhthan*, and never since, in virtue of the patron's legacy, has any one of the men of Ireland obtained power over *Eóghan*'s seed.

19   The seed of Niall is the outcome of the ancient blessings, the fruit of the holy man's prayer has now come to Turlogh, apple-branch of Tara's wood.

20   Son of Niall, son of Art *Óg,* son of Conn, descendant of the kings from Frewen, most righteous king that man ever saw of the mighty sons of *Míl.*

21   The difference between gold and copper, the difference between the moon and the stars, such is the difference whereby the lord of Bangor's fertile plain exceeds all other Irishmen.

22   A king who never allowed the men of Ireland to outdo the Ulstermen in anything, the king proven to be best, surpassing all Ireland.

23   A king through whom the men of Ulster are without war, without conflict; without envy, without resentment, without anger, without destruction of castles, without reaving.

24   A king who never broke his kingly word, the king to whom evildoers are most hateful: a king who will promise nothing under heaven save that which is certain to be done.

25   Even on the highway a ring of ruddy gold might be safely left for a year, such is the rigor of the law amongst the men of Ulster.

26   Under the glancing eye of the mighty hero of *Macha* the women of *Fál's* Plain might (each one) traverse Ulster singly, clad in garments of varied hue, broidered with gold.

27   If a ship laden with treasure were cast unguarded by the coast, such power does Turlogh wield that it would depart without infraction.

28   All the more wonderful is it for the man to have brought the Fifth into such a state, seeing that, save Ulster alone the whole of bright and fertile *Banbha* is one wave of depredation.

29   That deluge whereby God desolated the world, or
else just such another, has been sent upon Bregia's dewy
rampart; the happiness of *Banbha* has been extinguished.

30   In the land of the children of *Rudhruighe* there
is another conspicuous Noah, stately presence, whose
excellence is acknowledged, shielding it from the down-
pouring of the flood.

31   Now, out of all *Banbha*, Turlogh keeps the fifth
part of Tara's land unwetted by Ireland's deluge of
lawlessness.

32   Even thus of yore did the King of Heaven bring
Noah son of Lamech, fruitful scion, of word inviolate,
across the heaving sea of the Flood.

33   In the days of great Noah son of Lamech the world
lay beneath the darkness of mist through lack of reverence for creative God; a well-known matter ever since.

34   Save Noah himself and his three sons, the seed of
Adam then, all the people of the world, it is said, were
abounding in wickedness and sin.

35   The angel of God comes down from heaven on a
certain day to the son of Lamech, to prophesy to him
before the Flood, that most destructive downpour.

36   'The fierce, dark streams of the flood,' said God's
messenger to him, 'most able destroyers of them, will
overwhelm all simultaneously.'

37   'Let a firm, stout-flanked vessel be made by you,'
said the angel, 'ere the black, scorching brine come across
the solid plain of the earth.'

38   Upon the angel's entreaty the son of Lamech—
what courage—makes a graceful, smooth-masted ark, a
glistening watertight ship.

39   When the ark had been made ready the King of
the elements, God the Father, sent the Flood upon the
earth and laid it waste.

40 Until God in requital of their crimes had over-
whelmed the whole world, save eight alone, He ceased
not to harry them in His righteous anger.

41 It was not the comely, graceful ark that saved
them from the wrath of the Deluge whilst the tide was
rising, but the prayers and the saintliness of Noah.

42 The foreigners are the deluge, the Plain of
Conchobhar is the ark, and the Noah of that land is
Turlogh, noble, hospitable scion of Tara's fold.

43 Even as formerly Noah was chosen by Him, to-
day, according to His wisdom, God has chosen beyond
any of the warriors of the bright plain of the Gaels the
heavenly countenance of O'Neill.

44 Amongst the Gaels of Tara's Field God Himself
has chosen Turlogh, it is not easy to alter that choice
of the God of the elements.

45 It is not to be wondered at though a fierce,
powerful king such as he perform any of his actions,
considering the number of kings of Ireland that were
of his stock.

46 Twenty-six kings, in the reckoning of rulers, reigned
over the Gaels' land of dark yewtrees, from Niall son of
Eachaidh down to Turlogh to whom the forest bends.

47 Sixteen kings of *Eóghan*'s race preceded him, no
statement of an unlearned man, and ten kings, one after
another, of the long-speared seed of Conall.

48 Seventy-two kings, reckoning up from Niall of the
fair waving hair to proud *Míl* of Spain, ruled over the
pleasant, cool and dewy Plain of *Fál*.

49 Eight kings and four score ruled before him over
the field of the Gael: such is the resplendent pedigree
of the high-king, the latest generation is the best.

50   And further, if, as is not the case, the rest were of equal estimation with the race of *Eóghan*, the homage of Bregian *Banbha* would of necessity be given to the hero of *Annla*.

51   It is no season for Irishmen to oppose the power of O'Neill; it is no disgrace not to withstand thee now, since thou wert not withstood as (simple) Turlogh.

52   O Turlogh, grandson of Art, little short of woeful were it for any one who should see the homage of one Gael begrudged thee about *Flann*'s Field.

8

TO TURLOGH LUINEACH

1 At Christmas we went to the Creeve; all the poets of *Fódla* were assembled together by the smooth wall of the hospitable castle wherein O'Neill lay at Christmastide.

2 One of O'Neill's dwelling-places was the pleasant, lightsome Creeve—never was there built a court to excel it—wherein all the delight of Ireland was comprised.

3 It was then that the unopposed kingship was sustained by a noble scion from Tara's height, Turlogh, the fruitful branch.

4 It was ten years since the king had been inaugurated, and the gallant, famous branch of *Almhu* had built a dwelling in the Creeve.

5 We proceed to the Creeve to seek the white-toothed, bright-faced chieftain, we, the encomium-makers of the Land of the Fair, the poets of Ireland.

6 It seemed to us, when entering, as if the wall of the firmament had fallen, from the tumult of the sleek, yellow-bridled steeds around the lord of *Raoiliu*'s pathed plain.

7 And afterwards it seemed to us, from the sheen of weapons and accoutrements, that the whole place was aflame from roof to foundation.

8 The sounds of banqueting in the court of the descendant of Nine-fettered Niall we liken to a stormy sea coming against the shore, from the clashing of purple vessels.

9   When just in sight of the rampart even were I at the shoulder of any man I could not hear him because of the strains of music from the citadel.

10   Ere we had arrived beside it, it seemed to me that the brilliance of its bright-surfaced goblets, and the fragrant odour of its banquet ales were of themselves a sufficient enjoyment.

11   We seat ourselves, ordered and compact hosts, on the border of the lawn; in front of that noble dwelling amidst rich sward was a poet from every quarter of Ireland.

12   After a space there come to us the officers of Conn the Hundred-fighter's descendant, and they welcomed each one, with salutations to all from the high-king.

13   No glimpse of the high-king of Ushnagh was had by us that night; the slender, soft-haired hero of Bregia dismissed us to our sleeping chamber.

14   From then till morn the fair, haughty cupbearers of famed O'Neill plied us unrelaxingly with refreshment.

15   He sent a man to inquire of us if any of our poems contained tidings of his battles throughout Ireland, accounts of his triumphs and exploits.

16   "No," said the poets of Ireland, "but," continued the men of art, "we have, without any degree of un-certainty, the origin of the genealogical ramifications of Conn's descendants."

17   "We have," said the poets of Ireland then, "'The privileges of Niall's seed', the number of their race that ruled over the Bregian Boyne, and all that was rightful for them to do."

18   "We have said that the Rampart of Croghan, country of shallow rills, and the Rampart of Tí, humid and pleasing territory, are his by right, and that he is the sole heir to Ireland."

3*

19 The messenger went to seek the bright-faced, boldly-glancing chieftain, and on the morrow he related the speeches to O'Neill of Mourne.

20 "If their matter for encomium be what they have said," quoth the son of Niall, "rather is it their reproach; it is simply an exhortation of the race of *Eoghan*!"

21 "It were a great insult to the youths of Tara," said Turlogh, if Tara's plain should be wrested from Art's generous line and they should be unable to avenge it."

22 O'Neill of Tara of Trim declared that he would not listen to any of our poems, but—strange to think on—that he would give a reward for each one.

23 Thereupon there come to us the descendant of Niall of Callann and the race of Eoghan; and the ancient hazel-tree of Ulster's plain was full of reproach for our art.

24 The son of Niall O'Neill did not lift his kindly, gracious countenance, or his keen, heavy-browed, active eye to the poets of Eber's land.

25 From the sole of his soft, smooth, springing foot to his fine, abundant locks Turlogh's handsome, brilliant form became a crimson mass.

26 We all filled with fear of the high-king of *Conchobhar*'s race, for the red-lipped hero of *Bóroimhe* was thoroughly angered.

27 We attempted with pleasant speeches to distract his mind, seeking to turn away his wrath, but that availed us nothing.

28 The award we asked was conceded to us by the descendant of Nine-fettered Niall, but the noble chief of *Monadh*'s host would not hearken to one stanza of our art.

29 Ever since he hath borne an unchanging aspect of fierce anger, and the king of *Fál*'s noble, vigorous race hath found no abatement of it.

30   I ask of the high-king of *Oileach*, if it be timely to ask it; what caused the keen wrath from which the fierce glow arose in his fair countenance?

31   Wherefore this great anger which afflicts the son of Niall, in spite of having well rewarded everyone? What hath caused his clear countenance to flame, or was there any cause?

32   If one might say it to himself, as regards this great wrath which afflicts the son of noble Niall, he hath no reason for it; the easier is it to enkindle it.

33   His race are as dearly ransomed at the mouth of the Erne as by the limpid streams of the fair Finn, and the sweetly-murmuring *Trágh Bailc*.

34   Equally is he obeyed at the Drowes and at the Ards, at the glistening streams of *Srúbh Breagh* and at the green-banked Boyne by *Tailte*.

35   I do not find that the curly-haired king of fair Derg hath any reason for anger, but territories submitting to him, including kings and assemblies of Ulster (?) [1]

36   It is this alone, I know well, that causes the anger of the white-fingered, sleek-browed man, that no one recited to O'Neill a battle-roll of his exploits.

37   He would be waiting for them till the day of Doom, if the poets of Ireland were to versify the distant forays of the mighty and spirited one; the hostings and combats of Turlogh.

38   However, if all the people of Ireland were united against them they would be in no danger as long as he were on their side: in no place does any dare to contend with him. [2]

---

[1] Here **Ed.** has: ... anger; fitting was the poetry to his bright cheek, he is provoked without reason.

[2] **N** has: ... were against him while in their company it would be no marvel if he should spoil them.

The rest is too defective for translation.

9

TO CÚ CHONNACHT MAGUIRE

1 Free people are the seed of Colla, champions of *Liathdruim*'s homestead; stags of the royal herd from Conn's castle, vineblossoms from Frewin.

2 Manannans of western Europe, pure seed in kindly soil; smooth-fingered warriors from the stately Boyne of Bregia, twining stems of the bright host of the Gael.

3 Shore-defenders of the Plain of the Fair, Ireland's 'Children of Israel,' little does it profit to strive against their fortune — sustaining pillars of the House of Tara.

4 Furnace sparks from the mouth of a forge, deep, diluvian waves; mighty warriors to give battle, set stones of the land.

5 Favored children of the host of *Banbha*, fierce fiery heroes; few are the like of the men amongst the contenders(?) of Gall or Gael.

6 Never have we heard of any kindred fit to be pitted against the race of Colla from the confines of Oriel, or of any Irishmen such as they.

7 There has not been nor will there ever be found — what avails it to discuss them? — a perfect simile of the noble Ulstermen from the Bregian Boyne.

8 There is but one tale about the seed of Colla, the race of *Eachaidh* — that the heroes lost possession of Ireland by force of their exploits.

9 Of their own will the proud race of *Eachaidh Doimlén* have relinquished the kingship of *Fál*'s corn-abounding plain in exchange for other privileges.

10   Since the days of our ancestors the three *Oirghialla* of Bregia's soil have ever held privileges innumerable beyond (others of) the five blue regions of the Gael.

11   The king of the *Oirghialla* has not only the right to sit next to the king of Ireland, but I should think less of the best of the *Oirghialla* did he seek this privilege.

12   The plentifully attended king of Colla's tribe keeps vacant (at table) the space of his sword's length and his long hand between him and the freemen.

13   The kindred of noble Colla are entitled to a third of the honorprice, a third of the tribute and a third of the tax of *Fearadhach's* Plain, to be divided amongst them by the man.

14   They are entitled—what an achievement—from November to summer to quarter their steeds and their hounds from house to house on the plain of *Tealhbha*.

15   The king of Tara can claim from the *Oirghialla*— and did he mention any more he would not get it—once in three years a hosting of but six weeks.

16   Even as regards that claim upon the kingly seed of generous Colla, he does not send a man to bind their agreements throughout summer or autumn.

17   The wealth which any of them loses when he joins the high-king's army, the princely champion is bound to find seven times its value.

18   Twenty-one cows are due to every man from the firm king of the fair Gaels, when they are returning home from that army; an award which has ennobled *Eachaidh's* descendant.

19   Thirty blades—no small gift—thirty mantles, thirty steeds and thirty sharp elfin spears as well, from the king of Ireland to *Eachaidh's* descendant.

20   Despite the prohibition of the king of Inisfail, the shrewd lords of the Plain of *Eithne* can safeguard criminals for a year beyond the just term of protection.

21   If they are accused of crimes, this is what the high king of Ireland can have, the oath of the defendant in the case of every offence committed by the race of *Eachaidh*.

22   The learned ones of Bregia's land say that the king of the Field of the Gael gets no further homage from the warriors of the *Oirghialla* than an exchange of hostages.

23   Moreover the hostages of Colla's bright-sworded kin are entitled to take counsel with all in order to find the meaning of their judgment (?).

24   The soldiery from the House of Tara have no chain or iron ring confining slender hand or foot, nor is there a man's body (of theirs) in stone prison.

25   They are not to be ironed, the captives from the line of noble Colla: it is enough to take their pledges, all agree that they may have their liberty.

26   Each man has the attire of a chieftain when returning from the king of Tara, a privilege granted to the nobly feasting *Oirghialla* beyond other mighty hostages of the men of Ireland.

27   They have gold on the hilts of their blades, gold on the rims of their helmets; of fine-spun gold are their garments, the hostages from Bregia's dewy castle.

28   Therefore are they, rather than any other Gaels known as 'golden hostages', of ruddy gold are the fetters of their hostages when the *Oirghialla* are returning home.

29   When returning from the king of Ireland they have not so much as the heads of their javelins, the thongs of their spears or the fine greaves of their legs but is gold.

30   It is the right of the seed of Colla of smooth goblets that the men of Ireland should rise up before them, but they, warriors with whom women readily make peace, are not bound to arise.

31   Such privilege have they obtained from the king of Ireland that a hand is not dipped in a golden basin, nor yet is palm of hand or sole of foot cleansed therein until they have first washed in it.

32   In Tara of the hostages, then, it is not lawful that any bathe before the high-king of the *Oirghialla* shall have done so, or that any other man should be assigned an apartment in the sleeping house before him.

33   The high king of the land of Bregia might not seat himself until he should have sat, nor arise from wine until the champion of the Erne arose.

34   A third of Ulster, the great third of Connacht, according to the boundary, was the original share of the wine-quaffing race of Colla amongst the lords of *Fál*.

35   The Erne, the Finn, the Boyne and the Bann, and each territory that lies between them — brown-nutted soils where the sun shines — these are the boundaries of the land of the *Oirghialla*.

36   The privileges of Colla's seed have ceased: the fighting men of *Liathdruim* do not remember what hath long been owing to them from the peoples of *Tailte*.

37   Even were it feasible to claim it the *Oirghialla* do not seek to obtain from *Fiacha*'s kindred the due which was rightfully theirs.

38   It is not loss of power or of memory that affects the youths of Mourne; what is the reason that the privileges of *Banbha*'s bright-haired scions are withheld?

39   Many are their breachmakers of battle, many their stuff of high chieftains, sufficient is the abundancy of their warriors, the great host of *Maighin*'s fertile plain.

40   That they themselves do not unite, that, you would say, is the reason their rights are withheld from the three hosts of the Plain of *Codhal*.

41 There is good reason for resisting the power of the progeny of bold *Eachaidh Doimlén* — the seed of Colla are in three divisions, with a several king over each band of them.

42 A king over the seed of *Mathghamhain* from Moira, a king over the seed of *Maine*, son of *Eachaidh*, a king over the men of Fermanagh's bending woods, have the bright battalions of the men of Oriel.

43 It is wrong to have three kings over the seed of Colla, it is a cause of weakness; it were better to be depending on a single man, as a shepherd to all in general.

44 The three equal battalions of the kindred of Colla, warriors of Bregia's dewy mount, would do well to appoint a single man to rule them.

45 As for the true patrimony of Colla's tribe let the three royal bands deliver the kingship of the bright, blue-soiled plain, into the keeping of one man of the *Oirghialla*.

46 Why do not the race of *Eachaidh* put their trust in a valiant, rightly-judging king, over whom none (other) of the wondrous line of *Fiacha* would have any degree of superiority?

47 Let the three noble battalions of Colla's seed elect one king amongst them, according to wisdom and shrewdness; according to age and dignity.

48 What ails them that they confide not in *Cú Chonnacht*, son of *Cú Chonnacht*? scion . . . (?) of the House of the Three, guarding champion of his kin.

49 The only levying steward of the three battalions is the righteous king of Fermanagh: gently-moving foot, save when meeting spear-points, enemy to the wrongs of Ireland.

50 *Cú Chonnacht Óg* Maguire, protecting shield to his soldiers; senior of the seed of Colla *Dá Chríoch*, their surety for peace or for war.

51   Most precious jewel of Conn's Half, heir of great *Donn*, son of *Domhnall*, a man whom the wealth of this world never beguiled, the best nourisher of art.

52   Counseller in war of Bregia's land, chief of peace of the host of the Gael; a king who entwines the fair men of *Fáil*, the fulfilment of *Bearchán*'s prophecy.

53   Let your three united battalions assemble with *Cú Chonnacht*, the great host of *Eachaidh*'s descendants, valiant, rightly-judging kindred.

54   This is the intention of Joan's son, upon the coming of the three royal gatherings: to go and inspect the plain of Niall, it shall profit both them and him.

55   A man from fair *Cliú* shall recognize the son of great *Cú Chonnacht*, son of Brian's son,[1] as chieftain over your battalions, O fair kindred of *Eachaidh*.

56   From the beginning to the end of the world, ye have not found, nor will ye find a more princely chief than this king, ye three patrimonies of Oriel.

57   Son of Joan, and *Cú Chonnacht*—what king might one compare with him? a heart from which hardness hath parted, the latest generation of kindliness.

---

[1] See Notes.

10

TO MAGUIRE

1 Fermanagh is the hearthstone of hospitality; its men are more generous than hospitality itself; it is a land that hath put forth every goodly crop, a fount for the hospitality of all others.

2 For repute and hospitality there is not their like in *Banbha*; fame hath ever preferred the blood of *Odhar* beyond any in the Western Land.

3 The chieftain of the Manchian plain merits every gage of hospitality that may be found; it were fitting that those who journey *Cobhthach*'s Plain should deliver to him the gages of all others.

4 Short is the time of his opponent . . .[1] as the sea excels the tiny pool so doth he excel the pledgeworthy of *Féilim*'s blood.

5 The day Maguire is at his worst he overshadows the growth of other men's fame; their equal in one man confronts the choicest of the Gaels of the western land.

6 His word is enough to curb the host of *Banbha* when they are rallied in ranks of battle; from the wrath of the king of *Fiacha*'s land peace is made in five countries.

7 It behoves not Ireland to be independent of the king of *Odhar*'s race; the seed of Conn is powerful either to succour or to spoil the lords of the western land.

8 By his bold words a king was proclaimed through territories; a man banished by the seed of *Sfadna* did not find shelter throughout *Fódla*.

---

[1] Text corrupt and unintelligible.

9   Reavers dare not attack the Manchians of Gowra's Field; if the king of *Eamhain* be there he wards off those in the pass.

10   Heroes by whom the Dwelling of *Tuathal* is secured, whom nò man is found to face; the blood of *Fiachaidh* earn fame in the fighting, even when unwithstood.

11   They rule Ireland without reproach, from one corner of the western land; there is not sufficient might against them to attempt to spoil the race of *Odhar*.

12   *Cú Chonnacht*, by his qualities, deserved to be chosen beyond the Children of *Míl;* a king is made from the seed of Donn in preference to (all) the kings of Eber's land.

13   The king of the Erne can balance every known pledge of honor; it were a small pledge for the person of the Manchian if the pledge of (all) *Cobhthach's* Fold were got.

14   One would get from him at the feast a payment which should be denied every guest; the hospitality of *Craoidhe's* blood bears a repute which all Ireland never bore.

15   Consider has there or will there come a fortune which their exploits do not overwhelm; to people of repute the very faults of the host from *Bearta's* brink were matter for great praise.

16   With them is the custody of hospitality, to guard it from the western warriors; even if those against them be of the best the blood of *Odhar* will surpass them.

17   That which has been uttered in time of feasting is not denied when slumber is past; were an enemy seeking justice he never on that account made a biased award.

18   A cup brimming with the contents of goblets, it could not be tackled without a gathering of champions; the empty horn of the champion of Ulster brought a strong man's hand to the ground.

19 Greatly did the wonted trouble increase when *Banbha* was shepherdless; he goes to the House of *Tuathal*, that has removed the curse of the slaying of *Fiachaidh*.

20 The land of the Gael is thine as far as it extends, it is no boast for Maguire: since thou art pledged for the seed of Conn there is an end to spoiling in the western land.

21 Thou causest all *Banbha* to be without either reaver or watchman; all are thanking thee that no one is at the mercy of any other.

22 The race of Eremon and Eber have become one assembly; it enhances the exploit that it is no marvel that the Gaels themselves should do it for thee.

23 None but the soldiery of the Erne confront thee when rising forth upon the western land; not that one fears to oppose thee, but if it be gained it is by the blood of *Odhar*.

24 When thou comest single-handed into the conflict thou needest no exhortation; thou in the pass alone hadst power by which the Field of the Gaels was delivered.

25 Thy exploits on the brink of the pass suffice to guard them: on thy account the spoilers of *Connla*'s land pass through it unarmed.

26 In thy castle, Maguire, knowledge of territories is got from exacting companies; without quitting thy side a poet explores the whole of the western land.

27 Thou, from the extremity of the Irish soil, dost apportion the five lands; but a small thing mentioned by thee causes the hosting of the Sons of *Mil*.

28 The kings of Bregia are in thy steading in bands at feasting time, thou concealest under (as it were) a shelter of foliage(?) the royal throne of every other man.

29 The labor of thy sword hilt in the field of danger has spared thy companions: thy approach to the perilous pass robs(?) something of each man's vigor.

30   In the time which poets do not appropriate the
others wait in thy presence: the leaders of hosts, while
they are before thee, do not get an opportunity with thee.

31   The pledge of *Banbha* comes to thee, the utterance
of the prophets hath been confirmed; no man is envious
because the Gaels look for thy crowning.

32   Bending trees in the place of the pools which the
dry weather hath emptied; by reason of the produce it
hath cast on the strand the sea of the Champions' Plain
is empty.

33   A winding stream through a wood brown with nuts,
a hostage in fetters was never slower; the low bending
trunks, the shallow wave, are charters of ownership on
Feilim's land.

34   The envious could not discern any thing which
would be a reproach to the royal line; the seed of *Donn*,
(even) their enemies declare, are entitled to the tribute of
Una's soil.

35   The champions from *Oileach's* land were not
dreaded by the western country; without the wasting
of any territory *Odhar's* blood subdued five kings.

36   When they had enkindled every land it was not
long till a country was succoured by them; the peaceful
humour of *Fiacha's* blood pacified five territories.

37   In *Connla's* Land there is no refuge for him, till
he have requited (even) the damage he did not commit;
the reaver is accepted in no part of *Banbha*, because of
this new hound of *Eamhain*.

38   *Banbha* is guarded, though it be difficult, without
violence or enmity; no man has accused the blood of
Odhar of spoiling the Gaels.

39   The seed of *Connla* does not hoard up its great
gifts, golden bracelets have completed their time with it
the day they are fashioned.

40   After surveying the generosity of others never did
poet cool towards the warriors of *Oilcach*; having inspected
the whole of Eber's land he makes for the tribe of *Donn*.

41   *Cú Chonnacht's* vow protects them when they have
served like the Collas; the pledges of their fighting
men are released throughout *Banbha* by the warriors of
Eamhain.

42   After the battle the hostages of *Fódla* are proclaimed
on the green of his castle, in the house of the hostages
thou wilt find tidings of every man in *Úna's* land.

43   There is no danger of reaving on the coast, there
is no door to a hostel; the steward of Conn's descendant
is secure of tribute on the foot-hills of the western soil.

44   Hotter is every palm than the sparks from the all
but molten mass in smithy; weary must be the legs and
arms of the soldiery of *Rath* on returning from the battle.

11

ENNISKILLEN

1 Alas for him who looks on Enniskillen, with its glistening bays and melodious falls; it is perilous for us, since one cannot forsake it, to look upon the fair castle, with its shining sward.

2 Long ere ever I came to the white-walled rampart amongst the blue hillocks it seemed to me if I could reach that house I should lack nothing.

3 I heard, alas for me that heard it, such repute of the fairy castle of surpassing treasure, and how my beguilement was in store, that it was impossible to turn me back from it.

4 This was the saying of each man regarding the splendid dwelling of the lion of the Erne—no man in *Banbha* ever saw a dwelling to equal it.

5 And they used to say moreover, whosoever should see the bending wood or the verdant slope, the level beach or the green field, would not take one step away from it.

6 After hearing its description when I had slept for a while I beheld no other vision save the splendor of the noble spacious dwelling.

7 I proceed on my way, I reach Enniskillen of the overhanging oaks; through the fair plain of bending, fruit-laden stems I was in no wise loth to approach it.

8 Ere I arrived beside the place I was startled at the tumult; the baying of their lively hounds and their hunting-dogs driving deer from the wood for them.

E. Knott, Tadhg Dall Ó Huiginn

9 The strand beside the court, on the fairy-like bay of murmuring streams, was crowded with such groves of tapering ship-masts that they concealed the beach and its waves.

10 And hard by that enclosure I see a lovely plain of golden radiance, the moist-surfaced lawn of the bright-hued castle, the soil of Paradise, or else its very counterpart.

11 Thus did I find the green of the castle—upturned by the hooves of steeds; from the prancing of horses competing for triumph no herb flourishes in the soil of the outer yard.

12 The horses of the castle (were) running in contest, again I see them coursing one by one, until the surrounding hills were hidden, no mist upon them save an expanse (?) of steeds.

13 I make directly for the coupled fortress of the branch of *Lic*; those whom I found in the fair mansion— a wondrous content of a mansion were they.

14 I found the nobles of the race of Colla in the thronged court distributing treasure, and those who exposed the recondities of the genealogy of the Grecian Gaels.

15 I found, moreover, throughout the fortress plenty of poets and minstrels, from one bright, white-surfaced wall to the other — happy the dwelling in which they find room!

16 In the other division I found plenty of slender-lipped, satin-clad maidens, weaving wondrous golden fringes in the sportive (?) rampart with fair, sleek hounds.

17 All through the house is an abundance of soldiery, reclining by the side walls; their edged weapons hanging above the fighters, warriors of fruitful *Druim Caoin*.

18 A mighty band of elfin youth, either from the Fairy-mound of *Bodhbh* or from Lear's Hostel, such that eye dared not regard them because of their splendor, were on the battlements of the bright, wooded rampart.

19　A company of artificers binding vessels, a company of smiths preparing weapons; a company of wrights that were not from one land at work upon her — fair pearl of babbling streams.

20　Dyeing of textures, polishing of blades, fitting of javelins, exercising of steeds; captives in surety, drawing up of conditions, scholars surveying the list of kings.

21　Taking of hostages, releasing of hostages; healing of warriors, wounding of warriors; continual bringing in and giving out of treasure at the wondrous, smooth, comely, firm, castle.

22　Part of that day they spent in talking of exploits, in meditating on battle; and a while would be spent by the host of Ushnagh in feasting, in listening to music.

23　Thus till supper-time we spent the whole of the fair day in the bright, green-swarded, fertile enclosure; as one hour in length did that day seem to us.

24　All began to seat themselves by the smooth walls of the white rampart; hardly in any hostel is there a number to equal the party that was therein.

25　*Cú Chonnacht Óg*, son of *Cú Chonnacht*, supple form to which smoke clings, when all that were in his hostel have sat down he seats himself on his regal seat.

26　I sat on the right hand of the champion of Tara till the circling of goblets was over; though it had its due of nobles the king's elbow never disdained me.

27　After a while, when it was time for those in the castle to take their rest, beds of down were prepared for the noblest of the alert, instructed host.

28　Ere day overtook the people of the hostel a band of them were fitting spears; at daybreak horse-shoes (?) were being fitted within and men were going to catch steeds.

4*

29 Shortly after sleep I see around the hawk of *Síoth Truim* the picked ones of all in panoply of battle, in the gloomless, stone-built, firmly-standing court.

30 Ere the coming of morn the valiant youth of the king's court set out from us; a great, lengthy, dense, spear-armed mass, ignorant they of making treaties of peace.

31 It was not long until the gold-ringletted race of Colla rejoined us, after completely subduing every territory, happy the kingdom which is their homeland.

32 That day around Loch Erne there is many a stranger woman whose husband is no more; many figures of wounded hostages coming in after the conflict.

33 Precious treasures there were in that dwelling, which had not been theirs at the beginning of day: and hard by the place there were cattle which had not been near them the night before.

34 Then were the poets of the castle rewarded by *Eachaidh*'s descendant, who never shrank from combat: small harm was the dearness of their poesy, riches had been got beyond what he allowed to them.

35 I went with the school to take leave of Maguire; away from the lofty, brightly appointed court, alas that he suffered me to go.

36 When parting from me, he said, shedding tears down his brown cheek, even though I might not be near to the warrior, that he was not parting from me for good.

37 I remember that the day I turned my back on the household of the king's dwelling, such sorrow lay upon them all that the grief of any one of them was not distinct.

38 None the better am I that that household is no more, would I had consumed the end of my days; lest I be longlived after they have gone, it is perilous to me that I shall survive.

39   Never have I heard of a household so noble as
that in the castle—what excellence—under any that sprang
from the Collas; that is the pronouncement of every poet
regarding it.

40   Lifford of the bright lawns, none ever quits it of
his own free will; since it beguiles to the place a man
from every quarter—alas for him that beholds it.

HUGH MAGUIRE

1   I shall leave Hugh to the men of Ireland, they are enough for the white-handed one of the fine, soft hair; save myself alone all Ireland is his; he is her comrade, her companion.

2   I should not find room by Hugh, the best poets of the Irishmen are around him on every side; they do not permit me to approach *Criomhthan*'s descendant.

3   No matter, that is no harm; I shall look to Maguire to see if my king of Gowra will accept me since I am alone.

4   I must needs approach, even if it be wrong, the high-king of Fermanagh's soil; we have been forestalled with Hugh, supple-handed, foam-white form.

5   A curious little story concerning this I shall relate to Hugh Maguire—bright, fair-hued countenance fore which the wave ebbs for which it were unjust to reproach me.

6   Seventeen of the poets of Ulster went to study their art, the destination of the fair Ultonian band being Kilcloney in Connacht.

7   They purchased a pig and a beef, and forthwith these people I have mentioned, each of them in quarrelsome humor, began to apportion their shares.

8   The man of the house asked which of the undistinguished, bashful company should be set down to the beef, and which to the long, fat, substantial pig.

9   Unanimously they make for the pork, out of that senseless band there was only one man got for the beef, though it was a crazy proceeding.

10   "May I never come back alive," said one of them, turning, "it has parted me from this company of friends, I shall go to the sharp, bony thing."

11   Of the seventeen men — keen the liking — none selected the clear, succulent beef in the end save a single man; it was not possible to restrain them.

12   Consider, thou soft and white of bosom, how abundant ... (?) caused only one man to forsake the pork, thou shepherd of Cormac's Plain.

13   Today, thou son of Maguire, it is no fault in me not to approach thee; I am loth to celebrate thy praises amongst all the poets of Ireland.

14   Not rumors of niggardliness, not disagreement with thee, or hatred or distrust of thee, thou smooth-cheeked, wondrous, graceful one, keeps thee perpetually cut off from me, but (my) sulkiness.

15   Good as thou art, I would not forsake for thee my own man, *Cú Chonnacht*; my strength, my love, my affection; he would never abandon me.

13

TO BRIAN MAGUIRE

1 Fermanagh is the Paradise of *Fódla*, a tranquil, fruitful plain; land of bright, dry, fertile fields, formed like the havens of Paradise.

2 The murmuring of her waters is heavenly melody, her soil bears golden blossom, the sweetness of her rivers is a vision of sweet honey, the · tresses of her wood turning them back.

3 Gentle valleys beyond arable (?) plains, blue streams above the valleys, overhanging the flowers is a yellow-nutted forest covered with golden foliage.

4 Enough to take sickness from a man were the brownness of her branches, the blue of her waters, the ruddiness of her foliage, the gloomlessness of her clouds; heavenly is her soil and sky.

5 Like to the melodies of Paradise around the tender, blue-springed country is the murmuring of her pure, sand-bedded streams mingling with the angelic voice of her birdflocks.

6 No tongue — in short — can tell half her delight, land of shallow streams and clustering, succulent crops, what is it but the very Paradise of Ireland?

7 None interfereth with any other in this pleasant earthly Paradise; there is none bent on spoil, nor any man suffering from injustice.

8 Every man, moreover, finds in her glance a smile of love, so that even a veritable foe, if he enter, is not ready to do her harm.

9 There is no reavers' track in the grass, or trace of spectres in the air, or of monsters in the waters about the noble, gifted, dyked plain.

10 There are no ghosts in her woods, or serpent in her fens; no misfortune threatening her cattle, no spoiler plundering her.

11 They dare not traverse her beyond her boundary-dykes; little recks the bright, blue region of any of the spoilers of Eber's Land.

12 This land around Gowra's Field hath obtained by wondrous magic powers something that protects it so that it cannot be plundered.

13 It is not the properties of stones, nor is it the veil of wizardry, that guards the waters of its far-spread lands; it is not the smooth slopes, or the wood, nor is it the sorcerous arts of druids.

14 They have a better protection for all the boundaries —a shepherd sufficient for everyone is the man—one alone is their guard.

15 Brian Maguire of the bared weapons, son of *Donnchadh*, son of *Cú Chonnacht*; guarding buckler of Donn's Land, own fosterling of the fairy mound of *Sioghmhall.*

16 Towards Ulster he is the ocean's surface; towards Connacht a rampart of stone; comrade of the gentle, maidenly women of Bregia, boundary dyke of the two provinces.

17 A healing herb for the blood of *Eachaidh*; a gate of death to the Breffnians; a fiery bolt to the blood of Niall and to the *Oirghialla* of the other side.

18 Fermanagh of the fortunate ramparts is the Adam's Paradise of Inisfail; the descendant of the noblemen from Bregia's castle is as the fiery wall surrounding it.

19   If a single prey were taken from the race of Conn between the Erne and *Áth Conaill*, compensation for the spoilings inflicted on them would be got from the four quarters of Ireland.

20   He would not leave a dwelling unwrecked by the fertile banks of the Boyne, by the warm, bright, gentle Moy, or the very shores of *Bearnas*.

21   Equally would he lay waste the smooth hills around Creeveroe, and the wondrous country from Croghan of Conn as far as the borders of Corann.

22   It were attacking a dwelling of bees, or putting the hand into a serpent's nest, to plunder the man of his ancestral land—or it were to approach a blazing house.

23   Long hath she been watching for Brian himself to come to her aid; since every soothsayer hath foretold his coming to the bright, angelic plain.

24   Once upon a time the Greeks endured like this for a certain space, in great and grievous trouble, trusting to find help.

25   The flower of the men of the world march on warlike, valiant Greece, making upon her simultaneously, so that they deprived her of her magic (protection).

26   Since the youth of Greece had no means of giving battle, the king of the exceedingly valorous host said that they should abandon their fatherland forthwith.

27   "Do not abandon it," said the Grecian soothsayers; "it were better to keep your country; for people of your prowess it is a shameful thing to be ready to forsake your inheritance."

28   And then spake one of the druids: "All the fitter is it to preserve the land since there is one in store for it who shall be a shepherd over the whole world,"

29 "A babe to-day," said he, "is the man that shall deliver us; if we but endure the wrong we get, shortly shall we gain relief."

30 "Name to us more clearly," replied the rest, as one man, "who is, or will you trace to his origin the one you would say can accomplish it?"

31 The druid replied—sufficing weal—"great Hercules, the Grecian champion, it is he I have named as a protector for all, by virtue of his powers and fortune."

32 "The armies of all the world," he continued, "will gather under the terrifying, wondrous hero, the glowing form named Hercules, this fruitful palm-tree of a promised (deliverer)."

33 "No monsters, no human creatures shall have such strength as to attempt to contend with him or tell of the gains(?) of his kindred."

34 The druid who had spoken thus decided as a counsel for his friends that until that fair, bright, eager countenance appear, they endure the ordinances of all the islands.

35 "If ye do as I say," said the sage, "until Hercules come to manhood, all that the three continents have exacted is naught but a loan from us."

36 "We care not what wrongs, dangers or perils we undergo provided there is a prospect of help in store for us;" replied every one.

37 As for the Grecian high-king, he endured every ordinance that was imposed upon him, till the coming of the prowess of Hercules—ruddy, bright, soft cheek, never wont to do ill.

38 Nine queens of the Greeks ...[1] him, in order to hasten his maturity, a most promising company for his guarding.

---

[1] I have no other ex. of *branar* in any meaning that would suit here.

30 Never, moreover, would he leave the knee or the bosom of the high-king, such care had he for him: no negligent guarding had Hercules.

40 Thereafter it was not long till Hercules subdued the choicest of the world; what need to recount the deeds of the man—? he confirmed the prophecies of the druid.

41 He overcame the people of the world, he punished them for their unjust dealings; the Grecian treasures came back to him with a hundredfold increase.

42 Well did it serve his kinsfolk to wait for him in his youth—but why should I continue? Hercules is famed for his adventures.

43 Even thus were the far-raiding race of Colla as regards Brian, waiting for the ripening of his bright cheek sometime in his boyhood.

44 So that the men of Fermanagh, moreover, spent a time sorrowfully and woefully, ever watching for the royal champion of the men of *Oilcach*.

45 So that he was nourished—most fortunately — on the lap of Fermanagh's high-king, and by shining, white-handed women, this Hercules of the Sons of *Míl*.

46 Until he filled with courage from the excellence of his nourishing — ruddy cheek by whom peace is readily rejected and from his nursing in the bosom of the high-king.

47 So that there came to them after that the son of *Donnchadh*, son of Maguire, to rescue them, under omens propitious for the succour of his kindred.

48 As for the race of Colla, the tribe of *Eóghan* have levied and will levy what they owe by charter the blood of Colla.

49 Colla's race of *Dá Thí*'s Plain, these chieftains of Bregia have kept in their minds every decree that was made, in the hope of avenging it at last.

50   They cared not what wrong they should suffer from Ulster or from Connacht, since against the brigandage of Ireland, help awaited them.

51   Now will they demand satisfaction (?) for their grudges, from Ulster, from the territory of Connacht; since the prophesied Brian hath come reavers are marching from the north.

52   In front of all will come that son of Hugh's daughter, strong hand from which the javelin glistens, the Hercules of western Europe.

14

CATHAL O'CONOR

1   Let us make a reckoning, *Cathal*, of riches and of poetry; the occasion for making it is a heart's torment, thou star from the Plain of Calry.

2   This is a common saying, thou kindly countenance— "affection ends with the casting up of accounts;" it is not an utterance without sorrow for me, thou capital of hospitality to men of letters.

3   It is time for us to balance accounts—and yet, O star-soft eye and glowing cheek, O beloved of women, it was not timely for me that it should be done.

4   Too early for me didst thou determine to go into the reckoning, the end of my affection is a cause of grief, unhappy for me is the determination.

5   A bargain of gifts and of poetry I used to make with thee, O ruddy, gentle contenance, as was proper for me and for thee; sad is my share of the bargain.

6   There is no shape of all those which our craft has ever taken that I did not make for thy waving locks, from the poem to the weaving of a single stanza, thou noble chieftain of the host of Sligo.

7   There is no art, from playing the musical branches to the relating of soothing stories, and from that to extolling thy race, that thou didst not get from me.

8   Let us now make a reckoning anew, let me hear from thee how thou didst requite every quality in which, I served thee, thou surety for foray of the Plain of Cormac.

9   What is this silence which is upon thee, Cathal O'Conor, that thou recountest not against me whatever was bestowed upon me?

10   Why, son of Tadhg, dost thou not boast of all that I obtained from thee, thou bright and noble of presence, as a balance of my great account with thee, thou soft-haired hero of Bangor?

11   Were everything that thou hast granted to me put in the account, thou mighty ox of this land of Bregia, it were not easy to reckon it up.

12   The spur-strap and the belt would be got from thee, Cathal, mantle and goblet and steeds, thou scion of Sligo.

13   Alas, alas, one would get mares and the precious stone from thy slender hand, and the gilded horn and the ring, thou chieftain of the great plain of *Murbhach*.

14   Cattle would be got from thee, O clinging locks, land moreover, and the shepherding of those cattle, thou defending shield of the waters of Duff.

15   Found I a hundred times as much from thee, thou red-lipped, gently-speaking one, it is not the various wealth I received therefore that should be set against me.

16   Rather should thy favor be recounted, and thy prudent, kindly care, thou hostage of the fair Plain of *Fál*; more fitting were it to recount thy love and thy esteem.

17   I used to have thy confidence and thy counsel, thou branch of Leyney, thy elbow and half thy couch, an award which no gifts could excel.

18   It were just to give thanks for it to thee—from others, Cathal, I got plenteous gifts in consequence of being seen beside thee.

19   I could not recount, O bright face, one half of what I received amongst the host of the fair Dwelling of *Fál*, from appealing in thy honor.

20   Through thee I got my price from Clanwilliam
to the west, and, another time, from the battalion of
Breffney, thou twining stem of the host of Sligo.

21   I got—though I deserved it not—my share of the
wealth of Conall's race, and of the booty of the O'Neills
from the east, on account of thee, O waving, parted locks.

22   The Costellos, the *Gaileangaigh*, would be spared
for rewarding me: *Chlann Chúán* and Carra must needs
favor us.

23   From Erne's water to Slieve Aughty each chief,
each one likely for kingship used to flatter me: it was
no presage of exaltation of spirit.

24   Never before did poet get such honor as mine upon
the soft-swarded Hill of the Fair, from any king amongst
the men of Ireland.

25   *Eochaidh* the Sage had not such honor from Hundred-
fighting Conn as we from thee, thou ruling staff of Conn's
Banbha.

26   Consider even *Fithcal*, the soothsayer of Cormac—
from thy long palm, thou chief of the slender-handed
host of Bregia, I have had gifts such as *Fithcal* did not get.

27   In short—in the days of Niall or Corc of Cashel,
Torna, teacher of the learned poets of the men of *Fál,*
was not wont to obtain what I have obtained.

28   *Mac Coise*'s honor long ago, in the days of *Tadhg
Mór* son of *Cathal*, is not comparable to mine; harder
it is that thou shouldst perish from thy poet.

29   *Mac Liag*'s honor in *Leath Mogha*, in the time
of Brian of *Bóromha*, though good was the king of *Fál*'s
fair height, is not fit to set beside mine.

30   Never did the kings of Ireland give to the poets
of hilly *Banbha* half as much as I got from thy dear
countenance, or half my honor in a single house.

31 Since I cannot relate of thee sufficingly, Cathal O'Conor, it is grievous to me to speak of thee, alas that I did not perish by thy side.

32 None ever thought that I would remain after thee, it is shameful for me not to have gone with thee in requital for thy affection and thy bounty.

33 It is hard for the nobles of Innisfail, since I live and thou, O flower of the Gaels of *Connla*'s Plain, art no more, to have trust in any man of art.

34 Oft wouldst thou implore God for me that I should have a longer life than thine; O ruling hand of Bregia's dewy plain, thy boon hath perturbed my mind.

35 Thy boon hath harmed us, alas; thou hast obtained from God, O gallant form, that we live after thee, thou only hope of *Muircadhach*'s rampart.

36 It was no wonder, O white-handed, modest-worded, that thou shouldst obtain thy desire, who never didst refuse any under heaven, O gracious, gentle face.

37 Thine own boon, the wrath of the Lord, hath grieved me, thou bright and gallant form: in return for my loyalty to thee, through thee my devastation is come.

15

TO MÓR, DAUGHTER OF BRIAN BALLACH

1   Ah *Mór*, remember the affection, but in brief, thou eye with the hue of springing corn, there will be no difficulty in clearing away the charges which have sundered us.

2   In complaining to thee, thou soft of hair, I have— what unkindness—to confess, though it is no secret, an unworthy deed.

3   Alas, I have committed against my trusty lord, thou fruit of the branches from Bregia's citadel, an action whereat his disposition changed.

4   To my lord at first, and also to those who entertained me, I gave reasons for displeasure, it was a portent of sorrow to do so.

5   In short—a numerous throng of mischief-makers asserted to him that I had done wrong to the noble, sweetly-speaking hero of Bregia.

6   People are saying to me that in a poem I addressed to O'Donnell I am said to have committed an unjustice against the stately race of *Conchobhar*.

7   Great forbearance did the lord of Sligo, lord of the host from that moated stead of Conn, show towards me at that time, considering all the mischief he heard of me.

8   From that time on I have been wandering from one territory to another to avoid him, through the fierce wrath of Conn's race, and because of Donnell's displeasure.

9 Although I have not been outlawed, O *Mór*, for enkindling his wrath, throughout the fair, splendid Plain of *Féilim* I am as good as exiled.

10 For a year's space, and a little more, I have not visited my homeland, as long as a hundred years it seems to me, I have been away in the wilds of Ireland.

11 Moreover, for a year my credit amongst the race of Nine-hostaged Niall and the seed of Conall has been failing, the weather turning against me.

12 The noble princes of the men of *Fál*, those from whom I used throughout my days receive the choicest favor—exhaust their entertainment of me in one day.

13 In my own place, while I am in disagreement with the lord of the Suck's noble plain, I have no enjoyment save that of an exiled man.

14 Unless God and thou can protect me, O wavy locks, there is no might that can rescue me; such misfortune has befallen me.

15 If thou deliver me in the time of my distress, thou bright and soft of form—this is a decree which all have confirmed, I shall be in thy possession for ever.

16 According to legal decree, O soft, slender, womanly hand, it is right if thou canst succour me that I should be thine in return for my protection.

17 Hast thou heard, thou apple-branch from *Fál*'s fair Dwelling, of the three birds of a strange and curious kind, which came to an emperor in Italy?

18 Every day they were ever in the presence of the high-king, over his head when coming in, and above the couch where he reclined.

19 For seven years these were with him day and night, the bird-flock did not on any day return without him.

5*

20   Thus they were — trouble enough — without sleeping, without resting; not satisfying was the music of their discourse, wearying was their contention.

21   He offered his heritage, and also his daughter, to any man who knew the birds, and could tell what they were about.

22   Amongst the people there spake a youth, and vowed publicly forthwith, however hard it was for him, to rescue the king from his misery.

23   And thereupon he said: "As for the business of the three birds with thee, whosoever may be ignorant thereof, it is not hidden from me."

24   "These three birds, O emperor," said the youth, "have a delicate matter to lay before thee, decide it justly."

25   "These birds have for a long time had a case for judgment, and since justice is awaited from you it is high time for them that it should be instituted."

26   "A woman-bird and two men are these three that are with thee, a matter that will cause them to be discussed forms a curious dispute between them."

27   "Relate to us, as thou art certain, O youth," said the emperor, "the tidings of each bird, their origin, and their adventures."

28   "Conceal not from me, tell me what has been the reason of their sojourn with me, now is the time to reveal it."

29   "There came, O king," said he, "some time ago, a famine that lasted for a year, it afflicted the entire world throughout the globe."

30   "The bird-flocks felt it, the salmon of the ocean, the herds of the land; curious was it when considered."

31   "To one of the two birds belonged the woman-bird at first, throughout the famine he disowned her, when her protection was hardest."

32 "From the other man-bird, during that dreadful year, she got everything of which she was in need, as he had her in that time of distress."

33 "After they had come through that hard year, the former bird, he with whom she was in the beginning, proceeded to take possession of her, wishing to claim her by right."

34 "This is what the other man-bird says: that the woman is lawfully his, since it was he that brought her through that time so that she survived to the season of of prosperity."

35 "These were the words just now, of the first bird, who rejected her in the hard year: whosoever be the woman's first mate she cannot deny him."

36 "In order that you especially, rather than any other, might pronounce judgment for them, that is their object in remaining in thy presence, O king."

37 As a judicial precedent the king adjudged that when she had come through the time of hardship, the bird should belong to him who had succoured her.

38 That verbal decree of the emperor has been under seal ever since, it is an award by which one must abide, it cannot be changed.

39 O daughter of Brian, thou sleek of hair, even thus wilt thou have custody of me after dispelling my hardship, in return for rescuing me from my misery.

40 Never can I forsake thy gentle countenance, I would not, moreover, if I could, thou tender and white of cheek, if thou protect me in the hour of my strait.

41 Make of me one of thine own, O lady of noble Niall's Castle, it is necessary for me and thee that I render thee allegiance in return.

42 Essay my protection, O benignant countenance, if it were difficult I could teach thee how to do it with thy thick, silky locks, and thy white hand.

43 Do not raise to him the gentle eye until Donnell
and I be reconciled, neither spend nor husband his wealth,
do not say that good is to be increased.

44 Neither heighten the renown of O'Conor of the
plain of Tara, nor defend him from calumny; remain
melancholy throughout the feast, remember no man in
particular.

45 Enter not into securities for peace, do not pacify
the neighbouring territories, O prudent mind, O bright
of cheek, do not settle any suit or question.

46 Bathe not the hand or the bosom, or the pearly-
hued teeth; approach not the host of Sligo for feasting
or music.

47 Maintain not any rule or law, hinder not the quarrels
of thy assemblies—until peace is obtained for thy poet
from the wrath of *Conchobhar*'s race.

48 Many a thing dost thou do—if thou art attempting
to protect me, thou rosy lady of Bregia's Hill, which
is more difficult for thee.

49 Much harder is it for thee to bend the oak-trees
by thy counsel—subdue, even as thou dost the fruitful
wood, the displeasure of the head of *Conchobhar*'s race.

50 Calm the wrath of the high-king of the Duff, as
thou calmest the anger of the wave, soften the fury of
the man's storm even as the winter wind is silenced by thee.

51 As the melodious babbling streams are deprived
by thee of their eloquence, easier is it to control the lord
of Carbury in anything in which thou attemptest to
instruct him.

52 Even as thou curbest the forays of all others, let
some bridle be laid by thy ruddy, gently-speaking,
stately figure on the vengeful wrath of Donnell.

53   As thou makest shallow the streams, so that they
bear not the salmon, thus were it easy to abate the anger
of this descendant of *Fiachaidh.*

54   As thou causest the waves of the sea to ebb, and
abatest the bitter, cold, tempestuous weather, even so
make to ebb all the wrath which threatens thy poet,
that is the sum of what I have sung.

55   If thou, O *Mór,* join with *Meadhbh* while our dispute
lasts, there is nothing that can oppose me, despite all the
ill-feeling there is against me.

16

BRIAN NA MURRTHA

1 Towards the warlike man peace is observed, that is a proverb which cannot be outdone; throughout the fair forests of *Banbha* none save the fighting man finds peace.

2 If any one amongst the warriors of Bregia deem it well to pacify the Saxons, this will suffice for his protection, so it is said, let him spend a while in continually spoiling them.

3 The Gaels of civil behavior will not get peace from the foreigners, such is their warfare, these most valorous, royal hosts, that it is not worth a treaty of peace.

4 No object for pacification are the seed of Conall, or the seed of *Eóghan* of the standards, or yet *Cathaoir's* descendants, or the seed of *Sadhbh*, or the valiant race of *Conchobhar*.

5 The nobility of the blood of fair *Gaedheal* is vanished almost to a man: such hopeful quarry are they that pursuit of them is nothing to boast of.

6 They are being thrust on to the outskirts of *Banbha*, whilst regiments of foreigners are in the centre; of the seed of Eber and Eremon a one-sided ...(?) hath been made.

7 It is but fitting that the Saxon soldiery fulfil not terms of peace with the scattered band; it seems to them — alas that it should be so — that the hosts of *Banbha* are without a warranty.

8 It is because of their weakness in fighting men against the foreign battalions that beyond those of any land in Europe this wounded and unfairly — used people lack peace.

9 Lack of counsel it is that has rendered the people subservient to the wrathful, tyrannical band; alas that they do not find those who would exhort them through any single man of valor!

10 Great unfriendliness were it did none of the poets of the bright-knolled land say to the men of *Fódla* that they should declare war upon the foreigners.

11 Since our darling amongst the race of *Míl* is the son of Brian, lavisher of herds, with gentle utterances I shall counsel the scion from Limerick's vigorous, nimble host.

12 I would give the counsel of a friend to the head of royal *Fearghna*'s line, that he, ripe fruit of the vine, kindle a tiny spark in the embers.

13 I will, moreover, with brief discourse—what is it but a kindling of righteous wrath?—give to the king of rivered *Magh Sléacht* an incitement to foray.

14 Easy is it for him to give battle, from the sympathy of the five noble nations, from one coast to the other Ireland will join him in a united war.

15 Throughout fertile *Banbha*'s plain, the rest, both kings and princes, will kindle in sympathy with him, even as one house takes fire from another.

16 When the men of Ireland learn that the high-king of *Aolmhagh* is making war, throughout *Banbha* of the glistening showers there will not be a land without one to despoil it.

17 Eager for mischief are the men of Ireland, they will rise with him in their full strength; the Gaels will strive to unite so that Ireland may depend on a single surety.

18 Only by keen war for our plain of *Úna* can he wage them, his will be the profit or the blame there of—these forays on *Úghaine*'s isle.

19 Let stone castles become couches for wild beasts, let grass so hide each road that he leave the bright surfaced plain of Tara over-run with wild deer and wolves.

20 Let them leave such famine in the valley of the Boyne, and by the long-branched shores of Birr, that the woman in Meath's rich plain eat of the heart of her firstborn.

21 Let the white-limbed hero of *Gáirighe* effect that there shall be nothing of their precious treasures, or at all events of their limewashed castles, save the saying that once upon a time they were.

22 Let their fruitful orchard be cut down, let their corn-crops be shorn by the defenders of Croghan's province, spirited, ruddy-bladed warriors.

23 Beside Teltown let great towers be pulverised by him, let him sweep utterly away their mills, their kilns, their granaries.

24 Throughout Ushnagh let the level borders of spreading plains become moorlands, so that the man beside *Tealhbha* may not find a trace of the four roads.

25 Let it be treasured up for the passing guest as a marvellous thing if the lowing of a single cow be heard around Colt, or by green-swarded Usnagh.

26 From Naas of Leinster let powerful men carry away heavy burdens of massive (?) ancient gilt goblets and of the sides of their merchant's coffers.

27 Let, moreover, poor and friendless men become wealthy, and let wealthy and powerful noblemen be made poor.

28 After the deeds the seed of *Ruarc* slow to anger shall perform the foreigners of *Almha*'s fertile meadow will ask for a treaty of peace.

29 Messengers will come from them to seek a truce from the warriors of *Banbha*'s land; they will ply the graceful, affable folk with sweet, honorable speeches.

30   Their robes of satin, their precious treasures, they will bring to the host of ancient Sligo, whose nobles will be plied with golden rings by the surly, impatient band.

31   They will ask the leader of peace of bright Ushnagh's meadow to come with them to court, and they will not yet seek requital for what the seed of *Fearghna* will have done on that raid.

32   Let them not with honeyed words beguile Brian son of Brian from Breffney; woe to him who would approach them, ravenous, destructive barbarians.

33   Does he know of the case of the lion, once when he attempted treachery? To no one yet born does he show gratitude(?), this king of all the animals.

34   He summoned to him the quadrupeds of the earth, they go at the first asking; many a proud, headstrong band attended the thronged gathering.

35   The chief of the fox tribe came not at the beginning of the party, but kept away for the time, until he found a suitable opportunity.

36   On the same path then the foxes go to him together—it was not meet to contend with them in their crafts—a wily, stealthy pack.

37   When the host, not numerous enough for battle, had gone to look at the lion's cave, they filled with fear for their lives, a weak and spiritless hosting.

38   The first fox who approached the lime-white entrance of the gorgeous cavern bid those on the outer threshold return with one accord.

39   "Clearly can I see coming up to this the track of every quadruped, but there is no track leaving it, ye modest, youthful, prudent band."

40   "Did we go into that fortress," said the leader of the guileful company, "never would our returning tracks from the smooth, artful rampart be found."

41 Those foxes, then, turned away from the greedy cave, in brief, what they said is conceived by us to apply to the white-breasted swan of the Finn.

42 This court of the foreign battalions is the cave of the nimble lion, and the hosts of the Irish territory are the slain quadrupeds.

43 Let Brian, son of Brian, son of Owen, understand that none of bright *Banbha*'s warriors come from the foreigners safe from treachery or betrayal.

44 With such terror has the uniting thread of this land of *Lugh* inspired the Saxons that even if the rest surrendered him into their custody it would not be easy to capture him.

45 It is in his power, the chief of royal *Fearghna*'s race, to defend Tara; the rest cannot but guard him, blossom of the vine tendrils.

46 The nobles of *Banbha* could not rescue generous Brian, son of Brian, yet it were not difficult for the well-followed hero of the Duff to succour all the Gaels.

47 The hatred of the foreigners for him is his testimony(?); all have been proclaiming for long that she is his—he holds *Fódla* by the bridle.

48 It is easy for him to defend her against them, many are his allies, far and wide lie his forces, while he has naught to protect save Ireland.

49 The races from which his mother came will be around the son of Brian in phalanxes (?); each tribe like a precipitous flood (?), the seed of Niall *Caille* and the race of Conall.

50 The three *Laighne* will be around the chief of Breffney, a broad-shielded, numerous throng; the men of Tireragh, the men of Carbury, the men of Corran, will be with him in the fighting without delay.

51   The three MacSweenys from the march of *Bearnas* will also join him in one band; come weal come woe let them not part from him, steel of the bright host of the Gael.

52   The Hy Many will join the son of *Gráinne*, with crimson, blue-headed javelins — they will leave the foreign women wet-cheeked — and the haughty line of *Fearghus*.

53   From the Inny to Loch Erne all are with him, both freemen and wanderers, and from Boyle to stormy Loch Oughter, the men of Fermanagh, the O'Rourkes, the O'Reillys.

54   The three chieftains of Connacht will go with him in a bannered mass, three stately, mighty regiments, the valiant line of *Conchobhar*.

55   The *Clann Domhnaill* will be with him in their full strength, like oaks towering above the groves, a gay and wondrous band of the soldiery of *Fódla*, the mercenaries of Islay.

56   The lords of the Gael will then march to Dublin at the outset, many a stone castle will be laid in ruins by the stubborn, headstrong fighters.

57   From the generous seed of *Ruarc* the valley of the Boyne will be a mass of lightning, the foreign tribes from *Cliu* to Croghan . . .[1]

58   The fierce, heroic swarm will have many an ornamented goblet and basin, many sledges for shattering walls, many vats and shining cans.

59   Many a spit and hook will they have, and many heavy corded bundles, many tables and pots, and plenty of other booty.

---

[1] A line is missing in the text.

60   The slopes of Meath will be covered by them with the vastness of the spoils from the cities, the powerful, cunning host will make many a road about the bright-trouted Boyne.

61   At sleeping time, after spoiling *Magh Ccóil*, the children of kings will have in their camps plenty of half-cooked flesh for griddles.

62   The foreigners about Ushnagh's field will then say to the people of fair Boyle that they will not allow the blood of *Cairbre* to take their kine, their spoils and their manifold wealth.

63   The nobles of the Gael will not respect the utterance of the fair, splendid warriors, the children of *Cobhthach* will marvel greatly that the foreigners should contend with them.

64   Then will the Saxon battalions and the hosts of royal Tara take the field of battle, many deaths will the wondrous, fortunate host wreak upon them.

65   Then will they hack at one another till even; many foreigners, many Gaels will perish by the numerous, irresistible host.

66   Many a keen, razor-edged arrow from the bow will pierce the flesh of a nobleman; many a cold blade and javelin, and slender, shining battle-axe.

67   The land of Meath will be flooded with ruddy pools from the two vigorous bands, until blood rises above the shoulders on that bright-surfaced plain of Tara.

68   Then will the Saxon tribe be vanquished by the seed of keen-weaponed *Gaedheal,* so that from the proclamation of war there will never be any save Irishmen over the land of *Fódla.*

69   On the night following the battle on the hill above the beguiling streams of the Boyne there will be many a noble, comely body in death-throes (?) from the hero of the Maigue's fertile valley.

70 There will be many a scaldcrow tearing the flesh of stout-weaponed warriors, and many will be the ravens and wolves around bright, fertile, salmon-abounding *Chii*.

71 On the slopes of Meath many will be the wet-eyed queens over their dead, from (the deeds of) the host of the Erne many will be the keen, ardent cries over them.

17

MACWILLIAM BURKE

1 The land of *Banbha* is but swordland: let all be defied to show that there is any inheritance to the Land of *Fál* save that of conquest by force of battle!

2 No one man has any lawful claim to the shining land of the ancient Gaels. The law of this territory is that it shall be subjugate to him who is strongest.

3 The father does not bequeath to the son *Fódla*'s Isle of noble scions; until it be obtained by force it cannot be occupied.

4 Neither the Sons of *Míl* of Spain nor any who have conquered her have any claim to the land of *Fál* save that of taking her by force.

5 The spreading-branchéd forests of *Fál*'s Plain were taken forcibly from the guileful race of *Nemhedh*—most courtly line.

6 By force, moreover, such their tale, were the wondrous hills of Ireland—the best dispellers of sorrow— captured from the *Fir Bolg*.

7 By force, again, was the land won from the kings of the *Tuatha Dé Danann*, when the noble Children of *Míl* wrested from them the dewy plain of Bregia.

8 Forcibly was the Land of *Fál* taken from the Sons of Spanish *Míl*; the Hill of The Three Men is not wont to be obtained save by force.

9 Although the Gaels conquered the spacious, kindly land, it was reconquered in despite of them, and has passed into the power of foreigners.

10 There come across the sea in three battalions the warriors of France, the soldiery of Greece and the mercenaries of the eastern land, the wondrous youth of England.

11 The Greeks of swift steeds, the men of England, the nobles of France — bright, wonderful warriors — divide Ireland in three parts.

12 The men from fair Greece and the foreigners from bright, fierce England wrest from the war-seasoned race of Eber the share of *Augh Néid*'s son.

13 The warriors of the seed of Charles conquer from Limerick to Lecale, Conn the Hundredfighter's share of the ancient, green-isled land.

14 The descendants of Charles conquered from Cashel to the Ards, from ancient Tory yonder to the flock-strewn *Caol* of Aran.

15 Where is there, from the Boyne to Limerick of the ships, a single quarter of land from which they derive not a certain portion?

16 I forbear for a space, from fear of reproach, to recount their tributes, until their defender come.

17 Should any say that the Burkes of lion-like prowess are strangers — let one of the blood of Gael or Gall be found who is not a sojourner amongst us.

18 Should any say they deserve not to receive their share of Ireland — who in the sweet, dew-glistening field are more than visitors to the land?

19 Though the descendants of *Gaedheal Glas* used speak of the race of Charles, set stones of *Banbha*'s hills, as foreigners — foreigners were they who spoke thus.

20 Ireland cannot escape from them, for four centuries and ten years has the warm, ancient, humid land been under the fair warriors of the seed of Charles.

E. Knott, Tadhg Dall Ó Huiginn. 6

21 It is they who are the noblest in blood, it is they who have best won the heritage; from them—nobles to whom homage is meet—the Bregian Boyne can hardly be wrested.

22 There will not be, nor has there ever been a line equal in power to the race that sprang from William, rulers of the Dwelling of Tara.

23 As far east as the stream of Jordan there is no field that was not conquered by them; if the fair Plain of *Flann* should be overcome we need not wonder.

24 Of them was he who conquered London from the Saxons, although they were watching for him in a bitter, furious mass.

25 Of them was he who took Jerusalem by force— many things are related thereof—the centre of the fourfold world.

26 Twenty-one battles, moreover, as I know, they waged over Ireland, wresting the bright centre of the Gaels from the seed of Eremon of Bregia.

27 By Richard the Great was gained the Battle of the Cinders, the battle of *Calgach*, the famous conflict of Trim, the fray of the castle by Frewen.

28 Richard, moreover, gave in one month three battles to the blood of noble Conall and the race of Niall, stems from a single cluster.

29 The same man it is that fought the battles of *Loch Cuain* and of *Beannchor*, and—long has the result of the conflict been a benefit—the battle of *Annla* against the Ulstermen.

30 At *Ros Guill* by northern Tory, moreover, he gave battle to *Ó Maol Doraidh* and overthrew the race of Conall, it was a conflict of strength.

31 It is that Richard who divided *Leath Cuinn* with boundary ditches and into smooth acres yonder at his dwelling including Connachtmen and Ulstermen.

32   Under the favored offspring Sir Richard, him of the fair-browed, generous countenance, not a fastness or a hunting mound of victorious *Leath Cuinn* was left untilled.

33   From the Strand of *Baile*, son of *Buan*, to the shores of the Suir in its pleasant valley was his; his from the blue, sunny-banked Suir to the western Head of Erris.

34   He was lord over Shannon and Suir, over the murmuring waters of Cong, over the Moy, the babbling streams of the Bann, and all the rivers between them.

35   Salmon from Assaroe, from the pleasant shore of the Bann, and from Cashel's slender stream, used to be served on the same spit to that earl.

36   On one dish of ruddy gold the nuts of *Seaghais*, fragrant fruit of Derry, and apples from the banks of the *Boroimhe*, would be served to Sir Richard.

37   Never was there found the equal of his kinsman, Sir William, he continued the triumphs of the man, like to his father in disposition.

38   Eight battles are reckoned to William *Óg*, high-king of the Burkes, gained over the Leinstermen, over *Leath Cuinn*, by the imperious hero of *Umhall*.

39   The battles of Liffey, of *Magh Mail*. against Leinster, unkindly enough! The battle of Loch Neagh in Ulster, and four battles against Connacht.

40   The famous battle of Slievemurry, the battle of Inny, in the Annaly, the celebrated battle of Athenry, gained by the valor of the highking (*or* were amongst the exploits of the highking).

41   As for Scottish Edmund, none dared to oppose him: not so much opposition did he find as an attempt to speak disobediently.

42   Thomas, son of Edmund, was, in short, of the same bearing, and his valorous son Edmund, blue-eyed, smooth handed warrior.

43 Richard, son of another Edmund—no likely opponent was the fiery dragon—the fruit of the orchard from London did not receive homage from the blood of Conn.

44 There was no lair of the wild deer, in dangerous passes, or on the slopes of valleys, in Richard's day, that he did not despoil, so that he disquieted the isle of Ireland.

45 Richard—great was the power—a man by whom Conn's Tara was laid low, gave the spoils of Meath, the tribute of Kells, as wages to the men of *Umhall*.

46 In those days, of which ye have heard, the star of the Plain of the Champions brought the gates of Bregian Tara to Loch Mask on *Magh Tuireadh*.

47 The caldron of the king of Man across the sea, the smooth-framed harp of *Beann Éadair*, were brought to his house by the hero(?) of Tara, together with the chess from *Eamhain* in Ulster.

48 Long did great John, son of Richard, follow in his path, harassing the men of Ireland for possession of the bright, fresh-swarded Dwelling of the Fair.

49 Oliver, son of John, got John's heritage of the land of *Fál*; of those that took the grassy Field of *Fionntan*, no man's son excelled him.

50 John Burke, son of Oliver, is the man that will spend and defend the ruddy-nutted plains of the blood of *Cas*, and the boundaries of the shore of *Bearnas*.

51 The blossom of the apple-tree from *Eamhain* surpasses all his forbears, from Oliver back to William; to each man is his destiny apportioned.

52 An unfathomable ocean bed, a heart not to be doubted, a steed from the swift brood of *Eamhain's* rampart, a pious, subtle mind.

53 A brimming well in sultry days, a magnifier of every good, a resolve no less firm than are planted rocks, tokens of an adventurous prince.

54   The object of his enemies' blessings, instructor of
the lords, expected mate for the plain of Meath, herdsman
of his enemies' cattle.

55   Battle-stay of the land of Bregia, gate of death
to the race of *Ith*; smooth-fingered hand most unyielding
in battle, most precious treasure of the Burkes.

56   MacWilliam Burke, enemy of evil, capable to
banish unseemly customs; strong is his hand against their
wickedness, a prince like royal Caesar of the Romans.

57   There is no son of Gael or Englishman, from the
Ards in Ulster to Achill, that is not full of the same
affection for him concerning the possession of *Ughaine*'s
fair-sworded Plain.

58   John, grandson of John, has no enemy or friend who
has any reason to doubt his claim to *Cobhthach*'s bright-
walled castle.

59   From childhood's days until now, I defy each
learned man to show that the scion of Bregia's citadel
committed any deed of which his heart might repent.

60   In earnest or in play, in assurance or timidity the
star of Sligo's host never meditated anything which would
need confession afterwards.

61   The mischief-maker (even) is witness that he never
said, nor was there ever said of him — bright cheek like
the berry — anything he would conceal in a whisper.

62   Never was there said of his radiant face anything
which would be fitting to hide from him, and he never
concealed from anyone the reason of his foe's conspiracy.

63   Should it happen that a man were able to slay
those who surrounded him, once he submit to him he
need not fear vengeance.

64   Steeds have not been shod, nor has blade or corslet
been hasped since he, gentle grey eye, from which the
sea is calm, gained lordship.

65 There is no going into camp in his days, no weapon stirred from its rack; no one under heaven in dread, no rumours of ravaging parties to be heard.

66 No asking for tidings, no expeditions or hostings, no spoiling, no destruction, no conflict, no plundering of anything from an enemy.

67 Nothing which might make a woman tremble, no Gael committing injustice against any Englishman, nor any Englishman despoiling a Gael, no wrong of any man permitted.

68 From the prosperity of the peaceful kingship there is entrancing fairy music in the speech of each man to his fellow, around the defender of Curlews' plain.

69 Conn O'Donell — may God protect him! Precious scion of the race of the highkings; a man without lack of courage in exploits, leader of the warriors from Lifford.

70 Four score, five hundred and one thousand since the birth of Christ is remembered — the ... sorrow was destined — until the ... death of John.

EDMUND BURKE

1 What now delays Edmund? Surely we shall not endure to be as we have been for some time, like any captive at the mercy of the foreigners.

2 Everyone has noticed the length of this delay of Edmund's, ere the man's pride was enkindled, ere he found a reason for rebellion.

3 I know not what has hitherto kept the prince of the soil of *Umhall* like a hostage in English fetters, under the treacherous enactments of the foreigners.

4 Not weariness of battle nor peril of conflict, not lack of army or following has ever restrained the hero of *Bóroimhe* from setting forth.

5 Not . . .(?) days are responsible for (the delay of) the active, courageous one, hand by which the Fold of the Fair is overthrown, neither is it . . .(?) or bad weather.

6 When the man would be setting forth the prophecies of soothsayers or poets would not hinder his graceful form from spoiling or sacking Ireland.

7 Both to me and to himself has been known for some time past the sole reason for the delay of Edmund, chief of the people of Conn's spreading plain.

8 The amount of his riches and his wealth, the regality of his great princedom — these were protecting Ireland, warm bright-stoned Plain of the Three Fair Ones.

9 Edmund himself did not perceive — this certainly is the reason for the delay of his ruddy countenance — that there was a single thing lacking to him.

10 So long as he were permitted to be without trouble or hardship Ireland would be as a level pool from edge to edge.

11 As soon as he is attacked the English and the Gaels of Ireland will teem with treachery towards one another, with anger and discontent.

12 That which was never endured before let not the son of MacWilliam endure it; since there is a case for battle it is no day for Edmund to make peace.

13 Since conflict is kindling let him not leave it in doubt[1] but the hero of Bregia will requite their unjust deed.

14 The fight has been forced upon him without the leave of the dark-lashed youth, the more likely is he, pillar of battle of Corc's Plain, to avenge the matter.

15 Ever since days of old ... the man ... the man that begins the quarrel.[2]

16 What war has there ever been in which he that first started it was not vanquished? That is the way in wars.

17 Have we not witness enough in the assembly of Pompey, the hosting of Caesar? The descendant of the chieftain from the Plain of *Cnodhbha* is as in the case of the Civil War.

18 Pompey, if it be true, first made war against Caesar, and though victorious for a while, he was remorseful in the end.

19 Caesar, in fine, vanquished Pompey who first caused the conflict, and the valiant hosts from the eastern land, as they had begun the war.

20 Those who enkindle dissension are ever defeated in requital for making war, a work that does not meetly go unpunished.

---

[1] or, reading *cuiread*, 'let them not doubt'.
[2] Text imperfect.

21   Badly did it result for the Trojan warriors to make
the first day's war: they provoked the Grecian heroes,
who considered not an occasion of battle.

22   The people of Troy did not suppose at first that
in that fierce, ardent conflict—it was not long till they
felt the result of their wrong doing—the armies of the
world would rout them.

23   ...[1] the mighty Grecian soldiery, of admirable
deeds, a lasting example fit to be cherished.

24   Those that started the war—the Greeks did not
yield to them, nor did any of their seed since settle in
their native place.

25   Just such a war as that did Eber unjustly proclaim
upon Eremon son of *Míl* about the green-pathed plain of
the champion of *Fáil*.

26   The end of their battling was that Eber fell by
Eremon in his impetuous anger (fighting) for the bright
centre of the sunset land.

27   Great *Mugh Nuadhad* and *Mugh Néid*, well did
they expiate such an act—first renouncing peace with
Conn, a deed they could not maintain.

28   Conn beheaded both *Mugh Néid* and venomous
Mugh Nuadhad, ill did it result for the progeny of the
chief of *Fáil* that they did not uphold the law of battle.

29   May a like destruction, since it is he that is attacked,
be told of Edmund; a sure result[2] of all unjust dealings
in war.

30   He hath been treacherously dealt with: against
him the war hath been begun ...[1]

31   ...[1] spoiling in the midst of peace that is not
a seeking of disturbance for Edmund, object of the
glances of the noble English stock.

---

[1] Text imperfect.
[2] Reading: Ní cáil.

32　So long as they held from the son of MacWilliam the fertile portion of Connacht they would not need to pursue him to plunder the dangerous mountain ravines and morasses.

33　For the arrogant, stubborn band it would be putting the head into a lion's den to plunder the man of his ancestral land, or it were to approach a blazing house.

34　Or it would be plunging the bare hand into the griffin's nest in order to destroy her first brood, to meddle with his bright, softly-speaking countenance, or it would be plundering laden(?) bees.

35　Or it would be waging battle in spite of terms, or snatching treasure from fairy palaces or—woe to him that must face her—teasing a hound through her puppies.

36　Or it is handling the edges of naked weapons, or arousing a red bear, for the warmly-housed(?) soldiery from beyond the wave to attempt combat with Edmund.

37　Or does anyone suppose that when Edmund had been plundered he would leave anything of value in . . .[1] smooth, beautiful land of . . .[1] castles?

38　If any indeed so thought they had no justification; an evil not easy to repress is the surging of rapine from the kindling of Edmund's righteous anger.

39　. . .[1]

---

[1] Text imperfect.

19

EDMUND BURKE

1 Well mayst thou use this weapon, Edmund, O bright, pearl-gray eye; may it be an omen of danger to the enemies of thy fair-cheeked, lime-bright countenance.

2 May this weapon which is bestowed on thee, thou youth to whom such as we are dear, be a sign of protection of friends, despoiling of foes.

3 May it portend the exaltation of thy kindred, may it render time and occasion propitious, thou strong hand in quelling hosts—may it be a sign of the debasement of foreigners.

4 This weapon of mine is not as the weapons of others, though one would be glad to obtain it, dangerous are the conditions which go with it, thou smooth-footed warrior of *Bearnas*.

5 Thou shouldst not—if thou wouldst do so—take a weapon thoughtlessly from my hand in return for gold and silver, thou war-sprite of *Gabhrán's* bright Plain.

6 It will not suffer thy broad face to be unwatchful, unprepared, or that thy splendid form heed not to be active and alert.

7 It likes not that its companions sleep where they eat their breakfast, it endures not a refusal of battle, hard it is to accept its prohibitions.

8 Be the host few or many, be there peace or disturbance, this keen-edged sword which no blade rivals desires not to be even for one night on the rack.

9 Desisting from foray is one of its prohibitions, and this weapon thou hast received, thou hero from Art's lime-washed Dwelling, may not take one step in retreat.

10 Didst thou take a prey with it even on the seventh
day it were no harm; it is not possible for this weapon
to abide for the time of a month without spoil, without
trophies.

11 Were I thy suitor thou wouldst wreak, O bright
face, in search of the treasure of Conn's bounded Field
a hundred other injuries.

12 Thou wouldst not slumber on down or on quilt,
wert thou answerable to me thou wouldst not dare con-
sume a feast without a sentry keeping watch for thee.

13 Thou wouldst be one day beside the Duff, beside
the sunny slopes of Aughty, another by Croghan of the
battalions, and another at the borders of Tara's Dwelling.

14 Thou wouldst make conflagrations about Loughrea,
thou wouldst spend a day in spoiling thy gilt bucklers(?)
beside Bregia's plain, O bright form, or at ancient Loch
Key, having made a foray on it.

15 If Walter, thou slender of hand, be feasting or
playing chess, be thou in arms to win triumphs, until
his men of means(?) are despoiled.

16 The function of ...(?) with ships, the function of the
tongs in the smithy, O fruitful branch of *Ior*'s Dwelling,
is thine for thy high-king.

17 Unless thou do as I have said to thee thou wilt
get from this weapon as regards the treasure and the
booty of Conn's race naught but failure or death, O Edmund.

18 Their crimson mantles, their graceful hounds, their
women, their rings, their chessmen, their golden drinking-
horns are freely thine, their gifts of gold and silver.

19 If thou desire, thou warrior of *Codhal*, to be longlived and prosperous, let the conditions of this weapon
be maintained, never be they violated.

20

MAC WILLIAM BURKE

1   Much circumspection is due to the title of king, it must be guarded both from headstrong arrogance and lack of vigor, it is truly difficult to defend it.

2   If a man be headstrong he must needs be given to forays and wars, he will draw upon himself a contest for the kingship, and his land will be wrested from him.

3   Howbeit, let not one choose to be humble and servile; he will be despised thereby, not kingly is he who resolves thus.

4   Between arrogance and gentleness lies the golden mean of kingship; the king who is most moderate in his bearing is able to deal with disobedience.

5   According to this not many of us are fitted to assume kingship; it is not easy for a man to undertake it, considering these qualities which pertain to it.

6   Saving this only, might not Richard, son of Oliver — smooth hand like the blossom of the thorn — boast now that all follow his standard?

7   He seeks naught from anyone else, and he leaves none unsatisfied (?); despite the amount he spends of his wealth, there comes no ebbtide in his riches.

8   Although he has attained to kingship after winning every territory, it is enough for him to be as before, Richard, son of Mac William.

9   According to the judgment of the learned of Innisfail on Richard, grandson of John, he is the best, since he is the eldest, if he can answer for his comrades.

10　It is hard for them to displease the son of the queen from *Ráth Murbhaigh*; he of his race has the best claim, such might will be joined with him.

11　He is the most temperate in spirit, and has the best talents for lordship; the king of the Moy, chief in every fortune — by him is it most efficiently defended.

12　Never a day has the king of Cong been found humble or submissive — although he has plenty of prudence — hand which would not be checked in combat.

13　Neither is there any danger to the champion of Achill, high-spirited though he be, of being plundered on account of his arrogant spirit, fruitful branch of a lord.

14　Just such a warrior as he obtained the reward of his temperate spirit, the heir of the king of the Greeks, a deed most likely to be remembered.

15　The name of the youth was great Daedalus, son of Saturn, best warrior of the Greeks in valor, a graceful-fingered, kindly scion.

16　He coaxed — what greater affection? — the daughter of the emperor of the world to elope with him from sea to sea, without asking the leave of her father.

17　Along with him on his excursion, Daedalus, apple-branch surpassing the forest, brought his two brothers to guard the life of the warrior.

18　After exploring the lands they are wafted to a lonely isle, inhabited by no one in the world.

19　When this company of four had spent some time there, the maiden went of her own will to the green shore of the isle.

20　After a space a warrior of wondrous array came towards her; the woman, alone by the shore, regarded him for a while.

21　Never was there fashioned, of all human creatures, clay more beautiful than that warrior, face (radiant) as the moon, throat (white) as a blossom.

22 The young and giftworthy warrior saluted the modest maiden, such fear was in her heart that she made him no reply.

23 And then he asked: "What land is this in which thou art, or who has a right to dwell in it, thou graceful-handed, chaste beauty?"

24 "The children of the king of Greece, who never grudged wealth, Daedalus and his two brothers, they," said she, "are in possession of the land, three appletrees from a single stem."

25 "I shall bear thee away from the three heroes, maiden," said the warrior; "sorrowful are thy words," said the woman, "it would be an omen of conflict were they heard."

26 "Didst thou so deal with me," said she, "in despite of my husband, it would be difficult for all the world to shelter thee, from the terror of the high-king's weapon."

27 "I shall take their ship with me, and the three chieftains who are within shall remain in weakness of travail in this land until the end of the world."

28 He carried the woman into the ship, and then departed from the isle, having outwitted Daedalus, the generous, whitetoothed hero.

29 She cried as she left the shore, he rushed to her at once to see what was her trouble, or why she grieved.

30 He sees a ship under full sail, just visible from the strange land, speeding out to sea; he hears a cry from the vessel.

31 For seven days after, as it is told, Daedalus and the company who were ashore[1] remained without woman, without ship.

---

[1] lit. within. Cf. § 27.

32 "O brothers, it is poor-spirited of us," said bright-faced Daedalus, "not to escape with the wings of birds, and fly from the isle across the sea."

33 With strong glue they attach a bird's wing to the shoulder of each man; they arise from the slopes of the hills across the deep expanse of the ocean.

34 In arrogance of spirit the youngest of the eager heroes arises; from the sea he goes close to the sun, and ascended into the high heavens.

35 The sun's heat dissolved the fair glue, the wings gave way; he fell helpless headlong into the deep billows of the ocean.

36 The second youth kept close by the surface of the great streams, so that his stout pinion was struck from him by the cold flight of the water.

37 Upon the severing of the heavy wings by the harsh edges of the green waves the second warrior meets his death: an occasion of grief.

38 The elder of the joyous, fair youths, in a course between loftiness and lowliness, went unharmed across the surface of the white-foamed sea.

39 On coming to land the high-king seized his sword and his bright lance, and followed in the track of the couple.

40 He searched the whole world in pursuit of the pair, and when he overtook them afterwards he caused their bodies to be hacked in pieces.

41 He slew the ruddy, white-toothed woman and her paramour; he gave him due cause of remorse for seeking his wife from him.

42 The young maiden is the wand of kingship, yours was that woman at first: be not slumbering, thou bright of cheek, the maiden has been stolen from thee.

43   The ship, moreover, O soft of hair, answers to those places of sovranty belonging to the Seed of Charles which have been wrested from thee, as it is said; compensation is due for unjust deeds.

44   And the island upon which thou didst remain when the maiden had departed from thee, thou hand unflinching in combat, is the comfortable plain of peace.

45   The bird's wings whereby thou didst leave the island are the mercenaries of hilly *Banbha*, and the companies that surround thee.

46   And that glue which binds to thee the blue-armoured warriors, thou chief of Bregia's ever-roving host, is the stipend which is dispensed to them.

47   The other young brother, whose great daring submerged him, is the people who contend with thee, and the kindred which arose on thy behalf.

48   And the man whom his lowliness of spirit submerged answers to those who would tell thee to make peace about thy territory.

49   Thou, O chief of Cong, art come in the middle way between them; thou art the elder who wilt surpass the rest, thou star of the isles of Ireland.

50   Thy love who was borne away from thee unjustly, O sparkling countenance, if she be restored to thee let her not be received with humility.

51   Go forth, thou king of Carra, make fast to thee the wings to recover the maiden, thou fair forest-tree of *Bearnas*.

52   This maiden has from childhood's years been wooing thee, Richard, this smooth, long-cultivated, fertile land, this territory of the seed of Charles.

53   Thou art the most worthy of her, many are the reasons, thou stately hero of Bregia's hill, wherefore thy patrimony should be lawfully united to thee.

E. Knott, Tadhg Dall Ó Huiginn.

7

54   Thou hast the most numerous household, the largest number of veterans of battle: difficult it were for any to challenge thee, thou best of the sojourners of Ireland.

55   Let thy royal seat be filled, Richard, at the quaffing of ruddy draughts, with a number sufficient to guard the coasts of *Banbha*, a generous, peaceable host.

56   Let the northern side of the house be occupied by Sheela, daughter of Owen, and a flock of fair, modest, white-handed maidens, not of the daughters of the Sons of *Mil*.

57   Let the choicest women of the Irish and the English fill the apartment around her; a bright-cheeked swarm, ungrudging of cattle, disturbance of slumber to the warriors.

58   Many will be the slender-lipped, bright-cheeked beauties feasting with the daughter of the king of *Durlas*, like stars in time of frost.

59   A bevy of cupbearers with crimson beakers dispensing wine for her until after sleeping-time to the royal stags of the plain of Connacht.

60   After a time her minstrels, her music-makers, come to her; a forest of sweet-stringed, plaintive stems, about her soft, spreading locks and blushing cheeks.

61   The household of the queen of the plain of Cong— time passes swiftly amongst them: a noble throng, whom it is no wonder to love, abounding in witty converse.

21

MYLER BURKE

1 Subdue thine arrogant spirit, Myler, forbear, thou joyous countenance, to be perpetually plundering the children of Conn, thou accomplished, gracious one.

2 The disputes of Ulster, the wars of Connacht, are severally laid to thy reproach, thou fair and bright of face.

3 Thou art blamed respectively for what is despoiled in Leinster, or in Munster, land of gently flowing rivers, O clustering, ringletted tresses.

4 On thy account, thou broad, lean, gentle countenance, many a time, when thou art in repose, there are flights from thy reavings one after another in the four quarters of Ireland.

5 Because of the spoilings thou hast wrought thyself, thou son of Walter, thou art accused in every part of Ireland — noble land of sweetly murmuring streams — that is devastated.

6 No wonder that young and uncouth band which follows thee in time of stress should be blamed for forays, thou shapely, sleek, smooth head.

7 Men to whom a quilt of snow is a bed of down, amorous, ardent youths; a bright, adventurous, agile throng, wondrously equipped.

8 In no place are they so long settled, the young and spirited drove, the lawless, barbarian band, as in the gloomy cliffs of the heights of *Banbha*.

7*

9   Alas for him who is king over them, according to the look of this roving, active band; their couch grass, their feast cold water, these armies of the field of the Gael.

10   Thy followers are scarcely unlike thyself, thou son of Walter; troublesome, careless-minded men, scouting-parties of fierce warriors.

11   They sleep not, they eat not a meal, without discussing a battle or an encounter; continual pondering on forays and wars has dimmed the brightness of their glowing cheeks.

12   The time will come, Myler, when thou wilt regret the ways of thy followers, these warriors of keen, sadly-wounding spears; a company that will be intolerable.

13   As it is destined, if it be right to credit prophecy, thou wilt forcibly wrest the kingship of Connacht of the bright harbors from the hands of the foreign tribe.

14   They will continue, according to their wont, in wars, in roguish exploits, in doing hurt, O bright face, beyond any of the host of Croghan's dyked meadow.

15   As a king thou wilt not be able to suffer injustice or disturbance; then will thy dear face regret thy forbearance towards thy followers.

16   Thou wilt make all desist from their wars, thou, O waving tresses, wilt defend the Connachtmen from the might of reavers, and from the excessive burden of the foreign soldiery.

17   The soothsayers of *Fódla* were assuring the possession of the blue isle of the Gael, the fragrant soil of Bregian Tara, to thy father.

18   Thou, O bright, soft countenance, wilt fulfil what the druids foretold; thou wilt rescue the country of *Banbha* from the great oppression of the foreign hosts.

19   Of thee, O slender form, is foretold that which *Aoibheall* prophesied to the noble children of Brian *Bóromha*, three fair stems from the soil of *Lugh's* land.

20   Three sons of Brian, three lions of *Maicnia*'s Munster, three royal heirs from the House of Tara; gracious, comely men.

21   *Murchadh*, son of Brian, he of the bright hair, *Tadhg*, son of Brian, *Murchadh*'s brother—let one plant be chosen above the forest—nobly-born *Donnchadh* was their elder.

22   *Murchadh*, son of Brian, and Brian himself—these fell together, battling with the warriors of *Lochlainn* for bright, fertile *Clíu* and its smooth castles.

23   Those children of Brian, flower of the vine from fair *Clíu*, favorers of the sweet prophetess, were wont to obtain tidings from *Aoibheall*.

24   After a space *Donnchadh* son of Brian goes forth to speak with *Aoibheall* concerning the lovely Boyne, of smooth yew-trees.

25   "O woman," said *Donnchadh*, "declare to me who shall be king over the bright western plain in succession to Brian? it is not a curious thing to ask."

26   "*Tadhg*, son of Brian, thine own brother," said *Aoibheall* thereupon, "to him has the House of Tara, dwelling with varied vestures, been promised."

27   After this converse *Donnchadh* became filled with envy of *Tadhg* of *Banbha*; it is hard to bridle a woman's foolish speech, the hero's reason became subverted.

28   Therefore he fratricidally slew the heir to the kingship of *Fódla*, and said that he had refuted *Aoibheall* regarding that descendant of *Tál* and *Éibhear Fionn*.

29   *Aoibheall* came to reproach him when *Donnchadh* was left alone in . . . (?) Kincora, by the bright, fair, blue-streamed rampart.

30   "It is unjust for thee to say that my prophecy was false," said *Aoibheall*, "my words regarding the noble mate of Bregia's castle are certain," said the maiden.

31 "For the heir of a high-king and for the heir's son the prophecy is the same, it is said; have faith in what I say regarding the pleasant, flowery plain of swaying yews."

32 "What I promised to *Tadhg* of Tara, *Tadhg's* son Turlogh shall receive; stag of the royal flock of the noble line of Cas, finest vinestalk of the Fergus."

33 Turlogh, son of *Tadhg*, assumed sovranty over every part of Ireland—fair, pleasant land of graceful streams—even as *Aoibheall* had foreseen.

34 Even thus it will befall thee as regards this land, thou gracious form, thou wilt win supremacy over *Meadhbh's* Country, thou stately, white-footed youth.

35 *Aoibheall* promised the Country of *Lugh* to *Tadhg*, son of Brian *Bóromha*, and Turlogh—sustaining pillar of Tara's stead—had the profit thereof.

36 The druids of *Banbha* have ever been prophesying that *Cobhthach's* Plain—restful land of firm forest trees—would come to Walter, son of MacWilliam.

37 Walter, O crimson lips, died as he was about to become king, for thee, thou defending arm of Meath's hill, will the prophecy be fruitful.

38 The province, thou graceful form, was full of dissensions upon Walter's death, full of wars and battles and wrong and harm.

39 Since thou hast gotten warrior's weapons the rest have not dared to think of their enmities, to speak of war, or to use force, thou ripe fruit of the vine.

40 It was thy father's death that hid the fruits of the forests, the fish of the bay; and it is the reason wherefore the moon and sun were fettered.

41 There come with thee, as thou hast come, the flowering of those woods, the corn of the tilth, the produce of the streams; each element recognizing thy tokens.

42 Behold the fully sprung corn, behold the moon
shining brightly, why should there be any distrust of
thy claim to the bright-walled land of Connacht?

43 Moon and wind and sun, stars of heaven and clouds
of the sky are favoring thee, thou lord of Gorumna, the
sea is about proclaim thee.

22

A COMPLAINT

1 Thou messenger going across the moor, speak yonder with William Burke; tell him of the plight that I am in, without any prospect of help.

2 Tell him moreover, in secret, that there is no shelter for me on land or on sea; that no one before was ever afflicted with half of my injustice or one third of my wrong.

3 I have been paying my share for two years or three, and after that all the liabilities of others are levied from me.

4 When I saw the liabilities of the others being all wrested from me, I went to the courthouse to see if I could obtain right or justice.

5 In going to the court I myself spent—to my sorrow, and that is not all, in ridding myself of that trouble— whatever little I possessed.

6 I fetch with me a good warrant, and return full of spirits; I thought that I was safe after my visit to the great court.

7 I display my own patent to the . . .(?), when they had read my letters. I got even less consideration(?).

8 My captain, each of the two to whom I go again lamenting, swears by the glove of Christ that it is not his part to hinder them.

9 The sheriff that was in charge of us, this is what my precious fellow says to me: 'you trust to the creditors, it is not the soldier that will lack anything.'

10 It did not satisfy any of them to take one gage alone from me: in payment of the fines of the rest I had to render two or three gages into the hand of each man.

11 I spent a long time going from place to place in search of the gage; not only is my gage taken from me, but I redeem it twice or thrice.

12 When I would redeem it from the first man that held it he from whom it was redeemed in the beginning (?) would hand it on to the next.

13 I go promptly in pursuit of the gage, whether it be carried far or near; I never returned home till I had spent six times its price.

14 Then as for the President, to whom I would go to relate my case; with tears on my cheeks I used to make complaints to him, sternly and bitterly.

15 He says, gruffly, that not by his will would a gage be taken from me; that, however, I can give payment for it eventually.

16 It is not for my goods I am most grieved, but that when I lost my fortune none remained to support me, for I was left destitute in the end.

17 The horseboy, the cowherd, the quern-girl, the comb-woman—they all went from me at once, along with a soldier: a wretched deed.

18 This is what my own cowherd, of all those that deserted me, says, showing me(?) the fire: 'What keeps you from drawing up?'

19 I have been, there is no reason for hiding it, under dire oppression these three years; in hope for the coming of William Burke I did not make much of it.

20 God's curse on those dealers in lies that do not verify their stories; everyone whispers to me that William Burke is here.

21 Thou messenger going to meet him, pay no heed to fun or sport; speak with my own companion, and see if he has yet come.

22 Lion's whelp of Loch Con, salmon of the Shannon's bright streams, hound of the inlet of Assaroe, much do I expect from his coming.

22 a

RICHARD ÓG BURKE

1 Give heed to thyself, Richard *Óg*, do not forsake thine early disposition; if one might say so much to thee, it were more fitting to be as thou hast been.

2 Be, even as thou hast ever been, 'Richard son of MacWilliam;' alas, if thou shouldst assume any other rank, thou gentle, supple scion of *Mucroimhe*.

3 Thou wouldst do ill, O pure face, to change that former name, considering all it hath won for thy bright hand, with it thou didst increase in prowess.

4 The mantle from which a man derives customary good health, O pleasant countenance, he loves that garment, thou sacred stag of Bregia's fair territory.

5 The place where one succeeds in increasing his wealth, that is the post on which he is stayed, he is not easily expelled beyond its borders.

6 The boy who is sent to his own land from the country in which he is reared, after his nursing therein, thou bright of hand, the boy and its people are hard to separate.

7 Even thus it were not for thee to part from thy wonted title, thy well-known deeds, with every triumph that thou hadst of old, since from it was got all that thou didst win.

8 O son of Richard, gentle of heart, as for the foreign title thou hast got, never didst thou gain any advantage from it that the fame of the former title did not outdo.

9 Didst thou get the headship of *Flann's* Plain it would not advantage thee, thou gallant form, in thy native place, to reign over *Banbha* by a foreign title.

10 Even I—it were not worth thy while for the sake of a hazardous and shortlived title, thou warrior who hauntest the border of *Banbha,* that I should not get an opportunity of speech with thee.

11 Am I not all the more emboldened to say to thee, though it should mean an eric leviable against me, thou scion ordained above the blood of Conn, that there is a reproach between us!

12 Not happily didst thou obtain the strange title, or the horrid outlandish right, about which I make bold against thee, thou diadem of Connacht's first assembly.

13 Whatever land in which I might chance to fall, under any of the kings of Ireland, even though I should not seek a price for my blood I should deserve vengeance from thee.

14 Didst thou fail me of thine own part, thou wouldst still owe, thou offspring of high-kings, to bear the part of the queen of Galway's field with those who should avenge our displeasure.

15 It was seldom for us and for you, blood of the luminously judging Burkes, to whom shall fall the guardianship of Ireland, to be contending with one another.

16 Any offences that our people ever used commit against Clanwilliam, ours would be the honorprice there for, thou powerfully attended champion of Man.

17 Unfitting is it, if thou follow the dealings of their poets with their princes, thou charmed diadem from the fairy mound of Knowth, that the eric of such as I should not be paid.

18 Even as the fragrant blossoms of Clanwilliam ever did, do thou, O forest tree of Bregia's height, about thy poet's reproach.

19 In the name of poetry we forbid thee to change thy title: thou shouldst renounce the new appellation rather than lose thy patrimony.

20 Let me find thee again in thine own shape, thou champion of the Plain of royal Niall: thou must make speed, give up thy strangeness towards us.

21 Thou wert the sinew of *Banbha*'s land until thou didst get the outlandish title; the sheriffship of Conn's seed would not compensate for leaving sinewless the fair hunting-field of *Íor*.

22 Thou madest a deceptive bargain, an exchange not to be persisted in, thou triumphant champion of Bregia's hill, thou shalt regret the deed.

23 The worse for thee that thou didst not meet with the son of the French knight the day the new name was bestowed upon thee as a condition of receiving thy patrimony.

24 Once on a time the knight's son, feeling vigor in his arm, thought to explore the world, in hope to find marvels.

25 Despite his father's wish the youth set forth— what greater delusion?—active form, most steadfast of purpose, he would take no counsel to change.

26 A precious stone the full size of his fist did his father entrust to the youth, wrought with exceeding nobleness was it, and dyed in gold.

27 "Search the world from sea to sea with my gilded stone," said the father, "bestow it, thou bright, soft-limbed fellow, upon him who is most foolish of purpose."

28 The young noble bade farewell to his kinsfolk, courteous, firm in exploit, he left his fatherland.

29 After his sweetly-speaking, pleasant, sprightly figure had travelled the world, the youth—what greater strength?—found himself in a certain strange land.

30　He sees from afar a multitude of people, a great royal city; he hears many cries from the people gathered round the brightly-roofed, shapely castle.

31　He hears then, about the noble, stately city, on the hills hard by the enclosure, cries of sorrow and delight alternating.

32　Afar off, before drawing near the city, he enquired from the first man he met the reason for that assembly.

33　That man said: "those people thou seest before thee, clan by clan, are the inhabitants of the land."

34　"There is in this country," went on the young man, "a strange, alarming custom: their king, even though he break not their law, reigns over them but for one year."

35　"At the end of the year they leave him out on the sea, in a lonely island: alas for the king whose patrimony is the stately city thou seest."

36　"Every king who has departed from us will spend his life from this on without friend or companion, see if there be anything more pitiful under heaven!"

37　"This assembly around thee are making a new king to-day, having banished the former one, a deed to pacify a multitude."

38　"These hosts beside thee are choosing a new king, on account of nobility and birth, that is the cause of their gathering."

39　"These cries thou hearest from all, this is their import," said the young man, "a king being proclaimed by some of them, simultaneously with the lament for the former king."

40　The youth proceeded thereupon with his precious stone to meet them; the affable, ruddy, bright fellow remembered the admonition of his father.

41　That day into the hand of the king the youth — what greater contempt? — delivered the many-virtued, splendid stone, he earned thereby an upspringing of contention.

42 "What is the reason thou hast put into my hand this precious stone, or dost thou wish to sell it, thou strange youth?" said the high-king.

43 "My father," said he, "said to me: when thou hast searched the world, my son, bestow on the most surpassing simpleton the golden stone we have delivered to thee."

44 "By thee, now — therefore hast thou received the stone — has been committed a deed the most foolish under heaven, O glistening, kindly eye."

45 "Thy long life, and thine own inheritance, hast thou given, what senselessness, O noble, splendid form, for the sake of one year of supremacy."

46 The king paid heed to the pleasant speech of the young noble, and having found true guidance, he publicly renounced the kingship.

47 I would have given to thy bright face, if I had it, that man's stone, thou apple-blossom of Kincora, when thou didst change thy title.

48 Thou gavest, thou ruddy form, an abiding name in exchange for a temporary one; O fighter of Bregia's gaily-tinged hill, that was an imprudent deed of thine.

49 All that thou didst obtain from the beginning by that renowned jewel of a name was worth enough, thou star from Cormac's noble Plain, that thou shouldst not displace it.

50 With it, as Richard *Óg,* in youthful days long ago, thou hadst as profitable a time as ever man had, throughout the bright plain of the Gael.

51 Of yore thou wouldst spend a day in ravaging the shores of *Bóromha,* a day by the soft, shallow streams of the Boyle, a day by the flats of *Bearnas.*

52 A day by the babbling streams of Bonet, another in Erris: a day by Tara of Meath, and by noble, ancient Loch Sewdy.

53   Equally didst thou explore the brinks of *Forbhar*, the borders of Sligo; from them as far as Croghan of Conn, and from Croghan eastwards to the Shannon.

54   The track of thy steeds one would trace from Achill's point to Ushnagh, without a man swerving therefrom, from Bunduff to Loch Derg.

55   All would say, O kindly figure, that as 'son of Mac William' never, though thou borest no strange title, wert thou humbled in a fray (?).

56   The old name, O lord of Cong, well didst thou do to alter it did the fair curves of thy countenance find therefrom any reason to blush.

57   Those who know thee from childhood's years are challenged to say if thou didst ever meddle with anything on earth that would earn reproach for a man, thou lord of fair Loch Corrib.

58   Thou son of Joan, from the fairy mound of Trim, if there be variance between us, it should not be long persisted in, lest the fair curves of the cheek be scorched.

23

WILLIAM BURKE

1 God's justice between me and William! not well did the generous and gifted nobleman—even though it be possible to make peace about it—suffer such as I to be harmed.

2 It were not worth his while, without cause or reason, seeing that he, bright face, hath proper objects of plunder, to rob any man on earth of what he had gained by his art.

3 Even if his slender hand were continually plundering the poets of Ireland, surely the flower of those stems from the Bregian Boyne would have no right to despoil me.

4 Never before was there a portion that William and I did not divide—though it was destined for his bright cheek that by him I should be deliberately ruined.

5 I was his poet, but none the meeter was it that he should meddle with my goods because I was called his follower and there was a bond of art between us.

6 Long before, moreover, I was to William a pupil, a teacher: I used to impart learning to him, loyal, rosy countenance, and receive it from him.

7 All the parchments of learning, the strain of music, the improvised couplet, each one of these that he studied I used to expound to the man.

8 The book I used not to read myself he, bright face, would impart it to me, so that his fair hand was my noble instructor: it is a shawl which is the thinner from its folding.

9 Such learning and knowledge did he obtain from me that he was my special pupil; he to rob me is a sentence of bondage, he was my tutor in the elements.

10 I was his master, his pupil; his companion, his comrade: not well did he forthwith obtain my cattle; unjustly he went to despoil me.

11 Not well did he forget, when about to plunder me, that I was his follower, and that I and the fair, long-fingered fellow, William, used to be together over one book.

12 Moreover, even had I not been, as I am, his pupil, it was no meet action for him of the ...¹ tresses to snatch her gold from poesy.

13 Even had I not been tutor to the valorous champion of Fannad ...¹.

14 ...¹

15 I have served — alas for me that served — in all these forms ye hear, though the griffin of the Erne be now an enemy, the author of my hurt.

16 It was none the wiser for William to attack me because he knew that I would not avenge my angering or my wrong on the royal star of the lands of Connacht.

17 He himself knew that I would not satirize his bright cheek—alas, that any should see me plundered by the man—for anything in the world he might do.

18 I would not, it were not for me to do so, satirize the precipitous flood (?) of the blood of the earls, a plant of the fair-haired race of Conn I would not satirize for the gold of Ireland.

19 I would not, it were not for me to do so — satirize a griffin of Conall Gulban's stock, I would not, he did not fear it, satirize a dragon of the noble race of Charles.

---

¹ Text imperfect.

E. Knott, Tadhg Dall Ó Huiginn.

S

20   I would not satirize the serpentlike venom of the blood of sternly-judging Brian, or the keen, bright, leonine countenance of the true flesh and blood of noble Niall's descendant.

21   I would not for the sake of cattle dispraise the fierce, blow-dealing champion of the remnant of Corc's thirsty-speared seed, and of the progeny of famous *Ior*.

22   I know that the satirizing of the brown-browed warrior, oppressive though I deem his foray, would not be left unpunished by the kindreds of the high-kings of Ireland.

23   Even were no one on earth shielding him from me — bright, richly curling, waving tresses — I could not satirize William.

24

SORLEY MACDONNELL

1 Long has *Fódla* had a claim upon Alba, now is the time to urge it; provided she get her own rights it is not likely that Ireland will be left mateless.

2 For a long space of time that land of Alba has owed a due to *Cobhthach*'s lime-visaged castle; a cause of dissension to the Scots.

3 Alba of the shallow streams should deliver her dues to the isle of Ireland, indulating land of rippling waterfalls, lest there be disagreement between them.

4 What new claim to-day has the land of the Children of *Míl*, tell me if thou knowest—, whereby she sues the isle of Alba?

5 The heavy tribute which Balor imposed upon Ireland —it would be an awakening of conflict for her to do it— is that what *Banbha* would claim?

6 Or is it the isles in the east between *Fódla* and Alba, and each tract of the fair plain of Islay, or ancient Cantire with its limpid streams?

7 The land of Eber is not thinking of any of those things you suppose, but of something more difficult to levy, something about which she has been in want.

8 The three Collas, children of haughty *Eachaidh Doimlén,* this is the end of their story: they went to the land of Alba, three with whom it were unfitting to vie.

9 Two of the three came hither to Bregia's land of fairy hills, the choicest of the host have ever since remained away from us in the Plain of *Monadh.*

8*

10   It is strange that Colla himself and his ancient race, stately men with perilous weapons, from that time suffered their inheritance to be lacking to them.

11   Why should the Children of Colla, for whatever arose between them, render allegiance to a strange, foreign land rather than to *Banbha*'s plain of brightly-waving crops?

12   Who is the lord of the blood of keen-sworded Colla whom *Banbha* is expecting? If she has chosen one of the race of Alba, it were fitting that she should be freed from rivalry (?)

13   The best-beloved of Conn's Dwelling, Sorley, son of MacDonnell, the expected mate from *Monadh*'s Plain, he for whom Ireland is waiting.

14   Fruitful branch of Tara of the Fair Folk, bright sun after a downpour, fortunate spray from the apple-trees of Islay, star of favorable summer weather.

15   Most favored offspring of Colla's seed, arm that banishes foreigners, fruit of the apple-plant of Bregia's soil, sustainer of the five fifths.

16   ... cause of grief, until she sued Sorley, the land of *Banbha* under a burden of barbarians, their (her?) claim has remained unsettled.

17   Ireland, in brief, will separate the best warrior of *Domhnall*'s race, fierce, fair, splendid heroes, from the ancient, wondrous plain of Alba.

18   I have read in an ancient parchment a story which touches the race of Colla, the curious tale which will be unfolded will be fresh unto the end.

19   The hero of the story which will be unfolded to thee — Caesar, the famed high-king — departed from the land of Italy with an army of splendid warriors.

20   Westwards from Rome they travelled to Spain's yew-treed soil, a goodly band of adventurers, they had not come on an embassy (?)

21   Caesar of the scatheless hosts loved the west of Europe, he consented to remain away from Rome, yet separation was not agreable to both.

22   When he had remained away for some time, one day after retiring to repose he beheld a wondrous vision, it was a prospect of help for the king to behold it.

23   It seemed to him that he found beside him, in the guise of a lovely, graceful woman, Rome, recounting her hardships, matter for condemnation.

24   Rome with streams of tears down her bright cheek, with locks dishevelled in sorrowful aspect, was bewailing her wrong, fitting was it to lament over what she said.

25   "It should not seem fitting to thee," said Rome, "for me to be as I am now in thy absence, with no prospect of succour, overcome by outlandish men."

26   "To defend a fortress that is not thine own is astonishing for thee, thou keen-weaponed soldier, whilst thine own land, after being ravaged, is being wrested from thee by barbarians."

27   These were the words of Caesar: "O Rome of the smoothly-fashioned rampart, whether I be brought eastwards or remain here, I have striven to be obedient to thee."

28   "I would say to thee," said Rome, "bring with thee the full muster of thy following, gather thy splendid warriors to invade the soil of Italy."

29   "Hesitate no longer, shameful for thee is thy chamber of slumber since foreigners have arranged it (?) though it be terrifying to face them."

30   He took with him eastwards the warriors of Greece, the soldiery of Europe, it was a time for display (?), to defend stately Rome, a most righteous action when considered.

31   Caesar, in brief, after the tyrannies she had suffered, delivered the wondrous limewashed castles of Rome from the power of the wicked host of barbarians.

32   *Banbha*, spouse of Conn, like Rome of old, will bring her own man from the Plain of *Monadh*, that is the meaning of what ye have heard.

33   MacDonnell's son sees before him in a vision, ere he falls into slumber, fair and generous *Banbha* bewailing her oppression.

34   Even as Caesar came the son of Alastar will come now to the Bregian Boyne to aid everyone, with a following difficult to number.

35   Even as Caesar's hosts won to Rome, through *Lorc*'s Field, with the full muster of his following, will come the Caesar of Colla's race, the pick of a choice gleaning.

36   From the playful, melodious Moy, so famed for treasure (?) as far as the Peak of *Éadar*, son of *Éadghaoth*, there will spring forth from the edges of the strands a veritable forest of sail-trimmed masts of majestic ships.

37   He will discharge the debt of his forefathers to the land of Bregia, following in their wake he will occupy the plain of smooth standards and many ...(?) eastwards to the ancient castle of Tara.

38   Though Eber's land submitted not to that Colla *Uais* from whom thou art sprung, the ancient line of Colla possessed her, she is an inheritance unfit for division.

39   Do we count a single king, from Colla back to *Gaedheal Glas*, who did not seize the headship of Ireland, if that knowledge prove an exhortation to them?

40   Without leave from us, the three Collas, champions from *Baoi*'s clear, sail-bright bay, surrendered Ireland through envy, for one day's hard-won victory in battle.

41 Sorley, timely it is, will speedily issue a ban, he will not fulfil the ancient contract of the Collas about the land of Frewin.

42 About Cashel, about Croghan of *Aoi*, about the brightly-wooded Hill of Allen, and *Oileach* with its faultless steeds, the ancient covenant of all will be revoked.

43 Because of the ban which Sorley shall declare, *Banbha* is about to mate, a troop hath come to levy her, the Boyne will rejoice at that ban.

25

MAELMORA MACSWEENY

1 One night I came to *Eas Caoille*, till the Day of Doom I shall remember it; when the fortress itself shall have perished there shall still remain forever the events of that night, the doings of all (who were present).

2 The like of the men whom I found in the polished bright-hued castle, on the shapely benches of the crimson fortress, eye never saw before.

3 But few remain of the beloved company whom I found in the bright castle, the death of the four that were within was a grief from which *Banbha* did not look to recover.

4 I found Maelmora MacSweeny on the central bench of the graceful mansion, a man of generous and pleasant manner, favorite pupil of the schools of Conn's land.

5 Dear as life to me was the man I found in that domed castle with its ivory-hilted swords; as I have experienced twice its value of misery from (the loss of) it, the honor I received from him is the worse from its greatness.

6 Both pupil and fosterer to the poets of *Banbha* throughout his days was the chess-king of the Finn; the goal of our emulation, our ready gift, storehouse of the hearts of the learned.

7 Our healing herb, our sleep charm, our fruitful branch, our house of treasure; a piece of steel, yet one who never denied any man, most precious offspring of the Grecian Gaels.

8 I found beside the son of Maelmurray many men of
letters worthy of recompense, while the choicest of every
craft in the world were also reclining beside the chief
of *Derg*.

9 Till the day of his death the poets of the host of
the House of Trim were ever with the chief of Conn's
tribe in a gathering large enough for battle or assembly.

10 At that time in particular there sat by the warrior
of Loch Key — well did their scholarship become them —
three of the poets of *Té*'s Hill.

11 There was the poet of the Earl of the Burkes, and
also by his soft bosom was one of whom the very mention
was a surety, the poet of the famous race of Niall.

12 There was the poet of the chieftain of the Moy,
Mac William Burke of just awards — discouraging in sooth
are the changes of the world, that not one of these remains is in itself a sermon.

13 Brian O'Donnellan, kindly countenance, poet to the
lion of Loughrea; he with the schools as the moon above *compared* !
stars, peace to his gallant, noble form.

14 Brian Macnamee, son of Angus, poet to the
descendant of Nine-Hostaged Niall; a man whose attain-
ment (?) was the best of his time, he was fit to deliver *? take the price to*
wisdom's pledge.

15 Conor, grandson of O'Huiginn, poet to the lord of
Inishkea, almost equal to a prince was the poet, the head
of his kindred in worth.

16 The three poets that I found by the ruddy, fair-
skinned hero — let a trio such as they be found in the
land of *Banbha!*

17 With one accord they arise before me from beside
the chieftain who was my chieftain; often I think of
them in my heart, the utterances of the three drawing
tears from my eyes.

18 The soothing strains of . . .(?) harps, the sweetness of honey, the elation of ale — alas, that he of whom I had them no longer lives — these gave me pleasure.

19 For a while after my arrival they drank to me — gentlemen were their attendants — from cups of gold, from goblets of horn.

20 When we had gone to our couches of rest to slumber, ere the coming of day, he who lay furthest from me would not admit that to be thus was not a sentence of bondage.

21 I lay in the midst of the four, the four forms that were most dear to me, the three comrades who have grieved my heart, and the champion of *Magh Meann*.

22 To the blossom of Tara and his three companions I relate a tale in return for reward; its dearness was a portent of fame for them, golden youth of the north.

23 Four treasures endowed with virtue I take from them in payment for my story; that the like of the princely jewels may not be found — is not that enough to color one's tears?

24 As the first award I was allowed I took the dappled steed from the hero of steed-abounding Slieve Gamph, him at whose death hospitality perished.

25 The dappled steed that I took from Maelmora — woe is me that I took it — hardly is there its like in the world, a steed surpassing all the steeds of Bregian *Banbha*.

26 From Brian son of Angus I took the choicest hound of *Dá Thí*'s Plain: its excellence was such as to place it above all other hounds, it was one of the choice hounds of the world.

27 It had been easier for Brian to renounce one by one all of the treasures of Ireland — wherefore should this not depress my spirit? — than his treasure of a noble handsome hound.

28   From Brian son of Owen, ere the fair, rosy, kindly fellow slept, I got as a reward for my story a precious book, a brimming spring of the genuine stream of knowledge.

29   The 'Cattle-raids,' 'Wooings,' 'Destructions' of all the world were in the gift I received, with descriptions of the battles and exploits thereof, it was the flower of the royal books of Ireland.

30   Conor gave the magic harp, such a precious jewel as even a king would not bestow; long has that present been a sorrowful inheritance, it was no fitting gift from a poet.

31   The harp of the poet of the Burkes will be ever an object of reverence; he from whom it was got is no more, but it remains in freshness to day.

32   Alas for him by whom the givers of these were beloved, since it was destined that he should part from them; men never false in the house of election, men who loved to spread their fame.

33   Alas for my beloved four, my bed-fellows, my confidants: four stems from a fruitful forest, trees fertile in gifts for us.

34   My reason wanders, restless is my mind after that shortlived company; alas for him who remains on earth without them, departing, they have left Brian's *Banbha* without fruits.

35   It is a heartbreak that the chief of the band which was within should be lacking to us; never before did poet lack the generous gift of his stout heart.

36   May God requite Maelmora for the quantity of his wealth that I received; one who bestowed as much as any man gave, the benefactor of all.

37   Suave in utterance, stern in resolve, ruthless in deeds, modest in speech; guardian of every man of his kindred, judge, soldier, poet, soothsayer.

38 Treasure of contention of the race of *Breóghan*, winning of their game, defence of their pledge; satisfaction of the hearts of troublesome guests, love of melodious, merry, graceful women.

39 Prudent preparation(?), generous disposition, a keeping of word, a breaking of peace: bright countenance from which the eyes could scarce wander, nursing knee of royal rule.

40 Solving of problems, posing of counter-problems, Inisfail's anvil of knowledge(?): hate of perpetual ease, love of conflict, surety for the peace and war of all.

41 The son of *Gormlaidh*, a branch above the wood, keen in mind, gentle in response—where is his like for bestowing a troublesome award? sternness and generosity he has in equal parts.

42 Though I have been in poverty since he fell, I should be above all the land of *Fál* (in affluence) if only Maelmora — lime-white skin, countenance of amber — remained.

43 The remembrance of what I got from my friend will soon be but an omen of grief: I shall fear lest the greatness of my honor should come to me again in illusion.

44 Alas, not many of my comrades remain to me in their own shape: the world has cast me away, sending me travelling afar in solitude.

45 Pitiful it is to lack my three comrades, the race of *Gormlaidh*, from whom the day was short: *Banbha*, who looked for help from this clan, is now under a cloud of sorrow.

OWEN ÓG MACSWEENY

1 It is they themselves who repress the race of Niall, lords of the fertile land of *Fódla*; through the jealousy of Bregia's gold-decked host the glory of the Gael has ever suffered decrease.

2 The sunny soil of the isle of *Fódla*, upon the death of their father the eight sons of Nine-hostaged Niall—a band used to peril—divided it.

3 The share of *Maine*, fierce *Laoghaire*, *Fiacha*, and Conall *Críomhthainn* was the level of Bregia's ruddy-beakered Plain, the ancient territory of *Tailte*'s Dwelling.

4 To mighty Conall of wide renown, to *Cairbre*, *Éanna* and *Eóghan*, the royal slopes of the North were given by the fiery impetuous host.

5 There were two amongst the spirited offspring of the high king who surpassed the others, they resembled not the rest of Niall's noble progeny, although they were stems of the same tree.

6 *Eóghan*, son of Niall of the Nine Fetters, Conall Gulban, the fierce griffin, they and the other sons were not the same.

7 *Eóghan* and rightly-judging Conall, two sons of mighty Niall, son of *Eachaidh*, of one birth, it is said, were these princes with smooth, glistening skin.

8 On the day on which the two infants were born a contentious disposition inspired the noble, highspirited offspring, two stems from a single vine.

9 Upon their birth each one of the bright-faced, impetuous pair was found—omen of conflict—hugging the head of his companion in his arm.

10 As for these children of powerful Niall, Conall and valorous *Eóghan*, they were never afterwards free from a battlesome disposition or from the throes of war.

11 Their seed from that time onward have been following in the wake of that pair, ever full of envy towards one another about *Conaire's* hazel-abounding land.

12 Raid for raid, wound for wound, have been constantly exchanged between the seed of Conall and the race of *Eóghan*, much harm do we know them to be answerable for.

13 For a long time the seed of the two heroes of the land of *Ealg* were balanced in arms as regards the plain of Tara, hurtful to themselves were their ravages.

14 The fruit of the fertile stems held the supremacy of *Úghaine's* plain alternately down to the time of *Aodh Athlamhain*.

15 At *Aodh* the seed of *Eóghan* divide, it befell them — what disloyalty — to overthrow one another's power; they themselves revoke their own rights.

16 When their alliance (?) dissolved in the time of famed Aodh *Athlamhain* the clan *Suibhne* parted from the race of Niall, warriors who never earned reproach.

17 After that the race of *Suibhne* made with propitious counsel an alliance with the noble youth of the race of Conn in fertile Tirconell.

18 The lords of Conall's tribe gave to *Suibhne's* nobly-judging stock their choice of the spreading, pleasant, fertile land from sea to sea.

19 From that day forward — evil the bond which came X? upon them — the seed of *Suibhne* allowed no man of *Eóghan's* race to have possession of the kingship.

20 Since that the seed of *Suibhne* have levied throughout the fair, grassy plain a claim out of every part of Ireland for our tribe of Conall.

21 Until the race of *Suibhne* made conquests for our race of Conall, Ireland was held by the descendants of *Eóghan,* graceful scions from *Cobhthach's* fold.

22 From that day to this the chief of Conall's noble tribe has overcome the rest of the warriors of the Gael in every contest· for the land of *Flann.*

23 Now to the seed of *Suibhne* anew, and to the race of Conall of the plain of *Bearnas,* there has come an arm to maintain their rights upon the gracefully-spreading northern land.

24 Owen *Óg,* son of MacSweeny, guarding shield of the coast of Mourne; one fit to wage war for Conn's descendants, a spark in the embers for Conall's race.

25 Precious salmon from the stream of the Finn, a sunny day after a downpour; stately figure, cool in conflict, the Ulstermen's gilded stem.

26 The battle champion of *Dálach's* kindreds, a man who ennobles their annals; lucky treasure of the gentle race of Conn, shepherd of Conall's flock.

27 As long as MacSweeny remains with the hot-bladed seed of Conall it will be profitless for a man to speak of a contest for the apple-branched land of the Gael.

28 Never have the seed of Conall of the plain of *Ughaine* been mightier than they are now, thanks to the hero of *Bearnas'* varied plain.

29 While keen-weaponed Owen lives the king of Conall's race will not find a chief to oppose him in Ireland's bright-foliaged land.

30 A wood is stooped by the growth of its stems, the pledge of every man of *Eóghan's* kin is brought back by the son of Margaret to the deeply-wounding soldiery of *Bearnas.*

31 Had not the lords of noble Niall's race been attacked by their own side all Ireland would have been no match for *Eóghan's* line, the flower of *Monadh's* slender-fingered host.

32 Even thus was Troy overthrown, victorious city
bordered with flourishing woods, sloping plains with the
choicest of lime-washed ramparts—from the envy of
kinsmen about it.

33 The famed king Agamemnon and all his following
set out to capture it with the Grecian host, a band
dangerous to oppose.

34 Each day a fresh slaughter was inflicted around
Troy by the soldiery on both sides, famous, mightily
courageous warriors.

35 After more than ten years, piteous the siege, they
had not succeeded in taking Troy by force; to attempt
it was a formidable task for any man.

36 Had they remained around it from that day to
this, with the full strength of their forces, it is not likely
that the Grecians would have captured the green-branched,
turreted castle.

37 It befell it, treachery enough, that some of those
within delivered it to them, even when the attack was
repulsed and none remaining around it.

38 Had not the stately fortress of the bright ramparts
been forced from within, all the armies in the world would
not be likely to demolish Troy, you would have said.

39 Regarding the supremacy of *Lughaidh*'s plain even
thus it befell the soldiery of *Eóghan*'s race, the apple-
branches from *Eamhain*.

40 Until some of their own folk turned against them,
the land of Bregia was held by *Eóghan*'s race, without
desire of fight or attempt at conflict, neither refusing nor
accepting battle.

41 Had the men of all Ireland, from sea to sea, attacked
the line of *Eóghan*, it would not have been so grievous for their
soldiery as if the race of *Suibhne* alone were spoiling them.

42 Unkindly was it for the seed of *Suibhne* to levy
the dues of *Fódla* from the race of noble Niall for the
generous line of royal *Dálach*.

43   The seed of *Suibhne*, the noble seed of Niall, two vine-groves from a single root, fruit of one golden husk excelling all the wood, they have sustained the glory of the Gael.

44   They are called of the same stock, their pedigrees are the same, equal the nobility of their men, equal the patrimony of their fathers.

45   Did the spirited warriors of *Suibhne*'s seed but consider, no better is their claim to Tory yonder in the north, or to the calm, ancient stream of the Mourne,

46   Or to *Craobhruadh* of the children of Ross, or fair Carrickfergus, or to the green hills and bright lands of Dundalk.

47   No closer is Conn of the hundred fights, no nearer Niall son of *Eachaidh*, nor yet is spotless *Gaedheal* more akin to any other man than to Owen.

48   What should hinder Owen *Óg,* the Gaels' unique implement of battle, from following in the wake of Niall's seed of yore and taking hostages from the dewy hills of Bregia?

49   Empty houses around Croghan of Conn, from fear of the king of Conall's race; on Mac Sweeny the blame should lie — and castles by the Boyne are being wrecked.

50   What the daughter of Conn, son of the Calvach, gives to the poets — perpetual bestowing of treasure is an omen of praise — is a deprivation of which Margaret is none the worse.

51   Third generation from Conn, son of Conn, and from Manus, king of Conall's clan, though she be the most generous about riches what she does is nothing to boast of for her.

52   The kindreds of which she is, the wine-blood of Conall, the race of *Eóghan* — if she inherit their instincts — have hitherto been supreme amid the people of Niall's land.

MACSWEENY OF FANAD

1   The counterpart of Allen is in Ulster, for victory in battle, for wizardry; for defending the fair mansions of *Banbha,* for staying the rapine of Ireland.

2   For waging conflicts, for reddening blades, for music, for chessplaying: for seeking of killing and chasing, for desire of foray.

3   In the same guise as ever, Allen of the Field of the *Gailiain,* or its very likeness in a jewel of a firm house of stout masonry, is in Ulster.

4   Throughout Ireland, Isle of Bregia, away from the warriors of Leinster, until it reached Fanad of Ulster, Allen hath betaken itself.

5   The rampart which the *Fian* of *Fál* held is again in Rathmullan, or else a castle similar in structure to that ancient one of Allen.

6   There is in Fanad a likeness of soft-swarded Allen in its own guise: such as the warriors of Allen are in it, graceful, bright-weaponed, well-equipped stead.

7   Should it be that it is not Allen, this brilliant, marvellous rampart, this other dwelling is a <u>fitting pledge</u> X for the bright house of *Fionn* of Allen.

8   Though it were difficult to excel that first Allen of the tribe of *Baoisgne,* this second Allen — castle with firm, stately towers — is better when looked on.

9   Greater is its muster of valiant heroes, more its youths, more its companies of women: more numerous around the long-lashed scion of *Murbhach* are poets visiting the mansion.

10 More numerous the variety of its musicians, its reciters of soothing tales, more numerous the royal host of light-hearted women, ever weaving diverse gilt broideries.

11 More numerous the cupbearers dispensing feasts, the children of kings sharing fetters, greater the distribution of the wealth of all in the castle rich in flocks and gentle springs.

12 Nobler the household of the dwelling than the followers of *Fionn* of Allen; the pledge from the *Fionn* of old will go to the other *Fionn* of Ulster.

13 Thou, Donnell, kindly countenance, art that very *Fionn* from the land of Fanad — plain of limpid streams and stately rivers — protecting the men of Ulster.

14 No hardship or distress shall touch Tirconell of placid streams that thou art not bound to ward off from that country of untilled borders, of swanflocks.

15 As far as Moylurg on the other side, as far as the Finn, and to the shores of Tory, thou bright of cheek, it is thine to guard her bays and harbors.

16 Watching the couch when the king has lain down to rest, settling disputes, checking quarrels; going for him into battle on their behalf — the greater part of thine obligations I do not recount.

17 The rear in defeat, the van in an onslaught, thou, O lord of Fanad, dost form for the chiefs of Conall's glittering-bladed line in the country of the foe.

18 Therefore, Donnell, in the pleasant Land of *Flann*, bright with fair stems, ennumerable privileges are bestowed on thee by the seed of Conall.

19 Thou, gracious figure, art entitled to <u>hold</u> the ? <u>kingship</u> on the death of a high-king, until another king be found by whom she will be possessed.

9*

20   Thou, gentle of eye, art entitled to be by O'Donnell's right elbow, that thou, O king, shouldst occupy it ennobles the place.

21   When thou art dubbed MacSweeny, thou modest of countenance, yet menacing, the robe of O'Donnell of Derry is given to thee, thou heavy-lashed, stately eye.

22   Thou, modest countenance, hast the right to keep a fugitive under protection in thy country for a year without compensation being sought for his deed.

23   A cow out of every holding, a swine from every herd, this is thy stipend for defending the province; a ripe stem from the midst of a garden, thou hast the crop of every orchard.

24   The king of Conall's race may have sought to exchange estates with thee, thou ruddy countenance, we know of thee that thou hast never attempted to barter.

25   Did the race of *Dálach* give thee two or three times as much as they give, more honor even than that hast thou earned from that race.

26   Thou art the favored offspring of *Dálach's* seed, the pride of their annals, treasure-house for their peoples, herdsman for safeguarding their triumphs.

27   Thou art the eyesight of the host of *Bearnas*, the steward of their lordship; thou art the fruit excelling beyond all the wood, which succoured the noble race of Conall.

28   Thou art their protecting shield on the field of danger, thou leviest the heavy tribute which their fathers exacted from Ireland, it is imposed in every spot.

29   Thou art the leader of *Suibhne's* race, the *Fionn* of our Plain of Conall; it is thou that imitatest *Fionn*, thou king of whom *Aoibhcall* told.

30   Many prophecies have we from the noble saints of Ireland about thy sleek, soft, yellow head, foretelling the *Fionn* of Fanad.

31   Colum at first foretold to Ulster, land of bright
fruit-trees, what the *Fionn* of Fanad would accomplish
for the fair plain of heavily laden woods.

32   He foretold that this man would so deal with
Leinster, and the Peoples of Tara, that from lack of men
meadows would go unmown throughout that Dwelling
of *Taille*.

33   Beyond any other tidings that *Sèadna* revealed as a
young and truthful babe did the impetuously-affirming
youth tell of the long-haired *Fionn* of Fanad.

34   "Grievous to me," said the child, "it has filled me
with dejection, the slaughter that *Fionn* of the flowing
tresses will inflict on your warriors, ye men of Leinster."

35   "In the land of Leinster — sorrow enough – this
Fionn from Fanad will leave but women to till every
soil:" even as Colum had spoken.

36   Thou art that *Fionn* from Fanad, it is to thee thine
ancient rivals look to fulfil the prophecy, and banish the
usurping race from Ushnagh.

37   Thou wilt make a slaughter of the Leinstermen,
thou, graceful (?) of hand, wilt spread the hue of embers
over the white houses of the foreigners: surely Colum
will be believed.

38   Shortly, MacSweeny, wilt thou boast to the chieftain of our race of Conall the reaving of *Fòdla* from end
to end, and the banishment of the foreigners from Ireland.

39   Thou, son of Turlogh, hast given tokens worthy
of credit that thou art come to-day as the prophesied
one to reign over Fanad.

40   Allen of the fertile slopes of Leinster — thou, *Fionn*
of Fanad, hast built the counterpart of its timber and its
walls, the counterpart of Allen in Ulster.

41   A choice of the royal ladies of Ulster hast thou
made, thou dark-lashed eye; happy the man who hath
first taken her, happy he who made that choice.

42   A gentle eye, bright as crystal, hath the daughter of the king of Banagh; lips to which the hue of the berry might be likened, a glowing cheek that never was made to blush.

43   Every woman of Ulster would not suit the husband of *Gráinne* as a companion, none but a generous man would suit her, happy he of whom she is the mate.

INISHOWEN

1 Speak on, thou castle of *Oileach*, many a thing must one ask of thee, thou fair, long-standing dwelling, regarding the warriors of Ireland.

2 Let us learn from thee, tell us, thou ancient, bright-lawned castle, of those who invaded Bregian *Banbha*, of the forays and seizures of the Gael.

3 Each thing of which I have knowledge will be got from me, hearken, what time were better to reveal it? downwards from the pouring of the Flood.

4 I know, as a rare branch of knowledge, of six seizures in turn after the Flood on the cool, moist, white-surfaced, dewy plain.

5 The coming of *Pártholón* from the land of Greece, and of the Sons of *Nemhedh* to the country of *Fál,* the third age of the world, it is I that best remember them.

6 How wast thou at first, thou lovely, changeful castle, when *Pártholón* of Bregia's haven had come to occupy the Field of the Gael?

7 Upon the coming of *Pártholón* I was enduring my misfortune in this land, with no enclosed meadow or stone rampart, but all an oaken thicket.

8 How was it with thee during the sovranty of the Children of *Nemhedh*, when thy form had been changed? Tell us, thou castle of limewashed . . . (?) walls.

9 I was a smooth plain, without thickets, without woods, the border slope of my bright, steed-haunted lea was a splendid mound of assembly.

10 Of my bending wood with its graceful fruit-trees
not a root was left in the ground — small since that has
been the growth of my noble forest—from the might
of *Nemhedh's* saintly race.

11 How long wast thou thus, a smooth, brightly
glistening slope, without house or household, thou greens-
swarded castle of *Oileach?*

12 Until the coming of the *Tuath Dé Danann* to the
spreading woods of *Fódla,* I was, as such were unfitting
for me, empty of house or dwelling.

13 Dost thou remember who were the first of the
comely *Tuath Dé* who inhabited thee, thou tower amidst
supple, flowering stems?

14 The Children of mighty, honey-mouthed *Ccarmaid,*
keen-weaponed warriors, a glistening band from the
Bregian Boyne, were the first that entered into fellowship
with me.

15 For my smooth, fertile hills the Children of *Ccarmaid*
forsook stately *Cathair Chróoinn,* hereditary citadel of
the race.

16 A while after they had come to me the Sons of
Míl of Spain wrested *Banbha* from the Children of *Ccarmaid* without a division as profit of battle.

17 From that day to this the lords of *Míl's* race,
white-handed host, dealers of heavy blows, have been
defending Ireland within me.

18 From that time on I have never lacked one high-
king in succession to another, or a provincial chief who
excelled any in Ireland's swan-flecked plain.

19 From me five-and-twenty kings of *Róch's* valiant,
generous race seized the Dwelling of *Dá Thí,* thereby
my dignity is ennobled.   ·

20 And after the Faith there were crowned from me
six-and-twenty kings of the blood of fair Conall, and of
Niall's line, fruit from (?) each cluster were they.

21   Then was I held alternately by the noble kindreds of Niall's seed—a smooth . . .(?) plain with lofty stems, another Tara of the men of Ireland.

22   Since from thee all other tidings have been obtained, from the beginning until the end of time, thou fortress amidst pleasant, brown-surfaced hills, which company hast thou found the best?

23   The wondrous warriors from Ulster's soil, *Fiamhain*'s seed, the blood of *Dochartach*, that bright band are the best whom we have known from of yore.

24   O tapering tower of smooth, even walls, who is it that excels even amongst the lords of *Fiamhain*'s race, stems from . . .¹ of Frewen?

25   Were we considering it forever, John son of Felim, of the clear soft eye fore which the sea is shallow, would be the choicest of *Fiamhain*'s fair stock.

26   O'Doherty of the castle of *Oileach*—why should it be asked?—rosy, bright-hued countenance, he is my one darling in his time.

27   Though *Fiamhain*'s seed are the best of the noble stocks of Ireland, they are as stars about the full moon, John is the one choice of them all.

28   It is he that has most possessions, he is the one who bestows most gifts, in the benevolence of *Iomghán*'s valorous scion there comes no ebb.

29   It is unlikely that any should attempt to surpass Felim's heir in his name for generosity; as a plain lies beneath a hill so is every other renown in comparison with his.

30   Considering the fruitfulness of his territory, the goodliness of his kingdom, why would he not do all that he does?—no man should marvel thereat.

31   'The paradise of Ireland' is the name for that stretch of land which is his; never did eye behold a finer territory than the soil of its plains and hillocks.

---

¹ Text corrupt

32   From sea-locked Fanad to the bright streams of Loch Foyle, from Malin to the plain of *Bearta*, a lovely and most famous land.

33   Land where waves are gentlest, where granaries are loftiest, angelic country of shallow streams, 'Land of Promise' of the men of Ireland.

34   Well is it placed, between the sea and the woods, level strands beyond far-stretching plains, wondrous, fairy-like regions.

35   Smooth moors amidst its forests, peaked hills beyond the moors, a yellow-hazelled wood by the fair plain, a billowing sea as a hedge around it.

36   Good is this land ... [1], better is he who has custody of it; alas, if one should see over any part of Ulster a king that did not surpass Ireland.

37   Were his the supremacy of Bregia's plain he would spend it and defend it; if prosperity according to bene-volence be just the lord of Fahan should be prosperous.

38   If the contents of his house are considered, and the number of his household — it is not a superfluity which should be grudged to him — no superfluity (?) of riches is found.

39   Thou man who proclaimest what the high-king of *Fiamhain*'s stock possesses, grudge it not to the princely hero of *Fál*, greater is his spending than his gains.

40   If many speak truth, did not the house of *Oileach* fall to John, the thronged dwelling of O'Doherty would not be a shelter for any in Ulster.

41   This is the several statement of those who have journeyed the plains of *Banbha* — all the delight of Ireland would be found in the labyrinthine (?) four-towered court.

42   Since Tara received *Ruadhán*'s interdiction against the men of *Fál*, the lords of Conn's land have dwelt in the pleasant, fairy-like, comely castle.

---
[1] Text defective.

29

CORMAC AND BRIAN O'HARA

1 The repute of two is as a wood to each of them; they spare not to dispense their cattle: two fruitful branches of a fragrant forest, scions are they who have earned homage.

2 Two full moons of *Leath Mogha*, *Cian*'s two sons that never purchased peace; two palm-branches of the regal stock, choice ones of whom it is not apparent that either should be rejected.

3 Though the rewards of the first man were something to boast of, greater are the bounties that follow; until a poet obtained the wealth of Cormac, he glorified the gifts of Brian.

4 Long is it remembered by *Lughaidh*'s Country that the seed of *Cian* are no peaceable folk; either of them in ungentle mood was care enough for a land.

5 Whatever fight in which Cormac is is not believed to be wanting in forces; if he lacks a man he finds one in the house that is entered.

6 If a poet were leaving Cormac he would be coming to Brian: the company that did not depart from him last night will return as a fresh company to-night.

7 If it be that they avoid the rest of the seed of Eber that is no reproach to the excellent warriors, a pursuing party that has looked upon the children of *Cian* will not overtake even the most slowly-stepping women.

8 When Cormac joined the race of *Lughaidh* few believed that Brian would flinch, how many of the seed of *Sadhbh* abstained(?) from the conflict the number that were in the battle know not.

9 Through terror of Cormac under the shelter of night, through dread of Brian coming after him—they are both hidden by the hand of the foe · the grassy stalks have bent back.

10 As for spoils taken from the enemy, Cormac considered that what was in his keeping was not his own; only until a poet is seen does the hoarding of cattle trouble the race of *Cian*.

11 The gifts which Cormac keeps for travellers failed him at last; the guest is satisfied after his discontent, Brian's wealth hath made him so(?)

12 Oft of yore, in contending for the kingship of Leyney, has he sought his spears in the midst of slumber; he used to close the gates of his eyes when daylight came to his fastness.

13 *Una*'s son hath a bevy of warriors, of the hawk-like birds of the seed of *Blod;* in order to test the soldiery of *Tulach* in battle Brian allows a superiority over them.

14 Cormac only undertakes to get justice: Brian knows not contentment with justice, seizing a shield wrought with golden monsters, he seeks to levy claims which are not got.

15 No great regard had he for ancestral right(?) until she favored thee, Cormac: suffer poets to feast beside thee, that is an honor of which Brian thinks much.

16 Let those poets, too, be mentioned at the sewing of satin banners—it is difficult to abate the discontent of companies—utterances with the art(?) of gold rings.

17 Thou, Cormac, causing him to be forgotten, that is what has hindered the bestowal of her love; the woman who has sought thy companionship would not exchange Brian for any other man.

18 A word from thee is enough for a man, after that little doth he reck what place thou choose(?); a shattered flag of ice hath convicted thee of the foray.

19 People of means (?) after their discontent, if they rely on thee worthy is the support: all that the soldiery fear is lest their own king should wreck a tower.

20 Thou, Cormac, ruling a country, hath kept Brian from conquering it: thy stewards go beyond their limits to increase the liberties (?) of the kindred of *Cian*.

21 The warriors of *Banbha*'s isle are in fault that they knew not the manner of thy weapons; a lance which thou didst ply against them as a dart fitted the spearshafts of the rest.

22 From the shafts of thy javelins, after a space, there springs a wood from a champion's grave; so that it were the easier for thy attacker to wound thee, thou didst send such a number of weapons into him.

23 She gave her love in turn to the children of *Cian* of the glowing spears; the maiden looked on thee after him so that she was ready to chose another than Brian.

24 Amongst the great drinking-horns of another castle they must needs divide its measure, the head of thy spear, when its shaft is removed, excels the goblets of thy dwelling.

25 Thou hast for poets, Cormac, an entertainment ? reserve ? which is a cause of fame: in store for a passing guest thou keepest (but) a grass-green stream.

26 None the better does he like an attack in battle, since thou hast the supremacy in power; had Brian a longer cast he would not take the field of battle against thee.

27 Without its being red hot, without entering a forge, a feat none else ever could perform, thou wilt straighten — or it will break in pieces – a shoe ...(?) that never was worn by a horse.

28 It is he that first incurs the obligation, it were ?? better for the lips to be silent, any king that reproached thee for thy slayings denies it, or seeks honorprice.

29 Thou, Cormac, art celebrated by those who travel the three continents; the schools are not accustomed to thy going into obscurity, they do not seek thee there.

30   The warmth of the early spring joins the branches of great trees to the roots of the sward; the fruits bend the trees so low that there would not be safety on top for the bird's nest.

31   Bending woods and shallow pools, sweet springs over pasture plains, honey ...(?) tincturing green streams from the earth throughout an hour (?)

32   Scarcely is there anything to equal it in the days of Cormac, save the wondrous (?) havens of Paradise; what he drank of the waters of Leyney's plains takes from the child the remembrance of the breast.

33   The heavy tribute which Cormac gathered did not protect the land of the reaver: Brian thought his share of the settlement too small, he knew what it was before going on foray.

34   Gold is not lasting with the warriors of Cashel amidst the sparkling of hot ales; such fumes arose from the goblet around Cormac that brown mantles smouldered.

35   Lion's whelp of *Leath Mogha*, fortunate salmon of the race of *Cian;* whatever place he was in yester-eve he is enough as a guard for it to-night.

36   To a chosen soldiery who have followed them it would not profit to oppose them—the race of *Sadhbh* is not a fence without a top-rail, they fight to uphold Cormac's peace.

37   Her gray eyes flash crimson so that she cannot conceal her passion, because of him a woman can scarcely sleep, the branch of *Deirc* has confessed it.

38   For the castle of the champion of Leyney there is no danger that the complement of any house will excel it; all the mighty progeny of Eber the Fair arose from feasting along with our Cormac.

39   The spear-forest of Eber's race, scarcely is there a fruit that they have not won; it is not possible to rival them in battle, trees above the woods are they.

30

CORMAC O'HARA

1 Here is the guarantee, Cormac, take this hand in thy supple grasp, knit this heart to thine, thou forest tree of *Bóromha*'s shore.

2 Take this body upon thine own, thou chief of royal *Cian*'s race, against the law of the king of the bright isle of the English, let this life be guaranteed by thy life.

3 Accept me, upon thy mercy and thine honor, against both friend and enemy — O hand that rulest the race of Conn — thou art capable of protecting me.

4 Do not leave me. to contend alone with any, thou kindly, royal presence, since thou, O bright cheek, art our one friend amongst the lean-bodied host of Teltown.

5 In short, thou grandson of *Onóra,* that thou be with me in a rightful cause is no benefit from thy rosy countenance if thou do not also support me in wrong.

6 I am continually in the jaws of danger, because of all the gossip that has been made about me, having no one to protect me, unless thou canst undertake it.

7 To-day new laws are being imposed on the Sons of *Mil* by the noble, bright-handed English host, throughout the green-maned land of Frewen.

8 They summon the territories to them, and require from all in general, until they are all ascertained(?), a knowledge of every man, and of his native place.

9 Having assembled the territories the English of Eremon's Field write the names of their hosts, one after another, in a large, clean roll of parchment.

10   And when they have been assembled before them,
each of the men of Ireland, thou warrior of *Túl*'s Dwelling,
with manly following, must acknowledge an overlord.

11   They require that everyone under heaven have a
guarantor, or else—piteous the strait · which has been
wrought for them—die forthwith.

12   In brief, thou king of Leyney, on thee I set my
security, in all my days, as is meet, thy book shall be
my book.

13   Not because my inclination is towards thee, or
because I am thy poet, thou fruit of *Eaghra*'s cluster,
do I choose thee as lord.

14   For this have I chosen to be with thee, thou royal
star of Cashel's plain, both Gaels and English have agreed
to give thee the title of righteous king.

15   Because thou art full of kindness and generosity,
righteous and prudent—plentiful reasons for goodwill
towards thee—therefore art thou loved, Cormac.

16   In thine own books, thou high-king of noble *Cian*'s
line, under the knot that has never been loosened by
me, let the name of each of us poets be written.

17   Let the name of every man of my kindred, mine own
name in particular, thou precious treasure from the ancient
plain of *Túl*, be kept in those books.

18   Be thy gentle eye assured, since I have thine
affection, thou strong-aled scion from the waters of Duff,
that I shall merit it from thee.

19   I call thyself as witness to it if I live for the space
of a year during which thy love towards me will not be
beneficial to me or to thee.

20   I shall compose for thee the artistic, well-wrought
lay, the laboriously wrought (?) poem, and another time ·
the single stanza, thou noble chief of *Bóromha*'s shore.

21 I shall give thee, as is due, knowledge of thy genealogical branches, of the tribute taken by thy forbears from the plains of Ireland, the course of their triumphs and their exploits.

22 I shall tell thee, thou slender form, of thy nobility transcending that of the rest of the men of Ireland, and of every homage that were due to thee — the price of our friendship, Cormac.

23 In order to raise the envy of the rest, to thee, thou son of *Úna,* I shall devote the best portion of my poesy, and the best part of my converse.

24 In requital thereof, thou chief of Cashel, it is not too much for me that thou offer thy life and body on my behalf if I be captured.

25 Even were one on trial for his life in a courthouse, while depending on thy honor neither he nor thou need tremble; here, Cormac, is the guarantee.

---

26 Undertake my protection, Mary, on behalf of the chieftain of bright Galey, thou fruitful scion of *Suibhne's* race, whose safeguard is not in danger of violation.

27 O Mary, daughter of *Maol Muire,* until I entrusted to thee my shepherding, almost every fastness which I reached was forced, thou lady of clinging tresses.

31

CORMAC O'HARA

1 A good merchant is Cormac, *Cian*'s son for whom the yew-branch bends; a generous hand in bestowing cattle, the best barterer amongst you.

2 In Cormac's days never is anyone heard to cheat him in bargaining, that is what makes him of the pleasant, affable countenance easy to beguile.

3 *Cian*'s son, he of hardy achievements, the better bargainer is he—beloved hero from Bregia's hills—that each one coaxes him.

4 Behold is there any better exchange than the lasting, enduring honor that goes to the pleasant, kindly chieftain in return for vain, transitory wealth?

5 Not for long would the riches given by Fermoyle's lord remain, but the praises of his noble, ruddy countenance shall endure eternally.

6 None of the goblets or cloaks which all receive from Cormac, nor the . . . (?) engraved battle-weapon would endure for even a single thousand years.

7 Neither armour nor horse nor shining, carven helmet, nor tunic of soft, blue, sheeny satin, nor valued drinking-cup of variously wrought gold would endure.

8 If the wealth of the world were estimated—this is the gist of what ye have heard—save praise alone, there is naught of the earth but . . . (?)

9 A good merchant is he who exchanged the ephemeral flower that awakens envy—far from the flower is the coming of its fruit—for lasting encomium.

10 A good merchant is he who got in return for a worthless, transitory figment the sincerest of fragrant, lasting panegyric at a time when art was being rejected.

11 A good merchant is he that purchases when the discount is greatest the goods on which he depends, or those which he must buy.

12 It was for O'Hara, by virtue of his ancestry— unniggardly men of no mean figure—to purchase the fine panegyrics of everyone.

13 Cormac son of *Cian* would never find—the more fitting that poesy should be fully requited—a time in which the stately poems he buys from all would be cheaper than now.

14 Throughout *Banbha,* of the nobles of Bregia's soft, dewy plain, this warrior alone is seeking poetry from us now.

15 A hundred times as much as what could be got to-day for polished specimens of the poet's art shall be given for them later on by the hero of *Bóromha's* shore.

16 When it is cheapest and when fewest are seeking it, that is the very time to cherish the flower of perfect, durably formed poetry.

17 Since poetry is cheap to-day, Cormac, if the proph-esied one of *Crotta's* Plain survive, will have an unreckon-able store of the eulogies of all.

18 The rover of the hills of Bregia will leave provision for all, gathered when easiest to obtain, of the polished offerings of the poets.

19 Good was that man of yore, the mighty, valorous hero of Cashel, who, away in the beginning of time, made just such a provision.

20 Famous *Mugh Néid,* Cormac's gallant, princely ancestor, king of *Codhal's* strong-aled Plain, made a similar provision.

10*

21 The queen of keen *Alugh Néid* beheld long ago a vision; there was import in the telling of it, she related it to the high-king.

22 Seven goodly, thriving cows appeared to that wife of *Alugh*, she sees the bright, sleek, fair herd around the isle of Ireland.

23 And then, moreover, it appeared to her that from the bright, wondrous herd each fair, rosy, white-hazelled plain was flowing with new milk.

24 After that herd there appeared to her seven hideous cows, sickening to speak of were the aged, spectral kine.

25 With harsh, bitter cries, with ironlike horns: furious as a ... (?) flock; with sunken, burning eyes.

26 Not a trace of the young and marvellous herd was left by the frenzied, pugnacious, repulsive, venomous, serpentlike drove.

27 *Dearg Damhsa*, the king's druid, gave the reading of the dream, this is the truth thereof; he hearkened to the learned judgment, its great profit came to pass.

28 Thus said the druid, beginning: "The first seven cows are seven years of abundant milk, perfect in rule and sovranty."

29 "The other cows, moreover, are seven miserable years of hardship, for Ireland, land of sweetly-murmuring waters, it will be a portent of devastation."

30 "The woman shall devour the son she carries on her back, the heir shall deny the father, throughout Ireland, smooth, beautiful land of blue streams, from hunger."

31 "Therefore," said *Dearg Damhsa*, "let provision be made by you ere the first years come to a close, thou bright-limbed king of the Gaels."

32 "In thy tax or thy tribute from proud *Leath Mogha* accept not throughout the spreading land of fair, fertile, dewy hills one penny of gold or of silver."

33 "Do not accept from any in thy royal tribute,"
said the king's sage, "aught else save food as the universal
payment."

34 To each thing the druid said to him the king of *line's*
brightly-spreading land willingly agreed, he was of one
mind with the sage.

35 Upon their own summons the Munstermen unanimously attend the son of the high-king, in an ordered
multitude around Glandore, in return for aiding their
distress.

36 *Conaire Mór* and *Maicnia* did homage to *Eóghan
Mór,* after the assembling of the territories, most willing (?)
were the host to submit to him.

37 *Mugh Néid* was over Munster as a lofty stem
among saplings, by reason of his perpetual purchasing of
food for the comely assembly of Munstermen.

38 The better are his seed ever since that he waited
not for the time of high prices, he—bright form before
which the sea ebbs—purchased the cheap bargains of
the rest.

39 The high-king Cormac O'Hara imitates *Mugh Néid*
—two rightful owners of *Fál's* Cornfield are they—in
getting a profitable bargain from us.

40 *Cian's* son who never defended a wrongful deed,
it is right that he should be set to merchantry: flower of
the stock of *Sadhbh's* noble blood, a trafficker in the gold
of poesy.

41 Here is a propitious bargain of perfect work of
proven poets for his keen, eager, heavy-lashed eye, from
the learned of Eber's Land.

42 Till the Day of Doom all that he has purchased
of the gold of poesy will remain as an augmentation of
fortune and prosperity for the host from *Bladhma's* peaks.

43 The meeter is the time he hath thought to requite
the poetic faculty of Laoghaire's Land since the regard
of everyone else hath forsaken it: it is a flock without a
shepherd.

44 The blessing of the poets of Innisfail, the united
blessing of the holy men of Ireland; that is the requital
of his purchase; blessed is he by whom it is earned.

45 On *Cian*'s son who buys encomiums the fortune
of the blessing hath settled, from the sole of his soft,
smooth, gracious foot to his thickly-curled, stately head.

46 Not more to-day than when he was a child is the
love of all for his kindly features; the flower of Leyney
got as a babe fortune which shall not be denied him.

47 Some time in his boyhood he was left as a child,
after his kinsfolk had been cut off, ere his bright cheek
had reached maturity.

48 No trusty friend or comrade had the slender-
weaponed youth; he was in peril from his enemies, facing
them alone.

49 His territory, and moreover his kinsmen, had been
wrested from him, so that the builder of *Tál*'s Dwelling
was left as the only one of his kindred.

50 Then was the ownership of Leyney wrested from
him — unkindness enough! — the unrightful man was ele-
vated, and he for a time was outlawed.

51 Twenty-one years the man spent, during which
neither younger nor elder of *Cian*'s seed settled in their
homes, till he himself occupied the land.

52 The race of Blod entered into their old fortune[1]
when Cormac's wrath had run its course, so that the race
of *Cian* were brought in, and obtained their own award.

53 Full moon of the south — none the less did the
noble young scion obtain kingship for being left as the
single man of a kindred.

---

[1] Text uncertain.

54 None overcame him; it seemed as if those who
were plundering the race of Eber against the man were
on his side.

55 It was more than fortune (?) for the lord of Leyney
to obtain the tribute of the blue-surfaced land, after the
champions from *Túl*'s Dwelling, in despite of everyone.

56 Never before, either here or in Munster of *Maicnia*,
did God grant such fortune as this king's to any of
Dergthene's populous seed.

57 Pre-eminent fortune, choiceness of form, did the
bright-toothed hero of Bregia's castle obtain in the day
of his birth; the best of the Lord's first gifts.

58 Cormac's beauty was obtained from the Lord, both
as regards form and eloquence; from the dear heart to
the ruddy countenance are according to the will of Him
who ordained them.

59 From the sole of his foot to his bright, curly head,
there is not one member of the lord of *Gáirighe*'s fair
host without some special endowment.

60 The gift of agility hath the soft, white foot, of
which invaders will be wary; triumph in every activity
hath the white hand, a palm that is gentle save in conflict.

61 The gift of speech have the crimson lips that bring
discontent to women: the gift of intelligence hath the
sprightly heart of the spouse of *Maiste*'s Plain.

62 From God above he hath excellence of truth and
constancy; in the houses of election he hath triumphed
in generosity and prowess.

CORMAC O'HARA

1 Do you wish for the history of the seed of *Cian*, until they are traced to a single root? For the bright race of Eber the Fair one must do the utmost.

2 Or do you desire that from the spring of knowledge I have found there should be emitted a pure stream of recondite poetry about the affinities of the champion of Munster?

3 He was acknowledged as the best of the band, the Eber from whom they are sprung: another such as the torch of Bregia's castle was not amongst the Children of *Mil*.

4 There never was one to equal Eber the Fair in Spain or in Ireland, of the royal blood of his tribe, of the seed of *Bile* or *Breóghan*.

5 With him those sons of *Mil* of Spain came to the land of *Fál*; Eber was their senior, from across the ocean he conquered the Plain of *Té*.

6 Four sons of Eber the Fair gained the headship of Ireland; match of those four never sprang from the active, steadfast race of *Mil*.

7 Thereafter they all perished, save great *Conmhaol*, son of Eber, leaving no children in their places, the youthful, celebrated band.

8 *Conmhaol*, son of Eber of the steeds, the first king of the Munster warriors for whom a dwelling was prepared in Tara, a man about whom maidens were envious.

9 From *Conmhaol* to Brian of the horns there are of his kinsfolk thirty kings in succession in the regal list, reigning over the land of Ireland.

10   Thirty-eight of the line of Eber, son of *Míl*, ruled the stately, white-walled castle of Trim down to the time of *Oilill Ólum.*

11   From *Oilill*, son of *Eóghan Mór*, back to Eber of the red-gold weapons, Bregia's host—mild and noble of heart—were a single kindred.

12   The triumphant race of Eber the Fair divide then at *Oilill*—a thing which increased their mettle (?)—in three genealogical branches.

13   Nineteen sons are reckoned as the family of *Oilill Ólum,* and if you trace them there are only the descendants of three to be enumerated.

14   Fortunate he who had the three sons, *Eóghan, Cian* and Cormac; three fathers of the men of *Eamhain*, bright stalks of the vine-woods.

15   The line of *Eóghan*, which never refused combat, the race of *Carthach* in each of its species, there is much one need not trace, and the subordinate branches of the tribes of *Carthach.*

16   Cormac, son of red-weaponed *Oilill*, is the ancestor of the seed of Brian, north and south; children of one father are the blood of *Cas,* heritors of the grassy meadow of the Fergus.

17   Smooth-haired *Cian,* son of *Oilill,* was *Oilill's* youngest son; he deserves the pledges of the rest, a younger son to whom respect is due.

18   Never heard I of any to equal the progeny of *Cian,* son of *Oilill Ólum;* smooth-palmed warriors for whom the forest stooped, battle-props of the Gael.

19   Seventeen sons had valorous *Cian,* but none of his children occupied his patrimony save one, noble stem of a fragrant wood.

20   *Tadhg,* son of *Cian,* who never grudged cattle — from *Tadhg* are derived the kings over the long-grassed Plain of the Fair, and many of the patron saints of Ireland.

21 It was *Tadhg* himself who obtained the three *Luighne* from the king of Tara in battle; and not for gold, or in exchange for cattle, but as the price of shedding his blood.

22 The two sons of *Tadhg* of the beaked ships, *Connla* and Cormac *Gailcangach*, they are the two from whom the race of *Cian* sprang, two royal husks of kindred trees.

23 Descendants of *Connla*, son of *Tadhg*, are the seed of *Cearbhall*, of the smooth, vast plain, and—heavily fruited wood of crimson trees—the descendants of *Conchobhar* of *Cianacht*.

24 The host of Leyney, who never shrank from combat, are the descendants of Cormac *Gailcangach*: men steady in step towards spear-points, choice golden stems of Ireland.

25 Cormac *Gailcangach* took the land from the Plain of Mar to *Magh Tuircadh*; he had all the territory from Slievemurry to the Plain of Mar.

26 The same Cormac took from Loch *Laoigh* to Loch Corrib: from the east bank of Corrib he paused not until he reached the flowing Boyle.

27 One son was the offspring of Cormac, named *Laoi*, the long-handed; the son desisted not in his valor until he gained the inheritance of his father.

28 Two sons had *Laoi*, of the keen blades, nobly-born *Nia Corb*, and *Scisgnean*; peaceful scions from the rushing Moy, two royal heirs of the plain of Cashel.

29 One son had *Nia Corb* of the battles, named Art, the warrior of Tara; for twenty years did the man rule the hostages of the Gael.

30 For nineteen years after him was his son over his race; a king like Art was fair *Fiodhchuire*, for whom the cornfield of the *Gaileanga* was more fertile.

31 For twenty-one years *Fighcann*, son of *Fiodhchuire*, reigned: the land in which he was he held for a time as king without opposition.

32   Over the country of Leyney from end to end *Nad Fraoich*, son of *Fighcann*, followed for twelve years, it is said, the order of his genealogical branches.

33   *Bréanuinn*, son of *Nad Fraoich* of the feasts, reigned as a king worthy of homage for a year and a day without belying his promise (?), according to the testimony of the learned.

34   *Fionnbharr*, son of *Bréanuinn*, the archbishop, the high-king—the territories are sufficient witness—reigned thirty years.

35   Great *Diarmuid*, son of *Fionnbharr*, held the country of Leyney, land of glowing countrysides—the best of all reigns was the period of this champion—for six years without peril.

36   For twenty years *Ceann Faoladh* held the kingship, north and south; the wand of possession of the fair land was his, *Diarmuid*'s generous heir.

37   *Taichleach*[1], son of *Ceann Faoladh*, held the kingship of the pleasant land of Leyney—far extended is the time (?) of his fame—for twenty years without a break.

38   *Flaithgheas*, strong son of *Taichleach*, held Leyney of the bright gardens for—he neither lessened it nor increased it—the same length of time as did his father.

39   The door of no homestead was closed in the reign of *Béac*, generous son of *Flaithgheas;* for a hundred years he protected the churches, ruling over the blue lands of the *Gaileanga*.

40   *Saorghus*, son of *Béac*, of the golden horns, was made king by the others forthwith; for a year and a half the noble champion of *Modharn* ruled over Leyney.

41   *Eaghra*, son of *Saorghus*—it was most easy for him—held the crimson plain of Leyney for ten years in full rule and kingship.

42   *Maghnus*, son of *Eaghra*—alas for the land whose lord he was—attempted to take possession of the territories in despite of *Eaghra* his father.

---

[1] see Notes.

43 *Eaghra* of the green-edged weapons laid his curse upon *Maghnus;* he enjoyed the territory but for one day's space, he perished (?) ere he gained it.

44 For one hundred years afterwards, throughout three generations, they were without the title of royal heir, without a king, from the bursting forth of reaving and war.

45 Until *Aodh* of the plaited locks, son of *Taichleach*, son of *Muircheartach*, son of great *Domhnall*, son of *Maghnus,* took command of the host of the blue, green land.

46 For two and twenty years *Aodh* reigned over the fair slopes of Leyney; a clear-minded king worthy of pledges, ruling all in general.

47 Then *Conchobhar*, son of *Aodh*, most fearless king under heaven, face like a glowing ember, ruled Leyney but three quarters of a year.

48 It is said his rule over Leyney lasted but half a year—*Aodh* son of warlike *Conchobhar,* noble, heavily-fruitful scion of Tara.

49 For three score years *Diarmuid,* son of *Aodh,* the high-king, a king not faint-hearted before plundering-parties, reigned over the warriors of Leyney.

50 The son of *Diarmuid* of the generous gifts, the king named Art of the Horses—for four royal years the descendants of *Cian* were ruled by him of the bright, ever-radiant locks.

51 For twenty years in succession Art, father of *Domhnall,* left the kingship of the blue-brown, fertile plain in charge of fair *Domhnall* the Cleric.

52 *Seaán Mór*, the second son, obtained Art's inheritance without change (?)—enough was it as a king's rule—for twelve years without weakness.

53 Thirty-eight years he obtained—*Fearghal,* son of noble, loveable *Domhnall,* sincere heart which presaged affection, gained this land.

54 *Tadhg,* son of *Fearghal,* prince of the schools, for forty years ruled the bright, spreading plain of Leyney, restful land of ancient, warm rivers.

55 *Scaán* the swarthy, son of *Tadhg,* leader of the warriors, had—little enough for his bright cheek—the same period as his father.

56 For twenty years and twice nine, it is said, thus the extent of his rule when ascertained, *Tomaltach,* noble son of *Scaán,* reigned over the rest.

57 For five years at least *Muircheartach,* the other son, defended the bright slopes of Leyney, a task most difficult to perform.

58 The seed of *Cian* submitted to Cormac for twenty-nine years; strong, valorous scion, generous son of *Tomaltach.*

59 Neither *Ruaidhrí* nor his son *Maghnus* was called king, although they had the obedience of the men of Munster, for fear of wronging their seniors.

60 For eight years and five *Oilill,* son of *Maghnus,* a righteous king without violence, without treachery, held the kingship of all the territories.

61 For eleven years east and west the host of Leyney's crimson plain, companies who were no likely mark for hardihood, were in the power of *Scaán,* son of William.

62 *Cian,* son of *Oilill,* who never refused guests, did not wait to get his estate; when their lord perished the line of Cormac were not ready for action.

63 The period of *Tadhg,* son of valiant *Cian,* was four flowery years; a full moon causing most fruitful strands was the chieftain-tree from the plain of *Colláin.*

64 For eighteen years then it was in the power of Conn son of *Ruaidhrí:* he held the land without a rival, save that it was in peril.

65   After a space Cormac, son of *Cian*, son of *Oilill*, is made king by the rest: he takes possession in place of his forefathers, by the voices of English and Gaels.

66   He settles the land of Leyney, both as regards laity and church; the fragrant country with its fair vestures of soil Cormac apportions generally.

67   He settles in their own place all the assemblies of noble *Cian*'s line; wrongs are repealed, strongholds are erected.

68   The dues of his kindred he will levy on friends and enemies; the valor of the battle-lion of *Cian*'s blood has revived the fame of his race.

69   He gathers their books to discover their genealogical branches; every recondite matter concerning his stock he seeks in the regnal list.

70   The ancient charter of tributes of the plain of Leyney having fallen out of remembrance, it is renewed for his heirs, so that it is a bright, clear charter.

71   Many claims upon his own territory has the chief of royal *Cian*'s tribe: it is just that he, noble, fierce countenance, should obtain a spell of the patrimony.

72   Almost has it become prescriptive—for nine hundred and four years Leyney has been under the tribe of *Cian*, companies who never deserved reproach.

73   By means of battle and war was gained the land they have got—it were little but grievous to oppose them—and with the will of the high-kings of Ireland.

74   Claim enough for Cormac, did all consider it forthwith, are the troubles he met concerning it, armed, red weaponed hero.

75   A good charter on the land of his forefathers is the evil he suffered from childhood's years, shedding his blood on its behalf, till he displayed the fame of his exploits.

76   Leyney's territory, of glowing slopes, lay neath a covering of thievery and rapine, until he — the greatest war he ever waged — came to her help.

77   From that time on she has been a restful, fairylike plain; without pain, without enmity, without wrath, without desire of plundering or conflict.

78   The hand which had harmed repaired the land of Leyney in the days of Cormac; it is a land from which a veil hath rolled away, in one day it was settled.

79   Never has there been of his true race from *Tadhg*, son of *Cian,* to the son of *Úna*—the fame of his forefathers he has inherited from the warriors—a man comparable to Cormac.

80   The seed of *Cian* were in grievous perplexity, as ye have heard, until there sprang up the forest-tree from the Dwelling of *Tál,* who gives life to his kinsfolk.

81   The wooing was the beginning of fortune (?) [1], Cian's son, as the heir of a high chief, found in his hour of wretchedness the first mate he loved.

82   Mary, daughter of *Maol Muire*; regal in aspect, chaste in mind; a woman excelling those of Bregia's dewy castle, the favorite of all of her kindred.

83   Cormac son of *Cian* has got, if she be estimated in every particular — our choice of all her stock — the best of mates to love.

84   Those who preceded her of her line have fame as their inheritance, it is likely that she will possess the inheritance, rather than all the women of the ancient line of *Suibhne.*

---

[1] Text defective

33

A PRECIOUS WEAPON

1 Welcome art thou, fierce *Gráinne*! No ill case his who should depend on thee as his only weapon, thou shining one with the hue of ruddy drops (?), well-omened, keen-edged, perilous.

2 Thou surpassing jewel of a dagger; thou venomous, inimical monster; thou form so harsh yet most smooth, dark and graceful; thou veritable queen amongst the weapons of Ireland.

3 Thou fierce, hacking bear; thou best of all iron; thou bright-looped, swarthy tribal treasure; thou disturber of the hearts of champions.

4 Thou point that cannot be withstood; thou darling of high-kings; thou black opening of the great door, thou light of even before dark.

5 Thou slitting of the thread of life; thou high-king amongst weapons of all kinds; thou cause of envy in the heart; treasure of the eye of multitudes.

6 Thou gracefully shaped bar of steel; never did thy opponent in battle bear tidings from the conflict in which ye met, nor shall one ever do so.

7 Even the testament (?) in short, though the fee for leeching be small—great reproach doth it bring to thy bright form — is not procured for thy victims (?).

8 Never did any on earth experience a bad year from thy fortune, thou brightly-blossomed, comely sun.

9 It was a happy omen whereby thou didst fall to *Aodh Óg*, son of this *Aodh*, to a royal heir of Conn's race: a meet comrade for thee.

10   Thou art, such a precious treasure as sufficeth him, thou seasoned, keen, cool weapon, and he, the youth from Bregia's battlesome castle, is the one sufficing surety for thee.

11   Oft, as a pledge of much wealth, hast thou been lifted from the smooth, comely knee of Maeve's descendant, at the quaffing of the juice of the vine-fruit.

12   Oft, it is said, as stipend of a high-king's heir, did the salmon from the fertile, murmuring Boyne get much gold and silver by thy means.

13   Oft hath a hundred of each kind of cattle been readily got through thee by *Aodh* for the poets of *Criomhthann*'s line, to uphold the repute of the stately, heavy-lashed one.

14   Never was it expected, thou shining one that hast not suffered hurt, that the scion from ancient *Aolmhagh*'s slender streams would forego thee for the excellent weapons of any of the men of Ireland.

15   None of the men of the world could obtain thee from the white-toothed, graceful one—bright palm to which one must needs yield homage—save some man of art.

16   In exchange for gold or silver none might get thee readily from the prop of Bregia's white-footed host: and it is not likely that thou wouldst be obtained by force.

17   From the chieftain of *Eachaidh*'s race an exacting poet accepted nothing on earth save thee alone: thus was it easier to obtain thee.

18   Since one hath sought thee, after this *Aodh*, thou noble, alert, smooth, studded weapon, nobody will be forbearing towards any poet.

34

O'CARROLL

1   Either O'Carroll or the rest are mistaken, these are some of the stories about him: who is it that is really mistaken? it is time to consider.

2   There are some of them hoarding their wealth, those that never cared for hospitality: and some that bear the palm from *Guaire*, head of every company.

3   A question for the companies of the Five Fifths, it should be tackled: is it the bestower of kine who is most astray?

4   Wealth . . . (?), and castles the others cherish them: *Cobhthach*'s descendant has spent his own share, it is a wealth that endures.

5   The rest desert the professional poets of Ireland for common song, until (?) the man of *Clíú* checked their discourse, bright shield of Gowran.

6   It is a pity that the rest are not like O'Carroll, generous with cattle: given to (?) music and entertainment, blameless course.

7   *Maol Ruana*, king of *Cearbhall*'s stock, to whom Ireland rightfully belongs, to him the name is given as a just title — palm of hospitality —

The Feale and the Cashen are two rivers in North Kerry, and it is these two prime rivers with beautiful banks that form a fishing estuary for the men of West Munster, and as the Feale is plundered of her fish she goes and floods the Cashen, and brings a prey of fish with her when returning. In such wise O'Carroll, when the keen, pungent-worded poets of *Fódla* plunder his land and his territory of riches and treasures and wealth, he sets upon the dour, unintelligibly-speaking outlanders, and they are plundered and burnt by him again and again.

8   Again and again is the great plain of the Moy plundered by *Maol Ruana*; a man who never puts off a bardic company, so great is his pride.

9   ...(?) O'Carroll of the elfin blades; every man shall receive his own award if he reach the kingship.

10   It is not the son of Isabel, desirous of praise, who has made a mistake: all that hath joined him of the Plain of the Champions — bardic companies are its tax—

Doladh is a little town in East Munster, and nuns reside there, and a priest says mass every Sunday to those nuns, and good is the life (?) of that little town—

11   So that thence O'Carroll goes to raid Meath: to take cattle out of every town, firm is his courage ...(?) gone into the cauldron to dispense liquor.

12   *Maol Ruana* is the *Cú Chulainn* of Munster in greatness of courage : is the house in which he is better for him than the House of Tara?

13   The warriors of the Gael gather around him to exercise steeds: he has surpassed Ireland. *Éile* and *Oileach* in generosity.

14   Heir of *Seaán* son of *Maol Ruana*, wheel of prowess; man who could contrive victory, guarantor of hosting—

And it was a wonderful hosting the Vicar *Ó Conchobhair*, and the Stronglegged *Ó Léanaigh* (?) the Big made, having resolved to make an alliance and compact with one another, and to go without pause or delay to battle with O'Daly—

15   The fuller was robbed when coming from the forge, having ground his teasel: often ...[1]

16   In Limerick there is many a gentle young woman, and many a whistling man who awakens the fierce, cold-beaked, deep-crawed snipe.

---

[1] The remainder of this stanza in unintelligible to me.

17   It is not easy to collect the cattle of the man of
Éile . . . wrong and slaughter.

18   The cow of Athboy from its spancell, the cattle
of striped Slieveroe have been brought by thee, O torrential
champion, to *Éile*: many a running in their eyes for a
time from the warrior —

And the Monday after Michaelmas a mayor is made
in every big town in Ireland, and it is in this way he
is made, the shaven-lipped, big-paunched. bulging (?)-eyed
burgesses of those towns enter into courts built of gray
masonry and stout timber, and he who has the largest
retinue and following comes out as mayor, and it is a
great wonder that O'Carroll does not even so go to Tara
and gather the Gaels of all Ireland around him —

19   As did the spirited kin from whom he is sprung :
often is the fury of *Fearghal*'s descendants curbed by the
warrior of Limerick.

20   Many a heron (?) on the slope of *Turlach* and fawn
of *Leamhain* (?); no dull gathering on Sunday is the tribe
of O'Kearney —

And as for O'Kearney, he used to be in Cashel, and
it is for him O'Grady made the whisky, and sent one
of his followers for spice, that is pepper and aniseed,
telling him to memorise that well, like any lesson, and
the boy started learning it well, as he had been told,
and on drawing near the big town he got an extraordinary
and unfortunate tumble, and this is what he said as he
was getting up: 'pepper and aniseed.'

21   He brought a load of the same . . , to O'Grady's
castle: when he went to *Port an Phúdair*(?) he left distress(?)

22   Like to the cold Hill of Howth is the frown of
O'Grady, by the Grúda men nimbly cast trout into
boats.

23   I am frenzied [and (?)] every one in the country
around me, with love for the bright-toothed one, a love
unsupportable.

24   I am called O'Carroll's rimer in the land of Munster: him with whom I have the best place I shall make chief of the heroes.

The stag hath no natural liking for the bay of the dogs; Lorcan's descendant . . .(?) a miserable yeoman: there is many a heron and wild goose on the land of Ulster.

25   The like of O'Carroll have I heard of in the battle of Cnuca; he was foremost in all their feasts, large his pigs —

And Walter Mape was roasting two pigs for the king of England, that is, a fat pig and a lean one, and he took to greasing the fat pig with butter and oil, and he let the lean pig burn, and thus the English of lovely *Fódla* and the nobles of Munster act towards O'Carroll, for they give him gold and silver and manifold riches, while they give neither little or much to Carew, though he is nearer to the Lake of *Ribh*, son of *Muiridh* than the woman who comes from *Dún Mic Padraicín* to Owenogarney to gather limpets.

26   Over in *Trian Chonghail* there is many a breast in . . .(?) [1]

27   A Tara is that rampart of *Maol Ruana,* where there are companies . . .(?): in *Maol Ruana*'s castle there is many a gathering . . .(?)

28   *Magh Dreimhne* surpasses every other plain . . .(?) it is the darling child of the noble dwellings, praiseworthy are its people —

And as for the tribe of Munterhagan, they are in Meath, and they are wont to be killing and quarrelling with one another over the name of the head of the tribe, a name that no other of the men of Ireland would like to bear as tribal chief, and that is, The Fox — a fellow without clothing, without cattle, deceitful, false —

---

[1] The remainder of this stanza is unintelligible to me.

29   A gray-muzzled fellow, treacherous, shifty, crafty
. . . he would bring a hen from the marsh (*or* the Curragh?),
a guileful deed, he would not exchange for gold or cattle
a seal or a mackerel.

30   Generous-hearted O'Carroll, sought of travellers:
no one else hath such repute save Art the Lonely.

31   Art the Lonely or *Oilill* Bare-ear, from whom he
is sprung: it is shameful for all the bardic companies
in Cashel not to join him.

32   In fear of the champion the warlike English have
retreated to the coast; shortly will he leave the castles
of the foreigners deserted.

33   If the honor of all the men of Ireland be considered,
with accurate knowledge, the fame of O'Carroll should
be balanced with that of two kindreds [i. e. should be
handicapped by competing against two instead of one]
in the balancing —

And it is a wonderful leap that is taken by some of
the people in the eastern world, that is, to ascend the
lofty mountain overlooking Paradise, and they look
downwards and laugh, and go thence to Paradise, and
return from there no more: even thus, then, do the
landless men, the nobles, the travellers and men of art
of Ireland in the case of O'Carroll's castle.

34   As he competed with (?) the minstrels — attempting
a good division (?), the warrior for whom a blue vessel is
bright, our house of safeguard.

35   *Eile* of the ruddy appletrees whose fruit is good,
the produce of the fragrant branches conceals every path
in its way.

36   Murmuring streams running shallow at the beginning
of summer, from the heat of the winter every fish goes
a foot deep into the earth.

37   In the dwelling of O'Carroll of *Cobhthach's* Plain, who never loved hoarding (?), there is many a maiden in the spring and scores of hags —

And a hag who was in the house of MacDermot of Moylurg and ... save one year there, and that hag left ... honorable and famous always from that year, and that is wonderful, seeing that there are—

38   One hundred hags in O'Carroll's dwelling, God defend it: the King of all is with the youth, Mary and *Íde* (?).

39   ... from every man, no portent of conflict, however near in time (?) he gets in his castle hundreds of champions, bright, long visitation.

That man is deceived who would not wrest a passing pleasure from the goods of life, seeing they are but a phantom like the mist; to my mind it were better to lavish them justly therein, since assuredly none will carry them away from this dungeon of deceit.

35

HUGH O'BYRNE [1]

1 Despise not, O Hugh, the love of *Ior*'s spouse, grievous is it for thee that this land of Niall should be neglected: surely if thou comest — according to the words of Flann (*or* surely, it is said, if Flann's words come true) . . .(?) will be under tribute to thee.

2 Stretch forth thy (?) vigor as a woodbine enclasping a tree when . . .; the son of John is censured by the array of English, when he comes down on the land to banish the foreign soldiery,

3 And to take hostages of him who does not join with him, when thou art under the protection of thy armor and weapons. . . .(?) on the embroidery of banners, a full . . .(?) of silk on the bottom of a rough equipment (?).

4 A tough, seasoned blade against which English armor is no protection, and a sheltering gauntlet on thy forearm down to the fingers: a tall war-horse, none straighter leaps a gap, and a . . . (?).

5 A spear which the royal son of noble *Tuircann* possessed and was, it is said, for a time in the fairy castle of *Aonghus:* for thee was it destined, thou gallant son of John, the lines of the shield are written on thy name (?).

6 Scarcely a day but this hero of the six couplets has the gains of a king (?), when he puts on his armor; the shouts (?) of warriors facing battle-furies, and maniacs of the wind arising therefrom in the glen.

---

[1] The text has been transmitted in a very corrupt form, and many passages are unintelligible to me. In some cases the translation is from conjectural emendations of the published text, see Notes.

7 The clergy of the churches consider not half of his wealth enough as an additional tribute from those who used to go there (?) and from all who gather about the son of John at night, the poets seating themselves under his protection according to their rank (?).

8 ... under him, students of books, fairy *timpáns* praising him with harp-strings of ...(?); womenfolk with no useful craft save weaving textures ...(?)

9 ?

10 ?

11 Many a thing hath the generous son of John accomplished, Leinster's ancient plain without (need of) a shepherd over any flock, ...(?), while this best of men is king over the land.

FRIENDS BEYOND THE SEA

1   Delightful is this day in London, many noble, loveable youths of my friendship have gone from me eastwards to London for a time.

2   Many a darling, many a heart's core amongst my loving ones are there: many a wealthy scion to-day of the old nobility of the Children of *Míl*.

3   It were pleasant to be amongst them, those with whom my spirits would rise; many in London are my loved ones, my friends and companions.

4   Across the sea to London were taken the voices which were sweetest to my mind; the delight of the generous, white-footed scions, the converse of my comrades and my friends.

5   Just five of those who are away east should I see every day in London, [not evil were this journey]¹ from my house, it is not easy to treat of them.

6   Though we should never suffer any wrong or want save (the loss of) these five, no five of Bregia's land would equal these noble generous warriors.

7   *Donnchadh Ó Briain*, fruitful blossom, beloved *Donnchadh Ó Conchobhair*, two guarding griffins of *Banbha*'s shore, in cold, strange London.

8   Small is my share of repose since *Donnchadh* descendant of Conn the Hundred-fighter is gone, and my beloved companion, *Donnchadh* descendant of Brian *Bóroimhe*.

---

¹ The words in square brackets translate a conjectural restoration of the text. See Variants.

9 O'Farrell's son, my own *Irial*, is in bright, perilous London; it is unkindly for me not to fare across the wave since my three darlings are there.

10 Something more than twelve years has *Pádraicín* Plunket been in the gay court of fair apple-trees, without visiting the soil of Ireland.

11 Though never before did I see the dragon of Dunsany, he is before me every night, a graceful, bright, fresh-countenanced hero.

12 *Pádraicín*, my *Irial*, my loved ones; my two *Donnchaidh*, a gracious pair: it is a presage of pleasure for Conn's land that these should come to us.

13 The fifth man that is yonder, my soul, Brian *Mág Eochagán*, he went across the sea to London: it has lessened the glory of the Gaels.

14 *Donnchadh*, *Pádraicín* and Brian, my other *Donnchadh* and my *Irial*, if those whom I expect are there my day in London should be delightful.

15 My three darling companions, William, Richard, *Rudhraighe*: three that were never false to their side, three that are dearer than life.

37

THE BUTTER

1 I myself got good butter from a woman: the good butter—if it be good—I dont think it was from a cow, whatever it was of destroyed me.

2 There was a beard sprouting on it, bad health to the fellow's beard; a juice from it as venomous as poison, it was tallow with the taste of a sour draught.

3 It was speckled, it was gray; it was not from a milch goat: it was no gift of butter when we had to look at it every day.

4 Its long lock like a horse's mane, alas, knives to crop it were not found: long sick is he who partook of it, the good butter that was in our hut.

5 A wrapping-cloth about the sour grease like a shroud taken from a corpse: disgusting to the eye it was to look at the rag from the amount of its foulness.

6 There was a stench from that fellow that choked and stupefied us; it seemed to us to be of all colours, with a branching crest of fungus over its head.

7 It had never seen the salt: the salt had never seen it, save from a distance; the remembrance of it does not leave us in health, white butter bluer than coal!

8 There was grease in it, and not that alone, but every other bit was of wax: little butter did I eat after it, the butter I got that was flesh.

A FALSE FRIAR

1   Of what land art thou, friar? humility is one of the graces: give us plain information, that we may not be in ignorance about thee.

2   Is it a part of thy Rule? explain, friar, and relate, why are thy shoes sound and thy hat tattered?

3   Considering all the swamp thou hast travelled, thou valiant, wet-footed friar, I marvel at the cleanness of thy hose whilst thy hat is covered with dirt.

4   Was it in thy Rule, thou friar from Connacht, that thy shoes and hose should be stout and thy hat very frail?

5   Methinks I see not a single fault in thy long and correct costume, beloved, melodious friar, save that thy hat is not worth a farthing.

6   Including coat and cap, habit and hose, more than any other article of thy dress has thy hat been ill-fashioned.

7   I make no complaint of thy habit, thou contemptible friar; look behind thee and before, for there is a rent in thy hat.

8   Thy hat, student, from whomsoever in Ireland it has been stolen, that is not the hat of an honest man which is ever being secretly offered for sale.

9   It is not its faulty fashioning, it is not the badness of its colour, prevented it being from sold in Cavan, but the fact that it is a stolen hat.

10   Uttering it for sale, friar, that is what has brought about thy ruin; here is a proverb made, 'alas for him who brought a hat to Sligo.'

11   It is not the Earl's practice to suffer a friar to steal: if thou art sent in ...(?) the hat will be striped.

12   Good are thy shirt and thy vest, neat is thy step on the causeway, fine moreover is thy mantle, but badly doth thy hat become thee.

13   Why is thy habit short, and thy cloak down to thy heels, and thy hat damp and high (or broad?), of what land art thou, friar?

39

A VISION

1   There was a vision of a fairy woman here last night, alas for him who beheld the royal vision; a woman such as she we have never looked upon, the vision which perturbed my mind.

2   Dear the shape which came here to me last night in my slumber; the sleep of the night in which the dream came will ever be talked of by us.

3   Bright-cheeked countenance, the rose is not more red, had the maiden, such was her description; eyes like a hyacinth petal, and even, jet-black brows.

4   Slender lips, sweet as honey, had the maiden, with the hue of a budding rose.; every gentle utterance of hers was enough to heal the ailing.

5   In the softly speaking mouth were white teeth like a shower of pearl; about them a delicate resting place for her lips, like two couches of . . .(?)

6   Between the arms with long hands are placed these — the graceful mounds of fair, white breasts, with a covering of golden interlacement.

7   The covering of her feet was achieved by the gift of *Aonghus*(?), two shoes with golden borders were worn by the bright, sweet, fair, maidenly girl.

8   A purple mantle with satin fringes, a red-bordered golden tunic; fettered hostages of gold formed the vest around the loveable, fairy maiden.

9   The gentle, tender one greeted me with modest words, and thereupon I replied to the bright, noble-looking beauty.

10　A while after that I questioned the maiden: "of what kingdom art thou, from the king of what land art thou come?"

11　"Two divisions or three there are of the world, the easier is it to traverse them to seek tidings of me," said the woman, "my secret I shall not reveal."

12　"In search of thee have I come, come with me" said the maiden covertly, in a musical voice, gentle, sweet-substanced (?), modest-worded.

13　I know not—what beguilement—when I refused to go with her, whither the wise, tender-hearted beauty flew from me.

14　It was a separation of body and soul for the rosy, brown-lashed queen to leave me when departing, the fair, modest, justly-speaking maiden.

15　To the land of *Fódla,* long ago, there came before like this the woman who beguiled royal *Connla* the Red: more peaceful her deeds the second time.

16　The best son his father had, *Connla,* son of Hundred-fighting Conn—through the wiles of one woman he goes across the wave, there never went in a ship one to equal him.

17　Such another visit as that the woman with the brown cloak and the musical branch made from beyond the wave to the son of *Feabhal:* famous is the wonderful story.

18　Nine times nine of the children of champions from the nobility of Desmond did that woman carry away with her, even as she carried Bran, he was an additional triumph.

19　The beguilement of Bran, the coaxing of *Connla* across the sea by foreign women, thus also am I deceived, this seems the most wonderful of all.

20 *Midear*'s fairy mound with its bright-portaled (?) rampart, the castle of *Sanbh*, or the fairy mound of *Abhartach* — you know not of a woman in these castles to equal the gentle, softly-speaking one.

21 There would not be found in *Eamhain* of the Appletrees, or in the mansion of golden-weaponed *Aonghus*, a fairy woman comparable to the gentle, bright-formed, brown-browed maid.

22 Since the woman departed from us, I would fain, if it were possible, be not merely a sojourner, in her land (?)

23 After my love for her bright face, when the maiden had left me, as an ebb comes in every tide, the exaltation of my spirit was quenched.

A VISION

1 Art thou the woman who was here last night with me in a vision? uncertain about thee as I am, thou bright form, my mind is bewildered.

2 If thou be not she who came before, O slender figure, gentle and soft of hand, and dainty of step, thou art exactly similar.

3 Thy glowing cheek, thy blue eye — never were there formed from the four-fold element two more similar in form, O yellow, curly, plaited locks.

4 Thy white teeth, thy crimson lips which make sufficing lullaby, brown brows of the hue of the sloe, and all that lies between them.

5 Throat like the blossom of the lily, long, slender hands; supple, plump flesh, of the hue of the waves, dulling the whiteness of the river's foam.

6 Small, smooth, white breasts rising above a lovely, shining slope; gentle expanses, with borders most fair and delightful, they are to be likened to fairy knolls.

7 On the ends of thy luxuriant tresses are flocks not usual in winter, which have been bathed in pure gold; a most wondrous flock.

8 I am worthy of trust, thou art in no danger, tell me was it thou who came before to the land of *Fál* to trouble me, thou shining, white-toothed, modest-faced lady?

9 Or art thou she who came afore-time to visit the Round Table, thou head of smooth, fair, bright locks, to wondrous King Arthur?

10   Or art thou she who came to great *Aodh,* son of
Ughoine, from the seductive streams of the fairy mound
of Slievenamon to the mortal (?) plain of Ireland?

11   Or art thou she who came another time to the
camp of Brian *Bóroimhe,* to bear Murrough across the
Irish Sea, and eastwards across the surface of the ocean?

12   Or art thou she who came from bright, fruitful
Rathtrim to beguile the son of *Deichtine,* the valorous
Hound of *Culann*?

13   Or art thou she that came afore-time, thou bright,
angel-like form, to the land of battlesome *Banbha,* to
Mathghamhain Ó Máille?

14   Or art thou she who came again to seduce the
youths, in the days of *Conaire,* O bright cheek, to the
chosen host of Teltown?

15   Or art thou she, thou staunch heart, who bore
Bran, son of white-footed *Feabhal,* across the smooth
surface of the sea, to the chosen Land of Promise?

16   There came, perhaps thou art of them, to the
king of Connacht—a famous visit, beautiful women—a
gathering of power, to the shores of noble Loch Derg.

17   Or didst thou beguile *Connla* the Red, from the
host of *Banbha* of the cold, wet summits; O bright form,
not unseemly of looks, though he was guarded by the
sages of the people?

18   Or didst thou beguile myself before, thou shining
form, since thou, O slender, fairy-like lady, art continually
spoiling the men of Ireland?

19   All the more do I suspect that thou art the other
woman I saw, because there is none save thee to equal
her in beautiful, leafy *Banbha.*

20   There is not in the fairy mounds of the Boyne a
woman of thy beauty save that woman, nor in the fair
castles of *Síodh na gCuan,* thou gentle, white-formed,
pleasing one.

12*

21 Nor in the fairy mound of oared Assaroe, or in the castle of the *Ioldánach's* fosterfather, or in the smooth, warm-couched mound of Trim, or in the many-shaped castle of *Eochall.*

22 After her no woman shall we see in dream or in fantasy, until she comes to us again, returning in a vision.

23 Once or twice has my form been blighted by her soft face, it will happen a third time, the wondrous, shining beauty.

41

THE CALVACH O'CONOR

1   Hasten to us, O Calvach, advance across the darkly-eddying sea; thou goal of the poets of Conn's territory, come to us at the first message.

2   Thou kindly-faced son of Donnell, this message we send to thee, let it be a pressing business for thee, let it not be delayed over a jest.

3   Many fresh tidings have we for thy smiling, brown-lashed countenance, thou king of *Eine*'s grassy plain, which were a fit reason for haste.

4   The men of London, the warriors of Scotland are contending together, thou chief of the noble host of *Sioth Truim,* in one compact mass about us.

5   From fear of foray none, from the Shannon to the river of Sligo, O sparkling, heavy-pented, straightly-glancing eye, can sleep for one hour at a stretch.

6   Lest the others complain of thee, array thyself, come to our help, give to this district an opportunity of repose, have they not said enough?

7   Hasten thee, thou son of *Mór,* great is the reason for unrest, thou defending arm of the folds of Conn . . .[1]

8   . . .

9   The athletic feats of their champions, the courageous spirit of their youths, the shining, smooth, white skin of their women, the agreeable speech of their men of letters.

---

[1] The loss of some lines here obscures the trend of the remaining stanzas; but the poet is evidently describing the delights of O'Conor's country of Sligo, and seems to suggest that they may have an enervating effect on the warrior's courage and spirit of enterprise.

10   Headstrong children plundering hives, hawks in pursuit of birds; graceful stags bounding from height to height, ships, and hounds contending in speed.

11   Journeying over the slopes of Loch Gill: the produce of the stream of Sligo: nuts coming upon the white, thickly-growing hazel-trees about their border ditches.

12   The coupled mansion, with its golden goblets, precious treasures, red satin garments, bright, square, smooth battlements . . .[1]

13   Let not the excellence of their ale, or their quilts, or their charmed, stout, smooth ramparts cause thee to linger, Calvach O'Conor.

14   Let not the warriors of Carbury's swan-flecked waters, the noble clans of *Síol* Murray, beguile thee amongst them, thou hand ungentle on the iron of spear-shafts.

15   Away from them take, for another while, in a propitious hour and time, an unhesitating step against the foreigner, thou graceful stem from *Conchobhar's* plain.

16   . . .[1] thou slender-lipped hero of Bearnas.

17   Thou appletree from Paradise, thou precious, softly-worded jewel, thou hindrance of the suffering of Conn's race, thou art able to guard us.

18   If thy coming to us be heard of, O clustering locks, foeman [will not dare] to look from on high at the borders of this fair country from which one must go.

19   Were I not urging(?) thee, I would censure thy bright face concerning this dispute with thy fair cheek, in the white houses of Sligo's host.

20   Understand moreover, were I not dissatisfied with thy bright, steady glance, thy soft, white skin, thy supple form, I would not(?) forgive thee what thou hast done.

21   From the danger that I might reprove thee, rightly are thy censurers and . . .[1] giving thanks that we are at odds.

[1] Ms defective.

42

A COMPLAINT

1 This is an address to the race of Colla, to complain amongst them, the mighty youth from the Plain of Mar, of the misfortunes which afflict me.

2 Do not overlook a single man of Colla's race from the fertile borders of *Chii*, but address each of them severally, they are men who will not allow me to be refused.

3 Tell to my avengers, the progeny of Turlogh, son of Marcus, a company most modest towards poets, the sum of my wrong and injustice.

4 I shall tell thee, man, my complaint, my foreboding to the great affable, pleasant, generous throng, in the hope that thou wilt remember what I say.

5 Many scattered captains of bands, many quarterings and kern—alas for him who . . .[1] wrong me.

6 The kern of the house next to me are full of wickedness and surliness, entering my house every other day, they and the assembly which is around me (?)

7 . . .[1]

---

[1] MS defective.

43

A CONTENTION

Tadhg Dall Ó Huiginn sang:

The Macawards, mangy whelps, blind ...(?) of the Conall kindred; stuttering bards without a qualified poet over them: alas for any who is in their company.

A rejoinder from Mac an Bhaird:

The banner of foray of Conn's land is half-blind (?) Tadhg Ó Huiginn: is it not woeful for any who met that devil of a blind fellow who was whetted in the cave of hell?

44

A SATIRE

This is the satire Tadhg Dall Ó Huiginn composed on the people of the O'Hara family, for which they cut out his tongue *etc.*

1   A troop of six that came to my house, I shall give a description of them; scarce of milk was I the next morning, from the thirst of the six vagabonds.

2   It was a long time, seemingly, since a bit of cow's produce had entered their bodies, the twice three whom I have mentioned.

3   I was able—'tis a pity—to bring them from death to life: must needs they drink my milk, so great was the thirst from the dry bread.

4   I in want, and they in necessity—I am in a strait between the two: it is hard for me to repress these verses, yet is it sinful for me to make them.

5   It is best not to conceal the satire if any deserve censure; as I satirized the troop of six it is unfitting not to tell it.

6   The first that I saw, he was the best equipped of the band, a youth whose vest was not worth more than a groat; one whom feasting or gaming never impoverished.

7   The second man, as I found, coming in front of the company, was a miserable fellow whose marrow had gone from him, I shall not leave him out of the reckoning.

8   The munition of the third wretch was an old javelin and an untempered, gapped ax: he and his makings of an ax in an encounter, I pity such a battle-equipment.

9   The equipment of the fourth fellow who flux-smitten
marched with them, four shafts, that never knocked a
splinter out of a target, slung across his rump.

10   At the heels of the four others comes the fifth
rogue, in a short smock not worth a groat, I do not
think his mantle was any better.

11   The likeness of a fellow not worth a fleshworm
was along with the five; a gaunt (?), transparent sort of
fellow, he was a poor commodity on inspection.

12   I beseech God who shed His blood, since it is but
decay for them to be alive — it is scarcely to be called
living — that none may slay the troop of six.

NOTES

1

Conn, son of O'Donnell, was eldest son of the Calvach or Calough, as it is usually spelt in the State Papers. By Rose, daughter of Shane O'Neill, he was father of the notorious Niall Garbh, and Margaret, wife of Eóghan Óg MacSweeny. O'Donovan, FM vi p. 2384, and O'Gr., Cat. 422, state that his wife was Turlogh Luineach's daughter. They may have wrongly interpreted the entry in ALC 1585: *Roisi ingen I Neill dég .i. in ben do bi ag Conn mac in Calbaig Ui Domnaill.* 'Death of Rose, daughter of O'Neill, who was wife of Conn son of the Calvach O'Donnell.' It was a natural error to suppose the reigning O'Neill, Turlogh, was referred to. Sussex writes to the Queen, Sept. 1562 "Conn O'Donnell shall marry Shane's daughter." See CSPI, Sept. 29, 1562; Walsh's *Gleanings from Irish MSS*, p. 31. During his father's lifetime Conn sought the aid and protection of the English government against Shane O'Neill, whose policy towards the O'Donnells was not of a conciliatory nature. For some interesting correspondence relating to the Calvach and his son see O'Gr., Cat. 57-60. Sussex describes Conn at this period as "wise, valiant, civil, true;" "the likelyest plante that ever sprange in Ulster to graffe a good subject on" (CSPI, Oct. 1, 1562). When the Calvach died in 1566 Conn was disappointed in his expectation of succeeding to the headship of the clan: "This Chon looked to be captain of the country, but the bishops and other landlords of the same elected Sir Hugh [see 2] to be O'Donnell, whereupon there was great likelihood of great wars, which I quieted, establishing Hugh in the place of O'Donnell, and gave unto Chon the castles of Lyppar [Lifford, Donegal], and Finn [Castlefinn, Donegal], and the lands belonging to the same, being a good third part of all Tirconell" (Sidney, CSPI, Carew 1583 p.340). Amongst the articles set down by Captain Piers for the reformation of the North of Ireland is: "Con O'Donnell to be practised with. He ought to be O'Donnell after Hugh that now is O'Donnell" (ib., 1574 p. 491). Conn was eventually elected Tanist (CSPI, Oct. 30, 1567). Another of Piers' plans was to unite Conn with Hugh against Turlogh Luineach, but Conn eventually took part with Turlogh against Hugh (see FM 1581; O'Gr., Cat. 423) and his career of not greatly successful war and intrigue came to an end in 1583. The immediate cause of his death is not recorded. The FM praise his valor and generosity in an obituary notice of several lines, while in his elegy by Fearghal Óg Mac an Bhaird, *Fill t'aghuidh uain, a Éire*, he is likened to

Alexander the Great, and a large number of military successes by him are recorded. Such attention from the literati suggests that although Conn's attempt to reach the summit of his ambition proved no more successful than that of the luckless merchant's son in the poet's apologue, he did actually play a more important part than the rather meagre references in annals and State Papers would indicate.

§ 1 'Take the veil from,' this seems to be the general sense of *tógaibh eadrad*. I have no other exx. of the phrase, but cf. *na leig beind da bralaigh linsi adraibh 7 Eire* C ii 3³62⁰. O'Curry, RIA MS. Cat., H. and S. 599, translates 'A union between you and Ireland establish.'

fear aoinleabtha, cf. *lór le nech a nemchara mar fher a.* O'Gr., Cat. 384; similarly *lucht a.* infra 25. 130.

§ 2 'Isle of B. 'wife of F.', kennings or epithets for Ireland, see Introd. p. lvii. *Breagh* is gen. of the name of a territory including part of the present counties of Dublin, Wicklow and Meath. Thurneysen, Dic Ir. Held- u. Königsage i-ii p. 89, explains the word as gp. of *brí* 'hill.' This was also suggested by Hogan (Onom.). It survives in the present name of the township of Bray, Co. Wicklow. In the translation I use the latinised form Bregia, well-established in usage by O'Grady and other scholars. It is perhaps the commonest of the numerous kennings for Ireland in these poems. See Introd. lviii.

Flann, probably F. Sionna, king of Ireland † 914.

§ 3 'uncared for,' *cumhdach* is often used in the sense of 'protection,' as here and in 2. 98. Cf. *gan c. céile* Cúirt 179, *gan c. fir* Eóghan Ruadh 1903.

§ 4 'U. 's castle,' on Ushnagh Hill, Westmeath. Another epithet for Ireland.

§ 5 'one after another,' or perhaps 'one and all;' cf. 21. 15, 28. 13. *ceann i &c.*, like *láimh do láimh, druim ar dh.* 2. 113, 30. 35, is common in contexts where either or each of these renderings would suit.

'capitals,' *port aireachais* is used of a seat of government, the residence of a chief; *go mbáttar acc Loch Riach . . . ba hesidhe p. a. Iarla Cloinne Riocaird* FM vi p. 2200, see also ib. 1964, v p. 1562, and infra 20. 170, and cf. *Temair do dílsiugad ocus cathair airechais Erenn do chur dá treoir* SG 35. *cathair oirechais* "chief city" Marco Polo 3 etc. O'Grady renders *puirt oirechais* by 'tribal convention places,' Cat. 374-5. The word *aireachas* seems to be connected with *aire, gs. airech* (Contribb. 5 *aire*) 'chief,' and means 'chieftainship, sovranty:' cf. *a. athardha*, of the succession of Conn Bacach's son to his father's title, FM v p. 1564.

'weeds,' *clúmh* (Lat. *plūma*) 'down, feathers,' see 11. 108, 19. 45, 21. 25; for the meaning 'vegetation' cf. 13. 12, 15; Zfcp 8, 222, § 8; Ir. Gr. Tr., Decl., ex. 1261; GF ii 1, Unpubl. Ir. Poems xix 5.

§ 6 'round,'? It is in most cases impossible to determine the exact meaning of *corr*; a metrically useful word, it is very commonly applied to hills, buildings, trees, weapons, the human countenance, eyes (see note on 1 § 25), hands, fingers. See Vocab. and Meyer's Contribb. Further exx. are: *uaithne c.* 'smooth post,' K. Meyer Miscell. 366; *dá súil chuirrse* GF v 30; *súlchorr* ib. 32; *corrghlac* 'tape, hand' O'Gr., Cat. 452 = Unpubl. Ir. Poems xv 17; as subst.; *ar chuirr mo ghlúin* 'on the bend (or curve) of my knee,' Gadelica I, 294. In the present ex. it may mean round, smooth, or peaked.

'stripped', I take *maolaim* to be used here in the sense of 'laying bare, clearing.' Deforesting is probably meant. We know from numerous entries in the State Papers that deforestation was considered a necessary preliminary to the reduction of Ireland.

'firm,' *cuir* is also a difficulty; it is often applied to buildings, as here; to trees: *is é an bile ós chronn ch.* GF vii 45; *na bodhabhla c.* Ir. Gr. Tr. Introd. p. 24; *ní bhfuil tarbha na ttairthíbh. abhla c. nach ccumdaighthir* 3 C 12, 261 (= Ir. Monthly 1923, 586); *lubhgort c.* A iv 3, 861; *croinn ghegthegair choille cuir* L 17, 11a; *craobh . . . c.* 12a; to fences: *fál c.* (wrongly?) rendered 'twisting fences', O'Gr., Cat. 374; to plains infra 13. 9. The common phrase *cloch cuir* seems to denote a type of firmness, e. g. 17. 211. In I Chron. 29. 2 *clocha cuir* renders 'stones to be set.' Cf. *in cach crois fri hernól cuir gemm dermor do leic logmuir* SR 367. In the following instances 'building' seems to be the meaning: *fogus d'féin Murbaigh misi . ní féudaim a innisi mar do bhladh* (= *do bhlogh*, sc. *Brian Ó Conchobhair*) *a clacha cuir . . .* Bk. 326 b (No. 136); (of the removal of the stones of *Oileach* to Munster) *dar gluaisedh Grianan Oiligh . siar go Mumhuin . . . fá lucht iomachuir chlach ccuir . cath an fionnachaidh Olltuigh* L 17, 29 b. The word is apparently attrib. gen. of *cor* 'putting, setting;' of buildings it would then mean 'firmly founded,' of trees, however, the meaning 'planted, newly-set,' seems to suit the exx. above; similarly of fences; of plains it may be from *cor* 'sowing,' and mean 'cultivated.' In the Laws *cuir* is found as attrib. gen. of *cor* 'agreement, pledge,' e. g. *bean chuir ocus urnadhma* ii 398.

§ 7 'traces,' perhaps 'ruins;' cf. *Tá Druim Ana 'na thaisíbh ón tsárbhroid* Keat. Poems 497; *taise* 'remains, relics,' is common. See Wi., PH.; *as í an uaidhsí a bfuil an fer . as uaísle a tloigh na ttaisedh* Bk. 232a (No. 207).

'tapestried', *brat* is used of woven textures in general, also metaph. of a covering of any kind, *donnbhrat luisne* 'a red sheet of flame, Unpubl. Ir. Poems xv 17. In the present passage 'mantle' is a possible rendering; 'brightmantled' would apply to the inhabitants or frequenters of the castles. (Cf. *a slíos Tuir bhratghloin Bhreoghain* Unpubl. Ir. Poems ix 3).

"Niall" i. e. N. of the Nine Hostages † 405.

§ 8 '*Té's* R.,' a poetical name for Tara. As to this legendary princess who besowed her name upon the hill see FM, Keat. Hist., and Dindsenchus. — *Art*, son of Conn the Hundred-battler † A. D. 195. See Introd. p. lvii.

§ 9 For the lenition of *f* in *l.* 2, cf. perhaps *ĩnliaigh foirithneach Teamhra* A iv 3, 634; *ĩnliaigh fóirithne* [*foir*ithin MS.] *a huathbháis* Bk. 221 b (No. 310). 'enchantments,' *airmert* .i. *geis* O'Cl. See TBC 931, 2295, 4724 *var.* — 'take possession,' *tocht asteagh ar* 'entering into,' may be a technical phrase for seizing, but possibly the right rendering is 'it must needs come to pass,' and then we might take *l.* 3 as parenthetical, *ar* going with *tiocfa*. Cf. *fada a ndán 'sgo ttí asteagh* cited in notes to 10 § 11 and the use of *do-bheir asteagh* in: *a gheasa asteagh go ttabhair* 23 D 14, 63; *cóir t'oighre asteach ní thibhre* ib. 11.

§ 10 'C., son of' lit. Conn-son; here, as a metrical device, the proper name is placed as a qualifying prefix to *mac*, Similarly *Conallmac* : *chrobh-angslat* Ériu 4, 187; *Tadhgmhac* : *ardsla!* GF viii 21.

§ 11 'some encouragement,' I am uncertain of the correct reading here; *tallann* is of doubtful meaning. There are at least four distinct words (1) *tallan* 'talentum, talent,' *deich ttalluine fiched* 'thirty pieces of silver, 'MacAingil 52; used of mental gifts, the talent of poetry, Laws v 20; *tallann oir* Beatha Cille 80. Cf. *liog thalluinn* (of a tombstone) L 17, 21 ª. (2) *tír gan tallaind do thathaoir* 'land without a particle of blemish,' Top. Poems 96; cf. *tallann sceoil* Caithr. Congail 68, 156; *inneósad . . . tallann sgeóil a ngníomh ngaile* L 17, 127 ª, cf. Acall. 3193? (3) *talland* 'a siege,' as in *t. Étair* RC 8, 47; cf. MacCarthy 422? (4) *tallann* 're-proach,' Marco P. 64, P. O'C., cf. *talluinn* D. Ó Br. i, pp. 42, 138. Further *tallan* 'a turn or spell of anything', Dinneen, which may belong to (2). *tugann t. dá hinntinn* may mean 'adds something to her spirits;' the variant *tuilleadh* suggests the possibility of some such meaning.

'yew-timbered,' lit. 'yew-branched;' possibly 'with branching yew-trees.' Cf. *a chúirt ghéagthláith* (of Enniskillen Castle) Unpubl. Ir. Poems xix 1.

§ 12 'form,' *slios* 'side' I take to be used here in the sense of the general contour of the body; cf. *taobh*.

§ 13 'take to thee,' the rendering is uncertain; I take *téigh* as imperat. sg. 2 of *téighim* 'I go,' cf. *ná téig* SG 235. 33, RIA Ir. MSS Ser. 1, 176; this is supported by the var. *sin re cn.* 'lie beside.' It could, however be imperat. sg. 2 of *téighim* 'I warm, grow warm'; cf. *Tuathal Techtmhar lér théigh sí* (Ireland) 23 D 14, 33. There may be a play upon words. With *re cneas* cf. Mid. Ir. *fri cn.* 'beside,' Wi., Contribb.

Lugh, a legendary king of Ireland, see Keat., and *Celtic Irel.* 46. Cf. Introd. lvii 3 b).

§ 15 The story of Niall is published and translated in RC 24 and SG; a metrical version is edited and translated in Ériu 4 by Miss Maud Joynt, who points out parallels in medieval romance outside Ireland. Cf. also the story of Lughaidh Láighdhe, Cóir Anm., Celt. Soc. Misc. and Keat.

'united,' *fuaighim* is frequent in such a context; cf. *a heineing dofuaidh an gort* Bk. 238b, *gur fuaigh an aoibh athardha* Arch., Hib. i 92; the verbal noun *uaim* appears infra 1. 206, *snáth uama* 18. 171, *snáth uaime a oighrechta* Bk. 333 b (No 110).

The names of Eber and Eremon (*Éibhear* and *Éireamhón*) the two
sons of *Míl* who, according to the legends in *Lebar Gabála*, divided
Ireland between them, Eber getting the southern half and his brother the
northern, are very frequently used in composing synonyms for Ireland:
see Introd. pp. lvii-lviii.

§ 16 I have no other reference to this story about Brian.

§ 17 *ilgheas*, see note on I § 36.

'tearful,' or perhaps 'dewy;' *braonach*, and *braon-* (as an adjectival
prefix) are frequently applied to Ireland, but whether we are to understand
a reference to the humidity of the climate, or to take the words in a more
poetical sense, as rendered here, is generally doubtful. Cf. the use in
modern Irish phrases, Dinneen s. *braonach; ins gach aon pháirt de'n
domhan bhraonach*, Canon O'Leary in *Seanmóin agus Trí Fichid* ii 23.

'dark-lashed,' *abhraduibh* = *abhrad-duibh*, see Introd. p. lxix. For
the meaning of *abhra* see Addenda to Contribb. and Ir. Gr. Tr., Decl.
exx. 1299, 1301.

§ 18 'of great fins,' i. e. abounding in trout or salmon? *-eithreach*
I take to be an adj. from *eithre* 'end, tail, fin,' Lec. Gl., P. O'C. Cf.
Eithne (sic leg.) *agus Bóinn ós do bheinn . dá eithre óir a haoineirr*
L 17, 102a, *éigne ó Bhóinn bhūinithrigh Bhredh . dirimhthir ós ghlóir
Ghaoidheal* ib. 111a, *breac óireithrech ón Bhóinn bhinn . is dóigh fóirithnech
d'Eirinn* Bk. 221b (No. 310).

fóireithneach (cf. last cit.) is a form of the gen. of *fóirithin* 'help;'
a slóighfeithmhech na ttreabh ttais . fer t'fóirithnech ó fuarais L 17, 63b;
éinliaigh fóirithneach Teamhra A iv 3, 634; *d'iarraidh fóirithnech airm
7 eidigh ortsa* Celt. Rev. 2, 206.

§ 19 The following apologue is based on the story of the daughter
of Hippocrates told by Maundeville in his Buke (Roxburghe Club ed.,
p. 163) and discussed by M. G. Huet in Bibliothèque de l'École Des Chartes,
lxxxix, 1918, p. 43ff. Another apologue, essentially the same, though
differing in details, is used in a poem by Eochaidh Ó Heódhusa, see O'Gr.,
Cat. 476-7. Tadhg Dall's version, despite some slight discrepancy in details,
we may conclude to have been drawn from the Irish translation of Maundeville made by Finghin Ó Mathghamhna in 1475. An edition and translation
of this, which I shall refer to as GM (Gaelic Maundeville) was published
by Stokes, ZfcP 2.

'of fertile hills' lit. 'soft-hilled.' *bog* 'soft, tender, moist,' when
applied to human features, as in 15. 63, 27. 49, naturally means' tender,
plump,' hence of persons or dispositions 'agreeable, kindly;' when applied
to land as here and in 2. 63, 7. 83, 27. 71, 157; 28. 57, the meaning
'tender' would express something antithetical to 'arid, barren;' hence I
have ventured to give the rendering above. It is applied to grass in
27. 21, where the idea is probably expressed by 'thick' or 'luxuriant.'

Although Tadhg Dall places the scene in Africa, in Maund. and GM
it is in Cos, an island of the Greek Archipelago, reputed as the birthplace
of Hippocrates.

§ 20-22 *aderaid daeine co fuil ingen ac Ipocraitt annsan oilén sin i ndeilb draccuin . . . 7 goiritt lucht an oilein sin uile bantigerna an oilein di. Taispénaidh si hi fein fo thri cach bliadain . . . an uair dobi si 'na macaem docuir Deán annsa richt sin hi 7 aderaid daeine co mbia si mar sin nóco ti ridiri a hiarthur an domain 7 dobéra póige da bél, 7 mar doghéba si an póge sin dogena ben di.* GM § 33 (cf. RC 30, 403).

§ 20 'man of yore,' lit. 'first man;' *céidfear* is regularly used in referring to an actor in the apologue, to distinguish him from the personage to whom the moral is applied. Cf. **22** a, 186. Here, however, the literal rendering may be the correct one.

barrlagúir, 'soft and bright of hair;' *barr* 'top,' is frequently used for hair of the head, cf. **15**. 153, **23**. 91, **27**. 119; *lag* 'weak, limp,' when applied to hair means' soft, clinging, sleek,' cf. **2**. 129, **3**. 165, **4**. 165.

bandragúin is acc. sg. fem., though compds. with *ban-* usually retain the gender of the final constituent; *dragún* is of course regularly masc., as in next stanza.

§ 21 *Núl*, I have no other reference to the father of Hippocrates.

'a while,' the first vowel in *treimhse* may be long or short; rimes are *timcheillsi*, 23 F 16. 3; *bhraithfinnsi* ZfcP 2, 334; *oiléinsi* L 17, 48 b. The *-m-* is not regularly lenited in mss. (see **25**. 74, 170) but the modern form *trévshi*, and *trédhenus* etc. support the lenition. Originally it meant a period of three months (*tremsi co ba tri*, Ériu 1, 122), but is generally used of an indefinite period, *re tréimhsi chian* Acall. 76, *re treimsi do bliadnaib* 5548.

'difficult,' lit. 'a matter of conflict.'

§ 22 'gift of beauty,' or perhaps 'triumph of (i. e. surpassing) beauty.' Cf. *buaid* Contribb., Wi.; *ar bhuaidh ccrotha* L 17, 35 b; *mana derna eisde uaill, ga meisde búaidh ndealbha ar dhúil* Ir. Gr. Tr., Decl., ex. 1029.

'youthful,' here I have followed the reading of a single MS against all the others, which have 'serpentlike.' Possibly the latter is correct, the poet may be thinking of her dragonly aspect.

§ 23 'A merchant's son;' *macaemh ócc cennuige* 'a young merchant', GM 34. Here we may have the origin of the epithet 'Merchant's Son' applied to the Pretender by Aodhagán Ó Raithille (ITS iii, 1911, p. 12).

§ 24 'shining-haired,' *naoi (nua)* 'new, fresh', hence 'bright, shining;' cf. *úr* 1. 79 etc.

§ 25 'bright-eyed,' *corr* is frequently applied to the eye, see 1 § 6 n.; it probably describes the appearance of a well-opened, full eye.

'wondrous,' *sidh (-th)*, and *sidhe (-the)* are forms of gen. sg. of *siodh (-th)* 'elfmound,' used attributively in the sense of 'elfin', hence probably, 'wondrous, marvellous.' See Ir. Gr. Tr., Decl., §§ 39, 46; exx. 1116, 1265. 'Long-handed,' or 'supple-'. Cf. *laoi leabhra* 5. 11; *leabha(i)r* is used of hands (4 151, **14** 50), fingers (**4**. 119), spears or shafts (**2**. 4), the body or skin (**11**. 98), face (**21**. 14), hair (**27**. 132) of an army (**11**. 119), of ships: *longbhárca leabhra* A iv 3, 860. Cf. *liobhra* GF v 32.

§ 26 'I have forsaken . . .' there may be an idiomatic meaning in *do-chuaidh mé ó*, but I have no certain exx. Cf. *sgiath . . . do-chuaidh ón chath chathardha* GF viii 37; *do-chuaidh se ó oigreacht* TCD F 4. 13, 8 a.

'it cannot be,' the reading is uncertain; possibly we should follow Fr, 'I shall not be able' (reading *féaghadh* in preceding line).

§ 27 'modestly blushing,' *málla = mánla*, Keat. Poems, Eóghan Ruadh, etc., while *donn* seems to denote a dark shade of red; red-brown.

§ 28 *ó so, ó sin* are common.

§ 29 '*Féilim*'s Land,' a common epithet of Ireland. In GM she simply asks whence he came, and he replies, laconically, that he has come from a ship, but see citation above, §§ 20-22.

§ 31 'rage,' cf. Marco Polo 187, and *méad meanma* 'high spirits, arrogance,' **20**. 13 *etc.*; *cathaig red mhenma* 'do battle with thy spirit,' O'Gr., Cat. 457.

§ 33 Here 'rosy' includes *deirg* and *dhuinn*; as to the latter see note on 1 § 27.

§ 36 'in panic,' lit. 'in a rout of defeat;' cf. *mad remaib bus ráen romadmai* Alex. 228; *Cath Samhna . . . ann ba raen madma ar Ulltaib* Acall. 1193; *co ttangamar a raon madma* (sic leg.) ZfcP 1, 132. The older phrase was *roi madma*, see TBC 2311, RC 14, 408.

I do not know know whether *oil-* or *ilphiasd* is the older form; *oil-* might be from *oll* 'great,' and *i* < initial *oi* is common in the spoken language. Cf. *ilgheas*, var. *oil-* 1. 65, where the plur. pref. suits the context.

§ 38 'prophesied one,' i. e. one foretold by sages and saints of yore as a destined ruler of Ireland. Cf. **1** § 52, **6** § 17, **27** §§ 29-35. The ending of *tairngeartaidh* is curious, *-idh* usually denoting agency. Cf. *mina beith in maclairrngertaig Moisi* YBL 66 b, 22; further exx. Miscell. Celt. Soc. 404; infra **13**. 128; for decl. see Ir. Gr. Tr., Decl. 52, ex. 1329.

§ 40 For the gs. *dragún* cf. Ir. Gr. Tr., Decl. § 35.

§ 41 The Boyne is here used figuratively for Ireland, or the sovranty thereof; similarly **21** § 24 and GF v 43.

'disfigurement,' this rendering suits the context. The usual meaning of *éagruth* (*cruth* with neg. pref.) seems to be change (for the worse) of form, loss of beauty; often used of transformation through grief, rage or terror: *ní nár égruth Chruachan Cuinn . d'ég chaithleómhan chrú Dubhghuill* C iv 1, 177 a; *od-chualaidh an Modharn mhoir . beith ga haoradh go heccóir : teid an t-es a n-egcruth ann . do fes egnach na habhann* Bk. 12 b (No. 227); *aingcis éga a haois faire . cathaoir Chloinne Rughruighe : na clí nir chédmhothuigh sin . gur šní a n-égrothuibh Eamhuin* C iv 1, 177 a; *ionnlus a haghaidh ndorcha . . . gur šaor a héccruth uathmar* Bk. 220 a (No. 310; descr. by O'Grady, Cat. 476-7). See also *écruta*, Wi., *éagcruth*, Keat. Poems; O'Grady, Cat. 527 ('deformity'). When used in the pl., however, it may possibly be felt as a compd. of *éag* and *cruth*; cf. *i gcrothaibh báis* 'at the point of death,' Keat. ii p. 206.

§ 42 'descendant of Conn;' the official history traces most of the ruling Irish families to Niall of the Nine Hostages, who is derived from Conn; see Introd. p. lv, and Gen. Reg. & SS. Hib.

'C.'s Plain' Ireland is so called from *Cobhthach Caol Breagh*, see FM, AM 4658; ZfcP 3, 1 and Keat.

§ 45 'to win triumphs,' cf. **19**. 39, 59; *do denamh foghla* 7 *cena* FM v p. 1474; 'creacha or ceana i. e. raids,' O'Gr., Cat. 503 n. Ó Heódhusa seems to echo this couplet in: *do léigsiod diobh dénamh cen . tuirsech cogadh chlann Míledh* L 17, 94 b (== Ir. Monthly 1920, 595): *cean* is gp. of *cion*, apparently a u-stem, but perhaps declined in various ways at this period, cf. Ir. Gr. Tr., Decl. p. 48; Unpubl. Ir. Poems xi 31, **4**. 43, and *as ionann cion* 7 *écht* O'Cl. s. v. *mac ceanta*. For *tnúthach* here cf. **16**. 66; *gan tnúth le téarnamh* == *gan súil le t.* 'without hope of recovery,' *Filidhe na Máighe* p. 138. For the eclipsis see Introd. p. lxix, and also Ériu 5, 58. 91.

'man of the I.' *fear* is commonly used with place- or river-names to form an epithet; cf. **8**. 24. Whether it should be rendered by 'spouse' or by 'owner, ruler,' is not always clear. The meaning 'owner' appears in: *fear Baile Í Bhara .i. Seafrán mc Uillicc . . . fear Cáil Í Séighinedin .i. Seafrán mc Riocaird . . .* TCD H 1 18, 14 b.

§§ 46-7 Similarly **16** §§ 15-6. 'They ranne thorough the Towne, being open, like Haggs and Furies of Hell, with Flakes of Fier fastened on Pooles Ends, and so fiered the lowe thatched Howsies; and being a great windie Night, one Howse tooke fier of another in a moment.' Sidney to Council, March 1575, describing the burning of Naas.

cagaidh == *cogaidh*, see Introd. p. lxvi.

§ 47 'reaver,' *foghlaidh* (*faghlaidh*) often corresponds to the modern idea of soldier or fighting-man; cf. **9**. 198; **17**. 229. FM use it, along with *díbheargach*, in reference to members of the revolting clans of the 16th century, and O'Donovan usually renders it by 'rebel;' e. gg. v pp. 1500, 1736, 1748, see also vi 2304. The meaning 'brigand' seems indicated by the grammarian's specimen *riadh foghlaidhe* Ir. Gr. Tr., Decl. 52 n. 12. An interesting distinction is supplied in the following: *cisne trí báis ata ferr beathaidh . bás m. m.* (sic); *bas foghluidhi .i. iar forloscadh : bas bithbeanaigh .i. iar ngait no iar marbhadh duine.* Law Transcripts, O'D. 713. Cf. Triads 92.

§ 48 'wondrous,' for *sidhe* see note on 1 § 25.

'ruddy as the berry,' this I take to be the implied meaning in *mónanda*. Cf. *mónainn na móna* SG 364 (LL 297 a); *mónann* 'bogberry,' Acall.; *mónann* (fem.) Ir. Gr. Tr., Decl. 12, ex. 569; *mónóg* 'bogberry,' Arch. i 344.

§ 49 Frewen, a hill on the western shore of Loch Owel, was the site of an ancient stronghold. As the poets are studiously vague its use here is more likely to be figurative than to convey an actual instruction.

§ 50 'Donegal,' *Dún na nGall* 'Donegal Castle,' was a chief stronghold of the O'Donnells. See FM 1564. *Eas Dá Éagann*, 'cascade of the Two Fools,' was an old name for the falls of the Erne. 'L. Foyle' etc. lit. 'the wine-bright lake of *Feabhal*.' One is reminded of the kidnapping of Red Hugh, and the reference is evidently to the wine-cargoes which used to come to this haven. By L. Foyle we are to understand Inishowen, the country of O'Donnell's powerful tributary, O'Doherty (see **28**).

§ 51 *toireamhain*; cf. *tuaitheamhain* Ériu 8, 192.

coicéad evidently corresponds to Engl. 'cocket' a customs certificate, duty, see Iar Connaught 203-5 (cited in Wood-Martin's Hist. of Sligo pt. i p. 263) and cf.: *Ego Magonius ODonell, mee nationis Capitaneus, meo humanissimo Anglie Hibernie et Francie Regi Henrico Octavo ... mediam partem census mihi debiti in Ichdarconnachd, meisque antecessoribus, per tempora de quorum initio vix est memoria, ut chronicis et chartis antiquis apparebit, do ad presens et concedo, ac de omnibus navibus, que negociandi sive mercandi causa ad Sligaghe veniant, et a quibus ipse ODonell coquetum (ut vocant) habuerit, mediam coqueti partem do et concedo ...* State Papers (H. M. Comm. 1834), Hen. VIII iii I 481.

Of the Irish word I have only noted one other ex., viz: *aga sinnsearuibh do bhi coiced na Gaillue ... mar ata an da casc bradán is lugha is ole a nGaillibh 7 .u. .c. sgadan as a mbad mor da .c. go leth as a mbád bheug* TCD F. 4. 13, 1 a (on the prerogatives of MacWilliam Burke). Thus the form is not precisely decided, and cocket, according to the Oxford Dict., is of obscure origin, but one would expect *coicéad* on the analogy of *mailléad*, *gairéad*, corresponding to Engl. mallet, garret. Cocket is still used in parts of Ireland.

Tuathal, highking of Ireland + A. D. 106, FM; see note on **10** § 19.

§§ 50-1 are apparently an exhortation not to rest content with lordship over Donegal, Inishowen and Connacht, but to proceed without pause to kingship of the whole country, symbolized in Tara. Cf. the following, addressed to Turlogh *Luineach: Ná beanadh díod Dún Dá Leathghlas . an Lia Fáil ós fada a sgis; nó an Bheann Bhorb tar a feart féile . teacht ar lorg do fréimhe aris. Ar Dhún na Long nó ar Loch Feabhail . fiadh Taillean ná tréigeadh sé; dá madh sgur d'Ó Néill ni neamhghuth . gan dul do léim Teamhrach Té.* 'Let not *Dún dá Leathghlas* — since the *Lia Fáil* hath long been weary (for thee) — or yet Benburb, despite its miraculous hospitality, prevent thee from following in the wake of thy forefathers. For Dunnalong or for Loch Foyle let not O'Neill forsake the country of Teltown; it were no disreproach to him did he not go to conquer Tara of *Té* (text from 23 F 16, 209. I have normalized the spelling).

§ 52 'the salmon' etc. this epithet has not necessarily any geographical significance. *eó* is very frequent both in sacred and secular encomium. In the last line one would expect lenition of the F., as it follows a noun in the dat. and is a place-name; but it would spoil the metre. Cf. **3**. 168.

§ 53 'prophets,' similarly Brian Dorcha Ó Huiginn: *fáth reachta do floghthasa . bláth ar fedhuibh úrchasa* A iv 3, 620.

'promise,' *séan* in some contexts seems to mean 'sign;' cf. *s. dióghbhála a tteacht asteagh* Ériu 5, 56. Elsewhere a propitious sign, a blessing; see 13 188, **19**. 5, 6, 10; **31**. 162; O'Gr., Cat. 376; Acall.; *do athraigh s. catha Cloinne Cais* 'the success of battle of C. C. changed' FM 1559, p. 1572.

§ 54 'before summer,' for a similar extravagance see K. Meyer, Miscell. 176, § 28. 'Churches repaired,' cf. *a bhrath cumhdaigh na gceall* (where *cumhdach* may mean either 'roofing,' or 'protecting') Arch. Hib. i, 88; 'on May 19, 1542, O'Neil promised to rebuild all parish churches, now ruined, in my dominions,' citation from Carew MSS. in Wilson's *Beginnings of Modern Ireland* p. 137.

§ 56 'unlawful mate,' *céile cuil* cf. *ben chuil* PH 861-7; cf. FM ii p. 1100. The figure is pecul ar.

The 'closing' of the poem is not strictly orthodox; indeed it reminds one of that of Niall Ó Neanntanáin's poem, Parl. Cl. Tomáis 166, which is ostensibly an example of 'the way not to do it.' However the same kind of ending is found in other poets of standing: cf. the poem beg. *Cairt a siothchána ag siol Adhaimh*, which ends *fuighleach dir, Dán Dé* p. 6.

2

Aodh O Domhnaill, angl. Hugh O'Donnell, to whom the following three poems are addressed, was son of Manus (+ 1563)', by *Siubhán*, sister of Conn *Bacach* O'Neill. While Manus was alive Hugh took part with his uncle, Shane O'Neill, against the Calvach and Conn O'Donnell (1), but at a later period he and the O'Neills fought on opposite sides. He was elected O'Donnell in 1567, after the death of his brother the Calvach, and was knighted by the English Government the same year (Carew SP 1578, p. 149). Soon after his inauguration he made a successful hosting into Tyrone, and when Shane O'Neill made a return attack, Hugh, assisted by the three MacSweenys, inflicted on him the crushing defeat which brought about his fatal decision to take refuge with the Islesmen. O'Donnell continued to oppose the O'Neills until Hugh O'Neill, who married his daughter *Siubhán*, came into power. He kept peace with the English Government for the greater part of his career (see O'Gr., Cat. 423 n. 1), and having resigned the chieftainship to his celebrated son, Red Hugh, in 1592, died in Dec. 1600. O'Grady, Cat. 371, 423, 425-6 etc., wrongly styles him Black Hugh. Manus O'Donnell's father was *Aodh Dubh*, angl. Black Hugh and Hugh Duff, and Perrott, in his list of the chiefs who came to him at Dungannon In the summer of 1585 includes "Odonnell, and with him Hugh Duffe Odonnell the Tanist of Tirconell." (*History of Sir J. Perrott* p. 269); see also A. R. 52-4 and Carew SP, 1566, p. 374.

The following piece evidently refers to one of O'Donnell's expeditions into Lower Connacht to recover tribute; see Introd. xxvi. The second part of the poem (§§ 41-58) seems a diplomatic appeal for gentle treatment of the defaulters.

§ 1 'long-speared,' in the adj. *cleithleabhar* I take the first element to be *cleath* a wattle, spear-shaft. Similarly 7. 18S. Croghan is used figuratively for Connacht.

§ 2 'to the north etc.,' this may be a proverbial expression; cf. in TB Flidaise the words of Bricne urging Fergus to take up his quarters at Croghan with Oilill and Maeve: *is amlaid so rofhagbatar ar seanduine againn .i. tagall an tuaisgirt agus bliadain a Laignibh agus medarcuairt na Muman agus gnathcomnuidhi Connacht* 'thus we have it from our forefathers—a visit to the north, a year in Leinster, the cheerful circuit of Munster, and continuous dwelling in Connacht.' Celt. Rev. 1, 21S.

§ 3 'gentle (?)' I cannot determine the exact meaning of *dilligh* (or -*dh*). It is used of the human features and of natural scenery; *dillighe a dionn 'sa fairchedh* L 17, 11 a.

'the province of *Ol nÉ.*,' (gen.) an old name for Connacht: *Ailill tra, mac Rosa, 7 Mata Muirisc a mathair do feraib Ol nEcmacht; dibside congairther Connachta indiu 'A*, then, was son of Ros, and his mother was *Mata M.* of the men of *Ol nÉ.*; it is they who are called Connachtmen now.' LL 311 c 22.

§ 5 or 'to check with thy . . . the rivalries of the tribes of C.' *clanna Cuinn* seems here to mean the men of Connacht (cf. the early *Dál Cuinn = Connachta*, MacNeill, Popl. Groups § 40). In other contexts it is frequently used for the people of the Northern Half, or Irishmen in general, e. gg. 8. 63; Ériu 8, 193; Oss Soc. v 296, 297; Similarly Conn's Plain, Fold, Land etc. means either Connacht, the Northern Half, or Ireland, according to context, see Introd. pp. lvii-lviii. The Conn referred to is of course *C. Céadchathach* † A. D. 157 Fm, after whom the Northern part of Ireland was called *Leath Cuinn* 'C.'s Half,' according to the bardic scheme of history. The delimitations of *Leath Cuinn*, however, vary in different documents.

chommórthais this is the form required for the time but the -*t*- is unlenited in the MSS. I do not know the history of the word. Cf. Contribb. u. *commórtus*.

§ 6 'seed of S.,' i. e. the MacSweenys, who supplied fighting men to O'Donnell. See Notes to 25.

§ 7 'clans of N.' *clanna Néill* may stand for the O'Neills of Tyrone and their sub-branches, or for the O'Neills and O'Donnells, both regarded as descendants of Niall of the Nine Hostages.

'union and alliance,' this rendering seems required by the presence of the verb *do-nim*; *connailbhe* usually seems to mean 'loyalty to kin,' 'affection,' cf. Contribb. u. *condalbe*, and Duanaire Fhinn i, p. 5. With the use here compare: *bádar Conuill frinn aniar do-rónsad connailbhe is báidh* 3 C 13, 887. In some cases the meaning 'human feeling,' 'kindliness', is implied, e. g.: *iar ndol go hÁth Cliath don Iustis gusna braighdibh sin lais tainicc taom condailbhe ina cridhe go rochedaigh dona braighdibh sin . . . dul djiosrucchadh a ccaratt* FM v p. 1686; cf. also: *mar ghlacas conailbhe 7 báidh fris* Oss. iii 132; *araill d'uaislibh na bFionnghall . . . roghabhsat báidh 7 condalbhas fri Gaoideala* A. R. 12, and *ní dhiongna an Coimdhe th'oba ar aoi na connailbhe* Ir. M. 1921, 375.

For *combáidh* 'alliance,' 'confederacy,' cf. *hi combáigh na nGoideal* A. R. 160; *do-níd c. re chéile* 23 F 16, 7; *ar son chonnailbhe nó i gcombáidh* Hackett p. 91 = Keat. Poems 1329.

'great ties,' *rabháigh = báigh* (*báidh*) + intensive *ra-* (= *ro-*). This *báigh* is not to be confused with *báigh* 'boasting,' or 'threatening' (*ag b. 7 oce bagar* A. R. 128). Cf. *Olc do-rinne ciniodh Cuinn . buain re himlibh a fearuinn; dá dhonnghlaic nár dháigh* (sic leg.) *cogadh . báidh Chormuic níor chongmhadar* 3 B 14, 61; *Do cheangail Cormac . . . báidh go bráth re caomhchloinn Chéin* ib.; *is fiú a oineach . . . nach cóir gaolbháigh d'Cia air* ib. 62; *na Góidhil atrachtatar in bar mbáigh* A. R. 124. For the meaning 'love' see Ir. Review 1913, 624, 625; Unpubl. Ir. Poems i 16, v 14.

'king,' *branán* is the term for a piece in the game *brannumh* (*brandub* Contribb.). It is common as an epithet for a chief: *b. did chláir na ccuradh* L 17, 47b; infra **18**. 16, **25**. 22; *b. branduibh* Keat. Poems 1450. The word seems usually to denote the chief piece, but cf. *a bhranáin uaisle* 'his noble champions,' GF viii 15; *branáin Gaoidheal druim ar druim* Bk. 199a. The meaning 'chief piece,' 'king,' is supported by the following citations, which also throw a little light on the nature of the game:

Imleacán mhuighe Fáil finn . ráth Temhrach, tulach aoibhinn
si ar certlár an mhuighe amuigh . mar snuighe ar bhreaclár
bhrannuimh.
Gluais chuige, budh céim bisidh . ling suas ar an suidhisin
[leg. *snuidhisin*?]
riot, a rí, as cubhaidh an clár . as tí bhunaidh do bhranán
Do bhraithfinn dhuit, a dhéd bhán . saoirthithe bhunaidh branán
. . . suighter duit orra (the poet names the five capitals: *Teamhair,*
Caiseal, Cruacha, Nás, Oileach)
Branán óir guna fedhuin . tú is do chethra cóigedhuigh
tú, a rígh Bhredh, ar an tí thall . as fer ar gach tí ad tiomchall.

'The centre of the fair plain of *Fál* is Tara's castle, delightful hill; out in the exact centre of the plain, like a mark on a particolored *brannumh* board. Advance thither, it will be a profitable step; leap up on that square (lit. point, cf. the use of *tí* Coim. Y 607) which is proper for the *branán*, the board is fittingly thine. I would draw to thy attention, O white of tooth, to the noble squares proper for the *branán* (Tara, Cashel, Croghan, Naas, Oileach), let them be occupied by thee. A golden *branán* with his band art thou with thy five provincials; thou, O king of Bregia, on yonder square, and a man on each square around thee.' L 17, 26b (poem beg. *Abair riom a Eire ógh*, attributed to *Maoil Eóin Mac Raith*); *Atá*

brainech bhruighen lán . uime mar féin na mbranán, ib. 29b. The
number of pieces in the set was apparently thirteen, see Acall. 3949—50.
In *a b. óir ós fidhchill*, it is implied that *brannumh* and *fidhcheall* refer
to the same game, but cf. Acall. pp. 218-19. Both *brannumh* and *fidhcheall*
are used of the boards on which the respective games were played: *as tere
má do bhí ar bhrannamh bert mar í* 'scarcely has there ever been such
a move on the *brannumh* board,' L 17, 102b, and see above; for *fidhcheall*
see Corm. Y 607. This rather long digression may be pardoned in view
of our scanty evidence on the nature of ancient Irish games. The gloss
on *branán* cited from 23 L 34 in the glossary to Dánfhocail is apparently
by Peter O'Connell, as O'Curry states (H. & S. Cat.) that the additional
notes in this MS. are in P. O'C.'s handwriting. In his dictionary P. O'C.
has *branán* 'a pleasant agreeable witty fellow.'

§ 8 'one after another,' 'back to back' would hardly suit here; see
note on l § 5, and cf. A. R. 166. 12, where the ranks of an army about
to advance are arranged *druim ar druim i ndedhaigh aroile.*

'the seed of *Eóghan*' usually refers to the O'Neills, descended from
E. son of Niall (7), but here it may mean the MacSweenys, of the same
stock; see **26**.

For the rime *gríosmhálla : chíoschána* see Ir. Gr. Tr., Introd. § 38.
súir is curious, as *súr* is regularly a masc. -o- stem.

§ 9 'battle-allies; marriage connections,' I am not sure of the meaning
of *comhnáimha*, lit. co-enemy. Cf. the use of *námha* in **22**a. 191. Professor Bergin suggests that *cleamhnaoi* may be acc. pl. of a compound of
cliamhain and *ó(ua).*

I take *leas-* as = *lios-*, though I am not certain of the meaning. I think
its value is metrical rather than descriptive. Cf. *dá chúis doghra* [sic leg.]
leaschláir Luirc Ir. Monthly 1920 p. 109 § 11, where the editor connects
it, perhaps rightly, with *leas* 'advantage.'

Liathdruim, several places bore this name, including those from which
Co. Leitrim and Leitrim bar. in Galway are named; here it may be a
name for Tara, which was so called by the *Fir Bolg*, according to LG
(Macal. 252). See Macarthy 155 n. 3 and Met. Dinds. i 2. The -*thd*- in
this word probably = -*tt*-, see varr.

'Colla's kindred,' the Maguires, see **9**.

§ 10 'descendants of *Dálach*,' i. e. the O'Donnells of *Tír Conaill*
(Donegal).

'many-gifted ones,' *iolldánach* '(man) of many arts,' is commonly applied
to the mythological hero *Lugh*, see Oidhe Cloinne Tuireann, and Ridgeway
Essays, 332. Here the poet may intend a comparison with *Lugh*, but
the epithet is not rare: *iolldánoch íarthair Eorpa* (Maguire) 3 C 13, 513.
Cf. use of *sgolaidhe*, Ir. Monthly 1920, 109 § 14. The literal rendering
does not entirely bring out the meaning, which is that they are the only
ones in the five fifths of Ireland to merit the appellation.

§ 11 'fighting,' *cur feadhma* is often used of performing military prowess, 'going into action.' Cf. 21. 155; *rogha foghlama frith lais . cur fedhma, foghal ionnmhais* I. 17, 31 a (= Ir. Monthly 1920, 111).

§ 12 The families referred to in this stanza are, in order of reference: the O'Donnells (§ 10), the O'Dohertys of Inishowen (28), the O'Boyles and the O'Gallaghers. Capt. Piers, in his 'Articles for the reformation of the North of Ireland,' relates that "the lord's son is fostered with the best in the country, that is to say with O'Gallabor, with the galloglasses, t'w)o McSwynes and O'Boyle, the very pillars and strength of the country of Trynconnel." CSPI, Carew, 1574, p. 491. In 1599 the muster of the O'Boyles was 100 foot and 20 horse (ib. 1599, p. 299). In 160S Chicester reported "Divers gentlemen claim freeholds in that county [Donegal], as namely the three septs of the McSwynes, Bane, Fanaght and Doe [i. e. the MacSweenys of *Bóghuine* and *Fánaid* and MacS. *na dTuath*, see 4 §§ 42—3], O'Boyle and O'Galchare." CSPI, 160S, Oct. 14. "The O'Galloghers lived in the Baronies of Raphoe and Tirhugh, had a castle at Ballyshannon, were the Constables of the Castle of Lifford and commanders of O'Donnell's cavalry," Descr. of Ireland, ed Hogan, p. 32 n. "The midland of Tirr Conell is inhabited by the sept of O'Gallocars," Descr. of L. Foyle, Ulster Journ. of Arch. 5, 143.

§ 13 'raiders,' *sluaighsirthe* is npl. of a compd. of *sluagh* 'army' and *siridh*, nom. ag. of *sirim* 'I seek, search.'

§ 14 here 'the Champions of Tara's hill' refers to the four families just mentioned; in § 11 'the armies of Tara' means the rest of the men of Ireland.

§ 15 *tionól* may be gs. or gp., see 1 § 40 n.

§ 16 *Sreang*, the *Fir Bolg* chieftain who gained the province of Connacht as his share of Ireland, after the Southern Battle of Moytura; see Ériu 8. 56—7.

§ 17 'we know,' for *cadamar* see Gael. Journ. 1909, 310. It is noteworthy that the clause thus introduced is not in dependent form. Cf. *do-feadar* Ir. Monthly 1921, 114 § 22; *adamar* [sic leg.] 1920, 110 § 22.

§ 19 'to seek other aid', here *déanamh tar* seems to mean 'passing over, rejecting.' Cf.

> *rogha leaptha clúimh a cladh . úir tarar deacra dénamh*
>
>   A iv 3, 69S.

In Ir. Gr. Tr., Introd. §§ 1, 3 the phrase seems to mean 'do without.' 'shapely' is a tentative rendering of *sithseang*. I do not know whether *sith-* here is connected with *sloth* 'elfmound' or *s.* 'peace.'

§ 21 For *tarngartaidh* see 1 § 38.

§§ 22—33 refer to incidents narrated in *Cath Muighe Léana* ed. O'Curry, Celt. Soc. 1855; see also Keat.

§ 22 *maca samhla* is the older form of *mac samhla*. Cf. *séal samhli*. Marstrander has identified *maca* with ON maki 'match, mate' (*Bidrag* 40). Cf. Meyer, Miscell. Hibernica, Illinois 1916. The form *macsamhail* is a neologism.

§ 23 'fearless,' I take *neamh chorrach* as the neg. of *corrach* 'unsteady,' Contribb. *Mugh N.* = *Eóghan Mór*, Conn's rival, from whom the southern part of Ireland is called *Leath Mogha.* 'sheltering,' here I take *cleath-* as the noun connected with *ceilim* 'I conceal.' See Gael. Journ. 1909, 310; and cf. *clith* 'close, compact,' Contribb., *clithach* ib. xxvii. 'sleekly-waving,' lit. of the slack furrows; *clodh* is regularly used of the indulations of the hair, cf. 3. 188 and *gá chéibh nglannchlathaidh agrianoidh* Ériu 4, 64.

§ 24 'valiant', *catharda*, an adj. from *cathair* 'city, citadel', is used to translate *civilis* : *cath c.* 'bellum civile' 18. 68, cf. 16. 238; it also seems to mean 'civil' in the sense of 'gently-behaved, urbane', cf. 22 a 111 and we may have an instance of this in 16. 10; cf. *foraois oinigh fuinn Bhanbha róimh an oinigh chatharda* L. 17, 11 a; when applied to buildings or parts of buildings, as in 28. 60, 27. 31, it may mean 'stately'. When applied to warriors, as here, the correct rendering is doubtful; perhaps 'courtly, well-bred', or it may be that in such cases the word is to be referred to *cathar, cathfer* 'man of battle'; see Fél. June 3; SG ii 478. 11. From this we should expect the form *caitheardha*, really a preferable reading here, as *flaitheamhla* is the regular form of the rimiug word. P. O. C. has "*catharda* brave, stout, valiant; *cath cathardha* a brave battalion or legion."

§ 25 For the construction of this stanza see Introd. p. lx.

§ 29 'one and all', see 1 § 5 n.
céadóir céadóir; cf. *áig* in fourth line, and see Introd. p. lxvi.

§ 30 *lit*. 'the smooth-hilled host of T.' Here I take *Tailte* to be the placename preserved in the name of Telton tl., Roscommon.

§ 31 'to end', *gá dám(dú) dhó, gá d. ris*, is common in the sense of 'in brief, to sum up'. For further instances in these poems see reff. under *atá*, Introd. pp. lxxv-vi.

'diffident', I have rendered *anuallach* as if it were the opposite of *uallach* 'haughty' (cf. *uall* PH, *uallach* CRR p. 78, Keat. ii p. 40, Keat. Poems and infra 8. 55). But possibly the *an-* is intensive; cf. *anualach* Dán Dé xxviii 43, where 'proud' suits the context.

'Plain of the Champion', *Magh an Sgáil* may be a bardic name for Connacht, see Onom., and cf. *Machaire in Scáil*, otherwise *Magh Aoi*, Acall. Possibly the name refers to the Phantom (*scál*) which appeared to Conn the Hundred-fighter in Tara (ZfcP 3, 457; 12, 232).

d'éanldimh 'simultaneously' or 'with one accord,' has been inadvertently omitted in translating. Cf. *go ria a n-aithrighe d'é.* O'Gr., Cat. 467, "until with one accord their penitence should be accomplished."

§ 34 In the first line of this stanza three unstressed vowels come together, the middle one is elided, and the third, part of the surname, but a proclitic, having no more metrical value than the *ad-*, *do-* of compound verbs, is unstressed. ¡When part of a surname, or in the meaning 'descendant, one of a stock,' *ó(ua)* is regularly unstressed, e.gg. 7. 13, 201; 8. 40, 15. 22, 196. 'stately-eyed', lit. 'of slow eyelashes.'

§ 36 'officers', *aos gráidh(or grádha)* may mean according to context either 'lovers' or 'people of (official) rank' for the latter cf. infra 8. 40, and *robadh i ccarpat . . . roimchairsiot a muintir(no a thairisigh 7 a aes gradha) an Iustis* FM vi 2036. It may also mean those in holy orders, and this seems to suit the instance in O'Grady, Cat. 485.

§ 37 *Murbhach*, perhaps Murroe on the N. Donegal coast. Cf. 14 § 13.

§ 38 This is identical with 4 § 45. For Plain of the Fair see supra, Introd. p. lvii.

'summoned and pressed', for other variants to this line see 4. 178. I have selected the reading *tacair* as neither *tachair* 'of conflict' (RC 23, 437, O'Cl., Acall.), nor *teagair* 'of arrangement,' appears to me to suit the context. The meaning of *tacair* here is not quite certain, but the poet is apparently referring to followers not bound to the chief by ties of kinship. Cf. *tacar .i. ni bi bunadh* O'Don., Suppl.; *fine tacair* one of seven different kinds of tribes enumerated Laws v 318, and explained in the Commentary by *in fine tochuirid chuca .i. meic faosma* 'the tribe they call in i. e. the foster sons' (Atk.). In two of the following exx. the form of the word is not proved by the metre, but it is almost certainly the same:

ni thréicfea, damadh tú soin, do ghruag ar ghalldacht thacair
"for an artificial English mode," Irish Review 1921, p. 471.

d'fáth Banbha is baramhail soin . clár óir fa foirinn tacoir
ar ar bhfearoinne frioth seal . dith gealfoirne na nGaoidheal
Bk. 412 b (No. 82), 23 F 16, 26.

'This is the similitude of Banbha, a golden (chess)-board with an alien (?) set; for some time past our territory hath lacked the bright set of the Gaels'. Uilliam Óg Mhac an Bháird refers to Conchobhar O Briain, the scourge of the poets (see Notes to 3) as *Iarla tacair Tuadhmumhan (:bratuibh)*, Bk. No. 75. Cf. also *tacar* 'collection, . . . contrivance, . . . art, pretence' Dinneen.

With *tiomargadh* cf. A. R. 118. 24; *airecht do timurcain* Laws i 102, and *ro eirgissa a ndiaid na Feinde . . . 7 fecht ar a dó déc ro timsaigiusa lat. 7 ro timairgis ar in tulaigsea . . ., 7 in fecht déidenach ro fastissa lat tainic a chiall . . . féin d'Find,* Acall 4972 ("collected and mustered" SG ii 221). For the use of gen. vn. = pass. part. cf. *fear dearmaid* 'a neglected man,' GF iii 44.

§ 39 *Oileach*, older *Ailech*, Greenan Elly in Inishowen, Donegal. See notes to 28. The form *dreagan* seems a borrowing of Engl. dragon; the Middle Engl. loan *dragún* appears supra 1. 82, 106 etc. while the earlier borrowing *draig (draic, gs. dracón, dracoine* Wi. PH) from Lat., appears infra 13. 126.

§ 40 'hinders,' *turbhaidh* (*-adh*) is found in the sense of 'a period of exemption,' see Laws Gl.; O'Don., Suppl.; *cen turbaid cen dichell* Ériu i, 220; *turbaid chotulta* Ir. Texte i 97 seems from the context to mean 'prevention of sleep;' it is rendered 'sleeplessness' Hib. Min. p. 58. (Cf. *derbaid*, v. n. of O. Ir. *-derban* 'hinders,' and see Met. Dinds. i p. 68). I do not know if *turbha(i)dh* 'misfortune' O'R., P. O'C., infra **13**. 30, is the same word Further exx. are: *Gach lot ós aird nó gan fios . gach turbhuigh thig na bhflaithios* L 17, 83 a; *Gach triath a ttús a ratha . nach iomchair airm ardflatha; do as goire turnamh a tinn . turbhadh oile fa Éirinn* 83 b; *Timcheall tighernuis an tuaisceeirt . ní turb⁻ tarla ar thuir mBaoí; acht olc d'Íath cCobhthaigh a ccinnedh . nír locht orthaibh filledh faoi* 24 P 27, 149; of a land bereft of its chief: *Tainic dall ciach ós a cíonn . do leath a turbhuidh timchioll* C iv 1, 176 b; *Beag an turboigh da ttig olc . urasa m'fearg do dhúsocht* 3 B 14, 56; *lé Rughraidhe gur threabh Temhair . ben turbhaidhe d'feraibh hí* 23 D 14. 32. Cfr. also Ir. Texte ii², 196 § 14, Ir. Gr. Tr., Decl. ex. 545 and *Gleanings fr. Ir. MSS*. 34 § 32.

§ 41 *Fainn*, cf. Faing. Onom. The var. *Cairn Fionnaine* (not in Onom.) probably means 'fair *F*'s cairn,' *f* being omitted.

§ 44 'stately,' I have taken *neamhchranda* as opp. of *cranda* 'stooped' P. O'C., Contribb. Cf. *fuil cranda do chora i ccion . 'sna fola arda ísíol* Bk. No. 315.

'about,' *lit.* 'at the time of.'
leinibh, a by-form of *leanaibh*.

I do not know what was the poet's immediate source for the story of the Judgment of Solomon. A number of scriptural stories are found in Mid. Ir. in a more or less distorted form. For those already in print see Best.

§ 45 Whether the omission of the eclipsing *n-* after *inghean* here is in accordance with classical usage I cannot say. This instance is obscured by the final *-n* of the noun, and by the lateness of the MS. In the modern linguistic consciousness *cúpla* governs, not gp. but ns. We might expect *éagsamhla* here, but even in O. Ir. adjj. of this class may make gp. like ns. *Solmha* is a possible gen.: *Tempull Solma* (sic leg.) Arch. 3, 234.

'strange', I am not sure of the correct rendering of *éagsomhail* here. The original meaning is 'dissimilar' (neg. of *cosmhail*) and it is common in the sense of 'varied', 'strange', 'uncouth', and thence developes two different senses (1) 'uncomely, awful:' **13**. 126; **15**. 120; (2) wonderful, amazing, delightful:' *ingena áille examhla* Alex. 235, *do chruth áloinn examhail* Bk. 220 a (No. 310).

§ 53 'impatient men,' *lit.* 'the impatiences of the men' (?) But the phrase is strange. The word is properly *deinmne*, dat. *deinmnid*, but possibly there is a form *deinmnide*, dat. *deinmnidin*, on the pattern of *foighide*. If so *deinmnidin* might be the true reading here.

§ 54 'Telton,' see § 30. .

'dismantled,' thus I render *ar char eile* 'in another position.'

§ 55 *ní héidir*, perhaps we should read *héidear*, the usual form in these poems; see **4** § 17, **17** § 3, **23** § 23, but cf. **15** § 38.

According to Father Denis Murphy (A. R. pp. xxix-xxx) the Ineen Duv, daughter of James MacDonnell, Lord of the Isles, was Hugh's second wife. She was mother of Red Hugh and Rury.

'torrential stream' *déar* 'drop, tear.' I am not sure of the meaning of *d. díleanda*; cf. **16** § 49 n. Note the rime *díleanda : díbheargа -nd-*, *-ld-* may count as *-nn-*, *-ll-* or the *-d-* may have its normal value, see Ir. Gr. Tr., Introd. § 64.

3

In this piece the poet reproaches O'Donnell for refusing protection to his kinsfolk during one of the chief's punitive expeditions into Lower Connacht.

§ 1 'children of *Tál*' the O'Briens, or the Dalcassians (*Dál gCais*) *Tál* being a nickname of *Cas*, the ancestor of these kindreds, see O'Gr., Cat. 394; Keat. *Ros* was a more remote ancestor of the great Munster families, Keat.; LL 320 c 35.

'plunderings of', the gen. may be subjective: 'plunderings by (those of) C.'s Plain' in reference to the poet's immediate grievance.

§ 2 the third line is difficult: I take *thart thall* to go with *athaigh d'a.* (cf. mod. *thart* 'over, past'), and *i gc. dá gc.* to mean, freely, that the two kindreds were paired by the poets, the one to receive praise, the other a corresponding portion of censure. This suits the explicit statements in subsequent stanzas. Cf. however, *Dán Dé* xii 21, and in poem likening *Cú Chonnacht* Maguire to *Cú Raoi* and *Cú Chulainn*: *diobh Cú Connacht ... na coinsin . rú a ccomhar clú do cuireadh.* 'Cú Ch. is of those Hounds ... his fame is apportioned with theirs' ZfcP 2, 346. In the poem referred to below, note on § 9, stanzas in praise of O'Donnell alternate with stanzas censuring the Earl of Thomond.

§ 3 *Síl gC.*, for the eclipsis see Introd. p. civ. Only in quite Modern MSS., and then without regularity, is the glide written between *i* and a following broad consonant, so it is uncertain whether we should not read *síol* for all cases in these tribal names. The lenition of the *s* here accords with the rule that proper names are commonly lenited in the gen.

§ 4 '*Hugh (N.)*' see 2 § 23 n.

'valor's etc. *rómh, róimh* (1) 'Rome', Ir. Gr. Tr., Decl. § 42; infra **24** *pass.*; (2) 'cemetery', Fél. Wi.; *i rróimh adhnacail Síl Aodha* FM vi 2048, *rómha adhnaicthe* ib. 2298; (3) 'capital, headquarters'; infra **14. 8**; ZfcP 2, 342; *Forais oinigh fuinn Banbha . róimh an oinigh chathardha* L 17,

11 a; of Dunboy: *senróimh féile na hÉirenn*; *róimh oileamhna na n-éigeas* L. 17, 20 a; addressing Donegal castle: *Fa tú medh Emhna . . . nó an braoinlesa ós Bóinn bhinn . ba róimh aoibhneasa dh'Eirinn* Bk. 178 a (No. 12); *a rómh na riogh* ib. 178 b; *róimh aoidheadh chatha Cliach* 24 P 27, 148; *mar fine Róigh iar cCoin cCuloinn . ad-roigh ar róimh fuloing uainn* ib. 150. See also Ir. Gr. Tr., Decl. ex. 1, O'Gr. Cat. 456, 466; Keat. Poems 1479, KM. Miscell. 50.

§ 5 'even' for this use of *fiú* cf. *mé gan fiú an bhaird do bhuidhin* Bk. 84 a (No. 279), *ní bfuil fiu in ordlaig innaib . . .* O'Gr., Cat. 456, and Gadelica 1, 63, where Professor O'Rahilly suggests that *fiú* in this usage stands for *feadh*. This may be true of *go fiú*, but in the present and similar instances I see no reason for separating the word from the subst. *fiú*, especially as the tradition of the bardic schools is usually curiously accurate in preserving historical forms.

'humourous stanza', for *ábhacht* see Contribb., *Dánfhocail* 177, and *ádhbhacht*, Dinneen, and cf.: *Tré mhac Cathail na cciabh nocht . ní luidh mh'inntinn ar ádhbhocht* Bk. 319 a (No. 261); *déna dimbríogh dá ttéid thort . léig bhúr n-imsníomh ar adhbhocht* L 17, 90 b; *aithnim adhbhar do throda . riom a mheic Mheic Diarmoda ; ní fuil sí acht ag seilg mholta . ná bi ret feirg n-adhbochta* ib. 78 a (cf. ZfcP 2, 356. 21, where the text is incorrect) *ní mhaithfeadh sé a n-abraim d'ulc . gion go nabraim é acht d'abhacht* Ir. Monthly 1922, 416, and see infra, 17. 237. For the metre called *ábhacht* see Ir. T. iii pp. 100, 160.

'the race of C.,' Munstermen may be so called from *Corc,* the reputed founder of Cashel, and rival of Niall of the Nine Hostages. See Keat. and Contention.

§§ 9-10 This occurrence is recorded in FM: *Eoghan Ruadh mac Fearghail mic Domhnaill Ruaidh Mic an Bhaird, Muiris Ballach mac Con Coiccriche mic Diarmada uí Chléirigh 7 Mac Uí Mhóirín do chrochadh lá hIarla Tuadhmumhan, Concobhar mac Donnchaidh, 7 robdar saoithe hi senchus 7 i ndán an Muiris 7 an tEóghan remraite, 7 roba damhna aoire 7 easccaoine don Iarla an feillghniomh isin* 'Owen Roe *Mac An Bhaird,* Maurice *Ballach* . . . O'Clery, and the son of *O Móirín* were hanged by the Earl of Thomond, Conor, son of Donogh; and the aforesaid Maurice and Owen were scholars in history and poetry, and that treacherous deed brought much satire and malediction upon the Earl.' 1572. See also O'Gr., Cat. 341 n., and the note in YBL col. 98 (printed in Abbot-Gwynn Cat. 342). There is a poem on the subject by Uilliam Og Mhac an Bhaird, *Biaidh athroinn ar Inis Fáil,* in which the justice and clemency of Hugh O'Donnell and the nobles of Conn's Half are contrasted with the injustice and cruelty of Conor O'Brien and the Dalcassians.

§ 9 'perfected', cf. *adhbhur righ no ri ullamh* 'heir apparent or actual king,' Plummer, *Bethada NnE* i 262.

§ 13 'my unfairness', I am not sure of the meaning of the last line; *m'éagóir* might mean 'the injustice done to me', cf. 17. 268, or 'the inj.

I have committed', cf. *oc athi bar col 7 bar n-ćōra foraib (a mallacht-nachu)* PH 3638.

§ 14 The reference is, I suppose, to one of O'Donnell's expeditions into Lower Connacht to persuade O'Conor Sligo to his duty, see Introd. p. xxvi.

'firmly-walled', I have taken *-foirbhthe* to be used here in a sense approximating to its O. Ir. meaning, 'perfect'. The meaning 'mature, old' would be possible here, and also in **13** § 13, **16** § 40, **25** § 2, but in these three instances 'smooth, polished,' a natural development from 'complete, perfect,' seemed more suitable.

§ 15 *gan charaid* etc., the npl. is used here as *gan* governs the clause *caraid . , . d'imdhídean.* Cf. Ir. Gr. Tr., Introd. § 76.

'land of O.' may mean Connacht, referring to *Oilill (Ailill)* of the *Táin*, or merely a part of Sligo, referring to the son of *Eochu Muigmedón* from whom *Tír Oilealla*, Tirerill bar., is named.

§ 17 for gs. *cinéal* see **1** § 40 n., and for eclipsis see Introd. p. civ.

'unhappy' etc. I am not sure of the meaning of the last line, which may be a proverbial phrase. Cf. perhaps: *Dá dhoimhne asdeach théid an grádh . truagh a Dhé cor na gcompán; mó(mór MS) is doimhne ag tocht asteach . olc na foirne acht go bhfilltear* 3 B 14, 54.

§ 18 *B. Boirche,* an old name for the Mourne mts., see O'Donovan's *Leabhar na gCeart*, 38 n. g.

§ 20 'powerfully attended,' I have taken *meidheal (meigheal)* as a by-form of *meitheal* 'a band of reapers, a company.' Cf. Ir. Gr. Tr., Decl., §§ 53, 54; exx. 1340, 1377 (in § 54 *meidheal* and *metheal* are widely separated in the list, which suggests that they were distinct words, but the separation may be accidental), and *Ag atach Dé um dhénamh leathtaoibh . do Lúcás Díolmhain dreach thsaor; iomdha thsiar monghuire meidheal . is fonnghuidhe cliar nimheadh naomh* A v 2, 24 b.

§ 21 *gruadh ng.,* for the use of the gp. here cf. **3.** 143, **19.** 3, **20.** 223, **39.** 21 etc.

Almhu, the seat of an ancient court, is used as a synonym, or kenning for Ireland, see Introd. p. lviii.

§ 22 'unjustly' etc., I am not sure of meaning of last line. There are many exx. of *d'iomurcaidh* x, 'as a superiority over x,' 'to the disadvantage of x,' and I have taken this to be the meaning here: *do an an féile ag Olltuibh . a Éire dod t'iomorcuigh* L 17, 87 a, *Lé ríogh Uladh na n-ech seng . guala dhes airdrigh Eirenn : ó bheithir bhionnfocluigh Bhregh . d'iomorcuigh cheithir ccóigedh* 47 b. *. . . ní hí a innmhe acht a inntinn . tug ainm d'iomarcuidh gach fir . don bhaidhbh . . .* 31 a, *urchar bheirne do bhrisedh dom iomarcuigh* Bk. 325 b (No. 136); some other exx. of *iomarcaidh* are worth noting: *an ga bulg ag Coin Chulainn . iomarcuigh narbh ionfulaing* L 17, 42 a (cf. TBC 3850 var.); *Da ccoimeas g bé do bheath . mór an iomarcaigh d'Oileach : cuan long da gach leith* *don toigh . ní reith an tonn go Teamhraigh* F 16, 20; *Mór n-engnamh airmhid leabhair . . . do-chóidh a n-onóir d'Ulltuibh . dóibh ní foldir iomarcuigh* L 17, 47 b; *da roinn foirbfe ar nach antoir . gan poinn ortha d'iomarcaidh* Bk. 130 a, *dlighidh uaisle iomorcuigh* L 17, 86 b, *An cuigeadh gidh cia do chluin . cia tuigter as acht Uluidh: atá so d'uaisle ag Ulltuibh; no no uaisle d'iomarcaidh* Bk. 171 b (I. 17, 87 a), *Síol gCréidhi ōn Bhaoill bhinnealtuigh . éinfer dhíobh ní díommoltair; díon béime an chláir Chonnachtuigh . a ndáil th'féile dh'iomarcaidh* A iv 3, 620; *Eire agus airdrigh Berta . ní ffuil enbhann uaislechta: a thoil ní diomoltair dhi . d'iomarcaidh air nū uirrthi* Bk. 221 a (No. 310); *Iomad damhna ar druim nÉrenn . ag éirghe chlū a ccaithrémenn; san iomarcaidh ūd chéibh chais . ag fréimh fionnfortail Feorais* 23 D 14, 57; *beg do-chim d'imarcaidh air* "I see but few arrears accumulated against him," O'Gr., Cat. 501. See also Zfc P 2, 385; Ir. Gr. Tr., Decl. pp. 49. 4, 74. 8 etc.

§ 23 *Duibhlinn* may be Dublin, but more probably a river in North Connacht; perhaps the Suck. See Onom.

Calry, the name of a parish in Carbury bar., may represent *Calraighe*, the old tribal name of a territory near Loch Gill, Co. Sligo.

§ 25 *Maol Míolsgothach*, see § 37 n. The following apologue is based on the old tale *Airec Menman Uraird Meic Coisse*, edited by Miss M. E. Byrne in Anecdota from Ir. MSS. ii. According to the tale Mac Coise, poet to Tadhg O'Kelly of Hy Many, was plundered by some of the O'Neills because he had slain one of their kinsmen.

§ 26 'became incensed,' lit. 'their flame arises.' Cf. *tainic a losi* Anecd. fr. Ir. MSS. ii 12, *loise th'feirge* Ir. Monthly 1922, 31.

§ 27 'road-skilled,' I have taken *séad-arsaidh* as lit. 'road-ancient,' i. e. practised in expeditions and hostings, cf. 21 § 7, but this is uncertain, as the compound occurs in contexts where a different meaning is required, e. g. *tír sédarsuigh* C iv 1, 172 b.

'woeful,' *aigmhéil* I take to be = *acbéil, acbeóil* Contribb.; *aighmhéil* 'perilous,' wou'd also suit the context, but the *g* is not lenited in the MSS.

§ 29 Donnell, K. of Ireland, grandson of Niall *Glúndubh*, † 979.

§ 30 'enquired,' cf. *fochtuis* Marco Polo 54, Zfc P 6, 25 etc. and the hist. pres. *fochtuidh* ib. 90. The verb seems to be formed from the pret. of O. Ir. *iarmi-foig*, cf. *atfócht* TBC 5162.

tairsibh, the var. *tarstibh* (: *baistigh*) is noteworthy.

§ 35 'the breadth' etc. *comlethet a aigthi d'or* Airec M. § 32. This is a wellknown item of compensation in Irish and Welsh tales. Cf. *comleithet a enech di or 7 argut do Ailill* Mesca Ulad (LU 20 b) "as an atonement for the insult, he shall have a staff of silver . . . and a plate of gold of the breadth of his face" Guest's Mabinogion, ed. Nutt, p. 30 (*clawr eur kyflet a'y wyneb*); see Loth, *Les Mabinogion*, 1913, i 127-8, *Anc. Laws and Instt. of Wales* p. 3.

Gáinighe is unidentified. Cf. 31. 235, O'Gr., Cat. 367.

§ 36 'the slender-handed ... Bregia,' for *maicne* 'youths' A has *maoine*, a reading which would mean 'they (subj. of verb virtually *cloinn N.*) dispense to the poet the riches of the slender-handed scions (*géag*) of B.' In the rendering of the text given I have taken *géag mbastana* as lit. 'of the arms of slender hands,' for this use of gp. see § 21 n.

§ 37 *Orgain Cathrach Mail Milscothaigh* was the title which Mac Coise gave to the fable through which he related his grievance: *Ar ba he ainm do-rat Mac Coisi do fein ar duaithniughud a tsluinnti .i. Maol Milscothach .i. milisbriathrach innsin* "For this is the name M. C. gave to himself in order that his surname might not be recognized, Maol Miolsgothach, that is, 'of sweet words'" Airec M. § 8.

crioch, possibly we should read *crích*, object of *do-chuaidh*; *dith* is possible in next line, see § 34.

§ 38 The Plain of *Conchobhar* is probably Ulster, the ref. being to C. son of Ness, although he is traditionally connected with the eastern side of the province, not with Donegal. Cf. A. R. 164. 23.

§ 40 'did not become me,' cf. **28.** 47.

Line, this place-name, very common in epithets, is preserved in that of Moylinny (*Magh Line*) deanery, Co. Antrim.

§ 41 'red fist,' I take *duinndeise* as compd. of *donn* and *deas* or *deise* 'right hand,' see *dess, desse* Contribb.

§ 42 'to guard,' for similar use of *iomghabháil* see FM v p. 1584; *do ingaib é fen ar gach uile buáidred* Betha CC § 64. Cf. **20.** 1.

§ 47 If this is to be taken literally, Tadhg was evidently fostered in Donegal, where he is still remembered in oral tradition. See Introd. p. xxv.

§ 48 But see his poems on the O'Neills **6-8.**

Iomghán is one of the commonest of the place-names used in epithets. Possibly to be identified with Dunamon Castle on the Suck, Co. Galway, see *Dún I.* and *Caislen Dúin I.* Onom. and see ALC ii 364, 390.

§ 49 'make (great) people of them,' cf. *Mór doghnid daoine dhiob féin* O'Gr., Cat. 555, where *daoine* is probably obj. of the verb, although taken as subj. in the translation.

§ 50 I have not found any poems addressed by Tadhg to a Munster nobleman. If his threat was fulfilled the result has perished.

§ 52 Read *do ghéabhainn.*

§ 54 'connection,' for the use of *um* here cf. YBL 387a 34-7, Ir. Monthly 1920, 166 § 27 and *Atáid uime ... ocht ngluine déug uaisle fithcheid ... ó Aodh go Niall Naoighiallach* (to Tyrone) 23 E 26, p. 10a.

4

Drumleene, the anglicized form of *Druim Lighean*, is the name of a townland in Raphoe, Co. Donegal, but the Irish name was anciently applied to a hill near Lifford, on the borders of *Tír Chonaill* and *Tír Eóghain*. We should expect the border between O'Neill and O'Donnell to be the scene of much contention, but in this piece *Druim Lighean* seems to be used not altogether in its strict geographical sense, but rather as vaguely symbolic of the sovranty of Ireland. See note on § 18. The piece is somewhat ambitiously constructed, and as far as it goes, stands on a higher level than most bardic poems, but it is not 'closed,' and therefore appears to be unfinished. It is curious that the final stanza = 2 § 38 (see varr.).

The opening stanzas are based on some recension of *Lebar Gabála*, see the earlier chapters of Keat. Hist., FM, AM 2850 ff.; and Atlantis iii 385. O'Grady, in his interesting notes on the piece (Cat. 426), refers to some later and "more tangible" occurrences, from A. D. 1522 to 1583, and he supposes that a lively engagement between O'Donnell and Turlogh *Luineach* which took place in June of the latter year was the occasion of the composition. O'Curry, in Atlantis iii 385, states that the poem "professes to have been written on the eve of" this battle, and though there is no such decisive evidence as this statement would suggest, the specific reference to *Druim Lighean* makes the theory plausible. See FM *ad ann.*

§ 1 'Precinct,' cf. use of *maigen* in Laws.
'the valley' etc., "the glen of noble invers," O'Gr. He states that the 'invers' refer to the vicinity of the Foyle and of Loch Swilly.

§ 2 'crimson ... mass,' this is a merely tentative rendering of *rothnuall corcra*, an obscure term taken over from the early sagas. In the Táin, *Cú Chulainn* becomes a *rothmol* (-*mól*, -*nuall*) *corcarda* or *corcra* on awaking from slumber and passing his hand over his face (TBC 1256, 2496); also on emerging from his cooling bath (1370). In these instances it seems to mean that he became suffused with a pleasant glow. See Windisch's note, TBC p. 152. In later usage the phrase *do-rinne rothnuall corcra dhe* is applied to a person suddenly seized with anger: *atá fled agamsa duitsi, a Fergais, ar sé, agus as geis duitsi fled d'fágbáil noco tairsidh í. Ocus ótchuala F. sin dorindeadh rothnuall corcra de ó bhonn go bathis. Is olc dorinnis, a Bh.! ar F.*, Oided Mac nUisnigh, Ir. Texte ii[2] 129. Similarly infra 8. 97. Cf. also *rothnuall* (or *rathnuall*) *bairdne*, the name of a metre, Ir. Texte iii 141.

§ 3 'the lake,' O'Gr. identifies this with L. Monann, now Maghera Lake, Co. Tyrone; but possibly L. Foyle is meant.

§ 5 *Cruachán Lighean* 'the mound of *Lighe*,' another name for Drumleene, preserved in that of Croaghan tl., Clonleigh par., Raphoe.

§ 6 This seems to refer to the assault on '*Conuing*'s Tower,' traditionally located on Tory Island. We do not find in LG that Nemed or his

E. Knott, Tadhg Dall Ó Huiginn.   14 progeny fought any battle against *Conuing* in the neighbourhood of Drumleene. The reading *meic Flath* is doubtful; the name of *C.*'s grandfather is not in LG. The poet may have found it elsewhere, perhaps in the lost tale *Argain Tuir Conaind* (MS Matt. 590, Anecd. ii 47), if the reading is correct.

§ 8 This can only refer to the engagement known as the First Battle of Moytura, between the *Tuatha Dé Danann* and the *Fir Bolg*, which was fought, according to tradition, in the neighbourhood of Cong, Co. Mayo. See the text, ed. and translated by J. Fraser, Ériu 8.

'the ancient' etc., lit. 'by the ancient-dyked point of *C.*'

§ 9 'a space,' the form *athadh* is uncertain, as it is abbreviated in all the MSS, and the ending of the riming word is also doubtful. The noun *ealatha* (*ealadha*) has gs. -*an* or -*na*, but as npr. it may perhaps be differently declined. An acc. *athaidh* (-*gh*) is fixed by rime 1. 165, 13. 191; a gen. *athaidh* (-*gh*) 8. 45. Cf. Contribb. 3 *athach*, and *athaid*; and *athadh* (*othadh*) Ir. Gr. Tr., Decl. p. 53 y; exx. 350-1.

The battle referred to is the Second, or Southern Battle of Moytura, between the *Tuatha D. D.* and the Fomorians, in the par. of Kilmactranny, Co. Sligo. Text ed. with transl. by Stokes RC 12.

§ 10 'worthy to reign,' probably a ref. to nobles with ancestral claims to the high-kingship. Such phrases have acquired an interesting significance for us through Dr. MacNeill's essay on the laws governing dynastic succession in ancient Ireland in his *Celtic Ireland*.

§ 11 For *cean*, gp., see 1 § 45 n.

§ 12 'returned,' this rendering may give too precise a force to *aris* here; it may be simply transitional, 'then again,' 'moreover.'

§ 13 These chiefs are said to have been slain in the battle of *Tailte* (Teltown) in Meath. Save the tradition that *Íoth* was slain there (Keat. ii p. 56) I have no ref. to any battle between the Sons of *Míl* and the *Tuatha D. D.* at Drumleene.

'for whom' etc., lit. from whom hazels were fruitfully branched. The ref. is to the common belief in the beneficial influence of a just ruler on the earth's fertility; see Introd. p. lxii.

Cathair Chröoinn, the editor is solely responsible for this spelling. *Cathair Chrobhuing* regularly appears in 17th-18th cent. MSS for the earlier *C. Chrófind*, *C. Chroind*, *C. Chrouind*, *C. Chroffinn*, the name of Tara under the *Tuatha D. D.* (Met. Dinds. i 4, 28, LL 375 b w, MacCarthy 155 n. 3). I have no evidence for the quantity of the first -*o*-. The rime with *Bóind* (Met. Dinds. i 28) proves nothing, as both words are dissyllabic, and vowels in hiatus may both be short, whatever their previous history, see Thurn. Handb. § 45, and cf. Ir. Gr. Tr., Introd. pp. 22-3.

§ 14 LG only refers to two battles between the Sons of *Míl* and the *Tuatha D. D.*, that at *Sliabh Mis*, in Kerry, and the battle of Teltown. The third referred to here must be that fought at Geashill, King's Co., where Eber was slain by Eremon, Keat. Hist. ii 106.

§ 15 'moreover,' I have not attempted a precise rendering of the idiomatic *Gidh iad ann*; cf. *gér ïséin ann rob uasal a hincholnugad* SG 17 x.

§ 16 '*Ú*'s Land,' Ireland is so called from the monarch *Úghaine Mór*, whose death is recorded in the annals *A. M.* 4606. *Iúghaine* is the commoner spelling in the MSS of these poems, but the form in the text is established by rime, e. g. **16**. 72. In good early MSS *Úgaine* is usual, but an archaic form *Augaine* also occurs, e. g. Ält. Irisch. Dicht. i 29.

§ 18 'six,' i. e. those referred to in §§ 6, 8, 9, 13, 14. As none of these is recorded in LG to have been fought in the neighbourhood of, or in contention for, this particular hill, it is obvious that the site of the coming conflict is regarded in the preceding stanzas as a symbol of the sovranty of Ireland.

§ 21: §§ 21-9 are in imitation of the portents of the Civil War as described in Cath Cathardha (the Irish version of Lucan's Pharsalia) 818 ff.

§ 22 'folds,' I am not sure of the meaning of *cróbhuaile*; *cró* may mean 'blood,' 'death' (*cró. i. bás* O'Cl.), or 'an enclosure.' Stokes renders *cróbuaile* by 'deathfold' in Vocab. to CCath.; ib. 5378 he renders *c. catha* by 'fold of battle.' Some of the exx. in the same text seem to mean defensive enclosure,' 'phalanx,' e. gg. 5405, 5317. Cf. also TSh., Vocab.

'masses', I have no ex. of *morc* except in the phrase *m. teineadh*, which is found *Eachtra Lomnochtáin* p. 51, "pile, heap" and in the Irish Life of St. Margaret, ZfcP 1, 131; *is ionnan morc agus mór* Plunket s. v. *lues*. Cf., perhaps, *molc. i. tene* Lec. Gl.; *molc?* O'Mulc. 758.

§ 23 *Atconncadar araili rind ann co ruithnibh roedrochtaibh 7 co trillsibh tendtidib for esrediudh ass, in retlu mongach insin, 7 ni ro artraigh sen riam acht la cumscugudh flaitiusa, na clodh catha, nó la bás airdrigh.* CCath. 831-4.

'maned star,' i. e. 'comet;' cf. *in retla mhongach* "comet" ALC 1018. For the last word of the stanza we should perhaps read *iodhlannuigh*, see varr., and cf. *go rün n-udmhall n-iodhlannach* ZfcP 2, 359.

§ 24 This is probably a reminiscence of: *Atcluintea comtuaircnech na cnamh i mmedon na comrar i n-uilibh adnaictib* etc. CCath. 894-5.

§ 25 *No labraidis na ceithri tre glor ndaenda acco* etc. CCath. 885.

§ 26 There is nothing exactly corresponding to this in CCath., but it may be based on: *Ro tusmit geni torotharda imda isin Roim in tan sin, co met cuirp, co n-ilar lam 7 cos 7 cend, co linadh oman 7 imegla a maithri fein ica teancaisin* 891-3.

biasduidhe, see varr. Of many borrowed words beginning with *b* or *p* we find forms with either initial, as: *péisd : béisd* Ir. Gr. Tr., Decl. § 43 *príosún : bríosún* § 35, *punnann : bunnann* § 12 (cf. Marstrander's *Bidrag* 96 etc.).

§ 27 *Atcithea in badb catha gach n-aidhchi, 7 a haithinni giuis for derglassad ina láimh 7 a trillsi natharda nemidi ic dresechtaigh immo cend ic aslach in catha for na Romanchaibh* CCath. 902·4.
'isles,' possibly 'meadows.'

§ 29 For gs. *creachthóir* see Ir. Gr. Tr., Decl. § 50.

§ 30 'camp,' for the original meaning of *longphort* see MacNeill's *Phases of Irish History* p. 259. A later meaning is illustrated in a description of a 17th cent. hunting-party at Braemar, quoted from Taylor, the water-poet, in Scott's notes to Marmion C. 2: "... the first day, we travelled eight miles, where there were small cottages, built on purpose to lodge in, which they call Lonquhards."
'will ... before,' the varr. are: 'will have a golden shield on his elbow;' 'will have a golden shield on his breast.' The reading followed is that of the older and more correctly written copies; it has also the claim of being less simple than the others. Cf. *lainnrech na lethansciath lanmor ic a n-imurcur for uillennaib na n-anradh occus ar rightib na rigmiledh* etc. CCath. 5448-9.

§ 31 'whetting (?),' 'clasping (?),' I am not certain of the meaning of *ionnráithne* here. The -*th*- may represent an older -*ch*-, alternating with -*gh*-. Cf. *indráigne* 'detrimentum,' Wb. 16b 9. A different meaning is implied in: *glaodh na hindráithne* Ir. Gr. Tr., Decl. ex. 203; *Béara foirinn go hÁth Truim . a Airt ... um dhoirsibh tor nGall gáirfe . ar ndol tar am n-ionráithne* L 17, 102 b; probably a different word.

§ 32 'clang,' I do not know the precise meaning of *seasdán*, but the word is commonly used for noise of various origins; see TBC pp. 478, 721; *sesdán* [sic leg.] *na sochaidhe 7 muirn an morslúaigh, Buile Suibhne* 17; *sestán 7 seiseilbhe na ccenn ina dhiaidhsium* ib. 65; *sestan a sluagh* "the loud hum of its occupants," O'Gr., Cat. 474; *mar do chualaidh sestán sechránach ar na conaib* SG 306.
'ivory horns,' see *buaball* Contribb., and cf. *lionmhaire a bech 'sa buabhall* 'the abundance of its bees and its — (?)' L 17, 11 a. Here the word seems to be attrib. gp., unless it is an ordinary adj. Cf. *do seichid buabhall* Marco Polo 36, *clámh buabhuill* 1, 62, *go geloich buabhaill* Ir. Monthly 1923, 643. In referring to horn-blowing the poet may still be influenced by CCath.; cf. the descr. of horn-blowing and trumpeting in 5014 ff.

§ 33 'gaping,' *uaithmhéalta* may stand for *uaibhéala = óibéla* Wi., *óbéla* CCath, PH, FM vi p. 2176. Cf. *oillphuist ... uaithbhéalta* TSh. (Atk.) p. 185.
'fluttering,' O'R. has *gaothradh* "fanning, winnowing;" the only other ex. of the word I have noted is in an 18th cent. poem: *Do bhí gach rioghan liomhtha gléasta . is fleasc óir fá bhárd a céibhe; péarlaidhe is oscur go brollach gléigeal . sioda is sróll go leór ar gaethradh* Gael. Journ. 1905, 715.
For *eang* 'banner' cf. 29. 62, and *luaithealta ós cennuibh cháich . d'enguibh snaithenta sensnáith* L 17, 27a; *eang thana mhionsróill* GF iii 8.

§ 34 'clamorous,' *conghdireach* is formed from *conghdir*, which looks like a compd. of *cu*; 'baying of hounds;' *urlann do lis gan lúth greadh . gan conghdir gan chur ccraoitheadh, dob annamh* . . . Bk. 226 b (No. 90); cf. Unpubl. Ir. Poems xix 6; but though it would suit the context, it is nncertain if the piimary meaning is really intended in these exx., as the secondary meaning 'clamour' is well established at an early perid. Cf. Unpubl. Ir. Poems xix 16; *conghdir t'faighthe do uaignidh* l. 17,63a. The adjective in many exx. means simply 'noisy, clamorous;' *do boinfidis na cluigsin co congairech* Irish Bevis, ZfcP 6, 284; cf. ib. 285 *l.* 14; but in some cases a further development of meaning 'busy, crowded (?),' is implied, e. gg. *cathair congairech* Ir. Guy, ZtcP 6, 35; *fear caithmheach conghaireach* FM vi p. 1910, *ar a chaithmighe 7 ar a chonghairighe* ib. p. 2364.

§ 35 *Teach Truim* probably = Tara, cf. 8 § 22; or *Ráth Truim*, Met. Dinds. i 42.

'stately,' lit. 'heavy-headed.' If *ceann-* here means simply the human head the rendering given probably expresses the meaning; or *trom* might refer to the hair. If it means 'chief' we should render the compd. by 'strongly-ruled,' or 'having mighty leaders.'

§ 36 For further reff. to prognostication by cloud-gazing see Acall. 7579 ff., Ir. Texte ii 133, *Ridgeway Essays* 346 § 38 (Quiggin), Ir. Gr. Tr., Decl. ex. 1219; Keat. Hist. ii p. 348. Cf. TTebe 1196 (= Statius 460).

§ 38 'long-handed,' "with the long [i. e. taper, wellbred] hands," O'Gr., Cat. 427. See 1 § 25 n. In 2 §§ 12-14 the chief is apparently advised to rely upon his kinsfolk rather than upon hired swordsmen; in the ensuing stanzas we seem to have advice quite the reverse. The following is O'Grady's summary of §§ 37-45 (the brackets are his): "but does the Chief never consider, nor feel compunction, that the rank and file of Kinelconnelll complain of attending him now so long, without a sight of home? grumble at his constant maintenance of war? . . . the man from the Moy's side [county Sligo], from *srubh Brain* [Loch Foyle], from the Curlieus [county Roscommon], from Oriel [Mac Mahon's country of Monaghan], every one of them wearies for his house again; if O'Donnell must be so warlike he would do better to trust altogether to the trained fighting septs of the Mac Sweeneys, who are devoted to him and more effective than seven times their number of raw levies." Cat. 427. It is peculiar that § 45 of the present piece is identical with 2 § 38. In §§ 42-4 O'Donnell is obviously urged to trust in the three MacSweenys and his own immediate kinsmen, but what families are referred to in §§ 39 and 45? *Srúbh Broin* is Stroove, in Inishowen, and probably indicates O'Doherty; Oriel O'Grady takes to mean the MacMahons, but possibly the Maguires are referred to. The Moy and the Curlieus point to Sligo and Roscommon contingents, but it is not clear to me what particular families are meant.

§ 40 'Since,' etc. cf. 15 § 25.

§ 42 'The heroes of the *Tuatha*,' i. e. *MacSuibhne na dTuath* 'MacSwiney ne doe,' (See O'Gr. 464); scated in the present bar. of Kilmacrenan, Donegal; 'warriors of F.,' i. e. *MacSuibhne Fánad*, MacSweeny of Fanad, Inishowen.

'easy to fish' i. e. 'calm.'

The word rendered 'warrior' here is *onchú*. Stokes, in a note to Tog. Troi (2nd ed.) 1071, conjectured that this word was borrowed from Fr. *onceau*, but it is evidently a genuine Irish word like *dobhorchú* and *faolchú*. As n. pr. it is found along with other *-chú* words in early pedigrees: *m. Onchon m. Faelchon* LL. 317a 55; *Sil Onchon* ib.; *.h. Onchon* 314b 17; *Doborchu m. Onchon* 313c 15. See also Fél. Stokes afterwards noted that the literal meaning of the word was 'waterhound,' and suggested the rendering 'otter,' CCath., gloss. In SG 58 it is used of some kind of aquatic monster; cf. *onchú aigéin mara* 3 C 13. 460. In a passage in Anecd. ii 62 it seems synonymous with *cú*. O'Grady renders it by 'leopard,' Cat., 367 n. and in fact it seems in these poems to rank with *beithir*, *draig*, *gríobh*, as the name of some vaguely visualised monster, typical of bravery and heroic achievement; thence it may usually be rendered 'hero,' or 'warrior.' It has often moreover, the meaning 'banner,' 'standard,' evidently because these frequently bore, or consisted of, representations of some terrifying animal, and possibly the word refers in this sense to the heraldic lion or leopard. See Iar Connacht 267, SG 50, *fa onchoin seinlitrigh sróil* Bk. 298a (No. 283), *ag úaim onc[h]on sróil* ZfcP 2, 359, cf. Ir. Gr. Tr., Decl. cx. 432. P. O'C. has *onchú* 'a wolfdog; a standard or ensign with the figure of a wolf drawn upon it.' See also TBC and CCath. vocabb. We have a description of an *onchú*-standard in a poem by Maol Muire Bacach Mág Craith: *Tóigeóbhthar riasan ttor chleth . onchú dathchorcra dhuaibhsech; cló (clog* MS) *fraochda adchiú ar an ccoin . nach maolfa riú ar na rochtuin; Suil uirthe budh aimlesc linn . re huathbhasoidhe a hinill; pest uaibhrech nertmar nemhtrom . rechtmar uaibhrech ingenchorr* 'There will be raised on high before the bush(?) of spears the grim, crimson-hued *onchú*; a ferocious aspect I see on the hound, which will not abate when it is reached. We care not to regard it, so dread an armature it hath; a haughty, powerful monster, mightily venomous, furious, arrogant, sharpclawed.' Bk. No. 1. Probably the native *onchú* became assimilated in meaning to Engl. ounce.

§ 43 'hawks of *Beanna B.*,' *Mac Suibhne Bóghaine*, MacSweeny of Banagh, Donegal.

§ 44 this *Durlas* was probably in Donegal, see note by O'Gr., Cat. 386.

§ 45 See supra 2 § 38.

5

Lifford, one of the border castles between *Tír Conaill* and *Tír Eóghain*, and, according to Conn O'Donnell, 'the chief defence of O'Donnell's land' (CSPI Sept. 30, 1562), was built by Manus O'Donnell in 1527. The possession of it was frequently disputed between the O'Neills and the O'Donnells, and also between members of the O'Donnell family. Shane O'Neill demanded it in 1562 as a condition for releasing the Calvach from prison (CSPI May 1544, Sept. 1562 etc.; for Conn's estimate of the value of the castle see O'Gr., Cat. 59). The following poem was evidently composed in return for hospitality enjoyed at the castle during the residence there of Conn O'Donnell and his wife Rose, Shane's daughter (see supra p. 187).

§ 4 *D. Iomgháin*, see **3** § 48 n.

§ 6 *aird*, sic leg., for rime. For acc. after *ionmhuin* cf. *i. tigh* Ériu 8, 89.

§ 7 'chessplaying' is of course a provisional rendering; the precise meaning of *fidhcheall* has not yet been ascertained. See note on *brandu* **2** § 7 n.

'arches,' *sduagh* is not often used by the poets in its literal sense; cf. *caoin sduagh a righfuinneóg ruinn . mar snuadh mhínduilleóg mhemruim* 23 D 14, 120 (Eóghan Mág Craith).

§ 8 *Durlas* = *D. Guaire* **6** § 3.

§ 9 *Eamhain*, probably *Eamhain Abhlach* 'Apple-treed *E.*,' cf. the Avalon of Arthurian tales. See *Imram Brain* p. 7, note by K. Meyer, ZfcP 8, 194; and cf. Ériu 5, 56. 72; *Ridgeway Essays* p. 340, § 20. According to the poem beginning *Baile suthain Síth Emna*, printed in Skene's *Celtic Scotland*, vol. iii, this *Eamhain* was situated in the Isle of Man; in YBL 178a (= RC 24, 274), we read of four *Manannáns*, amongst them *mac Alloit*, a druid of the *Tuatha Dé Danann: 'is e in Manandan sin robai a nAraind, 7 as fria side aderar Eamain Ablach.* Meyer (l. c.) takes this to refer to one of the Aran isles in Galway bay, but in it is more likely that Arran in the Clyde is meant. This was understood by O'Curry, Atlantis iv 228. In the couplet cited by Meyer (l. c.) from Ir. Texte iii 34 *Arann : Manann* (cf. ZfcP 10, 286 w), and the name of the island in the Clyde has short initial, see Acall. 351. We might also compare the reference in the old tale of the sons of Tuirenn, or Tuirill, of the appletrees submerged beneath the sea in the neighborhood of an island between Ireland and Scotland (ZfcP 12, 244), a poetic myth which is curiously distorted in the later versions.

'children of *M.*,' these were seven heroes who fought on the Connacht side in the Táin; see TBC 166 etc., Keat. Hist.

It is a common form of compliment to compare the chieftain's stronghold with castles of other days, famed in history and legend; cf. **6** and **27** and *Ridgeway Essays* 366 ff.

6

This artistic little piece in praise of Shane O'Neill and his dwelling
only occurs in late, inaccurate MSS., and several lines are corrupt beyond
cure, though the elaborate metre enables us to emend confidently in a few
places.

§ 1 *Lios Gréine* I take to be a place-name, though I have not met
it elsewhere, and O'Grady, Cat. 525, renders the first line "A sunny liss
that to Ulster is an Emania." This seems to me a rather abrupt opening.
O'Curry, RIA MS. Cat., Betham 88, 416 renders the line "Lios Greine is
Emania to the Ultonians," while in H. and S. 527 he has "Lisgreine and
the Ultonian Emania." In A the poem is described in the heading as "on
Eamhain Macha, the residence of the kings of Ulster;" similarly in F vi 2,
a badly written copy to which I have not referred in the variants (*air
Eamhain Macha .i. dúnphort cómhnuighthe ríogradh Uladh 7 churraoi
na Craoibhe Fuadh* F vi 2. 240). But the *Eamhain* referred to is most
probably *E. Abhlach*, see 5 § 9 n.

Tailte is the ancient assembly ground near Navan.

With the construction in the third line cf. *sgéal nach deireoil
dhéireadh*, *Dán Dé* xii 23, *i n-aontaidh nach fríoth foircheann* xxiv 16.

The last line is imperfect; there is no rime with *fuil*.

§ 2 *Ealcmhar*'s castle seems to be identical with *Brugh na Bóinne*,
see RIA Ir. MSS. Ser. i 46, Met. Dinds. iii 30, Ériu 7, 210. The older
nominative was probably Elemaire, but gen. Elemair occurs, Met. Dinds.
iii 40.

'at variance,' I have taken *cur fá chéile* to mean 'set at odds' but
I have not noted another example.

§ 3 G.'s *Durlas*, the residence of *Guaire*, the seventh-cent. king of
Connacht so famed for his liberality, see Ériu 1, 43; Keat. Hist. For a
note on the ruins of *Guaire*'s castle see Oss. v 121.

§ 5 '*Dún Dealgan*,' Dundalk Fort, Co. Louth, traditionally associated
with *Cú Chulainn*, see ZfcP 2, 343-4.

§ 6 *Lios L.* is a name of Naas, according to O'Curry, MS. Matt. 478.

§ 7 'Hound of the feats' is a common epithet of *Cú Chulainn*. I do
not recognize the ref. here, nor am I sure of the correct reading or how
do thoirbhir should be rendered. The verb has the meaning 'to subdue'
(*tairbirim* Wi., PH), 'to yield, hand over' (Ériu 4, 114 § 13; FM v p. 1406 x,
vi 2170, 2220), and the v. n. *toirbheart* 'gift, bestowal' is very common,
e. gg. 14. 68, 25. 120, 28. 111.

'similar' etc., cf. *Ridgeway Essays* 340 § 16, Ir. Monthly 1923, 64t § 13,

§ 8. Cf. 11 § 11.

§§ 8-9 'exercising,' or perhaps 'trying;' for this use of *gníomh* cf.
11 § 20, ZfcP 6, 278. 3; Ir. Gr. Tr., Introd. § 78, O'Gr., Cat. 474.

The third line is corrupt. Ireland is called *Úna*'s land probably
from the mother of Conn the Hundred-fighter.

§ 9 'driving,' I conjecture that this refers to the shoeing of the steeds, but I am not sure of the meaning of *snlomh tairngeadh*. Cf. *mni snies trena brat .i. a dealg* O'Dav. 315, *nach taighlim na tri ceardcha . do shni fhaighlinn mh'aigeanta* Ir. Review 1913, 594.

§ 11 *R. Éanna* may be a kenning for Tara, perhaps from *É. Aighneach*, a prechristian king of Ireland (Keat. Hist., FM), or *É.* son of Niall N. G. Cf. *Dún Enna*, Onom.

§ 13 I do not understand *néalmhach*. In the fourth line we should perhaps read *do bhreith b.* 'to snatch bridles.' But the stanza is obscure to me.

§ 14 The rendering of this stanza is based on emendations, see varr. The first line is still unsatisfactory.

§ 15 *Lugh L.* a *Tuatha Dé Danann* chief appearing in the Second Battle of Moytura (RC 12; Oidhe Cloinne Tuireann, Atlantis iv etc.).

fádh, this form is common, see 13 § 23, *A. Ó. Dálaigh* p. 22 § 10.

'*Connla*,' perhaps *C. Caomh*, king of Ireland, whose death is recorded at A. M. 4757.

§ 16 Dungannon was at this period an important post for defence and parley. Shane's letters to Charles IX and the Cardinal of Lorraine, enlisting their aid in expelling the English, are dated from *Dun Genaind* (CSPI, April 1566, pp. 298-9). In May 1552 Sir Thomas Cusake reported that: ... "Shane O'Neill, the Earl's youngest son, came to Dungannon, and took with him of the Earl's treasure 800 *l.* in gold and silver, besides plate and other stuff. He sent to the Scots to give them entertainment" (i. e. to enlist them for his wars). After an interview with Shane on Mayday Cusake reported that he could see nothing in him "but pryde, stubboines, and all bent to do what he coulde to distroy the pore Countrey." CSPI, 1552, p. 126. Some interesting documents relating to Shane, including his letter to the Earl of Argyll (CSPI 1560 n. p. 160), are given by O'Grady, Cat. 524-6.

§ 17 *Bearchán* Propheta, of Clonsast, a saint to whom several prophecies about Ireland are attributed. See Fél. Dec. 4 (note LB), Keat. Hist., Betha CC pp. 420-22 etc.

§ 18 'hostage-cell (?), 'I conjecture the second element of *giaillbhrios* to be a form of *prios* 'press,' but I have no ex. of this. Cf. *prisún* Ir. Gr. Tr., Decl. § 35; ex. 909.

For ns. *greagh* see Ir. Gr. Tr., Decl. § 45.

7

The two following pieces are addressed to Tuilogh *Luineach* O'Neill, grandson of Conn *Bacach*'s brother Art. On the death of Shane in 1567 he was elected to the captaincy of the kindred, and for the remainder of his life waged a skilfully conducted opposition to his rivals and to the

English government, in the field, and by diplomacy. He died in 1595. O'Grady's notes on these poems, Cat., pp. 409-11, 432-4, are of great interest, and the following extracts from the 17th. cent. *History of Sir John Perrott* (ed. 1727) are illustrative of the old chieftain's attitude.

Of 'certayn Mocions' made by the Lord Deputy 'unto the Lords of the Privy Counsell in *England*', autumn, 1584).

"The sixth Motion was, that upon the Lord Deputie's last Entry into *Dublyn*, there came Letters to his Hands directed from the Lords of the Privy Counsell to *Turlough*, *O-Neale*, and the Baron of *Dungannon*. The Direction of it selfe seeming to attribute to much unto them (for *Turlough* was termed Right Honourable) the Lord Deputy opned the Letters, and finding the Contents agreable to the Direction, thought good, by the Advi-e of the Coun-ell, to make stay of the Delivery of those Letters, least they should have puffed them up to high as Thinges then stood. But the Lord Deputy besought theyr Loidships to writt theyr Letters in allo- wance of *Turlough*'s Dutie and Serviceablenes, in the Composition which he had mad, wherby he had strengthned hymselfe by the aide of lawful Peres under Government, with Caution, that theyr Lordships should not allow hym to high a Stile, for fear of Pride and Presumption, wherto his Place with any Applause would easily hurie hym, as the Lord Deputy knew best." p. 181.

"... *I understood the State of* Tirlaugh, Lenagh, O-Neale (*partely thorow his Want of Government) to be weakned and decayed after his Returne from this Parliament* [1584-5], *and his Shew of Obedience; insoemuch that his Followers forsooke hym, and refused to yelde such Duties, as he was to answer the Soldiers, wherby they were put in want, and the Composition in hazard of overthrowinge.* p. 209.

"He [i. e. Perrott on his visit to Ulster in 1585] found *O-Neale*, by reason of his Unweildiness (thorow age and otherwise inclined for Ease-sake) to yelde all the Hither-Partes of his Territories, upon reasonable Composition to the Erle of *Tyrone*, and his own sonne Sir *Arthur*. The Lord Deputy did the rather consent therto, thinking it a Meane to abolish the Title and Greatnes of *O-Neale* during his Life, and cleane extinguishing it, and drawing the Dependancie of *Friaghs* wholy to the State after his Decease. For these Considerations, and holding up of some Part of the Composition, and relievinge of the Soldiers Want, and allso for the keeping downe of *Shane O-Neale*'s Sonnes, this Agreement was concluded on between them by Indenture sealed and published in the Campe [at Dungannon p. 210]." p. 225.

"Articles of Agreement betwixt *Turlough Lenough* and the Erle of *Tyrone* were the rather condiscended to by the Lord Deputy and Counsell of *Ireland*, because they thought it a good Meane to abolish the Title and Power of *O-Neale* in *Ulster*, who because they had byn Princes of that Province, as longe as the Name remayned, they thought the Dignitie and Prerogative must ever follow; to extinguish which Opinion, and Operation of that Opinion, the Erle of *Tyrone* did then undertake to suppresse (upon the Assumption of this Stile and Partition). And soe for that Time a Peace and Unitie was procured betwixt the Lords of *Ulster*, that Contrie quieted, and the Composition maynteyned; yet *Turlough Lenough* had no sooner concluded these Conditions, but he began to repent his Bargayne, as beinge sensible of the least Losse, allthough it were of such Things as hymselfe knew he was not well able to holde; and soe shortly after would sometimes say, *They had put up a Whealpe, which they should not be able to pull down soe easily;* meaning the Erle of *Tyrone*, whose aspiring Mynde *Turlough Lenough* knew by former Experience as well in the Erle as in hymselfe.

The following piece is apparently an inaugural panegyric; possibly one of the 'rejected addresses' alluded to in **8** §§ 17, 22.

§ 1˙ 'privileges,' *sochar* consists of *cor(car)* 'agreement, contract' with the meliorative prefix *so-*. It is common in the sense of 'advantage, benefit, prerogative, privilege, special concession.' Such lists of privileges as appear here and in many other poems may be constructed in imitation of the verses in *Leabhar na gCeart.* Cf. **9**.

§ 4 *Uibh* (sic leg.) is unstressed, the words *neach* and *Néill* alliterating, see **2** § 34 n. In this piece the term 'descendant of Niall' is often used very vaguely, perhaps deliberately so, and it is seldom possible to tell if the Niall meant is N. *Ghundubh*, from whom the O'Neills of Tyrone are surnamed, or (as in § 8) N. of the Nine Hostages, from whom nearly all the noble families in Ireland claimed descent.

'no matter of doubt,' or perhaps 'there is no doubt at all,' cf. *dá mbiadh cuid amharais air* "were any modicum of doubt at all about it." O'Gr., Cat. 381-2. For further exx. of *cuid* with dependent gen. see **10** § 22 n.

§ 5 To accept hire from another was to acknowledge his political superiority, see *Phases of Irish History*, 274.

§ 7 Cf. **24** § 2, and also **9** §§ 36, 40.

§ 9 'not of them,' for *ó x amach* 'apart from x, besides x,' cf. *Gleanings from Ir. MSS.* 100 § 9, and *da n-ibhinn ó Aodh amach . ag righ eile fíon Frangcach* F 16, 170.

§ 10 'hilly,' *beann* by itself is vague, and here the context does not determine the meaning to be hill, turret, drinking-horn, or trumpet.

§ 11 O'Grady quotes and translates this and the three following stanzas, with the observation: "Hardly shall any poet of the Gael, projecting himself into the cosmic space of pure panegyric, have described a hyperbola much grander than this." Cat. 409. I have not noted any composition by Mac Coise containing the statements attributed to him here, but the idea in §§ 12, 13 appears in an opinion of the race of Aed Sláine, i. e. the Southern Uí Néill, found in the sayings of Flann Fina: *Caíte as dech rángaís? A n-as mesa do Síol Aodha Sláine 7 a n-as ferr díbsein as fri hainglib nime ata cosmaile.* Tecosca Cormaic vii. For a similar idea see Gibbon, *Decline and Fall*, ed. Bury v 392-3.

§ 12 O'Grady renders this stanza: "Said *Mac Coisi*: 'My testimony is this, that, as compared with all and several that are tribes of Tara, whosoever is the worst one of Niall's blood is nevertheless more excellent than they." I take the last line to be in apposition to *uathaibh* in the third, and to define the superior section of the stock. *Tuatha T.* seems to be used like *Doire* in § 13, *Liathdruim* and *Fréamhuinn* in 9 § 1, etc.

§ 14 *Cluain*, Clonmacnois. *Fionntan* is the celebrated antediluvian told of in *Suidigud Tellaig Temrach*, Ériu 4.

§ 15 'reasons,' I am not sure of the meaning of *cás* here.

§ 16 here we have a somewhat enhanced account of the blessing given by Patrick to *Eóghan* son of Niall; see *Tripartite Life of Patrick* p. 480.

§ 18 *Criomhthan* is probably *C.* son of *Fiodhach*, Niall's predecessor in the king-ship.

§ 19 'outcome,' rather 'object, objective.' The primary meaning of *fuidheall* is 'remnant, something unconsumed.' The defining gen. may indicate the material, as *f. fleidhe*, or the process, as to *f. áir*. Here it would be possible to take *fuidheall* as in apposition to *toradh*, and reading *síl*, render the line 'the remnant of the ancient blessings of the seed of N.' Cf. however, *Fuigeall beandacht brú Muiri* Arch. iii, 244, where *brú* and *fuigeall* are obviously in the relation of subject and predicate. In both exx., while the meaning 'outcome' suits the context well enough, it is not well supported, and we have several exx. of *fuidheall* where the defining gen. suggests a different meaning; see 17 § 54, and cf.: *d'fuigheall mallacht Fer nEreann .i. don iustis Saxanach lér milleadh Tomas Iarla* FM 1470 p. 1068 (O'Don. renders "wreck of the curses of the men of Ireland," with the note: "This is an idiomatical expression, signifying a person upon whom the obloquy and execrations of the Irish had been heaped."); *Fuigheall formuid fonn Sligidh . bés do—díochra a ainigin, tar chrích n-úir mbinnealuigh mBregh . cinnemhuin tnúith 'na timcheal* L 17, 53 a (O'Curry renders: "a victim of contention is the land of Sligo," H. and S. Cat. 598): *Fuigheall formaid full Dálaigh . tnúth dd mbuain na mbengánaibh* A v 1, 70 b; *fuigheall iaroinn aithleaghtha* (a complimentary epithet) L 17, 31 a; *Muca an Déganaigh ... ni bhia siad 'na bfuighioll sgéin . muna bfaghaid féin bás* Bk. 22 a; *f. tuisleadh* 24 P 33, 101; *Rí Caisil 'na chind ós chách . is eadh fil sunn co tí in bráth : fuighell beandachtan Dé duind . altóir Pádraic meic Alpraind.* O'Donovan's *Leabhar na gCeart* 54. Here though O'D. renders "consequence of the blessing," 'object' suits the context very well, as in our present instance.

§ 22 'outdo,' as to *iomarcaidh* see 3 § 22 n.

§§ 23-28 The picture of peace here is of course a conventional one, and could be paralleled from many odes and obituaries. Turlogh's rule is complimented in similar terms by Fearghal Óg Mhac an Bhaird (O'Gr., Cat. 384). Perhaps the English officials would have presented a different account; of the situation a few years later we read "South of a line from Galway bay to Dundalk respect for English law and order prevailed . . . in Ulster alone no improvement could be reported . . ." (Carew SP 1575-8 pp. xcvii-ix).

§ 28 'the Fifth,' Ulster is frequently referred to as *an Cúigeadh* in the literature, see supra p. 207 ll. 4-6.

'fertile,' lit. 'heavy-branched.'

'wave,' possibly 'surface,' but I am not sure how *tonn* should be rendered in this context. Cf. 8 § 29, and *no bhiadh dá chúicceadh Mumhan ina hentuinn bróin 7 basgaire* FM vi 2264.

§ 30 'whose' etc., lit. 'to whom a pledge (i. e. a gage of submission) is recommended.'

§ 31 'fifth part,' for *eang* see 10 § 11 n.

§ 32 'heaving,' the word so rendered is an adj. either from *dromchladh* 'dorsal surface' or from a compd. of *druim* 'back, ridge,' and *cladh* 'ditch.'

§ 33 'wellknown' etc., lit. 'an ancient cause (or material).'

§ 37 'firm,' the reading I have selected is that of a good copy and seems the most probable; *taidhleach* ,shining,' would make fairly good sense, while *taidhleach* 'stout, stiff,' (P. O'C.) would suit admirably, but there seems no reason why any scribe should alter this into *teigfioch*. Cf. *Sáithid Gaoidhil is Goill Bregh renna a rosg, rún a ccroidhedh, lot sith do éignidh orthuibh, san ccrich ttéiglidh ttorchorthuidh.* L 17, 53 a. *don chrich ttéigligh ttonnmhaoinigh* ib. 54 b, *coicceadh Uladh ina linn láin, ina thopor thecht 7 ina thuinn teccle isin mbliadhainsi gan guais catha . . .* FM vi p. 2142; *clár téiglidhe* 13 § 1.

'solid' see note to 9 § 4.

§ 41 See O'Grady's note, Cat. 410.

§ 42 Plain of *C.* i. e. Ulster *Conchobhar* son of Ness is referred to. 'hospitable' lit. ale-ancient, cf. O'Gr. 433 n. 2.

§ 43 'His wisdom' I am unable to decide whether *do dhruim eólais* here means as a result of (God's) knowledge, 'or' on account of (Turlogh's) knowledge.'

§ 45 Cf. 20 § 6.

§ 46-7 As to the 26 kings, 16 of Cinel *Eóghain* and 10 of Cinel Conaill see Giolla Mo Dhubhda's metrical chronicle *Éri ógh, inis na naemh* BB 49 b (MacCarthy 408 ff.). The last high king recognized in the official histories is Maol Seachlainn, who was dethroned by Brian:

> *Air éis Mael Sechlainn sona*
> *mic Domnaill mic Donnchadha —*
> *do scar saerbrigh re cach clainn —*
> *nogor gabh enrí Érinn.*   BB 52 b 44

MacCarthy renders the last line "Until Henry occupied Ireland," but probably we should read *nochor ghabh aenrí Érinn* 'no single king took possession of Ireland,' i. e. his successors were all 'kings with opposition.'

'in the reckoning' the reading in the text is probably wrong I have no other ex. of gp. *flath*. Read with AGLC 'who never shirked battle.'

It is noteworthy that in accordance with this accepted scheme of history the 16th century poet in hailing an O'Neill, an O'Donnell, or even a de Burgo as rightful king of Ireland speaks of Maol Seachlainn as his immediate predecessor in that office.

§ 49 'eight and four score, 'that is sixteen of the race of *Eóghan*, and seventytwo' Milesian predecessors of Niall. With the last line of this stanza cf. the following from Muircheartach Mhac an Leagha's ode to the Calvach O'Conor of Offaly:

Mac do Mhurchadh ri Ruidhe Calbach an chuilg ordhuighe;
saor an glun degenach [leg. *deireanach*] *dhiobh genealach ur na*
                                                    n-airdriogh. LL 394

and see Ir. Monthly 1922, 72 § 8, *Dán Dé* xxix 18.

§ 50 *Annla*, not in Onom.

§ 52 'a single Gael,' variant 'the Gaels.' 'in *Fl.*'s Field,' or 'for,' 'as regards, *Fl.*'s F.'

maoidhimh is used here as in mod. Ir., see Fr. O'Leary's *Mionchaint* iii 37.

8

In this piece the poet celebrates a Christmas banquet given by Turlogh to the poets of Ireland, probably in order to ascertain his standing in public opinion, and increase popular feeling in his favor. Cf. Gofraidh Fionn's address to William O'Kelly, Ériu 5, and *Phases of Irish History* 344.

§ 1 The Creeve was on the west of the Bann, near Coleraine: "On the Bann, near to Coleraine, is an important salmon-leap called *eas na craoibhe* (angl. 'Asnacreeva': a barbarous denomination discarded happily for that of 'the Cutts Fishery') and on the Derry side at this point may have stood the house . . ." O'Grady, Cat. 432.

'smooth wall,' see note on *slios* 11 § 24 n.

§ 4 'ten years,' this dates the poem to 1577, two years after his treaty of peace with Elizabeth. In Sept. of that year the Council of Ireland informed the Queen: ". . . The North is in greater quiet than it has been of long time, for Tirloghe Lenoghe has come in to your Deputy without protection or hostage. If troubles should arise there by means of the Scots, Tirloghe is to be framed as an instrument and scourge for them." CSPI, Carew Mss. ad ann. p. 110.

Almhu is probably the Hill of Allen, Co. Kildare.

§ 6 With F.'s reading of second line cf. *Atá teach aoibhinn innte .* *dá las li na firminnte*, *Ridgeway Essays* p. 344. The form *firmint* may

be old, cf. Ml 42b 10, 22. In Ir. Gr. Tr. I have only noted *(f)iormamhaint*
(Decl. § 13; ex. 657).

'pathed,' I have taken *rian* as 'track,' but it may be the old word
meaning 'sea,' and *rianmhagh* might be rendered 'sea-washed plain.'

Raoiliu is very common in such epithets; the word seems identical
with *Roiriu* (*Roeiriu*, *Rairiu* Onom.) which Hogan connects with Mullagh-
Reelion in Kildare.

§ 7 Cf. Unpubl. Ir. Poems xix 14.

§ 9 *mun aimsin*, the demonstr. suff. *sin* can attenuate preceding
consonant, cf. **15**. 135 etc., and see Ir. Gr. Tr., Introd. § 150.

§ 11 with second couplet: *tnú fán mBanbha bféaraird bfinn . faghla
ann gach ēnaird d'Éirinn* (Tadhg Camchosach ó Dálaigh), F 16, 55.

§§ 16-18 This is a just summary of the vague and general compliments
of which the court poems usually consisted. It is easily conceivable that
at this period especially, a body of poets from different parts of the
country would hardly care to put, as it were, all their eggs in one basket
by detailing Turlogh's individual claims too minutely. He complains,
reasonably enough, that their compliments might apply to any of *Eóghan*'s
descendants; so at least, I understand § 20. See O'Grady's note, Cat. 434.

§ 21 This I take to mean: so far from being a compliment to the
line of *Eóghan* and Art to say that they can retain the kingship, it were
a gross insult to suggest that anyone could think to wrest it from them
with impunity. The Art referred to may be Turlogh's grandfather, brother
of Conn *Bacach*. From the latter Shane and Hugh O'Neill were descended.
See A. R. p. xlv.

§ 22 ... *Teamhrach Truim*, cf. *oc temair truim* ZfcP 8, 306. 25;
11. 44 § 62. As *temair* originally meant 'a height, eminence,' (O'Dav. 1546)
there may be some connection with *síoth Truim* (**11** § 29).

§ 23 Niall of C., king of Ireland, was drowned in the river Callann,
A. D. 844. See FM, Cóir Anman, ZfcP 12, 234. He was grandfather of
Niall *Glúndubh*, from whom the O'Neills of Tyrone are surnamed.

'hazel-tree,' or possibly 'forest-tree;' *coill-* may be *coill* 'forest,' or
coll 'hazel,' with attenuation before the component -*bile*.

§ 25 'crimson mass,' see note to **4** § 2.

§ 28 the identification of *Monadh* is uncertain, see Onom. and cf.
24 § 9, **26** § 31.

§ 29 Perhaps *fa aontuinn* etc. should be rendered 'under one wave'
cf. *cosmhail re Coin na hEmhna, a Briain* ... *do thonn feirge a ngoire
gliadh* Bk. 327b (No. 148), *do linn feirgeisi* ib. See **7** § 28.

§ 33 'mouth of the Erne,' in the text *Inbhear dá Éagann*, otherwise
Cuan Easa dá Éagann, see **1** § 50 n.

§ 34 *Srúbh B.*, the reading is very doubtful here, see varr.

§ 35 The last line is doubtful. In Ed. the reading is altogether different, see footnote. We should get a satisfactory sense by taking *righ* and *oireacht Uladh* (N-reading) as place-names, but I have no support for this. For *sbroigeacht* (Ed.) see Ir. Gr. Tr., Decl. § 24.

§ 38 'them,' i. e. the poets. In N's reading I take 'their' to refer to the poets and 'them' to the people of Ireland.

§§ 39-41 The last line of § 40 means: 'Anna would be likely to aid me.' As § 41 opens with a ref. to *Síol gColla* it is clear that these additional stanzas are a tribute to Turlogh's wife, Agnes Campbell, to whose 'fayre speaches and lewd counsell' Sidney attributed the chief's rebellious tendencies. Sidney also described her as 'a grave, wise, well-spoken lady in Scottish, English and French.' She was daughter of Archibald, 4th Earl of Argyle, and by her first husband, James MacDonnell, Lord of the Isles, was the mother of Ineen Duv (**2** § 55, Carew 1580 p. 297). She was married to Turlogh in 1569, see CSPI 1509-73 pp. 420, 439 etc).

9

The three following poems are in praise of Maguire, Cú Chonnacht, son of Cú Chonnacht. In **9** he is also called son of *Siobhán* 'Joan.' If Tadhg Dall is the author this can only be the Cú Chonnacht who was elected to the captaincy of the Maguire kindred in 1566, and died in 1589. He was the father of Hugh Maguire who was slain in Cork in 1600, and of the Cú Chonnacht who succeeded Hugh in the captaincy. Hugh's pedigree is traced thus to Donn Carrach by O'Clery, 23 D 17, 80 a: *Aedh m Con Connacht m Con Condacht (.i. an Comarba) m Con Condacht m Briain m Pilip m Tomais m Pilip na Tuaighi m Aedha Ruaidh m Flaithbhertaigh m Duinn Carraigh.* 1302. In **9**. 217 we must therefore assume an error of transcription, and read, as I have emended, *mheic mheic* for *mhóir mheic,* see varr. For a collection of poems on the Maguire family, mostly addressed to our Cú Chonnacht, see Stern's paper *Ueber eine Sammlung irischer Gedichte in Kopenhagen,* ZfcP 2, 323 ff.

Cú Chonnacht's first wife, so far as I can discover, was Hugh's mother, Nuala, daughter of Manus O'Donnell (FM 1592, p. 1924; Ó Heódhusa's poem *Cuirfead so ionnat, a Aodh*). His second, Margaret, the mother of his son Cú Chonnacht, appears to have been daughter of Shane O'Neill; Ó Heódhusa concludes his poem for our Cú Chonnacht, *Anois molfam Mág Uidhir,* with stanzas in praise of O'Neill's daughter (*Inghean Uí Néill.* See Stern 354; C iv 1, 148 a), and in a poem addressed to him by Fearghal Óg Mhac an Bhaird, *Cia re bhfuil Éire ag anmhuin?,* there are stanzas in praise of Margaret daughter of John (*Mairgréag inghean Seaáin.* See Stern 337; these stanzas are lacking in the copies in C iv 1 and 3 C 13). In *Fada óm intinn a hamharc* Ó Heódhusa refers to the young Cú Chonnacht as grandson of John son of Margaret; *bráthair of*

Hugh Maguire (Stern 359-60; O'Grady, Cat. 454. Lughaidh Ó Cléirigh, however, calls him Hugh's *derbhráthair*, A. R. 228). Stern quotes from two poems in which a *Bé bhionn*, wife of Cú Chonnacht Maguire, is mentioned (339-40). It is unlikely that she is to be identified with Nuala, as he suggests, and if he is right in dating the poems c. 1558 they can hardly refer to our Cú Chonnacht. Siobhán, Cú Chonnacht's mother, I have not been able to trace. As he is sometimes referred to as *ua Seadín*, Seaán was probably the christian name of her father.

Cú Chonnacht succeeded as Maguire his brother, or half-brother (*bráthair*) Seaán (son of Cú Chonnacht, son of Cú Chonnacht, son of Brian), who had been banished by Shane O'Neill. He kept on good terms with the English government; Sidney writes in Dec. 1575 "O'Donnell, Lord of Tyrconnell, and McGuire, Lord of Fermanagh, who wrote humbly unto me, live wealthfully and deny not to pay rent and service to her Majestie (so as that they may be discharged from the exactions of others)," CSPI, Carew 1575-88 p. 30. In the Description of Ulster in 1586 it is reported that The county of Farnmanagh [*sic*] contains all Farnmanagh, Tyrmangrah [=*termon még craith* Onom.] Tirmin O'Mingan [see *termon uí moain* Onom.]. Its Captain is Sir Conohour [*sic*, for "Coconagh," i. e. Cú Chonnacht] McGwyre, under the rule of Tur(logh) O'Neyle, but desirous to depend on the Queen. He is able to make 80 horsemen, 260 shot, and 300 kerne." See also O'Gr., Cat. 430-31 n. In recording his death in 1589 the FM describe him as generous towards churches, poets and soldiery; skilled in Latin and Gaelic. He attended Perrott's parliament at Dublin in 1585.

Sir John Davies, in his Letter to the Earl of Salisbury in 1607, writes: "Touching Fermanagh, otherwise called M'Guyres country; that country was never reduced to the crown, since the conquest of Ireland, neither by attaindure, surrender, or other resumption whatsoever, until Sir John Perrott's government, who caused Coconaught M'Guyre (father of Hugh M'Guyre, who was a principal actor in the late rebellion, and slain in Munster, upon an encounter with Sir Warham St. Leger), to surrender all the country of Fermanagh in general words unto the late queen, and to take letters patent back again, of all the country in the like general words, to him and his heirs; whereupon was reserved a rent of one hundred and twenty beeves, arising out of certain horse and foot, and a tenure in *capite*: but this English tenure did not take away his Irish customs and exactions; he was suffered still to hold his title of M'Guyre, and to exercise his tyranny over the queen's poor subjects, of whom the state took no care, nor notice; albeit there are many gentlemen who claim estate of freehold in that country by a more ancient title than M'Guyre himself doth claim the chiefrie. Coconaught M'Guyre, having thus obtained letters patent, died seized of the country; and after his death, Hugh M'Guyre, being his eldest son, took possession thereof, not as heir at common law, but as Tannist, and chief of his name, was created M'Guyre, and held it as an Irish lord until he was slain in actual rebellion, which we hold an attainder in law, in this kingdom. Davies; *Hist. Tracts*, ed. 1787 pp. 219-20.

E. Knott, Tadhg Dall Ó Huiginn.

For the traditional history on which much of the poem is based the reader should refer to the legend of the Three Collas, of which versions are found in Keat. ii pp. 356-64, *Silva Gadelica* ii pp. 461, 505, ZfcP 8, 317. See also Skene's *Celtic Scotland* iii 397.

The Maguires are derived by the genealogists from Colla *Dá Chríoch*, one of the three sons of *Eachaidh Doimlén* son of *Cairbre Lifeachair*, hence in bardic verse *Síol gColla*, *Síol* (*Fuil* etc.) *Eachaidh*, are standing epithets of the family. These epithets of course, can be, and regularly are, applied to other families derived from the Collas, such as the MacMahons and O'Kellys, from the same ancestor as the Maguires; the MacDonnells of Antrim and the Isles, the *Meic Dubhghaill*, from Colla *Uais*. This source of confusion may account for the inclusion of the first forty stanzas of the present poem in *The MacDonald Collection of Gaelic Poetry*; the scribe of the MS may have thought he was transcribing an encomium on the Lords of the Isles. The editors of the collection certainly took it as such, for it is thus described in their table of contents (p. vii): "This panegyric on the race of Colla Uais, from whom the Family of the Isles is descended, is from a manuscript in the possession of Clanranald, and is in the handwriting of Cathal MacVurich [cf. Abbot-Gwynn Cat. pp. 155, 360], who flourished in the latter half of the 16th and the first half of the 17th century. The name of the author is not given, but it was probably composed by one of the MacVurichs early in the period of the Lordship of the Isles when the MacVurichs were bards and senachies to the Island Lords." In the absence of more definite evidence we must leave it for the present unproven whether the Scottish scribe made an extract from Tadhg Dall's poem, or Tadhg himself borrowed the portion dealing with the privileges from some Scottish bard's panegyric on one of the Mac Donnells. It may be noted that the only known copy of the prose version on which this part of the composition is based (see notes to §§ 11 ff.) is found in juxtaposition with folios containing matter of Scottish interest.

§ 1 *Liathdruim*, see 2 § 9 n. The kindred of the Collas are called *sluagh Liathdroma* in LgC. 144.

§ 2 *Manannán* is connected with the sea in early Irish mythology, see *The Voyage of Bran*, TBC p. 366, C. O'Rahilly's *Ireland and Wales*, p. 95, and supra 5 § 9 n. In Cormac's Glossary and in Cóir Anman he is euhemerized into an excellent pilot who dwelt in the Isle of Man. Possibly his name is used here with reference to the boatcraft of the lords of the Erne, unless we are to take it as a tribute to their various talents.

'twining stems,' in 22 a § 21 I have rendered *féathlonn* by 'sinew,' but I doubt if that is correct. Cf. Tor. Gr. Gr. 149 (féil); *do innsaigh E. airdrí Eirind et do timcill E. eisium amal timceallus feigh- figh* (var. *amhail thimchiallus feithlionn fiodh*) RC 39 pp. 18, 31; TBC 6054.

§ 3 'Shore-defenders,' in 24 P 33, 144 *foireann chalaidh* is contrasted with *f. allmhardha*. The literal meaning being 'the shore crew' it may mean the holders of the isle as distinguished from the invaders, hence the true natives. Cf. *foireann chobhsaigh Cláir Feidhlim*, of the *Meic Dubhghaill*, C iv 1, 179 a.

'Children of I.', i. e. the Chosen People.

§ 4 'furnace sparks,' cf. Ir. Gr. Tr., Decl. ex. 1296.

'set stones,' P. O'C. has "*tuinidhe .i. daingean* fixed; firm . . . immoveable. Ex. *clocha tuinidhe* for *clocha tuinighthe* immoveable stones." The adj. *toinighthe* (*tuinighthe*) is evidently connected with the verb *doneuth* 'I remain.' For the verbal noun, *tuinide*, see Laws, *Cáin Ad.* p. 46, O'Clery *s. v.* and cf. Acall 2811, Luke xix 46 (O'D.). In the FM *cloch thuinighthe* is apparently used of a stone in the formation of a building, e. gg. vi pp. 1982, 2012, 2028; A. R. 106. Here, however, it may mean a stone socketed, as it were, into the ground, hence one which may be said to have acquired a prescriptive right of tenancy (cf. the use of *tuinide* in ZfcP 12, 363. 26) or a rock of such size and weight that it is impossible to stir it. Cf. **7** § 37, **17** § 19, *tamhan t.* MR. 98 and *táin trom-thuinighthe* Ir. Monthly 1920, 315.

§ 5 'Favored,' or 'Privileged; 'similarly **17** § 32, **24** § 15, **27** § 26. For *sochar* see **7** § 1 n.

'contenders,' I have no other ex. of *iompadhaibh*; it may be dat. pl. of **iomthaidh*, nom. ag. of *iomadh* 'contention.'

§ 6 Oriel, see § 10 n.

§ 7 'avails,' in *gá dás*, lit. 'wherein is it' we have the same verbal ending as in O. Ir. *oldás*. Cf. **9** § 48, **13** § 40, Unpubl. Ir. Poems xxiii 1, and *cidh tás do shúil* Betha Moling 35.

§ 9 *Eachaidh D.*, see p. 226. The correct form of *Doimlén* (see varr.) is uncertain; 17th-18th cent. scribes usually lenite the *-m-*; sometimes the first syllable is spelt *Duibh-*; in older MSS we find *Domlén, Domplén* and *Damplén* (ZfcP 8, 317; Rawl. B 502, 139 b 41, 140 b 40, 141 a 45, etc.).

§ 10 *éidir*, see **2** § 55 n.

Oirghialla is applied in written tradition to the kindreds derived from the Three Collas (supra p. 226). The older form is *Airghialla*, and MacNeill explains it as meaning "the eastern subjects," (lit. 'hostages'), *Phases*, 126, cf. Meyer's *Zur kelt. Wortkunde* § 193. As a territorial designation the meaning has altered more than once (*Phases* 185, 278; Onom. s. v.) eventually the anglicized form Oriel or Uriel became attached to MacMahon's Country, that is Monaghan and part of the present Co. Louth: "This Countie [of Monaghan] was in tymes past called Oriel," Descr. of Irel., p. 22. "This county [of Louth] beinge anciently called Iriell," Dymmok's *Treatice*, (Tracts rel. to Irel. II Ir. Arch. Soc.) p. 21. This county [of Monahan] was anciently called Iriell," ib. **23**. "The Countie of Lowth anciently called Uriell or Eorgall," R. Downing's History of Louth, RIA Proc. xxxiii C 1917, p. 500. See also Maxwell, *Contemporary Sources*, pp. 81-2, 260. The etymology of *Oirghialla* offered §§ 27-8, and in the document quoted in § 11 n., seems

15*

intended as a kind of pun, but it could only have been suggested at a
time when the original form had gone out of use. In the translation I
use Oriel when the territory is referred to.

§ 11 The following account of the privileges of the *Oirghialla* agrees
substantially with that in O'Donovan's *Leabhar na gCeart*, pp. 134 ff., but
more closely with that given in a fragmentary tract in H 3. 1S, which is
referred to by O'Donovan, LgC. 36 note e, 139 etc. and has already been
printed, not quite accurately, in Skene's *Celtic Scotland*, iii 463 ff. I print
here, from the MS, with a translation, the part which is of interest in
connection with this poem. In the course of the translation I have
bracketed after each item the stanza of the poem in which it is referred to.

H 3 18, p. 783
(the letters in square brackets are illegible in the MS)

This fragment on the *Oirghialla* begins on p. 785, in the middle of
a sentence, and ends p. 780 (pp. 780-91 are bound and numbered upside
down). It is on paper, in dark ink, and in an inferior 17th cent. script.
After narrating the story of the Three Collas down to the battle of
Achadh Leithdearg in Farney, AD. 331 FM, the author proceeds:

Do chuir rí Éireann .i. M*ui*readhach *Tíreach* gairm ar cloinn
Each*aidh* Duiblén .i. na trí Cholla 7 tuga*dh* go Teamraigh iad.
Tug saoirse 7 sochra dhóibh fein 7 da n-oighreadhuib 'na
ndiaigh go síordhuidhe 7 do maith marbadh a athar doibh ar
a ccongnamh do beit leis o sin amach, 7 tug an oiredsa do
dhúth*aigh* dhoibh os cionn a ngabhál[tuis] a nUltuibh .i. triocha
céd in gach cúigedh eile d'Éirinn 7 baile in gach triocha chéd,
7 teach 7 garrdha in gach baile. Ag so an chuid eile dona
s[ochruibh] fuaradar .i. coimhéirghe rompa ar feruibh Éirenn a
n-aonach 7 a n-oirechtus acht rí Éirenn amháin 7 gan iadsan
d'éirghe re ccách . Trian édála a ccuantuibh long dóibh, tús
dighe; tús leapta 7 ionnalta re míledhuibh Éirenn [i]ttighib
riodhcuarta aca. Coinnmedh da ndaoinibh ar feruibh Éirenn
an f . . . beid gan bhuannacht d'faghail. Gan éiric fola do dul
uatha. Coimhéd ghiall Éirenn aca. Giodh bé do rachadh ar
a n-ionchuib coimairce go ceann mbliadhna aige. Gach arm
nochtar a n-aonach nó a n-oireachtus do beith aca. Ni raibhe
ag rígh Éirenn acht braighde ar braighdibh uatha. Leatghuala
ríogh Éirenn ag rígh Sleachta na cColl*adh*, 7 fad a láimhe 7 a
loinne d'folmughad eidir é 7 cách. Coinn[mheadh] eachra 7
chon ó Samuin go Bealtuine ar fedh Éirenn aca. D[á] mbeantaoi
creach 'na ndiaigh dhíobh 7 siad ar sluaigheadh rí [ogh] Éirenn,

sé ba san bhoin dóibh uadha. Bó ar fiched tuarasda[l] gach
aoin da maithibh ó righ Éirenn ar sluaigheadh. Tríocha [782]
colg ded, tríocha balt (?) airgid, tríocha sleagh, tríocha brat ó
righ Éirenn do rígh sleachta na cColl*adh* iar bfilleadh da
sluaigheadh, 7 da mbeidís geill uatha ag righ Éirenn ní biodh
do chuibreach ortha acht slabr*adh* óir, no a mbeith fa réir a
ccuideachta riogh Éirenn ; óir as uime adeirear Oirgiallaigh riú —
ór as glais da ngiallaibh. Ag sin a sochair, maille re sochruibh
eile nach air[i]mther annso.

    As iad na ceithre haibhne as uaisle a nUltuibh tóranna
feruinn chloinne na cColl*adh* .i. Bóinn, Banna, an Éirni, 7 an
Fíonn. Iomtúsa Cholla Uais : níor bfiú leis fuireach a nÉirinn
ar a chuid don dúthuigh no dona sochruibhsin adubhramar, o
do bhí Éire 7 an ríogacht aige féin roime sin. Fágbhais a
fearann 7 na sochairsin aga braithribh. Dála Colla *Uais* anais
a mbun a gabháltais féin a nAlbain 7 bFionnlochlannuibh o
soin a le, 7 a ngabhluigheann uadha, acht ar fill go hÉirinn
diobh a mbun a nduthcusa. As é so craobhsgaoileadh śleachta
ríogh Éirenn .i. Cholla *Uais* .i. Clann Domnuill a nÉirinn 7 a
nAlbain, 7 a ngabhluighenn uatha, mar atáid Clann Raghnuill
atuaigh, 7 Clann Eóin Aird na Murchann 7 Mac Dubhghuill
Lathairn 7 Clann Alasdair a nÉirinn 7 a nAlbain 7 Clann
tSíthigh na Mumhan, 7 mórán do maithibh oile nach airemhther
annso. As iad so sliocht Colla Dá Críoch .i. derbrathair ríogh
Éirenn, Cholla Uais .i. Mag Matgamhna, Mág Uighir, O Ceallaigh,
Í Maine, O hAnluain, Mag Cana, O Floinn Line 7 Mág Aodha
o Oilen Rinn Sibhne & mórán eile is ísle ionáid sin nach
airimther annso, 7 ní faghann croineicil sliocht ar Colla Meann.

    Trí céd (deg *added with different ink and pen*) bliadhan o
ionnarbad Cloinne Rugruidhe 7 ó marbad Fergusa Fogha gus
an mbliaghainsi, no gus an aimsirsi 1634.

    The remainder of the fragment is on the pedigree of the
MacDonnells.

TRANSLATION

    The king of Ireland, *Muireadhach Tíreach*, sent a summons
to the children of *Eachaidh Doimlén*, that is, to the Three Collas,
and they were brought to Tara. He bestowed freedom and
privileges upon them and their heirs who should succeed them

in perpetuity, and he forgave them for slaying his father, on
condition that he should have their aid from that out, and he
gave them patrimonial territory in addition to their conquests
in Ulster, as follows: a cantred in each of the other fifths of
Ireland, a townland in each cantred, and a house and a garden
in each townland. The other privileges they obtained were:
all the men of Ireland, save the king of Ireland only, were
bound to rise before them in meeting or assembly, while they
were not to rise before the others (§ 30). One third of the
spoils of sea ports [lit. harbors of ships, cf. note cited from the
memoirs of Charles O'Conor, *Tribes and Customs of HyMany*
p. 4, and see also *ib.* pp. 62-6. From these passages it appears
that the 'spoils' were wreckage and sea-waifs. § 13 may be
based on this item]. In drinking, in couching and in bathing
they have precedence of all the warriors of Ireland in banqueting
houses (§§ 31-3). The men of Ireland must give coigny to
their followers [as long as (? MS illegible here)] they are getting
no billeting. No blood eric to be paid by them. They can
keep the hostages of all Ireland. Whosoever puts himself
under their protection is safeguarded for a year (§ 20). Any
weapon bared in meeting or assembly is theirs [i. e. is surrendered
to them?]. The king of Ireland could only have hostages from
them in exchange for hostages (§ 22). The king of Colla's
race to sit next the king of Ireland, and the length of his arm
and his blade clear between him and the rest (§§ 11, 12).
They might quarter their steeds and their hounds all over
Ireland, from November to May (§ 14). If a prey be taken
from them in their absence, while on the king of Ireland's
hosting, six cows for each cow are due to them from him
(§ 17) Twenty-one cows is the stipend due to each one of
their nobles on hosting from the king of Ireland(§ 18). Thirty
ivory-hilted swords, thirty silver belts (?), thirty spears. thirty
cloaks are due from the king of Ireland to the king of
the Collas' race on returning from his hosting (§ 19). If the
king of Ireland had hostages from them, the only fetter
upon them would be a chain of gold, or else they would be
at liberty, in the company of the king of Ireland (§ 25),
for this is the reason they are called *Oirghiallaigh* — gold
are the fetters of their hostages (§ 28). Those are their

privileges, in addition to other privileges which are not enumerated here.

The four noblest rivers in Ulster form the boundaries of the territory of the race of the Collas, namely, the Boyne, the Bann, the Erne and the Finn. Colla *Uais* did not consider it worth while remaining in Ireland for his share of the territory or privileges we have mentioned, since the kingship of Ireland had been his before. He left his land and the privileges to his brethren. As to Colla *Uais* he and his descendants, save those who returned to Ireland to rule their patrimony continued in sway over his own conquests in Scotland and Norse territory [i. e. the Norse settlements in Argyll and the Western Isles; the writer seems to be ignorant that the Norse invasions did not begin until more than four centuries after the time of Colla *Uais*, but more probably he is including the territory won by Colla and his descendants in one statement. Cf. in this connection *Ó Gnímh*'s address to the first Earl of Antrim, published by Fr. MacKenna in Irish Monthly, 1920 p. 314], The following are the branches of the race of the king of Ireland, Colla *Uais*: the Clann *Domhnaill* [MacDonnells] in Ireland and Scotland, and their ramifications, as Clann *Raghnaill* from the north, Clann *Eóin* of *Ard na Murchann*, the MacDowells of Larne, Clann *Alasdair* in Ireland and Scotland [cf. Lgc. 141 note r], Clann Sheehy of Munster, and many other nobles not enumerated here [the Clann Shechy were famous mercenaries, see Rev. P. Walsh's *Leabhar Chlainne Suibhne* p. xviii, for notes on some of these clans].

These are the descendants of Colla *Dá Chríoch*, brother of the king of Ireland, Colla *Uais*: MacMahon, Maguire, O'Kelly, the *Í Mhaine*, O'Hanlon, MacCann [Magan? but cf. Top. Poems xxiii 144] O'Flynn of *Line* [or O'Lynn, see Top. Poems xx 112] and Magee of the Island of *Rinn Seimhne* [i. e. Island Magee, see *Rinn S.* in Onom.], and many others of lesser rank, who are not mentioned here. No chronicle gives any descendants from Colla *Meann*. [According to the pedigrees in LL 333b, 338c and ZfcP 8, 319 C. M. was ancestor of the *Mugdornai*, a Monaghan people. See LgC. 140-1].

There are thirteen hundred years from the banishment of Clann *Rudhruighe* and the slaying of *Fergus Fogha* until this year,

or this time, 1634. [FM place the battle of *Achadh Leithdearg*
under 331; the synchronism published by MacNeill, *Ériu* 7, 113,
places it in the 20th year of Constantinus, A. D. 329, our scribe
probably omits the odd years deliberately, preferring round
numbers. The remainder of the fragment is on the pedigree
of the MacDonnells].

§ 13 'F.'s Plain,' Ireland.

§ 14 *Teathbha*, sometimes anglicized Teffia, was the name of a plain
comprising parts of Longford and Westmeath counties. The version of
H suggests that here it may be used vaguely for Ireland.

§ 16 i. e. they could not be compelled to mobilize in spring, sowing
time; or in autumn, harvest time. Cf. the privileges of the *Í Mhaine*,
Tribes and Customs of Hy Many, p. 56.

§ 17 Read 'princely champion of *Fál*,' i. e. the high-king, who is
bound to give them this compensation. Cf. *gur chuir comhairle Saxan
d'eacht 7 d'forcongra ar an iustis an Rúta do thabhairt* ... FM v 1818,
and see 31. 45.

§ 18 'from that army,' possibly *ó* is partitive here: 'every man of
that army.'

§ 19 'elfin,' *sidh* is often applied to weapons. Cf. Ir. Gr. Tr., Decl.
ex. 816.

§ 20 'despite etc.' cf. *Tar chruas airdrigh Innse Fáil . dá chéd
dég—dia do thromdháimh: ga ndaighréir don féinn Ultuigh . 'na ccléir
aimhréidh iomarcuigh* L 17, 48a.
'*Eithne*' there were several princesses of this name. Probably the
mother of *Tuathal Teachtmhar* is referred to.

§ 21 *ni icait i ngait do gniad acht luga merlig* Lec. 378 b ay =
LgC, 134.

§ 23 Perhaps 'to take counsel with all, and learn the purport of
their declarations.' I am not sure of the precise meaning of this couplet.
There is nothing corresponding to it in H, but LgC. gives as one of the
privileges of these hostages *a mbeith a rúinibh righ* 'to be in the secrets
of kings.'
The phrase *crúdh comhairle* is common in the sense of 'taking counsel,'
'considering plans;' see FM v 1860, vi 2030 (cf. *ag c. cest 7 caingen*,
2160, 2164), 2334; Unpubl. Ir. Poems xiii 5, 7. Cf. perhaps, *conad hi
comairle rocraittea leo* "believed in" Marco Polo 129 (*ro-crúittea?*). In FM
v 1396 *sgrúdadh comhairle* is used in the same sense. In some MSS
crúdh in this usage is confused with *cruthughadh*, e. g., in a late 17th cent.
copy of Acall.: *rocruthaighedh comhairle leo andsin .i. tocht go Teamhraigh*
24 P 5, 312. Cf. *dochuaidh i gcruth ceasta agus comhairle do dhéanamh
leo, Me Guidhir Fear Manach* p. 131.

§§ 24-5 Cf. LgC. p. 134, where it is stated that it was sufficient for them to swear by the king's hand that they would not make their escape.

§ 25 *fa réir* is also used in the corresponding passage in II, and the meaning is clear from the ex. in *Leabhar Chl. Suibhne* p. 40. It is evidently identical with Sc. Gael. *m'a réir* 'free' (Tr. Gael. Soc. Inv. xxi 255; xiii 74).

§§ 26-7 Similarly LgC. 146 § 4.

§ 28 'golden hostages,' this explanation of *Oirghialla* (also in II) is arrived at by arbitrarily lengthening the initial, which rimes and the older spelling prove to be short; see § 10 n. According to Tadhg Dall and LgC. no fetters or chains whatever were placed on the hostages given by the *Oirghialla*, H states that a golden chain might be used for them, but this may well be merely a suggestion put forward by the compiler of the tract in support of the explanation which he gives of the name. Taken with the following stanzas it seems probable that Tadhg Dall uses *glas* in a figurative sense here; the only fetters on their hostages, he means to say, are the gold fittings of the accoutrements furnished to them by the king of Ireland on their departure homewards.

The custom of exchanging hostages formed an important part of governmental machinery in ancient Ireland, at a time when militarism was predominant, and on the election of a new king hostages were delivered to him by the disappointed candidates, as surety for their loyalty. The importance of the custom is recognized and proclaimed in the legal dictum: *ní rí lasna biad géill i nglasaib* 'He who has not hostages in fetters is no king.' (See Laws iv 50).

§§ 30-33 not in LgC.

§ 30 This seems suggested by:

In cheist-sea for chloind Colla
for sluagh luchair Liathdroma
can fis a dtuarastail tall
ó rig Fuaid na findfearand. Lec. 378ᶜ a = LgC. 144.

but *can*, rendered 'without' by O'Don., may mean 'whence.'

'owing to them,' cf. *tarrla tri .xx. marcc do deiredh a fuasgailte amuigh ar MacS.* "unpaid by MacS.," *Leabhar Chl. Suibhne* p. 54; *ocus na fiacha amuigh ag MacSeadhain . . .; sin amuigh re .xx. bliadain gan ic; sin amuig o O. . . . tar ceann Taidhg* Irish Deeds IV. Similarly in modern Ir.: *ní díolfar cómhar anois leat, mar níl an cómhar amuich agat*, Canon O'Leary in *Seanmóin*, etc. ii 101.

§ 39 "Many they have that are fit to stand in battle's gap," O'Gr.

§ 40 'Plain of *C.*, 'i. e. Ireland; see O'Grady's note, and cf. *Benn Chodhail* "Ireland's Eye," Onom.

§ 42 'seed of *Mathghamhain*,' the MacMahons, to whose territory the name Oriel or Uriel (*Oirghialla*) was at this period appropriated; see § 10 n. Sir John Davies testifies that "the M'Mahounes undoubtedly are the proudest and most barbarous sept among the Irish; and do ever soonest repine and kick and spurn at the English government." *Hist. Tracts*, ed. 1787, p. 228; *Maine*; according to Keating's genealogies (Keat. iv 35), and *Tribes and Cust. of Hy Many*, p. 24, *Maine* son of *Eochaid Fear Dá Ghiall* s. o. *Domhnall* s. o. *Iomchaidh* s. o. *Colla Dá Chríoch* was ancestor of the O'Kellys of Hy Many, but in LL 338 g the *Uí Maine* are derived from *Mane m. Echach m. Domnaill m. Fiachach Sroptine m. Carpre Lifechair*; cf. Laud gen., ZfcP 8, 292. 28. *Manchachaibh* is dat. pl. of *Minchaigh*, the people of *Feara Manach* 'Fermanagh,' Maguire's country.

§ 44 In line 173 read: do-ghéabhdaois.
'mount,' possibly *tolcha* is part of the place-name here; *Tulach Breagh* may be a name for Tara.

§ 46 'superiority,' for *iomarcaidh* see 3 § 22 n.

§ 48 'scion . . .' I do not understand *-acla*. Other exx, are: *suinn aobhacla gan chall ccen . a n-am chaomhanta a céimeadh* (of *Clann Dubhghuill*) C iv 1, 177 a; *laoich dhaghacla lér téigh toil . samhalta a ccéim a chosnaimh* 175 b; *re hucht ccosanta chliar bFáil . don bhosacla fial armcháidh* A v 2, 32 b.
'House of the Three,' i. e. Tara. The Three may be the *Tuatha Dé Danann* kings, *Mac Cuill, Mac Céacht* and *Mac Gréine*, as to whom see Keating, or the Three Fair Ones, see Introd. lvii.

§ 50 As to *Mág* see 10 § 5 n.
síol see 3 § 3 n.
'surety,' similarly *orra sidh orra eissidh* ZfcP 2, 343. Cf. *urra creachfaghla cuain Breagh* 23 D 4, 305, and see 16 § 17.
'for peace etc.' perhaps rather 'for pacts or for conflicts.'

§ 51 *Donn*, son of *Domhnall* † 1302, was the first Maguire to become lord of Fermanagh, FM iv p. 1242, AU ii 398.
'wealth,' lit. 'leaf,' or 'leaves;' *duille an domhain* seems used in contemptuous reference to worldly wealth; cf.: *grás Muire . . . ná tréig ar dhuille an domhnáin* Ir. M. 1922, 386; *lámh dhearluiccthe dhuille an bheatha* F 16, 67; *beanfoghlaidh duille an domhnáin* (of a generous lady) ib. 10; *Inghen Diarmoda, drech náir . a ttimcheall dhuille an domhnáin . . . ní fuair oilbhéim ó aoinfer* L 17, 43 b; *Duille in domhnáin-dobeir Mac Diarmada ar dhuanaibh: a ttabhair do Dhia is do dhaoinibh . cia nach ccualaidh* 24 P 9, 284; *Duille an bhetha bhudh blath breige . . . ger[r] go (m)buinfuighear do dhuille dhiot*, Rel. Celt. i 136; *A. Ó Dálaigh* lii 40. For prose instance see TSh., Gloss. Prof O'Rahilly refers me to a similar use of *duilleabhar*, BCC pp. 138, 442. Evidently the transitory nature of material possessions is referred to, but one would expect *bláth* rather than *duille*. Probably the phrase is of exotic origin, and first appeared in the religious verse. Cf. perhaps, the standing phrase *loise an tsaoghail* 'the brilliance of the world,' 'worldly splendor,' Ir. Gr. Tr., Decl. § 1, *Dán Dé* iv 28.

§ 52 'entwines,' see **9** § 2 n.

§ 54 O'Gr. renders this: "Ardent desire of Joan's son is this: that on the advent of the three grand battalions he should go and with them 'have a try' for the land of Niall [a step] which will serve both them and himself."

§ 55 *Cliú*, i. e. his kingship shall be recognized so far away as Munster.

10

This piece is addressed to a reigning Maguire, Cú Chonnacht. The name of his father or of his mother is not given, but the only Cú Ch. whom Tadhg Dall could have addressed as Maguire is he who died in 1589. See above, p. 224.

The metre is *rannaigheacht bheag*, with full internal rime in the second couplet, rime or assonance in the first, and consonance of the end-words throughout each stanza. Several pieces similar in tone and form are found in the Maguire MS. described by Stern, ZfcP 2. These highly artificial metres usually clothe a complimentary strain so peculiarly extravagant and involved as sometimes to lean towards the consciously humourous. Each stanza expresses a carefully wrought compliment, often wrapped in a metaphor obscure to modern ears, and the unravelling of the meaning may be compared to the task of tracking the involutions of the lines in our old interlaced ornament.

§ 1 'fount,' lit. 'vessel' but the idea seems to be that of a replenishing source, cf. *Tobar fir einigh Fir Manach* ZfcP 2, 340.

§ 2 *Odhar*, the ancestor from whom the Maguires are surnamed, fl. c. 1050 according to the genealogical lists; see LL 338 d.

§ 3 'Manchian,' a member of the Fermanagh kindred, renders *Manchach*, an adj. from *Manach*, which has been taken by some scholars as gp. of *Manaigh* = Manapii; see ZfcP 11, 170, 182.

'should deliver,' etc. i. e. those who have travelled over Ireland must acknowledge that the chief of Fermanagh excels all others.

§ 4 'opponent,' cf. *a cceleadh comhlainn* 'of their antagonists' FM v 1646; *céile comhraic* ZfcP 2, 356, Gadelica 1, 276. The second line of the stanza is corrupt, and without another copy emendation is impossible.

§ 5 The change of *Mac* to *Mág* (gen. *Méig*) in Irish surnames is regular before a vowel, and also occurs before certain consonants; see Ó Maille, *Annals of Ulster* 51 n. When part of a surname both *Mac* and *Mág* are treated alike: fully stressed when no christian name precedes; unstressed when coming between christian name and surname (see Introd. xcvii).

§ 6 *Fiacha, F. Fionnfolaidh*, k. of Ireland; see § 19 n.

'five countries,' the five fifths of Ireland; cf. *snadhmthar síodh ar chóig chánaibh . fá lámhaibh rígh fhóid Éimhir* 3 C 13, 542.

§ 8 This stanza is ambiguous: another possible rendering is: 'a king proscribed through territories was emboldened by his (Maguire's) words; a man,' etc. as above.

§ 9 'G.'s Field,' cf. *Sgriath Gabhra*, the site of a castle near Enniskillen, where the Maguires used to be inaugurated, FM vi 1876. *Eamhain* probably stands for Ireland; Gofraidh Fionn addresses one of the MacCarthys as *sgoth Eamhna*, Ir. Monthly 1919, 342, or in each case it may be the *E.* of **5** § 9.

§ 10 'dwelling of T.', Tara, or Ireland, from *Tuathal Teachtmhar*. 'fighting,' see Contribb. under *cliath*. In the meaning 'hurdle' *cliath* may have been formerly applied to defensive erections in mountain passes etc. (cf. *cliatha draigin is derg-sciach gniset moa n-áth dia aire* Met. Dinds. iii 316), and thus acquired the meaning 'skirmish, battle;' but the meaning phalanx, in the military sense, is often implied. Cf. *cuirit a caithcliatha diobh, 7 fágbhaitt a ttighe troda* A. R. 106 (of a retreating army), *an ionbhaidh . . . bhus tana bhar ccliatha ghabhala* ib. 124.

§ 11 'they rule,' *tilim* is very common in bardic poetry: *an ríghe an tann fa ttiltear . a míni as ann aithintear* 3 C 13, 637 (Bk. No. 109); *Mac Pilib fán lia do loigh . a ttilid nocha bía ar bail, na Manchaigh ar n-ég an fir . créd libh a mharthain 'snach mair* ib. 539 (Bk. No. 236); *Leat do tiledh teagh nimhe . do dheich n-ordaibh ainglighe* 23 D 14, 116; *mar dhlúíththilfe* [: *chúitighthe*] *Gort Gaoidheal* ib. 119; *Cing Artúir . . . do thil clár na cruinne cé* Unpubl. Ir. Poems v S. Exx. of the verbal noun are: *fada i ndún 'sgotti asteagh .* [ ] *Clar Dá Thí do thileadh* 24 P 33, 144; *Trian Conghoil mur thiltior tuaidh . congmhaid gan tiledh gach tír* ib. 189; *fa ruire tilidh na ttuath* 24 P 27, 81; cf. *seas tilidh* 'stern seat' (modern) Arch. i 157. For the adj. *tilte* see Ériu 5, 58-9; Unpubl. Ir. Poems xxiv 13. If the original idea in the verb is 'directing, steering,' perhaps we might compare *til* 'patibulum' Ml 50ª 7, the shape of the rudder might explain the connection. Cf. Ir. Monthly 1923, 641 § 14.

'from one corner,' similarly *a héineing do fuaidh an gort* Bk. 283b. The origin of the phrase may be in the following lines from a poem to one of the Burkes, attributed by O'Curry to Maol Seachluinn na nUirsgéal (probably the attribution is wrong; a different poem, of which the first line is identical with the first of this, is commonly assigned to M. na nU.):

> *A hoilén Gréige do gheabh* [sic leg.] *. Alexandair . . .*
> *neart deighríghe an domhainsi . . .*
> *Goill eile — ní fuilim dáibh . sgél ort a oighre Seádin*
> *eang thíre d'Éirinn agaibh . ríghe a héineing fuaradar*
> *Ríghe an domhain — dia do séan — mar frith a héineing d'oiléan*
> *dóigh leinn an gort do ghabháil . a heing do phort Pharthaláin*
> 3 C 13, 781-2 (Bk. No. 275)

For *eang* 'piece of land, territory,' see also **7**. 121, **13**. 83, **24**. 23, **27**. 112, **28**. 122, 143.

With the second couplet compare Flann Óg Mág Raith: *Tonn lán fa urphort n-oirir . gan musgladh fá Mág Uidhir: ní bhí ar neart do thuinn thoraidh . teacht do chabhair fuinn fuinidh* 3 C 13, 446.

§ 13 'can balance,' cf. *Ge atá geall ag cru Cobthaig . clu ortaibh na cheann cuirfidh* ZfcP 2, 332, see also ib. 333 n.

§ 14 *Craoidhe*, I have not been able to identify this ancestor of the Maguires.

§ 15 *móir*, an instance of predicate adj. agreeing in number with its noun; similarly 31. 19. See Strachan's Middle Irish Declension, p. 16. *Bearta*, see 28 § 32 n.

§ 16 'custody,' see *airlám* Contribb., and : *na bailte baoi ina n-orlaimh* FM vi 2302, *ro fáccaibh araill ele diobh i n-o. Iarla Desmumhan* 2164 *um [= im']urláimh* Unpubl. Ir. Poems xxi 14.

§ 18 'contents,' I have taken *bróin*, doubtfully, as dat. of *bró* 'mass' (ll. 119). It may be from *bró* 'quern' (Ir. Gr. Tr., Decl. § 84; Contribb.). Cf. 16 § 26, and *Do chumhdach a ccolg leabhar . iomdha ór dha aith-leaghadh ; 'sas iomdha bruighean óir ann . do bruigheadh do bhró[i]n bhuabhall* L 17, 111ª.

'could not,' for *dóigh* see 16 § 5 n.

'brought,' etc., I am not sure how this couplet should be translated ; I take the general meaning of the stanza to be that Maguire's drinking-bowl was of such size that a powerful man could not hold it even when empty; full, it required a number to sustain it. Cf. 29 § 24.

féinnidh, the lenition of the initial suggests that the epithet is felt as a proper name.

§ 19 A figurative reference to the legend of the slaying of *Fiachaidh* (or *Fiacha*) *Fionnfolaidh*, k. of Ireland, by the plebeians, A. D. 56. By this deed Ireland was left shepherdless until the return from Scotland, as king, of *Fiachaidh's* posthumous son, *Tuathal Teachtmhar*. See Keating; ZfcP 11, 56 ff. The poet would liken Maguire to another *Tuathal*, ready to take possession of Tara, and rescue Ireland from her neglected state.

§ 21 Similarly Fearghal Óg Mhac an Bhaird: *cóig slóigh ag breith a bhuidhe . gan duine ar bhreith fir eile* 3 C 13, 476.

§ 22 'it enhances,' etc.; the translation is uncertain, as *nách* is a doubtful extension. The MS has *n* with a bar. Possibly we should read: *téid i gc.— ni cuid mh.—* with *téid i gcéim* compare *Do chuaidh a cceimionnaibh Cuinn . a ccath mór Muighe Tualuing, ar merghlonnaibh Mogha Néid* Bk. 176ª 'C.'s exploits . . . excelled those of *Mugh N.*' (?); *ni deachaidh riamh clú a ceimibh . nar eiligh tu* ZfcP 2, 338 ; *teid a bladh dáibh a ndoilge* 'her fame increases their trouble,' 340. See also 22ª. 12.

'no marvel,' I take *cuid mh.* to mean 'something for boasting,' 'a matter for remark;' cf. Ir. Monthly 1920, 544 § 37, and *Ní cuid mhaoidhimh do a dhénamh . ciu heile do aineghadh . an ccrích . . . ar rinn ccogaidh* L 17, 53 b; *fuair aoinfer da n-aicme sin . ceannas Eirenn . . . gér chuid maoidhimh nir mhór dháibh . glór gach aoinfir dha admháil* C iv 1, 179ª; *Ulaidh do chuir fa chánaidh . a ccumha nior chuid mhaoidhimh* (of a dead chief) F 16, 73. Similarly *cuid rúin* 13 § 49. Cf. also *cuit péne* TTr.² 639, 1483 (Ir. Texte ii). See also 29 § 3 n.

§ 24 'exhortation,' *laoidheadh*, lit. 'lay-making,' is used of the exhortatory riming by which warriors were encouraged in the onset, and shamed from retreat; P. O'C. renders the word by 'an exhorting, provoking.' Cf.: *mór a dhiol do lucht laoidhidh gniomh aoinfir i ngurt ghábhaidh* (sic leg.) Zfcl' 2, 332, 'a great reward to the rimers is the action of one man on the field of danger;' *ní mór feidhm fir a laoighidh . Gaoidhil libh a mbeirn baoghail*, 3 C 13, 543; *fá chumhuidh riogh rátha Breagh ní rigthi a les ar laoidhedh ... a inghena* L 17, 61 a (where the poet seems to address the keening women). Further exx. in the vocabulary to Meyer's *Deathtales*, u. *láidim*.

§ 25 *Connla* is an archaic form of *Colla*, cf. ZfcP S, 319. 32 and Rawl. B 502, Facs. Index u. *Conla*. Possibly this is intended here, as evidently in § 39.

§ 26 Cf. *Iul Éirionn sgan é ar mh'aire fuair meisi is mé a n-énbhaile* Bk. 240b (= 3 C 12, 446). I take *le* in the first line in the sense of *apud*, though possibly it indicates the agent with *fríoth*, in that case the meaning would be 'knowledge of territories is (was) gained by exacting poets.' The meaning may be that poets from all parts flocked to Maguire, and thus his castle was a likely place in which to gather information; or the reference may be to hostages, or mercenaries, or craftsmen of various nationalities; cf. 11 § 19.

§ 27 With the first couplet compare lines 41-2. As to *orloinn* 'extremity' cf. *airlann* 'end,' Contribb., *erlond*, *irland* TBC Glossary, Anecd. i 16. 15, 'end of a spearshaft;' *ó rinn go hurlainn* 'from point to end' (of a spear) *Eachtra Lomnochtáin* § 74. It is possible of course that *urlann* 'an enclosure' (see 11 § 11) is used here figuratively for a 'territory." Cf. *dob í cúigeadh sughdhonn Sreing . an cúigeadh urlann d'Éirinn* (sic leg.) 3 C 13, 696.

I am not sure how the second couplet should be rendered; the third line may be parenthetical.

§ 28 'concealest,' possibly 'protectest;' cf. *Dreach lé bhfolchair gach fáidhfile* Ir. Monthly 1920, 485.

'shelter of foliage,' similarly in a poem addressed to the same chief by Irial Ó Huiginn: *Moltar uaidhe d'aitle comlaid* (leg. *comluinn?*) *clanna righ do reir a lámh; sé dá maoidhiomh fa dion duille gniomh gach aoinfhir uime a nagh* ZfcP 2, 340, in a poem by Brian Dorcha Ó Huiginn: *Tú ag dion do ghég ngeiniolaigh . mar ghéig fa dhion duilliobhair .* A iv 3, 620, and one by Cú Choigcriche Ó Cléirigh: *tú aréir fa dhion duilleabhair . d'éis na ccríoch do ehreachlosgadh* 24 P 27, 86.

§ 29 'robs (?)' I am not sure of the meaning of *tógbhaidh cuid* etc.; in the translation given I have assumed that 'each man' of the foe is referred to, but possibly the chief's own men are meant, and we should render *t. c.* etc. by *adds* to.

§ 31 'the pledge,' etc., i. e. Ireland submits to thee.

§ 33 'a hostage in fetters,' a vivid figure; see 9 § 28 n. The metre requires dat. *géibhinn*, instead of the MS *-ionn*, but the only other ex. I have noted of this form is *gébind* LL 5 b; see Hogan, *Cath Ruis na Rig* p. 167.

With the second couplet compare: *fuighle mine tonn ttirim . sgríbhinn fire ar fonn Féilim* 3 C 13, 545 (Flann Óg Mág Raith). The trees bending under their burden of fruit etc. show that the true king reigns.

§ 36 'humour,' for *móid* cf. Glossary to *Dán Dé*.

§ 37 *Connla Caomh* is the name of a prechristian k. of Ireland; but here the ref. may be to *Colla Uais*, see § 25 n.

'till he have requited,' the translation here is not literal, *gur dhíol* is of course perfect, but the sense of a future perfect seems implied. The meaning is obscure: until he has paid for damage for which he was unjustly blamed? or which he intended to do?

'accepted,' *gabhthoir* might mean 'is traversed' here: 'no reaver traverses any part of B.,' but the translation given is supported by *díon* in first line. For *gabhaim le* 'I accept, take to myself,' cf. *Gabh a Féilim ... liomsa mar thogha tochmairc* 3 C 13, 909; *Gabimsi ... leatsa a Féilim d'éinchéile* ib. *Gabh tar mo lochtaibh linne . maith dhúinn airde m'inntinne* Bk. No. 179 (3 C 13, 610).

§ 38 A different rendering of this stanza is possible, taking the second and third lines as parenthetical: 'without violence or enmity—though troublesome is the defence of *Banbha*, not a single man opposed them — have the Gaels been ravaged by the blood of *Odhar*,' a rhetorical way of saying that as no man in Ireland gainsaid their claim to rule, the inaugural prey was a merely nominal ceremony.

§ 39 For *Connla = Colla* see § 25 n. I give 'bracelets, 'as the most likely rendering of *idh* 'spancel, tie,' in such a context. Cf. *An chnu chumhdaigh an igh óir do bhir as na tulchoibh thuaidh* 24 P 33, 189 and *iodh* 'ring', Keat. ii 218. The meaning of 'completed' etc. is that they are given away as soon as made.

§ 41 'C.'s vow,' the rendering I have given of these lines was suggested by Prof. Bergin. The Collas, though guilty of his father's death, served as soldiers under Muireadhach Tireach, who vowed that he would not take vengeance on them; see the sources cited on p. 226. For *cor feadhma* see note to 2 § 11.

§ 42 'of F.' i. e. from all parts of Ireland. This apparently refers to a custom of proclaiming the names of hostages on the castle green.

§ 43 Cf. *ar cach uile as teand dtabaigh* ZfcP 2, 354: *a C[h]uilliend gan tend dtabaigh* ib. 344.

§ 44 In the last couplet 'the poet adopts,' as O'Grady might have said, 'a much flatter trajectory;' in fact, one would suspect some corruption, were not the metre irreproachable. Cf. perhaps *sgithe a lamha ar luas a ledradh* in a mid-17th cent. Scottish poem, H 3. 18, 788. *Rath* I take to = *Magh Rath*, Moira, in Co. Down.

11

This piece is a record of a visit to Enniskillen Castle in the time of the same Cú Chonnacht. O'Grady translates the first stanza, and gives a synopsis of the whole in his own imitable style, Cat. pp. 430-2. Cf. Ó Heódhusa's poem on the recapture of the castle from the English forces in 1595, Unpubl. Ir. Poems xix. Lughaidh Ó Cléirigh calls Enniskillen Castle *dúnáras agus port oireachais Még Uidhir (Aodha) agus gach aoin no hoirdnithe hi ccennas na críche* 'the fortified dwelling and seat of government of Maguire (Hugh) and everyone who should be ordained in the chieftaincy of the country.' See A. R. 66. The glowing description in the following poem is evidently not intended of the castle alone, but of Maguire's whole demesne, including his "36S" islets, referred to in a report from Miler Magrath cited by O'Grady, Cat. 455 n.

The translation given above has already appeared in Miss C. Maxwell's *Irish History from Contemporary Sources* (London, 1923), a few verbal changes will be noticed, but they do not affect the general sense.

§ 7 'bending . . . stems,' *feir-* is the attenuated form of *fiar* 'twisted, stooped.'

§ 8 'driving deer' etc., as to the method of hunting referred to cf. Chamberlin's *Private Character of Queen Elizabeth* pp. 107-8.

§ 9 *doire carbh*, a favorite figure. Tadhg Óg uses *doire long* in a description of Loch Erne, YBL col. 175. Cf. **24** § 36.

§ 11 'outer yard,' Enniskillen Castle being an erection on the Norman pattern *orlann* may be here applied to the base court or bailey. We know from numerous references that it was a place where there was constant prancing of steeds, baying of hounds, and similar bustle. See supra, p. 213 *l*. 2. In some instances *orlann (urlann)* and *faithche* seem synonymous, though no doubt originally distinct terms; A. R. 24, n. 2; 50. 23, 52. 11; ZtcP **4**, 34; *Rel. Celt.* ii 321 and Joyce's *Social History* ii 61 (*aurla*).

§ 12 'expanse (?),' I am not sure of the meaning of *aghaidh* here; one might get a tolerable sense by reading *adhaigh* 'night,' but the expression would be foreign to the style of these poems. I think the rendering given is likely; *aghaidh* may be used in the sense of 'surface,' cf., e. g. *aighthe do leirge* Unpubl. Ir. Poems xix 14.

§ 13 'coupled,' cf. **25** § 5, and Ériu 5, 60 where *cúplach* is rendered, rather freely, by 'domed,' It is probably formed from a borrowing of the architectural term 'couple,' the joining of two beams at one end to make an arch. Cf. *sreath cúpladh gcorcra ós a cionn* Ir. Monthly 1923, 643 § 33.

Lie is inferred from the gen. *Liag*; the place referred to may be the neighborhood of *Áth Liag* on the Shannon (Ballyleague) or the place of the same name on the Suck; see Onom. u. *Ath L.*

§ 14 'Grecian,' see Introd. lix (for **17** § 9 read **17** § 10).

§ 16 'sportive,' The meaning of *conchair* is doubtful; 'hound-loving,' hence 'fond of sport' (?), see Glossary to *Dánfhocail.*

'weaving,' etc., similarly GF iii 40, Ir. Gr. Tr., Decl. exx. 375, 887, and cf. ZfcP 13, 268. 24; *Eachtra Macaoimh an Iolair* 52.

§ 17 'their' etc., see Keat. ii pp. 250—52. 'fruitful,' *cnuaisdigh* is gen. sg. m. of a compd. of *cnuas* 'cluster of nuts, fruit,' and *tiogh* 'dense.' See Ir. Gr. Tr., Introd. p. 11.

Druim C., a name of Tara, see MacCarthy 155 n., Met. Dinds. i 4.

§ 18 'elfin,' for *sithe* see 1 § 25 n. The Fairymound of *Bodhbh* is said to have been on Loch Derg, near Killaloe; Lear's Hostel, otherwise *Sioth Fionnachaidh* on *Sliabh Fuaid*, in the Fews, Armagh.

In the 3rd line of this stanza read *lamh* for *lámh*, see Add. and Corr.

§ 20 *gormadh*, cf. *gluedhi aga ng*. Irish Guy, ZfcP 6, 29, 'exercising,' for this use of *gníomh* see 6 § 9 n.

'surveying,' or possibly 'in charge of.'

os cionn, see Introd. pp. xcvii, xcix, and Gadelica i 157 n.

§ 21 'wounding,' O'Grady takes this to refer to the chastisement of malefactors.

§ 23 'spent,' as to *rugsam as* see Gadelica i 65. 40.

'the whole . . .' *car (cor) an chaomhlaoi* is common in verse and the more artificial prose; see FM vi pp. 1982, 2198; RC 29, 112, *Eachtra M. an Iolair*, Vocab. The first word is probably the verbal noun of *cuirim*, used in the sense of 'a turn, revolution.; cf. *anais cor an foghmair*, in an early text, Ériu 7, 197; *Car* (var. *Fedh*) *an faghamhair* Ir. Gr. Tr., Decl. ex. 950.

§ 24 'walls,' see Keat. ii p. 250; *slios* 'side, vertical surface, side-wall of a room,' may mean 'bench' here. O'R. has 'bench, seat' amongst other meanings of the word. In an account of Irish customs written in Latin by an unnamed foreigner towards the close of the 16th century, the seating arrangements at a banquet are thus described: "The more honorable person sits in the centre; the second (in rank) on his right, the third on his left, the fourth on the right again, and so on until the hall is filled to the walls. All sit facing the door, none turning his back to it, which is said to be done lest enemies should come upon them unprepared." (Arch. Hib. v 17; *Contemporary Sources* 320; see also O'Grady, Cat. 424 n. The 'central bench' mentioned in 25 § 4 was probably by the wall opposite the entrance, and the 'side walls' of 11 § 17 were those running at right angles to it, on the chieftain's right and left. The custom of placing the company according to rank is noticed by Martin, *Western Isles*, p. 108 (1716), and see AR. 230.

§ 25 'smoke clings,' i. e. heated from valorous effort; cf. *Duach Dalta Deghuidh drech mhiolla . meic Cairbre Luisg da len dé* L 17, 23a.

§ 27 *cúilte*, see Ir. Gr. Tr., Decl. p. 69. 7; ex. 688.

múinte, cf. *laoich as múinte a méin chogaidh*, 23 D 14, 133.

§ 28 'horseshoes,' cf. *ag craithedh a n-each* FM iv 1014 (1461); *craidhthi aga cur fo . . . caomechaibh* ZfcP 6, 29.

E. Knott, Tadhg Dall Ó Huiginn   16

§ 29 *Sioth Truim*, on the left bank of the Boyne, E. of Slane. Cf. *Temair Truim* **8** § 22 n.

§ 31 According to Sir John Davies, the men of Fermanagh had no just claim to a military reputation, as their triumphs were mostly won for them by warriors from other territories: "for albeit Hugh M'Guyre that was slain in Munster were indeed a valiant rebel, and the stoutest that ever was of his name: notwithstanding generally the natives of this county are reputed the worst swordsmen of the North, being rather inclined to be scholars, or husbandmen, than to be kerne, or men of action, as they term rebels in this kingdom; and for this cause M'Guyre in the late wars did hire and wage the greatest part of his soldiers out of Connaught, and out of the Brenie O'Relie [i. e. Cavan], and made his own countrymen feed them, and pay them; and therefore the jury enquiring of Escheates, found only two freeholders in this country, besides Hugh M'Guyre himself, to have been slain in the late rebellion." *Hist. Tracts* p. 255. The poets are not always to be taken seriously when eulogizing the warlike behavior of their patrons.

§ 40 Lifford; the reading here is doubtful. Each of the three MSS containing this stanza spells the word differently. One has *láithfir*, which if genuine could be rendered 'of the champion,' taking it as a compd. of *láth*, as in *láth goile* 'a champion,' and *fear*. This however would involve including the st. in the poem, as we could only suppose Maguire to be referred to, but as the poem is already closed, we should expect § 40 to be in compliment to another patron, and I think we are justified in taking *Baile Lithbhir* 'Lifford,' as the real reading. As this stronghold was claimed both by O'Neill and O'Donnell the omission of the occupier's name is possibly diplomatic.

12

This piece is addressed to Hugh Maguire, son of the Cú Chonnacht of the three preceding poems, and his successor in the captainship of Fermanagh. It may be that it was composed during Cú Chonnacht's lifetime, and he is referred to in §§ 3, 4, and 15. If, however, we adopt the reading of Bk. in the first line of § 13, we must assume that it was composed while Hugh was Maguire, consequently, after his father's death; §§ 3 and 4, as well as § 13, would then refer to Hugh. This assumption however, would render some of the poem unintelligible — why should the poet tell us in § 1 he is going to let Hugh alone, and in § 4 that he is going to approach him? Yet on the whole the simplest explanation is that the piece was addressed to Hugh after Cú Chonnacht's death, and the transl. in § 15 should be: I would not have forsaken; he would not have abandoned.

§ 1 Text and transl. of second couplet doubtful; possibly we should read *a s. a ch.*

§ 2 Read *an éigse* (collective); *-se* in the preceding line is the emph. suff., 3rd sg. f.; cf. *fuairse* 22a. 104.

§ 3 *féachfa mé re*, cf. *ionadh ríogh d'adbor ollaimh . dá nderna ...
dam . le neach oile ní féghabh* (sic leg.) ZfcP 2, 348.

Gowra, see 10 § 9 n.

For *gabhaim le* see 10 § 37 n.

tarla etc., cf. Unpubl. Ir. Poems xviii 2. The older construction would
be with the infixed pron., cf. e. g. *cid cian om thír domrala* Hib. Min. 83.

§ 6 Kilcloney, Professor T. F. O'Rahilly has supplied me with the
following note on this: "*Cill Chluaine*, Kilclooney, about seven miles to
the north of Tuam, in the barony of Dunmore. Here there was a settlement of the poetic family of O'Huiginn. In 1574 'Donell Ohigin' owned
the castle of 'Kilclune' (Galway Arch. Journ. i 117). The same person is
mentioned in Perrott's Composition, in 1585, as 'Donyll O'Higgin of
Killclona, gen.' (Hardiman's ed. of O'Flaherty's *H-Iar Connaught*, p. 330).
In 1590 were pardoned 'Tho. O Higgan, of Kilclony, Donell oge O Higgen,
Brian O Higgen, and Towhill O Higgen, of same, gentlemen' (Fiants of
Eliz., 5447). The first of these appears in an earlier Fiant (4895, A. D. 1586)
as 'Tho. O Hugin of Kileloan' (leg. Kilcloan). We also find members of
the family associated with the immediate neighbourhood, in Fiants of Eliz.
So the well-known Tadhg Óg Ó Huiginn died in 1448 in Cill Chonnla (FM)
i. e. the present parish of Kilconla, adjoining Kilclooney." See also
App. C infra, under Brian.

The apologue which follows reminds us of the story told by Stanihurst:
"No meat they fansie so much as porke, and the fatter the better. One of
John Onels household demanded of his fellow whether beefe were better than
porke? That (quoth the other) is as intricat a question, as to aske whether
thou art better than Onele." Holinshed's Chronicles, Irel. p. 67 (1808). The
anecdote is given in Stanishurst's *De Rebus in Hibernia Gestis*, 1584 p. 38,
as follows:—"porcos praecipuè opimos nimiopere appetunt; faciunt pluris
omnium obsoniorum nihil. Interrogatus, à convictore, quidam de O Neli
satellitibus, an caro vitulina porco esset delicatior? id, inquit, perinde est
ac si quis percunctaretur utrùm tu O Nelo sis honoratior? permoleste
nimirum tulit, opinatorem de re minimè controversa pueriliter dubitare."

§ 14 This can be taken as the last st. of the poem proper; the final
letter recalling the initial; § 15 is added in compliment to Maguire, Hugh's
father.

13

The subject of this panegyric, Brian son of Donnchadh Maguire, was
nephew of the Cú Chonnacht of the foregoing poems. The FM record his
death at 1583. The piece seems to celebrate some warlike operation. In
his praise of Fermanagh the poet is not more enthusiastic than Sir John
Davies, writing to Salisbury from Enniskillen, in the autumn of 1609:
". . . Fermanagh, which is so pleasant and fruitful a country that if I should
make a full description thereof it would rather be taken for a poetical
fiction than a true and serious narration. The fresh lake called Lough

Erne . . . divides that country into two parts. The land on either side of the lough . . . is the fattest and richest soil in all Ulster." Hill's *Plantation Papers* p. 153 (CSPI ad ann. p. 2SS).

§ 1 *téiglidhe* 'tranquil,' cf. 7 § 37 n.; *co tarrla in muir ina clár comréidh taethéglidhi* CCath. 1927. *sruth téigle ná tuil ré baois . éigne ó Dhuibh is ó Dhrobhaois* E vi 2, 374; *in tir do boi ina hoentecli toraid* C iii 1, 3ª b.

§ 2 'the sweetness . . . honey' (*omit* sweet), I am not sure that I have rendered this line correctly, but the couplet evidently refers to the fruitful woods bending over the stream, and the honey dripping into the water from the tree-trunks, cf. *Teas ag téghadh na meala . ag dénamh meadha d'eas abha* Ir. Gr. Tr., Decl., ex. 1550; *Lindte o mil ar minsiobal . fa bfillter fiodh fiarroigeal* ZlcP 2, 339. See also 29 § 31.

§ 3 'arable (?),' for *cuir* see 1 § 6 n.
fiodh etc., cf. *Ní hi an choillsi ar cúl na sreabh . na 'n chlochsa ar cúl na ccoilleadh, do dhaingin, a bhadhbh Broine . ná 'n mainnear arm n-iudhloidhe* (from a poem addr. to an earlier Maguire by Giolla Íosa Ó Sléibhin) 3 C 13, 458. For *ar chúl* see also 28. 137.

§ 4 Cf. the Hawk's reasons for clinging to Achill, Anecd. i 25. 5.

§ 5 'tender,' *taidhiúir* refers, I think, to the sounds of the birds, the running waters and the breezes. It is commonly used of music, or tales. The melody of birds is of course a favorite theme in Irish literature, also the music of running water, *is fleadh d'fior 'sis oirfideadh*, says some earlier poet (I have mislaid the reference). See also Ir. Texte iii 195. 35; Anecd. ii 23 (Mo lLing Poems), etc.

§ 8 'in her glance;' similarly Ó Heódhusa, in praise of Sligo: *cnuas tirmsreabh teirce a sriobh . tibhredh seirce 'na silliodh* L 17. 53 a; and the FM, of a person, vi 229S. 7.

§ 9-14 Cf. the following, from an inaugural ode to O'Conor Kerry by Mathghamhain Ó Huiginn ("about 15So," O'Curry, H. S. Cat.):
Dar leat atá le tréimhse . ar lucht foghla an oiléinsi
tir chormfoirfe na ccuan ngeal . fordhoirche dhruagh dá dhíden.
Nó atáid siodhuighe bhenn mBreadh nó as fé fia atá 'na ttimcheal
oirer sriobhghlan na síth bhfionn . dá din ar fionnmhadh Éirionn.
Ní trén faolchoin 'na fedhuibh . ná onchoin 'na hinnbheruibh
gan rian torathuir dá tuinn . riamh tar chladhachaigh
Chríomhthuinn
Lór (leg. *lorg*) *ilphiasd dénta dochair . ní bhí a loch ná a*
lionnsrothaibh
fá chrich ghormghlóin na ccolg nocht . ná lorg foghla a bhférghort.
Ní fé fia ní draoigheacht druagh . atá a[g] caomhna a crioch
mbennruadh
ferr berta riogh ó Rosa . do dhíon deera a dhúthchosa L 17, 4Sb

§ 13 'veil of w.,' this is a free rendering of *fégh fiagh*, or *fé fia(dh)*, some kind of enchantment by which persons or objects could be rendered invisible. See Atlantis iii 386-8, Thes. ii p. lx, TBC p. 550; *Ceilt a grádha ar an ngruaidh bfaoilidh . fada ar inghin 'na fégh fia* 23 D 14, 35.

The correct orthography of the term is uncertain, and I have simply followed the reading of a good manuscript. The rime fixes *fiagh* or *-dh* for the second word in this instance, and in others; e. g., *Boing cheasa do dhreachtaibh druadh . feasda ní leamhaid a lán, masa ceas eóil an fé fiadh . do-chiam ad dhebígh é ar an dán* 23 H 8, 47 b; but in some exx. *fia* is required, e. g., *do dhealbh sé reultonna is ré . thall dar ccédaittrebh fé fia; tainic san chruine a ccli mná . rí atá 'na dhuine 'sna Dhia* Bk. No. 183, similarly *A. Ó Dálaigh* p. 24. We have (as suggested in Atlantis iii 386) undoubtedly the same phrase in the title given to Patrick's hymn, *Faeth fiadha*. According to the Middle Irish preface to this hymn it was chanted by Patrick as a protective charm for himself and his monks, and through its virtue they appeared as deer. There we have the same idea of protective disguise, 'camouflage,' which is implied in *fé fia(dh)*. Cf. *fiadh* (var. *fianchruth*) *draideachta* Acall. 7505, *féth fithnaisí*, Wi. p. 552, and Acall., Gloss s. *féth, feth, fethana*. The idea is still to be found in oral folklore, e. g. in a tale printed in *An Stoc* May 1924.

§ 15 'D.'s Land,' i. e. Maguire's country, from Donn mentioned supra **9** § 51. *Sioghmhall* dwelt at Síoth Neanta, in Roscommon, see Metr. Dinds. ii pp. 8, 91; LL 10a, Acall. 271, 1982. Cf. Cog. 78, where the name represents the Old Norse Sigvaldr (Marstrander's *Bidrag*, p. 93).

§§ 16-17 Ó Heódhusa uses similar terms in a poem addressed to Hugh Maguire:

> *Gus faolchon go bfeirg bfiadhaigh . ucht aille re hOirghiallaibh*
> *mír cruadha achaidh na nArt . guala ré cathoíbh Connacht.*
>
> *Lámh indheghla Fher Manach . muir thécht ré hucht nEóghanach*
> *gruaidh roithe go rún cconfaidh . múr cloiche ré Conallshaibh.*
>
> Bk. No. 310 (= 3 C 12, 366)

doras báis, is this of Scriptural origin? Cf. commentary on *portis mortis* Ps. 9. 15, Thes. i 54. Somewhat similar phrasing is used in describing the power of Mo Laise's relics, SG i 32. The Breffnians are the O'Rorkes of Leitrim and the O'Reillys of Cavan; the blood of N. the O'Neills of Tyrone; the *Oirghialla* . . . may be the MacMahons (see **9** § 10 n.). The blood of E. are of course the Maguires, see p. 226.

§ 19 *Áth C.*, probably *Béal Átha C.*, 'Ballyconnell,' Co. Cavan.

§ 22 Cf. *Miscell. Ir. Provv* §§ 379-80; *Ir. Aen.* 751. The second couplet is repeated infra, **18** § 33.

§ 25 *bhfear nd.*, *forgla* may be an old neut., but *fear* (gp.) is often irregularly eclipsed in such phrases, probably on the pattern of cases were the preceding word was formerly neuter, e. g. *trian bhfear nÉireann*.

'her magic,' see § 13 n.

§ 30 'will you trace . . .,' cf. *Toirrdealbach mc Taidhg nar tubadh . triath Fer gCeall bérad gó a bhun* (in a versified pedigree by Muiris mhac Briain Óug (I Mhaoil Chonaire) C iv 1, 169 a.

§ 32 *thairngeartaidh* is an identifying gen. here; for the form see 1 § 38 n.

§ 33 1 am not sure of the meaning of the last line; cf. *Gasraidh óg na n-arm bhfoirfe . nir chleacht siad seal aonoidhche, gan facht Goill nó goradh lis . do thoill an foghail d'aithris* 3 C 13, 636 (var. *a ha.,* unmetrical, 23 D 14, 136).

§ 35 'all that . . .,' cf. *Lucht tabhuigh cíos do chinil . da maire a meic Caitilin , ar thaibhdhedar ni bhia ar bail . budh lia a n-airleagadh oraibh* I, 17, 54 b. *na tri r.* see **29** § 29.

§ 38 For *branar* as vn. cf. *Cuimhnig mullach Uisnigh dh'ar . dioghail an brugh do bhranar; síol branair Bruighne Dá Chog . biodh cuimhne ar t'falaidh agod* L 17, 101 b.

§ 39 'never,' for *tre bh. s.* see **15** § 18 n.

§ 40 *gá dás,* see **9** § 7 n.

§ 46 'by whom peace is . . .,' the meaning of *soidhearaidh* is doubtful, I have only one other ex.:

> *Ar eachtra ó airdri nimhe . mar tám as tuar oirbhire*
> *mé soidhearuigh on toigh thall . toil don oileamhuin agam.*
> in a poem by Niall Mór Mac Muireadhaigh A v 3, 62 a

It is evidently a compd. of the pref. *so-* and *dearadh* , a verbal noun of which exx. are very rare, and the meaning so far undetermined: *Ben nar fhéd duini do deradh* Ferm. 199 a, *ní ben dertha deighriagla* ZfcP 2, 339 seem to require the meaning 'refuse,' or 'renounce.' Thus *soidhearaidh* might mean 'easily rejected,' a rendering which would suit our context.

§ 47 'rescue,' cf. the Mayo usage of *tugaim i dtir* cited by Prof. O'Rahilly, Gadelica i 65.

§ 48 This is obscure to me, and I am not sure that I have rendered it accurately. From the vague references one can conjecture that the poem was occasioned by a triumph over the O'Neills by Maguire's forces, Brian being in command of the latter.

§ 51 *Fóchtaid,* see **3** § 30 n.

14

This is an elegy on Cathal son of Tadhg O'Conor, brother of O'Conor Sligo of **15**. See Wood-Martin's *Hist. of Sligo* i 387, 393-4. Cathal was slain by Scottish mercenaries in 1581, see Introd. xxviii; O'Grady, Cat. 381.

§ 2 *deireadh* etc., this is cited in *Miscell. of Ir. Provv.* (323) from O'Grady's extract. I have noted other occurrences of it in verse, e. g., in a religious poem by Uaithne mhac Uilliam Í Chobhthaigh, 23 D 14, 117; *deireadh cairdesa comaireamh* C ii 2, 25 b, see TCD Cat., Index.

'capital' as to *rómh* see 3 § 4 n.

§ 7 'musical branches,' cf. Unpubl. Ir. Poems xxiv 8, Ir. Gr. Tr., Decl., ex. 1165 and *gan reic ndrecht nó nduan bhfiledh, re glór bhúr siodhchraobh senma . fá ól bhfionchaor bhfinemhna* ('without reciting of poems to the sound of . . .') Ó Heódhusa 23 L 17, 63 b (= Ir. Monthly 1920, 542). Is the instrument referred to in these passages to be identified with the *craobh* of the old tales (*Imram Bram* 1, Ir. Texte iii 193, SG i 272, etc.), which emitted beautiful, soothing melody when shaken? or is it not rather some reed instrument?

§ 11 'mighty ox,' *damh ré* seems to be virtually synonymous with *d. dile*, 'a diluvian, that is, an ante-diluvian ox, or stag'. It is often used as an epithet, see 22 a § 4, Keat. Poems 739; *dlighidh sé saoradh Teamhra . aondamh ré na righealbha* 23 D 4, 239. Both *ré* and *díle(ann)* may be corruptions of proper names.

§ 13 'mares,' *groigh* may be sing. or collect., see Ir. Gr. Tr., Decl. § 45; 'precious stone,' I follow partly O'Grady's rendering of *caor bhuadha* ("precious jewel"). Perh. 'magic st.'? cf. 13 § 13.

§ 14 As to the bestowal of land upon poets see Introd. xlii, Keat. iii 94, and Unpubl. Ir. Poems xxi. Duff, a river in Sligo.

§ 16 'favor,' *muirn* frequently occurs in contexts where the meaning 'favor, esteem, credit,' is implied; also 'the advantage derived from the possession of respect or honor.' In §§ 28, 29 it is used as an equivalent of *cion, anáir*, similarly in the wellknown line *Mairg mheallas muirn an tsaoghail* (O'Grady, Cat. 357). Cf. 15 § 12; *diograis muirne* O'Grady, Cat. 475 and see Ir. Monthly 1923, 586 §§ 1, 2; 589 §§ 32, 34; *mac muirnech* 'favourite son' SG i 5. I do not know if the word is to be identified with *muirn* 'clamor' (TBC, Gloss.; *Buile Suibhne* p. 22; TTebe 1901) or *muirn .i. buidhean* P. O'C.

§ 17 'elbow,' i. e. the seat next him at table.

§ 20 'Clanwilliam,' the Burkes of Mayo; the battalion of B., 'the O'Rorkes of Leitrim.

'twining stem,' see 9 § 2 n.

§ 21 'C.'s race,' the O'Donnells of Donegal.

§ 22 'The C., the G.,' the Costellos of Costello bar., Co. Mayo, and the ruling families in the bar. of Gallen, in the same county: "The most part of this Countie [Mayo] is possessed by the Burkes, whose Capten they commonlie call McWilliam . . . The rest of the Countrie is inhabitted by the McJordans, McCustulaghes and the rest above Specified (Omaylies, Clandonels, McMorice), who be dependers upon McWilliam, and in a manner his Vassals." *Descr. of Irel.*, p. 141. The other families referred to in this stanza were seated in the bar. of Carra (anglicized form of Ceara). The name Cl. Chuán (the older spelling) is preserved in that of Cloncuan deanery.

§ 23 'flatter,' the phrase *tuilleamh buidhe*, common in prose and verse of this period, is very old; see Ml 39 d 18, Thes. i 655 note f. *Ridgeway Essays* 327 § 56; '*na thuilleadh buidhe bidh sinn . gach duine astír a tteighim* 23 H 8, 68 b, *am tuillmech buide fri trén* SG i 43. Cf. *ní tuill díomdha* [sic leg.] O'Grady, Cat. 116.

§ 25 I have no further ref. to this Eochaidh. For two poets of the same name who flourished at a later period, see Ériu 8, 155; ZfcP 8, 328.

§ 26 *Fitheal*, legal adviser to Cormac mhac Airt, see Keat. ii 338, *Hib. Minora* 82, Ir. Texte iii 199, 227; Best, *Bibl.* 263.

§ 27 Torna Éigeas was fosterer of Niall of the Nine Hostages, see Otia ii 88. He appears in the story of Niall edited and translated by Stokes in RC 24 and by O'Grady in *Silva Gadelica*. See also *Iomarbhágh na bhFileadh* pt. i p. ix.

§§ 28-29 Iorard Mac Coise was, according to tradition, attached to Tadhg O'Kelly, of Hy Many, while Mac Liag was the poet of Brian Bóromha. See the poems attributed to the two poets, ZfcP 8, 218 sq.

§ 29 For the rime *fionntolcha : ionchomtha*, cf. *fochla : dolta* Ir. Gr. Tr., Decl. ex. 140, and **2**. 19, where the MS. reading should perhaps be retained. *anáir*, cf. *dfiachaibh ar Mhuintir Slatra onoir bidh acus eadaigh do tabart don tsliocht sin Meic Seain* Ir. Deeds xviii.

§ 34 The poem proper ends here, the last letter reflecting the initial; §§ 35-7 form, as it were, a little appendix having a fresh initial and a final corresponding to it. These stanzas seem modelled on the following, from an elegy on Eóghan O'Conor († 1444) by Maol Seachluinn na nUirsgéal Ó Huiginn:

> *Munab í an itche do iarr . tug gan ar n-éag ar aoinrian,*
> *créad fa mairim ó nách mair . da mairinn ar n-éag Eóghain ?*
> *Do sir ar Dia, díoc[h]ra an crúdh . m'fagbháil tar éis mo chompán,*
> *misde a aomhadh ó Dhia dham . saoghal budh sia iná saoghal.*
>
> 3 C 13, 705.

15

This piece is an appeal to Mór, wife of O'Conor Sligo, to intercede with her husband on the poet's behalf. O'Conor's displeasure, he relates, was aroused by some statement in a poem Tadhg had addressed to O'Donnell; Hugh son of Manus, evidently. Possibly **2** is the poem referred to, as in that piece he asserts O'Donnell's claims to Connacht perhaps too explicitly.

Mór was daughter of Brian Ballach O'Rorke, and sister of Brian na
Múrtha (see **16**). Her husband, Donnell, was son of Tadhg O'Conor († 1552),
and brother of Cathal of **14**. Both Brian Ballach and Tadhg O'Conor
married daughters of Manus O'Donnell, the one Gráinne (**16** § 52) the
other Siobhán, or Joan († 1553 ALC). The name of Donnell's mother,
however, was Caitilín, according to Ó Heódhusa, 23 L 17, 54 b. Cf. Wood-
Martin's *Hist. of Sligo* i pp. 387, 394.

The Calvach O'Conor (**42**), only son of Donnell and Mór, died in
1581, and in 1582 the Annals of Loch Cé record the marriage of Meadhbh,
their daughter, with Brian MacDermot of the Rock. Donnell died
in 1588.

§ 3 'trusty,' I am not sure of the sense of *tairise* here; the word is
common in the phrase *t. liom* (Wb 23a 18, Acall 5765, TBC Gloss. cf. *tairis
linn do theacht d'ár dtír* O'Gr. Cat. 605). For the use of the word as here
cf. *Mairg fuair mar fuair mise . moirn a tigerna t.* Tadhg Óg, Bk.
No. 261; *maigistir t., cara t.* PH 6724, 5328. TSh.; *aos t.* A.'R. 30. 14, 32. 8.
'disposition changed,' for *athraigh aigneadh*, cf.:

Car an chaomhlaoi do chaith soin . ag múnadh a mhic ionmhoin
bláth na ccraobh ó chathraigh Bhreagh . da thaobh do athraigh
aigneadh.

(Of Fionn, endeavouring to amend the manners of Mac Lughach) 'The full
length of the fair day did that man, flower of the branches from Bregia's
citadel, spend in admonishing his beloved son; thereupon he altered in
disposition.' 3 C 13, 614 (Bk. No. 179). *Ní biú de ní sia na sin . cuir
me ar aithearrach n-aignidh . . . gé gníomh docair a dhéanamh.* 'I shall
not pursue the matter further; put me in a different frame of mind . . .
though it be a difficult thing to accomplish.' ib. 615.

§ 4 'entertained' *oileamhain* is not always to be taken in the strict
sense of 'fostering, rearing,' cf. **5** § 4. In **3** § 47 it is implied that poet was
fostered in Donegal; his homeland was Sligo. Here however *l. oileamhna*
may refer to the O'Donnells, implying that he had contrived to offend
both families. Then we should render it 'my fosterers.'

§ 5 'done wrong,' I take *iomarcaidh* here as = *iomarcraidh* in : *fer
na ro leicc a fairbrígh na a iomarcraidh lasna tighearnadhaibh battar
ina chomharsain* FM v p. 1594; *doronsat fairbricch 7 iomarcradh foirn*
ib. 1670, A. R. 326. 19.

§ 6 'am said to have,' *más fíor* 'if it is true,' often corresponds to
'so they say,' sometimes with the implication that the information is un-
reliable. The lenition after *más* (*másu*) is regular in the older language.
'stately,' for *ceanntrom* see **4** § 35 n.

§ 7 *'sa bhfuair* . . . cf. *Cred fuarais oram, a Aoidh* 23 D 14, 131.

§ 8 *do bhíthin*, cf. *dá mhíthin sin* Oss iii 148; *do bhíthin asluigh
an uicc . las fuidh crithir san choguilt* 3 C 13, 794 (Bk. No. 246) and O'Gr.,
Cat 461 *l.* 15. In the form *do bhíthin*, Keat. Poems 1487, which I have

not noted in strict verse, the length of the vowel may be due to the influence of *do bhriogh*. Cf. *dá bhíoth* KM Miscell. 49 n. 2.

'D's displeasure,' O'Gr. misread this line, Cat, 411 *l.* 12.

§ 11 *an tsíon*, similarly *síon im aighidh ag iompúdh* Ir. Monthly 1923, 586 § 9.

§ 12 'choicest,' cf. *sgoth toirbhert*, *sg. innmais, dldla*, O'Gr. Cat. 475. For *muirn* see 14 § 16 n. The second couplet is difficult; the translation gives I think the sense required. I take the literal meaning to be: 'the noble princes . . . spend my honor (i. e. whatever largesse they bestow upon me) in one day.' Heretofore he had been accustomed to prolonged hospitality. Possibly *caithim* is used here with the meaning 'I finish with,' 'relinquish.' I have no exact parallel.

§ 13 *aoíbh*, cf. *fá buaidh díbhe ocus onóra* SG i 31, and *anaoíbh* Ir. Monthly 1923, 588 §§ 23, 26.

§ 15 *síorruidhe*, this is the more usual spelling, but the older *síordhuidhe* also occurs; see 7. 55, with varr.

§ 18 'ever,' this form of the phrase is common in early Irish, side by side with *tri bhith sír* (see 13 § 39); see Fís Ad. § 34, Contribb. s. *bith*. I know of no precedent for the lenition of the *s* here, as in C.

§ 20 'wearying,' *sódh* here seems to have the sense of *sás*, 'a sufficiency for,' 'a cause.' Cf. *Mac Con Mara . . . sódh a charad do chothucchadh* 'supporter of his friends' FM. v p. 1650. For *sódh* 'pleasure' see 22 § 16, O'Gr., Cat. 357; Ériu 9, 107 § 42. Cf. *sódh (ón digh)* Ir. Gr. Tr., Decl. § 38.

§ 21 'what they were about,' or perhaps 'their customs.'

§ 22 *tar*, etc. cf. *Luaghaill an leómhain . . . dénta do Niall im chró cCuinn . tar a mbiadh dhó dá doghruing* 23 D 14. 29.

§ 24 'delicate,' lit. a matter from which there should be shelter: *sgáth* 'shade, shelter, protection,' hence 'desire for protection, nervousness.'

§ 25 'since,' etc. cf. 4 § 40; 'instituted,' lit. 'awakened.'

§ 28 *ciodh* as interr. pron. is fully stressed, here *aniogh*: *ci(o)dh*; *gi(o)dh* 'though it be,' 'even,' is an *iarmbéarla*. I do not think the form *teisbéanadh* is countenanced by the 16th cent. grammarians; the form *t. isbéanta* is not amongst those given in Gr. Tr., Decl. p. 39. This stanza is only in L.

§ 30 For gen. sg. *aigéan* see 1 § 40 n.

§ 31 'her protection,' varr. are 'her rejection' (i. e. by him); 'his rejection' (i. e. of her). Either of these is possible. In each 'hardest' would refer to the effect of his action on her.

§ 34 see 8 § 9 n.

§ 38 Cf. *ní breath óné gus aniudh . an bhreathsin . . . as cosmhail a beith ar bun, ar breith arsaigh da n-antur* 3 C 13, 479. Probably we should read *éigean : éidear*; see note on 2 § 55.

§§ 42-46, 50 are quoted and translated by O'Gr., Cat. 411-12.

'Essay,' O'Gr. renders this line: "In sheltering of me, O face of magic, now co-operate," apparently taking *cuir re* to mean 'add to,' like mod. Ir. *cuir le*; cf. however 3 § 17. The general context is in favor of the rendering given here; cf. § 48.

§ 43 Cf. **17** § 53, Ériu 8, 173; *dia mōrad gach maith* Arch. iii 315 n. 21; *ní romōra olc* ib.; *ní náir mar chaithes a chrodh . cáir a mhaithes do mhóradh* [sic leg.] L 17, 22 b last line and see *Ir. Proverbs* § 285.

§ 51 Carbury bar., Sligo.

§ 54 The poem is properly concluded with this stanza; the next (only in L) is added in compliment to Meadbh, Mór's daughter.

16

The title of this poem should read Brian na Múrtha. The form which appears above is based on Charles O'Conor's heading in E., *múrrtha*. The mark of length is not very distinct in the MS, and the doubled *-r-* would usually imply a short vowel preceding, but the form *múrtha* is so common in MSS., and in the modern language (e. g. Canon O'Leary's *Mo Sgéal Féin*, 101, that it cannot be rejected. For the spelling *múrrtha* cf. *tulach uí Róigh mórdha na múrrtha mbeann* KM Miscell. 50. The word has been rendered 'of the bulwarks;' but more probably it is connected with the verb *múraim*, and refers to Brian's skill and practice in demolishing castles in order to prevent his enemies from occupying them. The correct form is probably *múrthadh*, as in A. R. 188. 1.

The date of the piece cannot be precisely fixed, even to a year. It is natural enough to assign it to 1588, the year in which Brian was attacked by Bingham, but it may belong to the period of his conflict with Malbie, 1580-3. O'Grady observes that it "is exceedingly well constructed; nor need Teigue *Dall's* energy of expression scandalize any that will first of all recollect when it was that he wrote: Sir Richard Bingham's time in Connacht namely, and will then (after ascertaining what that implies) just put himself in the poet's place." Cat. 415.

Brian Ó Ruairc, son of Brian Ballach and Gráinne, daughter of Manus O'Donnell, attained the headship of his kindred in 1566, and in 1567 was knighted by Sidney, who records that he was the proudest man he ever dealt with in Ireland. In the autumn of 1580 he was *"esumhal do Ghallaibh"* (FM), and was attacked by Malbie. In 1585 he again made peace with the English government, and attended Perrott's parliament. Bingham marched against him in 1588, after the Spanish wreck, and in 1590 he was forced to flee from his territory and take refuge with MacSweeny na dTuath (**26**), with whom he remained for a year. He then crossed to Scotland, in an ill hour, for he was promptly handed over to Elizabeth by James, and was executed in 1591. For some interesting notes on his career and personality see FM 1591, Hardiman's *Irish Minstrelsy* ii 426 ff., O'Grady, l. c., and ib. 422, 447, 482-3.

§ 3 *riodha*, I take the MS *riogha* to represent *ri* + the adjectival
suff. *-da*, as in *rioghdha*, where the long form of the stem is used, see
Introd. p. lxix, last paragraph.

§ 5 'such hopeful quarry,' for *dóigh* 'a likely mark, a likely subject
for conquest,' cf. 26 § 31, 10 § 18; *cia haca acht dóigh deaghdháimhe*
A iv 3, 618. In modern Irish *dóichin* is used similarly; *is eól duit nách
aon dóichin* [sic leg.] *me i gcomhrac aonair* Canon P. O'Leary's *Lughaidh
Mac Con*, p. 24; see *Foclóir do Séadna*, s. v. For a somewhat similar use
of *ionntaoibh* see *Dánta Seáin na Raithineach*, p. 29. Cf. also the use
of *do-nim dóigh de* in the following, addressed by a poet to a patron who
is unaccountably displeased with him: *an trid do-rinnis dóigh dhíom .
nach ttapruim fuil na n-airdriogh ad gruaidh . . .?* 23 D 14, 131, i. e.
'didst thou think it safe to attack me because I never made thee flush
(at my satire)?'

§ 6 'one-sided . . .' for *airc* 'strait, difficulty, tight place,' see Contribb.;
leithimeal may mean simply 'outer edge,' cf. A. R. 98. 1; *bun agus bárr,
lár agus leath-imeal an sgéil*, Seanmóin ii 136. But the phrase *airc
leithimil* is obscure to me. "to whom did King Henry the second impose
those lawes? not to the Irish, for the most part of them fledd from his
power into the deserts and mountaynes, leaving the wide countrey to the
conquerour." Spenser (Globe ed. 514). The 'conquerour' did not, however,
win his land so simply.

§ 7 'warranty,' i. e. 'protector.' Cf. *buidhean bhriste bhearnach gan
bharánta* TSh p. 185; *do chaill sí seadh a hágha . asi an bhean gan
bharána* C iv 1, 176b; *biaidh Eire aigesiomh óir as é baránta as fearr
dhí caitheamh aga dhá cosnamh é* Cath Muighe Léana, ed. O'Curry, 106;
barántas Maoise ar chloinn Israel Keat. ii p. 28.

§ 9 'exhort,' for *laoidheadh* see 10 § 24.

§ 11 Read áirgheadha áilgheana; in the second word the length
of the initial is well attested; it is usually accented in MSS. The first is
evidently ap. of *airghe*, see Ir. Gr. Tr., Decl. § 3, *l.* 28; ex. 146; Ir. Texte
i 40. 19. The initial of *airghe* 'herd' etc. is not usually accented but the
fact that the *-r-* is not doubled points to a long vowel. The word may
be connected with *árach* 'spancel.'

§ 12 *Fearghna*, a remote ancestor of the O Roikes, LL 338 f.

'kindle' etc.; this is a favorite figure, similarly *adudh do chor i
gcoiccill an choccaidh* FM v 1792.

§ 13 *M. Sléacht*, a plain in the bar. of Tullyhaw, Co. Cavan. *Bréifne
Uí Ruairc* consisted of the present Co. Leitrim increased by the baronies
of Tullyhunco and Tullyhaw, which were aded to *B. Uí Raghallaigh* to
form the present Co. Cavan. In the text here the gen. *Moighe Sléachta*
is curious, and does not support the old explanation of the name, 'Plain
of the genuflexions' (Keat. ii p. 122; see Metr. Dinds. iv p. 379).

§ 15 O'Grady prints and translates, with commentary, §§ 15, 19-25,
32, 43, 47, 55, 62, 63, 69-71, Cat. 415 ff.

§ 16 *Aolmhagh*, in Dromahaire, Co. Leitrim. This word belongs to a class of proper names which can be declined like *magh* 'plain,' or as -*o*-stems. See 33 § 14; *a thuir Aolmhuigh (: suibh)* 3 B 14, 45; cf. 1 § 14. *Sligeach*, *Imleach* are similarly treated, but as these seem derived from adjectives, they are not quite the same.

§ 17 *éinearraidh = éanurraidh*, cf. *go ndech Eiri dh'enurraidh* Tadhg Óg, YBL 374 a 16; and see 9 § 50 n. and Ir. Gr. Tr., Decl. § 7.

§ 18 perhaps: He must needs make a hosting for our plain of *Ú.* — his will be, etc. Cf. YBL 380 b 22.

§ 21 'at all events,' cf. Unpubl. Ir. Poems ix 8. "their distinguished lime-dashed burgs," O'Grady.

§ 24 *Teathbha*, see 9 § 14 n.

§ 25 Colt, a district between the Boyne and the Liffey.

§ 26 'massive;' *bróintibh* may be dp. of *bró* 'quern,' or of *bró* 'mass. see Contribb. s. *bró, bróin*; and cf. 10 § 18.

§ 29 *miadhchardha* is a doubtful emendation (see varr.). Cf. *miadchar*, varr. *midchara, midhchuir* Tec. Cor. 3, 38; *fáilti midhchuir* Anecd. i 78; *miodchar : ciothmhar* Ir. Monthly 1924, 587. Above we should perhaps read *iothBhanbha : miodhchardha*, the second word seems to be connected with *miodh* 'mead,' and might be tentatively rendered 'cheerful.'

§ 30 'Sligo,' here *Sligeach* is used of Connacht in general. It was originally the name of the river, see Arm. 15 a 1; A. R. 76.

§ 44 'uniting thr.,' see 1 § 15 n.

§ 47 O'Grady renders this: "The magnitude of the pirate young men's hatred for him [has this fount]: for him it is that in general opinion's course it does prevail, and of him the multitude long time proclaim it, that he [as good as] holds Ireland by the bridle." The brackets are O'G.'s. The sentence "for . . . prevail" renders the second line, evidently; but I do not quite understand it.

§ 48 *comhanta*, gen. of *comhnadh*, or *cumhnadh(-ódh ?)*, see Irish Guy, ZfcP 6, 39, 48, 52, etc.

§ 49 *mbodhangaibh*, cf. Ir. Gr. Tr., Decl. 13; ex. 643.
'Precipitous flood(?)' *déar aille* is a common epithet, e. g., 23 § 18; cf. 2 § 55; *déar dochaithmhe dileanda* (of Cú Chonnacht Maguire) 3 C 13, 513; *der dilinne an eoil* ZfcP 2, 350. We may have the same idea in *atráchtatar Laigin amail buinne dilenn do aillib* SG i 380 (LL 304 b), see *Miscell. of Irish Prov.* 418. The O'Neills (see 8 § 23 n.) and O'Donnells are referred to in the last line.

§ 50 The three *Luighne*, possibly the two O'Haras, *O Heaghra Buidhe* (29-32) and *Ó Heaghra Riabhach*, and *O Gadhra*. But *na trí L.* may be used here simply for the families occupying the territory of the *Luighne*, see Hogan.

cliathchaibh, dp. of *cliathach* a derivative of *cliath* (10 § 10 n.)' see Contribb.

§ 51 'the three MacSweenys,' see 2 § 12 n.

§ 52 Hy Many, perhaps the O'Kellys; *clann Fearghusa?* possibly = *ceinéal F.* of Donegal, see FM 1215, or the Clare families reputed to be sprung from Fergus and Meadhbh. Cf. A. R. 84 z.

Brian's mother, Gráinne, daughter of Manus O'Donnell, died in 1551.

§ 54 O'Conor Sligo, O'C. *Donn*, O'C. *Ruadh*.

§ 55 *clann D.*, i. e. the MacDonnells, see supra p. 231 *l.* 20. The soldiery of F. are the Irish branch, the others are the Scottish mercenaries 'entertained' by Brian. In his struggle against Malbie in 1581 he was reported to have 900 Scots, and later on G. Fenton writes to Leicester: "O'Reworke has entertained 500 Scots to revenge his private wrongs upon some of his neighbours." Carew, 1584, p. 375.

§ 61 'griddles,' cf. *lann .i. greideal no roistln* P.O'C (O'Cl.). *lóisdin* < Engl. 'lodging,' Gad. i 286.

17

The historical portion of this piece is illustrated by the tracts entitled *Historia et Genealogia Familiae de Burgo*, as to which see Abbott-Gwynn *Cat. of Irish MSS in TCD* 318, and O'Grady, *Cat.* 428. Imperfect translations of portions of these tracts have been published in Galway Archaeological Journal vi-vii; Knox's *History of Mayo*, and elsewhere; a complete edition of the whole would be of interest.

Irish tradition connects the de Burgo family with Charlemagne; according to O'Hart they are derived from Charlemagne's ancestor Pepin le Vieux. A connection with William, Duke of Normandy, the Conqueror of England, also seems to be hinted at (§ 24); this may be explained by the tradition cited in O'Hart that Harlowen de Burgo had by Arlott, mother of William the Conqueror, two sons, of which one, Robert, became the great grandfather of William FitzAdelm or FitzAldelm, the ancestor of the Irish Burkes (cf. Orpen, *Ireland under the Normans* ii 195).

The two main branches of the de Burgo family in Ireland are the Upper or southern Burkes, of Galway, ancestors of the earls and marquises of Clanricard, whose reigning chief was anciently styled MacWilliam *Uachtair*; and the Lower or northern Burkes, (or Bourkes) of Mayo, led by MacWilliam *Iochtair*, from whom are the earls of Mayo. Tadhg Dall only addresses the latter branch. The subject of the present piece, Seaán son of Oliver, became MacWilliam in 1571, was appointed Seneschal of Connacht by the English Government in 1575, and † in 1580. See Introd. p. xxx; Knox, 179 ff. His mother was daughter of O'Donnell, see MacFirbis Geneal. 804; O'Grady 404, 428 n. 2.

The poem may have been composed any time between 1571 and 1580. According to § 20 it was composed 410 years after the Burkes conquered Ireland. From what year are we to date this conquest? Not from 1175, the year in which William FitzAldelm was appointed viceroy, for that would bring us to 1585, five years after Seaán's death. It reads like an inaugural ode, but deducting 410 from 1571 we get 1161, five years before Dermot's appeal to Henry II. Possibly we should take 1169, the date of arrival the first of the Cambro-Norman adventurers: that would date the poem to 1579.

On f. 54a of the *Historia* is a drawing of a mail-clad knight holding a long lance, and mounted on a white steed with red and yellow trappings. At the top of the page is the title:

Ag so Mac Uilliam a Burc Seaan mac Uilveruis mic thSeaain mic Ricaird í Chuairsge 7 dá dhóchus fein as e as mo [an erasure] *fuair d'olc a cosnadh a dhúchais fein* [an erasure] *dha taineig ruimhe anuas .i. tug se fein 7 a chinadh seacht madhmanna ruibh a* beith *a tigernas dó ré na linn féin.* See Galway Arch. Journ 1911, and Knox's *History of Mayo.*

This assertion of the claims of a Norman family to the possession of Ireland disgusted Charles O'Conor, who has written in Irish on the margin of the copy in Bk.: 'Curse you, Tadhg. This is a shameful poem you have left.' Similar language had been used before Tadhg's day, however, in fact §§ 1-8 seem to be modelled on the opening stanzas of another Burke poem, *Seanóir cuilg cairt an Bhúrcaigh.* I have not been able to satisfy myself as to the identity of the individual addressed in this poem (he is called *Riocard mac mic Riocaird*, and *mac mic Mairgrég*). The only copies of it I have found are that in Bk., and O'Curry's transcript therefrom in 3 C 13. The author's name is omitted. The poem's position in the MS., sandwiched between a poem by Tadhg Óg and one attributed to Maoil Seachluinn na nUirsgéal, supports the conjecture that it belongs to the middle of the 15th century. Precisely the same arguments are used as here:

> *Cairt cloidhimh, cá cairt as fearr*
> *cairt Ricaird ar Ráth Raoileann;*
> *cairt gach deaghslóigh asl sain*
> *ar seanróimh Dhá Thí is Thuathail.*

No charter other than this had the children of Neimheadh, Lugh Lámhfada, or the Sons of Míl:

> *Os cairt chloidhimh chosnas sin*
> *ionann ceart chloinne Mílidh*
> *'sna mBurcfear dar ghiall goil*
> *ar iath ccúirtgheal ó gCobhthaigh.*   3 C 13, 764-5

That Tadhg Dall had studied this piece is suggested by § 58, see note below.

§ 1 'swordland,' i. e. gained by force of arms, by right of conquest; see Keat. ii p. 362 and O'Grady's note, Cat. 428. Similarly *tír c.* Cóir Anm. 76, ZtcP 8, 318.

'let all be defied,' cf. *ón ló theosda an té fá táim . do slán, a Dhé, feasda fúin* (a father lamenting the death of his only son) 23 F 16, 154;

ar slán fód' geasa Oss. vi 34; *slán cogaid fá chloinn Uilliam* O'Grady, Cat. 376, seems to mean 'a defiance of any war against Clanwilliam,' a warning to all not to undertake one.

§ 2 Similarly Tadhg Óg, urging the claims of *Siol gColla : Ac so breath is breiti ar Éirinn . d'eis gach cuir dar cuireadh di, a beith acun ti bhus treisi . ge beith ri budh deisi dhi* YBL facs. 384 a 17 (col. 176).

§ 5 'courtly,' for *cathardha* see **2** § 24 n.

§ 10 the 'three battalions' is of course a rhetoical phrase; the 'warriors of France,' are the de Burgos, traditionally derived from Charlemagne, hence known as the 'seed of Charles;' 'the soldiery of Greece' are the FitzGeralds; Irish historians derive this family from the Trojan Aeneas, and this is possibly the origin of the epithet 'Grecian,' see Kilk. Arch. Journ. I 3rd ser. 1868-9, p. 361; IV 4th ser. 1876-8, p. 257; Br. Dominic O'Daly in Mechan's *Geraldines*. As to the English contingent O'Grady's brief explanation "this term [Saxon] includes all other aliens," may be adopted.

§ 12 'the share of *M.*,' i. e. *Leath Mogha*, which here seems to include Munster and south Leinster. The FitzGeralds made settlements in Waterford, Cork and Kerry.

§ 13 The de Burgos obtained power in Limerick, Tipperary, Mayo, and east Ulster.

§ 16 Cf. *leigem secuinn seal go se . an clann so acht Ros fionn Failghe* LL 394. Of certain of the perquisites of MacWilliam the author of the *Historia* says: *is leis féin é an uair is toil le Dia* 7 *leis an phrinnsa he* 'it is his when it so pleases God and the sovran.'

go reich, cf. *Dán Dé* vi 11, where it seems to have the force of a prep.; GF i 9.

An English rendering of the portion of the *Historia* detailing the lands and perquisites of MacWilliam is printed by Knox, but it is not always accurate.

§ 19 'set stones,' for *toinighthe* see **9** § 4 n.

§ 20 'four' etc., see above p. 254-5.

§ 24 William, Duke of Normandy, the Conqueror of England, is evidently meant here; see above p. 254.

§ 25 The *Historia* relates that two noblemen of the de Burgo family named respectively Ball-du-uinus a Búrc (Baldwin) and Uilliam Búrc took counsel as to which part of the world in which they should make conquests. Baldwin went eastward and seized Jerusalem and the kingdoms of the Persians, Saracens, and Ascalonites; see O'Grady's note, Cat. 428-9.

'centre,' a mediaeval belief; *"bidh a fis accatt curab é Ierusalem certlár in talman"* Gael. Maund. 156.

§ 27 'Richard the Great' see FM 1232 n. p. According to the *Historia* (8 a) the Clanwilliam Burkes were descended from Richardus

Magnus, son of Ullialmus Aldelmson. The Battle of the Cinders, against Ruaidhri Ó Conchobhair, high-king of Ireland, was fought in 1178; Ruaidhri was defeated and, according to the *Historia*, his hand was struck off by Richard; *et nemo deinceps preter principem erat rex in Hibernia. Historia* f. 8ª; MacFirbis 798ᵇ.

The references are rather vague in §§ 28-38, and it is not easy to identify each individual. The Sir Richard of § 32 must be the Red Earl of Ulster, and Sir William of § 37 is evidently one with William Óg of the following stanza, victor in the battle of Athenry, in 1316, where Feilim O'Conor and nearly all the Irish nobility of Connacht were slain. Not a battle for an Irish poet to exult over. The other battles I have not been able to identify precisely.

§ 29 Read *Loch Cuan* 'Strangford Lough.'

§ 30 *Ros Guill* peninsula in Donegal; see Walsh's *Leabhar Chlainne Suibhne* p. 140.

§ 31 *Risdeard*, see var. The poets seem to use Riocard (Ricardus) and Risteard (Richard) indifferently. See §§ 32, 36; 44, 48 for rimes, cf. 20 § 6 n. Risteard is sometimes re-latinised in documents; e. g. in a document of 1497 *Ricardum alias Risterdum de Burgo : Uluk filius Ristardi Mc Tomas*, in a will of 1468; *Ristardus de B.*, in a MS copy of Papal bull, 1511, Iar Connaught 176, 207, 171.

§ 32 *Sior*, this is stressed; cf. §§ 36, 37, the form is decided in: *planda tiogh in gach teannta . an sior Gallda Gaoidhealda* (Sir James Dillon), A v 2, 29 b.

§ 33 Strand of B., at Dundalk.

§ 34 *Cunga*, Cong in Mayo.

§ 36 *Seaghais*, i. e. Roscommon and Sligo, according to O'Grady; *Seaghais* is the older name of the Boyle river, A. R. 76. The term *cna Seaghsa* could, apart from context, mean the 'nuts of knowledge,' told of in the lore of the Boyne and the Shannon, see Metr. Dinds. iii 130, 529; that would hardly suit here, however.

Bóroimhe, on the Shannon, north of Killaloe; see Ériu 4, 71.

§ 37 Sir William Liath de Burgo † 1324, see ALC, FM and Galway Arch. Journ. vi 228, vii 1 ff. The poet calls him Uilliam Óg as his father's name was Uilliam. He was cousin of the Red Earl.

§ 38 *Umhall*, now the barr. of Burrishoole and Murrisk, Co. Mayo.

§ 39 *Magh Máil*, a plain between the Barrow and the Nore.

§ 41 'Scottish Edmund;' son of Sir William Liath. According to the *Historia* he was brought up in Scotland by his mother, the daughter of the king of Scotland. After the death of the Brown Earl, heir of the Red Earl, "*do-chuaidh bádhadh fine ar Búrcachaibh*," i. e. the line failed, and Edmund went to this mother's kin in Scotland. There he remained for twenty-two years, and on his return to Ireland he wedded the daughter of O'Malley, Sadhbh, daughther of Diarmaid s. o. Eóghan s. o. Tadhg Ruadh Ó Máille (*Historia* f. 6a). Edmund's obit is 1375. See Galway Arch. Journ. vii 23-7.

§ 42 Thomas † 1401; Edmund † 1458.

§ 43 i. e. Richard son of Eamonn na Féasóige otherwise Riocard Ó Cuairsge, or Ó Cuairscidh (ALC ii 178) † 1479. The rendering "R. of the Bent Shield" (Gal. Arch. Journ. vii 22, Knox 158) is not supported by Irish documents, which, so far as I have noted, treat the Ó as the word for descendant; gen. *Uí*. In one of the Burke pedigrees MacFirbis has: . . . *m Riocaird Uí Cuairsgd no na ruag ttimchill* (Geneal. 808).

§ 44 'so that . . .;' "so that he upset Ireland's whole island" O'Gr.

§ 46-7 I have not noted the legends referred to here. The only connection of Richard with Beann Éadair I have read of is the following legend told by MacFirbis: *As e an Riocard ceudna do ghabh Tighearna Binne hEudair 7 rug les i tTir Amhalghaidh e, 7 nir bhean do fuaslugadh as acht dorus a chuirte do bheth osluighthe ar chuid meadhoin laoi* 'It was the same Richard who seized the Lord of Howth, and bore him off to Tirawley, and took nothing as ransom for him save that the door of his castle should be open at the midday meal.' (Geneal. 804). This is an earlier version of the famous 'Granuaile' story; see Elrington Ball's *Howth and its Owners* pp. 68-9.

§ 47 *le drithlinn T.* might mean 'together with the spark from Tara,' but I have nothing to support this.

§ 50 'spend and defend,' cf. 28 § 37, and see *Miscell. of Ir. Provv.* 403 and Knox 176.

§ 51 'apple-tree from *E.*' see 5 § 9 n.

§ 52 'unfathomable,' *forus* 'foundation, bottom' (?); see 25 § 40 n.

§ 53 'planted rocks,' (?); for *cuir* see 1 § 6 n. O'Gr. renders the line: "of resolution firmer than a corner stone" (Cat. 430). Was he thinking of *cuirr*?

§ 54 'object,' for *fuidheall* see 7 § 19 n.

§ 55 *doras báis*, cf. 13 § 17.

§ 58 The second couplet recalls a couplet from the piece cited above, p. 255: *Ceart Riocaird ar Chathraigh cCuinn . ar gach adhbhar dá n-abruim, cia aga mbiadh amhorus air . fa iadh ccladhsolus cCobhthaigh* 3 C 13, 774.

§ 60 *dár iribh*; possibly the rule cited Introd. p. cvi should be followed here, reading *ni ariribh*; but the usage may be one on which the grammarians differed. Cf. 23. 16.

§ 64 *barradh*, cf. *ag barredh úirierna a n-each 's mainder crūiniemhdha a ccraoiseach* ZfcP 2, 359.

§ 68 A favorite figure in early Irish literature; e. g., Br. DD. 17, 66 (RC 22).

§ 70 I do not understand *duitheanta*, *suitheantha*; cf. *duaithnidh*, *suaithnidh*?

18

From the meagre data it is impossible to conclusively identify the Éamonn son of MacWilliam addressed in this fragmentary piece. Possibly he is the Edmund Burke of Castlebar, son of Uilleag, who tried to secure the MacWilliamship in 1586, or Edmund son of Richard *an iarainn*; both are mentioned in the "true discourse of the causes of the late rebellion of the Burkes", Nov. 1586 (CSPI 1586 p. 200 ff., cf. ib. p. 174 and see Knox, ch. 24). Edmund of Castlebar was eventually hanged by Bingham in 1595, in his 80th year, after attempting to escape while imprisoned in Galway as a hostage. Seaán of **17** had a son Éamonn, and his brother, Richard of **20** had a son Éamonn *allta*, † 1582 FM, ALC.

§ 1 for *eadamar* see **2** § 17 n.

§ 2 'pride,' *uaill* evidently = *uall* Wb 15 d 40; gl. 'elatio' Ml 57a 11 cf. **2** § 31 n.

§ 5 *corra* should perhaps be rendered 'unsettled.' Cf. *síona carracha* Ir. Monthly 1920, 108
dailtion, I have not noted any other ex. of this word.

§ 10 'level pool,' *linn lán* is used elsewhere as a similitude of tranquillity or prosperity; *do bhámar 'nar linn láin . sinn ar ttrághadh ó a tteasdáil* Bk. 231 b, *Coicceadh Uladh ina linn lain, ina thopar thecht 7 ina thuinn teccle isin mbliadhainsi gan guais catha na creiche gona na gabhála forra a hentaoibh d'Erinn* FM 1599 p. 2142.

§ 11 Cf. **33** § 18.

§ 24 The construction of this stanza is not clear to me; I have rendered the 2nd line as though the verb were intransitive, but this does not entirely solve the difficulty. The general sense is of course plain enough. For *ó soin* see **22**a § 36.

§ 25 See Keat. ii p. 104.

§ 33 See **13** § 22 n.

§ 34 'laden (?)' I am not sure of the meaning of *óghlán* here.

§ 37 'anything of value,' this is a free rendering of *athmhaoin*, which may perhaps be used in the general sense of wealth, as well as in a special one. Some of the exx. I have noted seem to require a meaning indicated by the pref. *ath-*; *munbhudh leó cosccar an la sin na biadh a n-a. da éis acht a marbhadh ... "... no prospect remained for them but ..."* FM vi 2068; cf. 1958, 2038; v 1850; Ir. Monthly 1921, 68 § 10.

19

It must be admitted that there is no specific reference in this piece to connect the subject with the Burkes. The warrior addressed is not a chief, and may indeed have been a professional fighting man. *Eamonn* is a common name in more than one of the soldier septs. The connection of *Bháitéar* (15) with the man addressed is not clear. If the rendering given of *lucht adhbhair* is correct he is evidently a rival.

§ 2 *dearlaicthir* does not make a good rime with *aithghin*. The form of the verb is not quite certain; historically there should be *gh* in stead of -*c*-. Cf. *derloicctech : soichlech* Ériu 4, 218.

§ 15 *lucht adhbhair*, I do not know the meaning of this term; cf. *maithmhechas na n-aindligheadh . do thabhairt do lucht adhbhair* G. B. Ó Heó lhusa, T. C. 230; *Gar tád do Mhuigh Muiredhaigh . do sguir cách dá gcomhfalaidh; lucht a. Fóid Feradhaigh . d'armuibh ar chóig comhadhuibh* A iv 3, 621. *Feadh do dhiomdha um oirear nÍr . ní loighfiod a bhfiodhbha féin; gér bhfada fer adhbhair uaibh . ar adhbhuidh fuair nír bhean béim* 3 B 14, 85. See also **29** § 19.

§ 16 *cogthach* 'man-of-war' (?). I have only one other ex.: *coisrig a Chríost cairbh Dhonnchaidh . . . bi ar a chogthach ad chrann seóil . dá chur tar feirg n-aigeoin* L 17, 12 b.

§ 19 *Codhal*, see **9** § 40 n. 'maintained', for *ar bun* see cit. **15** § 38 n.

20

This piece is addressed to Richard Burke, own brother of the MacWilliam of **17**; see Introd. p. xxx. O'Grady suggests that is was composed while Richard was contending for the title with Richard *an iarainn*, or before the contention began. •See Knox, 191-7. It may, of course have been composed shortly after the death of R. *an iarainn*. At any rate it is not addressed to a holder of the MacWilliamship; he is merely Richard, son of MacWilliam.

§ 4 I am not sure how the second couplet should be rendered: the most moderate king is he who bears himself without humility (?). For *iomchor* 'enduring' cf. **28** § 7. For *méad meanma* see **1** § 31 n.

§ 6 *Risdeard*; so MacFirbis names him, using the form *Ríocard* of another brother. See **17** § 31 n.

'standard', lit. 'tokens, signs;' cf. *Tucus grad d'airrdenuib Uilliam* O'Grady, Cat. 338, where O'Gr. explains tokens by "i. e. outward and visible signs of in ward qualities of head and heart."

§ 10 His mother was daughter of O'Donnell; see p. 254 w above.

§ 14 ff. O'Grady observes that this apologue "consists in a somewhat free handling of Daedalus and of Icarus, of Ariadne and of Theseus (with a few supernumeraries) grouped not unskilfully in an unmistakably Irish setting" (Cat. 437).

§ 25 'conflict;' *cliachdha* = *cliathcha*, see **16** § 50 n.

§ 27 'weakness' etc. See TBC p. 30, Thurneysen's *Ir. Held. u. Königssage* i 359. The phr. is probably a petrified figure by this period, used to express 'captivity, powerlessness.' Cf. *Danta Grádha* p. 1.

§ 33 *togbhaid ortha*; cf. *thógbhus C. air* SG 282; modern Donegal *tóg ort*, Quiggin 451, Similarly in Sc. Gaelic; *thog iad orra* RC 1, 195; An Deo Greine 1921, 68. For a similar use of *tógbhaim* with *um* see *Buile Suibhne* §§ 15, 17 etc.

§ 36 *muinchibh* 'surface' (?), the form is doubtful, see varr. and cf. *muinchinn .i. uachtar* O'Cl.; *muinchend cumung* 'a strait' LU 1b z; *tar muncinn Gaididoin* "the sea of Gadidon" Ir. Nenn. 54 (see note); *tar muinchind an maighsléibhe* A. R. 20x. P. O'C. quotes this couplet as an ex. of the pl. of "*muineach* a back or hill, a ridge or wave." He also cites, similarly, the ex. in G. B. Ó Heódhusa's Poem printed Gadelica i 11, with the reading *muinchibh*.

§ 39 'lance,' *omhna* is common in this sense, see varr., and **29** § 22. The -*m*- is usually lenited in MSS, but seems to be doubled in some dialects; see *Tor. Gr. Gr.* 40. 3, and *omnai* (var. *ommna*) Trip. 218.

§ 42 'wand of kingship;' see Keat. iii pp. 10-12 for the wand handed to the lord or king on his inauguration.

§ 54 'challenge,' or 'enhance,' cf. **10** § 13 n.

21

From the allusions in this piece we gather that it is addressed to a Myler Burke whose grandfather had been MacWilliam, and whose father, Walter, had failed to attain the title. The apologue further suggests that Walter had been slain in order to clear the way for another candidate. All this points to the identification of the person addressed with Myler son of Walter *Fada*. Walter's father, David, who was MacWiiliam, † 1558. In 1545 or -9 (the annalists vary) Walter was slain by Donnell O'Flaherty at the instigation of Finola, mother of Richard *an iarainn*, who wished to secure the succession for her own son. Myler himself was hanged in 1586, and the prophets were falsified. The piece may be connected with his "aggressive walk" into Tirawley in 1582, see Annals.

§ 4 *ceann i gc.*, for the metre here see Introd. p. lxxxix.

§ 7 'adventurous,' this is a tentative rendering of *séad-arsaidh*, see **3** § 27 n., and cf. **24** § 36.

§ 8 I am not sure how *do bhunadh* should be rendered. Cf. **39** § 10, and *ní mhaireann grádh do bh.* ('love does not naturally endure (?)'), *Dánta Gr.* p. 14.

§ 11 "But grow like savages,—as soldiers will,
That nothing do but meditate on blood,—
To swearing and stern looks . . ." Hen. V 5 ii.

§ 19 ff. This apologue is also used by Gofraidh Fionn, see Irish
Month'y 1919, 457.

§ 34 'befall,' *imdhéabhas* = *imdhéaghas*, ē-fut. of *imdhighim* (= *im-thighim*).

§ 36 'firm,' see 1 § 6 n. and cf. Ir. Monthly 1922, 416 § 8.

§ 41 For *túr* see Ériu 7, 26.

§ 43 Read: about to proclaim

22

The meaning of this piece depends ou the proper connotation here of the illusive legal terms *fiach* and *geall*, and without a precise knowledge of the circumstances referred to this remains in doubt. Something due, a debt, a rent payment, a tax or fine can all be denoted by *fiach*. The person liable is usually indicated by the prep. *ar*. The word *geall* 'pledge' is generally used in the 15th-16th century land deeds somewhat in the sense of chattel-mortgage, e. g. it is used of number of cows given for a piece of land, the latter being redeemable on the payment of cows equal in number and value on the date specified in the agreement; it is also used of land mortgaged. See the Irish Deeds published by Hardiman, RIA Trans. xv, and Appendix to the xxixth Report of the Deputy Keeper of Publ. Recc., Irel., p. 42.

§ 1 *Uilliam Búrc*, see note on **23**.

§ 2 *clampar*, cf. Cúirt 88; *Réilthíní* Óir, s. v.; c. *fiach*, *Amhráin P. Mhic Gearailt* 654

§ 3 *ag d. mo choda*, cf. *gach combrathair bhias a nioc a choda fein do i baile* (of land held by a number of kinsmen) App. to xxixth Rep. p. 40 x.

§ 4 'the courthouse;' at Ballymote?

As *cách* in the previous st. evidently means the persons liable I suppose it must denote them in this st. also, although the gen. after *fiach* is also used of the claimant, e. g.: . . . *an tEasbog . . . ag tógbáil ciosa annsan bfearann . . . as si cedrama fagbamaoid ug an Easboig, an cedrama ara suideocar fiacha an Easboig do bed an c. lá* ('the quarter originally charged with his dues'). Ir. Deeds XXXIII.

§ 6 'warrant,' cf. in the assignment of the lands of Baile Slatra to Muintir Slatra by the Mac Shanes: *acus dfiachaib air an sliocht san Meic Seain a mbaravtus acus a lamha acus a litir do bheith aig M. Slatra re ndul a ccúirt acus a ccomhairle do chosnamh a nduchuis agus a ngill doibh a mBaile I Slatra:* 'The Sept of MacShane are bound to give their warrant deed and sign manual to the Slattery family that they (the Sept of MacShane) should go into court and to █████ncil to make good their inheritance in Ballyslattery' [transl. might also be: 'that they, the Slatterys may be able to go in to court etc.,' i. e., that they should have the deeds of assignment in their possession, produceable on any attempt to disturb them in their holding, and this I think would correspond with the reference in our poem. I leave it to legal experts to decide which rendering is more likely]. Ir. Deeds XVIII.

22 a

This piece is ascribed to Tadhg Dall only in Bk.; it is usually ascribed to Brian (son of Eóghan Maol) O Domhnalláin (**25** §§ 13, 28). O'Grady points out that the individual addressed is evidently one of the Lower Burkes, but declines the task of indentification: "The stirring members named 'Rickard Oge' were far too numerous to admit of their claims being weighed here." (Cat. 401). However a Richard son of a MacWilliam named Richard whose date would suit either poet can hardly be other than R. Og son of Richard son of Seaán an Tearmoinn. R. son of Seaán † 1570, and his son Richard Óg, nicknamed 'the Pall of Ireland' was hanged by Bingham in 1586.

The title with which Richard was tempted is not clearly specified, but if we may take a hint from § 21 we may safely conclude that it was either the sheriffship of Mayo or a seneschalship (cf. Knox 185, 197-8). The shrieval function does not seem to have been very clearly defined to the Irish mind at this period. To the annalists a sheriff's seizure was simply a *creach* (see Introd. p. xxviii n.), and our poet's son, who was made sheriff of Sligo, is described by a 17th cent. writer as *comitatus de Sligo toties Capitaneus* (*vulgò schirriff*) (*Anatomicum Examen* p. 133). At any rate the position of heir-presumptive, even, to MacWilliamship, with all the excitements it involved, was a superior one in the poet's eyes.

§ 2 *Mucroimhe*, the name of a plain between Athenry and Galway.

§ 3 'thou wouldst do ill,' for *olc do-gh* cf. *ge deruid aroile gurab olc do frith an gniom sin ní héidir a radh nach maith fuair .h. C a chuid féin de* ALC ii 444.

'former name,' i. e. 'son of MacWilliam.'

§ 5 *éir*, see Introd. p. lxxxii-iii; another ex. of the form as pres. ind. is *gar bheag dh'ionnramh chean ó gCéin . sreabh nach éair tar fiodhruigh bhfeaoir* [sic], 3 B 14, 86; *co n-ēir, Proleg.* 47, seems to be fut.

posd cothaighthe; I am not sure that I have rendered this correctly; cf. A. R. 108. 5.

§ 11 Read: lamhaim

§ 12 *an t-a. anma*, see **24** § 18 n.

§ 14 'the queen,' Richard's mother or his wife.

§ 19 Cf. *Ná tréig choidhche, crosaim ort . do chuid féin a ccrich Chonnacht* 3 B 14, 121.

§ 21 'sinew,' (?) cf. **9** § 2 n.
for, son of Mil, ancestor of the royal line of Ulster.

§ 36 possibly we should read *a s̄. ó so*; in such phrases the demons. pron. may be lenited or not, cf. *ó sin* **7**. 131, **15**. 149, **28**. 39, but *ó sin* **8**. 113, **15**. 29, **26**. 141, **28**. 69.

§ 53 *Forbhar?* See Index of place-names, infra.

§ 54 L. Derg at Killaloe.

§ 56 Reading *ní fríoth* (with Bk.) we might translate: well wouldst thou do to reform (*i. e.* re-assume) it; never did, etc.

§ 58 I have not been able to identify his mother. The reference to *Sioth Truim* need not be taken literally.

23

The William to whom this piece is addressed is probably the Uilliam Búrc of **22**. No surname is given in this, but relationship to Conall Gulban, Charlemagne (§ 19), Brian (Bóromha) and Ó Néill (§ 20) is suggested. Possibly he is to be identified with the Uilliam Búrc son of Seaán [of **17**] and Máire [dau. of Ruaidhri MacDiarmada, MacFirbis 806] to whom Fearghal Óg Mhac an Bhaird addresses a *crosántacht beg. Mairg um dhiaigh chenglus cumunn* (23 I. 32).

§ 4 *Ní dubhraidh*, cf. *ní dubhradh riamh roimhe soin . . . do ghuin i n-aisgidh ó fíor*, F 16, 7 (Bk. No. 305).
ar-iribh, cf. **17** § 60 n.

§ 7 'the strain of music;' for *adhbhann* see Contribb., where the emendation *adhbha(nn)* is unnecessary; cf. *adhbh(chiúil)*, decl. as fem.-ā-stem, Ir. Gr. Tr., Decl. § 39. Possibly *adhbh* and *adhbhann* are distinct; the former is applied to a musical instrument, Ir. Gr. Tr., Decl. § 39, ex. 1078. Here either meaning would suit, and *adhbhann* is used figuratively of a musical instrument Ir. Gr. Tr., Decl., ex. 455. For the var. *adhmad* cf. Unpubl. Ir. Poems x 11; Carsewell p. 24.

'expound,' *aiteacht* may be *aith-teacht* 'returning to; going over again;' cf. O'Grady, Cat. 392. 5 where the riming word requires *aitecht*.

§ 8 *brat* etc., see *Miscell. of Ir. Provv.* § 316.

§ 9 'elements,' I do not know what is the precise meaning of *adhbhar* here.

24

This piece is addressed to Somhairle Buidhe Mac Domhnaill, Lord of the Route, and Constable of Dunluce Castle, known in English as Sorley Boy; youngest son of Alastar Carrach Mac Domhnaill and father of Raghnall, first Earl of Antrim (see Ir. Monthly 1920, 317 ff.). It may relate to his landing at Marketon Bay, Nov. 1567 "with six or seven hundred redshanks, in whose presence he swore never to leave Ireland with his goodwill." The news of this landing was the cause of "considerable consternation" in official circles (DNB).

§ 1 'Alba;' the rendering 'Scotland' might be misleading, as the poet may be thinking merly of the western portion, *Airear Gaoidheal.*

For the use of *cóir* here and in the following stanzas cf. 7 § 7; 9 § 40, and *Mó do šaoilesa cóir cáigh . do bheith agam at anáir—do-chóidh an uairsi am aghaidh . ná ar ccóir uaibhsi d'fanamhain* 23 D 14, 132.

§ 4 'the isle of A.,' *inis* may be used here in a special sense, as in *Inis Eóghain,* or the poet may be thinking of some passage in which Alba is used in its older sense as the name of the British island.

§ 5 *aigéaradh,* sec. fut. of *agraim (ad. gair);* cf. Ir. Gr. Tr., Decl. ex. 1253.

§ 8 For the Collas see pp. 226, 228 above.

§ 18 'a curious tale,' *aoighe sgeóil* 'a stranger of a story,' i. e. a wonderful tale;' similarly 39 § 17; *Gleanings fr. Ir. MSS* 16; cf. *a. anma* 22ᵃ 12. For the story cf. perhaps CCath. 402 ff.

§ 19 'hero' (in the sense of principal character) this may not be exactly the meaning of *urra* here (see varr.), it might perhaps be rendered 'warrant,' i. e. guarantee of worth. Cf. *sgel oirdeirc ... ni bu scel é gan urraidh* H 1, 14, 105a; *sgél oirderc ... ó dhraoíthibh Fódla frioth linn, tarla sé san rolla rempa . as hé orra a reactha rinn* 23 D 14, 32. Cf. *orradh* in 25 § 11.

líon g. is an emendation; cf. *l. gliadh on Bhúill* A iv 3, 621; similarly *l. foghla an tansoin do thriall* L 17, 54a.

§ 20 'on an embassy;' *ar c. teachta* 'for a coming' (?) (i. e. in order to return). Cf. *do-chuaidh is ní ar ceand techta . ceann eachtra uaibh, a Ulta* (of a dead chief) 23 F 16, 73.

§ 32 'like,' lit. 'by the judgment of.'

§ 36 'forest,' etc., cf. 11 § 9 n. and *fidbaid ... do séolcrandaib* TTr. (Ir. T. ii) 843. *séad oirdhreic?* cf. *séad-arsaidh* 21 § 7. In first line read: Diolfaidh.

§ 37 Another possible emendation in the last line is: iliodhnach 'manyweaponed.'

§ 38 Colla Uais was banished from Ireland with his brothers by Muireadhach Tireach in A. D. 326, when he had held the kingship for four years.

§ 41 lines *a* and *c* go together. I am not sure of the meaning of *cuirim crois ar* here, but cf. 22a § 19, Unpubl. Ir. Poems xxi 5. In § 42

the meaning of the last line can hardly be other than the rendering given.
The 'fiery cross' may evidently be ruled out. The 'ancient contract' I
take to be the prophecy of the druid that if Fiachaidh Sraibhtine was defeated
and slain in battle by the Collas none of their descendants should ever
be king of Ireland (Keat ii p. 360).

25

This piece recalls a visit to the house of Maol Mórdha son of Maol
Muire MacSweeny, who was slain in 1581; see Introd. p. xxviii, and
O'Grady's notes, Cat. 423 ff. According to the Rev. P. Walsh, *Leabhar
Chl. Suibhne* p. xxxvii, Maol Mórdha belonged to the branch called
Mac Suibhne Connachtach, seated in Tireragh bar., Co. Sligo.

§ 1 *Eas Caoille*; location uncertain, but the name may be preserved
in that of Ballysakeery tl., Tirawley, Co. Mayo; see Onom.
'when . . . perished,' O'Grady's rendering is also possible: "our visit
to that dwelling shall [in memory] abide for ever."

§ 2 'benches,' see 11 § 24 n.

§ 4 *slíos m.*, cf. *for míodhslíos na bruighne* A. R. 230 z.

§ 5 'domed,' see 11 § 13 n.
fríoth etc., similarly *a fhagháil as meisde mé . m'anáir ré ré fleisge
Lí* 3 C 13,533; *Mac mic C. . . . fríoth a mhuirn, meiste a fagháil; ni
faghmaid dí ar ttocht i Tháil . ní as budh olc ar n-anáir* 23 D 14, 93.

§ 6 For *branán* see 2 § 7 n. and add to the exx. cited the proverbial
clár nocha bí gan branán Unpubl. Ir. Poems xxvi.

§ 7 'charm,' cf. *ortha, artha* Ir. Gr. Tr., Decl. 8; *créd fa n-iarrfadh
árrtha grádha . acht gruadh ghairthe nár ghríos sgoil* 23 D 14, 35.

§ 8 *Derg*, perhaps the Derg lake or river in Donegal, cf. 8 § 35.

§ 9 'house of T.,' probably Tara, see 8 § 22 n.

§ 11 'Earl' . . ., i. e. Richard *Saxonach*, second earl of Clanricard;
see O'Grady, Cat. 375 n. 3.

§ 12 'chieftain of the Moy,' i. e. the head of the Mayo Burkes, or
Bourkes, to use the chosen orthography. Here probably Seaán of 17.

§ 13 Brian son of Eoghan Maol Ó D. was slain in 1582 during a
raid into Tirawley by Myler (21) and Theobald, sons of Walter *Fada*, and
nephews of MacWilliam, Richard *an iarainn*, see ALC.
'Loughrea' (?), this seems to have been the headquarters of the Galway
Burkes, but the Irish form of this name is regularly *Loch Riach* (see note
on 1 § 5). *R. Raoibh* would seem to be identical with *L. Rí(bh) mheic
Luireadha*, which is regularly identified with Loch Ree in Roscommon.
See Keat. (Ind.); Met. Dinds. iii 450, 560. Cf. *L. Ríogh* Ériu 5. 64. The
name of the son of *Muiridh* seems to have been troublesome to early

writers. In Met. Dinds. *Rl* is given as nom. and gen.; elsewhere we have *Ribh*. We should expect *Ríach*, if a pr. name, to be gen. of *Reó* or *Ré*, but in Dinds. it is the same in all cases.

§ 14 Brian Mhac Con Midhe; I have no other ref. to him.

§ 15 C. grandson of O'H., possibly Conchobhar son of Éanna, † 1587 ALC.

Inisbkea is the name of an island off the Mayo coast. The 'Lord' (lit. highking) is MacWilliam Burke of Mayo (§ 12).

§ 18 I do not know the precise meaning of *meannchrot*. It is common in Mid. Irish tales in the phr. *binnithir téta m*. (Br. DD.). Later, *meann-* is confused with a commoner word, *beann-*, and we get *beannchr*.; see TBC p. 743; Acall. Gloss., *Dánfhocail* § 26; and cf. **35** § 8.

§ 22 'portent,' for *mana* see TBC Gloss.; *m mōrchumhadh dia cairdib* "cause," ALC ii 430.

§ 29 'Cattle-raids' . . . The early Irish scholars classified their stock of tales according to the general subject; see the list is printed from LL in O'Curry's MS Matt. and see also Anecd. ii 43 ff.

§ 32 'election,' i. e. of kings, or heads of kindreds; cf. *innsoighidh bar n-inat coinne . . . na beiridh a tigh na togha . libh acht deimin roghu rīgh* YBL 380b 8.

§ 38 Read: commórtais (see note on **14** § 29). With the phrase compare *gein n-imarbaga* Br. DD. 106 (RC 22).

§ 39 'preparation;' perhaps 'protection;' cf. *rún toirbhertach, tegar séd* L. 17, 64a; *lámh lér sgaoileadh teagar gach tighearna* Ir. Monthly 1920, 651; *teagar gach tíre a mbearnna* (complimentary epithet) 3 B 14, 100.

§ 40 'knowledge;' this is a doubtful rendering; cf. *ro múradh . . . an t-oilén* [i. e. *Dún an Óir*] *iar sin lás an Iustis jo dháigh ná badh carracc cothaighthe 7 ná budh inneoin forais do dhiberccach é ní budh síri* "strong retreat," FM v 1742; *inneóin f.* as a complimentary epithet, "anvil of solidity," ib. p. 1408. Other exx. of *forus* are: *forus meanman na macaomh* (ep. of a woman) F 16, 10; *do snaoi sinn . . . linnte foruis na bhfiliodh* L 17, 97a; *linn forais gach ealadhan* (of Ceann Coradh), A iv 3, 706; see also **17** § 52; Triads p. 40y.

§ 41 *Gormlaidh*, "most likely O'Rourke's sister of that name, † 1585," O'Grady, 425, see p. [   ] infra.

26

The subject of this piece, Eóghan Óg, son of MacSuibhne na dTuath (angl. MacSweeny Doe) succeeded his brother Domhnall in the headship of the kindred in 1570, and the verses may refer to his hopeful candidature. In §§ 27, 49 MacSuibhne does not appear to be used definitely of the subject of the poem, but of the head of the kindred, without special reference; in § 24, on the other hand, Eóghan is explicitly designated 'son of MacSuibhne,' which implies that he had not yet attained the headship. The stanzas in praise of his wife Margaret, daughter of Conn O'Donnell and Shane O'Neill's daughter (p. 187 above), must have been added later. They are only in one copy, and were probably taken from the chief's own poem-book. Eóghan was tutor or fosterer of Red Hugh and the harbourer of Brian na Múrtha in 1590 (p. 251), and † 1596. See A. R. 10, O'Grady, Cat. 420, 464.

§ 2 For Niall's sons see Keat. iv 28-29, 58; ZfcP 8, 293.

§ 4 Conall, i. e. C. Gulban, ancestor of the O'Donnell's.

ón chaoir, similarly ón chaoir shluaigh "from the fiery host," Unpubl. Ir. Poems xxi 5.

§ 9 dtuismidh, probably the -m- should be lenited.

§ 14 Aodh Athlamhain, see Walsh, Leabhar Chl. Suibhne pp. xii -xiii, 2, 80, for the division referred to in this and the following stt.

Athlamhain seems a doubtful form; cf. § 16. In L. Chl. S. athlomhan appears as nom. (p. 78) and gen. (p. 80); on p. 2, ib. the gen. is athlamhain. In Keat. i 26, iv 28, the gen is athlaimh. According to Keat. and L. Chl. S. this Aodh was son of Flaithbheartach an Trosdáin, king of Oileach, whose father was greatgrandson of Niall Glúndubh, but cf. Laud Genealogies, ZfcP 8, 294. 13ff., where Aodh A. is not mentioned.

§ 16 'alliance;' reading rabháigh : Athlamháin, which is possible, though not certain.

§ 17 'fertile,' -lachtmhar may be from lacht 'milk,' or the compd. may be craobh-luchtmhar 'branch-laden,' i. e. with heavily-laden fruit-trees.

§ 21 gur chuirsead . . . fúthaibh, cf. 11 § 31; rochuirset an mbloidh tíre . . . co fomamaighthe fóthaibh 7 ba héccen i ngéill . . . do thabhairt dóibh A. R. 34.

§ 32 'bordered . . . woods,' or 'of bright-wooded banks.' A city usually implies a river at hand. The meaning of géag in compounds is often obscure.

§ 33 'a band' etc., or 'a band (lit. flock) whose avoidance was a perilous undertaking.'

§ 36 'turretted' renders gairéadach, from gairéad, corresponding to English 'garret' in its earlier sense of 'watch-tower.' Cf. Do bhendoibh do ghaired ngeal . do-chímis . . . Bk. 178 a (No. 12), ri gan fius ar ardghairéd A iv 3, 619 (Brian Dorcha Ó Huiginn), and the pl.-name Móta Gairéad 'Mountgarret.'

§ 39 Eamhain, see 5 § 9 n. We may add that in the poem Baile suthain etc. the region is called Eamhain mheic Lir mheic Mhdhir (23 II 8, 59 a), and that there is a similar doubt about the situation of the land of the *Fir Falga*, which is localized now in the Hebrides, now in the Isle of Man (ZfcP 9, 201-2).

§ 42 i. e. to levy tribute for O'Donnell.

§ 46 *Craobhruadh*, this seems preserved in Creeveroe, the name of a tl. in Eglish par., Armagh.

§ 47 *Gaedheal*, i. e. G. Glas, ancestor of the Milesian race. Cf. 16 § 5, 17 § 19.

27

This is addressed to Mac Suibhne Fánad, Domhnall son of Toirdhealbhach, who was cotemporary with Eóghan of 26. From his castle of Rathmullen, here celebrated, he and Red Hugh were enticed on board Perrott's ship in 1587; see A. R. 8, *Leabhar Chl. Suibhne* p. xxx ff.

The Mac Sweenys, as we have already noted, were soldier kindreds, and the poet is fittingly reminded of the famed leader of an earlier fighting line.

§ 1 For Fionn's fort of Almha see Keat. ii p. 330, and the story of Cath Cnucha, RC 6.

§ 3 Read: Gháilian, see ZfcP 15, 96. Field of *G.*, i. e. Leinster, The Gáiliain of Leinster are well-known from a famous passage in the Táin (TBC 414 ff.), see also Keat., *Duanaire Finn* i p. xxxi, ZfcP 11, 173 ff.

§ 4 *Fánuid* is a peninsula in north Co. Donegal, west of Loch Swilly.

§ 5 Rathmullan, see FM 1516, *L. Chl. Suibhne* p. 66. "From the entrie of Lough [Foyle], until you come to a poynt of land a little short of Ench, there is neither castle nor fort, but then uppon a poynt of lande is a castle and an abbey called Ramellan (*in marg.*: Mac Swyn O'Fane's chief countrey house)," Descr. of L. Foyle (1601), Ulster Journ. of Archaeology v 141.

Almhunda is an adj. formed from the long stem of the noun, with the suffix -*da*. The -*nd*- is of course to be sounded as -*nn*- here.

§ 10 'variety,' cf. *is imdha atherrach creidium innti*, "variety", Gael. Maund. 145.

§ 26 'pride of their annals,' I am not sure of the precise sense of *oireas* here; -*oiris* might be retained, see *oiris* (*ón aimsir*) Ir. Gr. Tr., Decl. § 13; *Ua M. an tráth do thuit . ug cách 'na oiris orrdhruic* ex. 669; but *oireas*, masc., occurs in similar contexts; cf. the epithet *calaind oiris*, the and masc. *oires* (*ó dhá chéill*) Ir. Gr. Tr., Decl. § 38.

§ 29 *Aoibheall* the prophetess is usually associated with the Dál gCais; see 21 § 23 ff.

§ 31 Colum, i. e. Colum Cille.

§ 32 'throughout,' rather 'around.'

§ 33 *Séadna*, a prophetic child; cf. ZfcP 3, 31.

§ 42 leg.: inBághoine? cf. Ir. Gr., Decl. ex. 1446; Metr. Dinds. iv 392, and Onom. s. *benna bogaine*. See 4 § 43.

Gráinne may have been dau. of MacSweeny Baghuine; I have not succeeded in identifying her.

§ 43 last line, read: dan hi

28

This piece is in compliment to Ó Dochartaigh, Seaán son of Féilim, who † 1582. His father Féilim † 1556.

"From the Derie three miles within the land, towards Lougswillin, is the castle of Elloghe, O'Dougherdie's chief house" Description of Lough Foyle, from MS tract in SP Office dated 12th April 1601, Ulster Journ. of Arch. v 140.

§ 4 'branch,' *gobhlán* (*gabhlán*), from *gabhal* 'fork,' is used in the sense of 'branch, section, division, tributary;' *deimhinnsgne ... asi sin ... an treas gobhlán don Ghaoidheilg* 23 D 14, 53 (Gofraidh Fionn); *tucus gablán o Dubglais dom thig* LL 284 a 43; cf. also Keat. ii 212 y.

§ 5 *trian deiridh* I take to mean 'the latter third'.

§ 8 *amlach?* Cf. *sciath a*. Unpubl. Ir. Poems xi *l*. 70, *Bardachd Ghaidhlig* 3127, *na n aolchlár na*. L 17, 63a, *amhluigh dh'or* 64a (= Ir. Monthly 1920, 541, 543; *sduagha amlacha* Marco Polo 77 ("full of emblems" see the glossary), *inair amlacha* CF 249, *cóta amalach* Trans. Gael. Soc. Inv. xiii 71 (Tiree folk-tale); *amladh* Ir. Gr. Tr., Decl. p. 55. 13, may be related; see *Dán Dé* xxxi 4 n.

§ 10 'growth,' similarly *techt in talmhan* L 17, 81b; *teirce tochta ar tholchuibh oir* 14 b.

§ 14 *Mhirbhéal*, similarly O'Clery's LG, ed. MacN.-Macal. 182, but *Cermait Milbél* LL 11b 4 Lec. 562 b BB 35b 20.

§ 15 For *Cathair Ch.* see 4 § 13 n.

§ 16 'division,' cf. *ba lais Mumha gan roinn ris* "M. was his alone," GF vii 26.

§ 19 '*Róch*'s race,' I take this to refer to kings of the line of *Rudhruighe*, see Keat. iv 25. 62; *Gen. Reg. et SS.* 24 ff.

§ 20 Cf. 7 § 46 n., and see MacNeill's *Celtic Ireland* 132-3.

cnú seems to be collective here; in form it must be either nom. sg. or acc pl. (Ir. Gr. Tr., Decl. § 83); *as* may be for *ós*, see Introd. p. xcvii.

§ 26 *taoibhneambán*. when *neamh-* (*neimh-*) is prefixed to an initial *b-* the *-mh* becomes delenited and eclipses the *b-*; cf. 41. 55.

§ 30 Read: a ndéanann?

§ 32 *Bearta*, this name apparently survives in Buit House, near Bridgetown, Donegal. "From Ellogh, five miles up into the country, at the syde of Lough Swilly, is another castle of O'Dougherdie called Birt" ... Descr. of L. Foyle, U. J. A. v 141; this is O'Sullivan Beare's *Bearta arx*, cited in Onom.

§ 35 Cf. **13** § 3.

§ 36 'surpass,' I am not sure of the meaning of *iomarcaidh* here; cf. **3** § 22 n.

§ 37 *Faithne*, see Fathan, Onom.; "over against Elloghe, in O'Dougherdie's country, is a castle and a church called the Fanne" Descr. of L. Foyle, U. J. A. v 140.
'would spend,' see **17** § 50 n.

§ 42 A ref. to the cursing of Tara by Ruadbán Lothra, and its subsequent desertion; see the story of the Death of Dermot, in *Silva Gadelica*. Cf. MacNeill's *Phases* 233-4.

29

This poem is a curious panegyric on two brothers, Cormac O'Hara, otherwise Ó Heaghra Buidhe, chief of Leyney, who is directly addressed in some stanzas, and his brother Brian. Possibly it may be assigned to the year 1578, as in August of that year the following grants were recorded: "Grant to Cormocke O Harree of Collannye [*Cúl Áine*], co. Sligo; of the office of seneschal of the country of Magherye Leynye alias O Harree Buye's country. To hold for life, with all lawful customs hitherto received by the seneschal or captain of the country. 1 Aug. xx." (Fiants of Eliz. 3390) "Grant to Brian O Harree of Carrhewnecryvye [= *Ceathramha na Craoibhe* MacFirbis 227, 'Carrownacreevy'], co. Sligo, being the eldest and fittest of that name; of the place of second person in O Harree Buye's country. To hold during pleasure, with such possessions as the second person or tanyst of the country has had. Recites that Brian ought to be as well by birth as by years the second person or tawnyst in that country, according to the customs and usages heretofore used there. 1 Aug. xx." (Fiants of Eliz. 3391).

At a later date Cormac won a firmer hold on Leyney, see notes on **30**. Brian's career was curtailed by Bingham, by whose order he was executed in Galway in 1586.

§ 2 *dioghna*, cf. *ni chualamair dighna dibh* Ir. Gr. Tr., Decl. ex. 262; *ni chuala dlogha dibhséin* 23 D 14, 28.

§ 3 *gér chuid mh.* see **10** § 22 n. In the neg. exx. *ni cuid* x might of course mean 'no small x' but this is doubtful. Cf. the O. Ir. use Wb 14ᵃ 8; Ml 102ᵃ 15; differently 67ᶜ 2.

§ 5· 'fight,' or *bruidhean* may have its older meaning of 'hostel' here; possibly a pun is intended; as to the general meaning of the stanza cf. *Ní chleachtann sibh seachna éinfir . a ua B. . . . mór (nior* MS) *bhfear le bhfagar an adhbha . teagh folamh* [sic] *na ttarla tú* 23 F 16, 211.

§ 12 Cf. *Ag dáil der . . . nir fégh derc dhá doirseóraib* Ir. Gr. Tr., Decl. ex. 1305; *riandoirse ar nderc nach dúntoir* I. 17, 117ª.

§ 15 This stanza seems corrupt; we might read *cheard* or *cheird* 'the hereditary (poetic) art' (?). In the last line the pron. seems to agree with *uirrim*. The couplet may be an echo of *Beith d'araidh ag ól ar h'uilland . lór don fagail d'uirrim uait* Ir. Gr. Tr., Decl. ex. 648, which does not, however, help us to discover the meaning of the lines here.

§ 19 For *lucht adhbhair* see 19 § 15 n.

§ 22 Similarly *corba coill comdluith do slegaib . . . a sciath* TTebc 3282-3; we may also recall Jack Cade, who fought so long against a troop of Irish kerns that his thighs with darts "Were almost like a sharp-quilled porpentine."

§ 25 *stil re,* so 22a § 24; in 22 § 19 the addition of the prep. seems the most likely emendment of a short line. The point of this stanza is not clear. The meaning may be that Cormac is so lavish to poets that he hoards nothing but a drink of water for chance visitors.

§ 26 'hast . . . power,' or 'hast begun the battle;' the brothers are perhaps conceived here as fighting side by side, and it might be better to render the verb in the last line literally, 'he would not share the field with thee;' the ambiguity may be intended. We might fill up the second line by reading: ó luair sibh, which is translated.

§ 27 I do not understand *ré ngl.* here; it may be corrupt.

§ 29 'three continents;' *Is and sain ro rannad in domun i tri rannaib .i. Eoraip . Afraic . Asia* LU 1 a (Orosius c. ii). SR 2650 sq.

§ 31 *congalȝ* Cf. *ni beithte ar ti chongail chnó* 23 D 14, 96 = Ir. Gr. Tr., Decl. ex. 741.

donnadh: cf. Ir. Monthly 1921, 112; *bile dar donnadh gach dair,* F 16, 174; *na tuill do ghruaidh dearg do dh.* 23 L 32, 50.

§ 33 'reaver;' here *faghlaidh* may mean 'enemy.' For the gs. see Ir. Gr. Tr., Decl. § 52.

§ 36 Read: would not be profitable; 'they fight,' etc.; or 'their fight is under Cormac's protection;' (he will secure their terms).

Sadbh, wife of Oilill Ólum, from whom the Ui Eaghra are derived (32 § 13 ff.).

30

Sometime between the death of Conn son of Ruaidhri in 1581 (32 § 64) and 1585 Cormac son of Cian O'Hara secured himself in the headship of Leyney, see 31 § 51. He was one of the signatories to Perrott's Composition in 1585 (see Introd. p. xxix); aided O'Neill and O'Donnell in some of their campaigns, was pardoned by James, and died in 1612, much lamented by the literary and the needy. He appears to have been married three times, if I have rightly interpreted the reff. to feminine names in the poems addressed to him: I in **30** §§ 26-7; **32** § 82, and in poems by Írial son of Aonghus Ó Huiginn (3 B 14) and Fearghal Óg Mhac an Bhaird (ib), we have compliments to Máire dau. of Maol Muire, a scion of Clann Suibhne: the same lady may be alluded to by Maol Muire Ón Cháinte as *banua Bhriain mheic Eóghuin* (3 B 14). Brian son of Eóghan is evidently the father of Brian na Múrtha (**16**), and as O'Grady suggests (Cat. 425), the latter's sister, Gormlaith († 1585) is probably to be identified with Gormlaidh mother of Maol Mórdha Mhac Suibhne (**25** § 41). Máire then, would be sister to Maol Mórdha. **II** In other poems to Cormac, e. g. by Domhnall Óg and Maghnus Óg, sons of Aodh Ó Huiginn; and by the same Írial and Fearghal Óg cited above (3 B 14), we find compliments to Caitilín dau. of Toirdhealbhach, of the kindred of Raghallach. **III** In Pat. i James I vii p. 23 there is a pardon to 'Cormac O'Harie otherwise O'Harie boy of Teaghtemplae, gent. Une ny Gallothoire wife of said Cormac, Cormac oge O'Harie of the same, gent.' (i. e. Cormac's son, who † 1646, 3 B 14, 5). Úna was the name of Cormac's mother) **29** § 13, **30** § 23.

§ 4 'D . . . any,' other exx. of *ná léig idir* are: *a Thríonóid . . . ná léig eadrom is m'feitheamh* Timth. 1918, 43; *ná leig eadrainn agus inn* 'do not leave me to my own devices (?)' *Dán Dé* xxii 17; cf. the positive use: *lig edruinde 7 cách* ZfcP 6, 36 (Ir. Guy); similarly 6S; Acall. 2228, 3565.

§ 13 In the first line there is no elision between *Ní* and *ar* (*leg.* har?), but in the second the *a* must be elided. Cf. **32**. **83**.

§ 20 'laboriously,' or 'hastily (?);' but *d. saothair* seems to be a technical term, like *d. díchill* ZfcP 2, 252.

§ 26 *Gáille* 'Galey,' on Loch Ree, Co. Sligo; see Ériu 5, 68.

31

Here the poet has a theme beloved of panegyrists of all ages and climes; the transitory nature of material wealth contrasted with the permanence of panegyric:

At-chuala ra senaib sund . ferr molad [i]ná cech mod,
ná fitir Finnachta fial . co nach cian maras in crod. LL 306 b 24

§ 17 *Clár Crot*; in Tipperary? Cf. *Sliabh C.* Onom.

§ 20 ff., this apologue is taken from the story called Cath Maighe Léana, see O'Curry's ed., p. 4 ff.
Codhal, see **9** § 40 n.

§ 25 I do not understand *ealtuin sgean*; possibly it = *altain sg.* 'razors of knives,' 'i. e. their horns were as keen as sharp blades (?).

§ 26 *tánaigh*, *tána*; *tánaidh* is a form of the dat. sg. of *táin*, see TBC Gl. s. *tánad*. For dat. *tána* cf. *comha*, ds. *comha* or -*aidh*. Similarly *cánaigh* from *cáin* 31 § 32; see Contribb.

§ 33 -*monadh* 'money' (*moneta*); *dob fiú gach pinginn díbh sin .x. pinginne do monadh coitcinn in tírí* Lib. Flav. 11 6 b 2. 9. Cf. **44** § 8 n.

§ 34 *Áine*, Knockany, Co. Limerick.

§ 42 *b*. *Bládhma*, 'Slieve Bloom,' a vague allusion to the southern origin ascribed to the family.

§ 51 According to **32** § 64, Conn, Cormac's predecessor, held a perilous tenure of the land for eighteen years. Probably we are to add three years after Conn's death in 1581 to make up the twentyone, this brings us to 1584.

§ 59 *Gáirighe*: for decl. cf. *im Gháiridhe nglainiobhraigh* (: *d'áiridhe*) 23 D 14, 30 (Bk. No. 120).

§ 60 *leamhoid*; in the note in Introd. p. lxxxiv read *dhréachtaibh* : *léamhaidh*.

§ 61 *M. Maistean*, at Mullaghmast, Co. Kildare.

32

In illustration of this versified pedigree of Cormac Ó Heaghra I print here the

Genealogy of Cormac O'Hara, from O'Clery, the earlier part compared with MacFirbis, LL 338 h and Rawl. B 502 145 d.

RIA 23 D 17 p. 110.

38 Corbmac	23 m. Muirchertaigh (Murchada LL)
37 m Céin	
36 m Oilealla	22 m Domhnaill
35 m Magnusa	21 m Murchaid (Murchada LL)
34 m Ruaidri	20 m Maghnusa (Murgiusa LL)
33 m Seaáin Bhuidhe	19 m Eghra
32 m Taidhg	ó tá an sloinnedh (Egra
31 m Fergail Mhóir	Faprigh a quo .h. Egra LL)
30 m Domhnaill Cléirigh	18 m Saorghusa
29 m Airt na gCapall	17 m Becc (Becce LL and
28 m Diermada Riabhaigh	O'Gara Gen., O'CL)
27 m Aedha	16 m Flaithiusa (Lathgusa a
26 m Conchobhair Guitt	quo Cland Lathgusa LL)
25 m Aedha	15 m Taithligh (om. LL Taichligh
24 m Taithligh Urmhumhan	O'Gará Gen. O'Cl.)

14 m Cinn Faeladh
13 m Diermada
12 m Finnbairr
11 m m. Brénainn
10 m Nat Fraich
 9 m Hidin (Iden *no* Eoin LL)
 8 m Fidhchuire (Idchuir,
       Ithchaire LL)

 7 m Airt Chuirp (Airt Chirp LL)
 6 m Niadh Corb
 5 m Lui a quo Luighni (Loi
       o filet Lugni LL)
 4 m Corpmaic Gaileng
 3 m Taidhg
 2 m Céin
 1 m Oilealla Auluim

24 taichlig LL (urmhumhan *om.*). *In the ped. headed* .g. lugni connacht LL 338 h, 8-6 *are as follows*: m idchuir m niad corp m loi; *in that
headed* .g. lugne, *ib.*, 14-7 *are*: m cind faelad m findbairr m diarmata m dala
m coin m ithchaire m airt chirp. *Variants from MacFirbis* 666: Gnl. Uí
Eaghra Buidhe 28 diarmada riabhaigh no ruaidh 26 conchabhair nuid no
guid .i. bailbh 24 taithligh o r*áiter* loch tailtigh urmumha*n* 19 eaghra
paprigh a quo uí eaghra 17 bece 16 flaithghiusa ó ttad clann ílaithghiusa
15 taichligh 9 fidseng no fin*n*en no idhén no fidhen no iodhain (10-9 *cf.*
nat Fraoich mcEach⸗ mcFiodhcuire, MacFirbis 665ª) 7 airt ci*r*b 5 loi ó
ttáid luighne.

In Rawl. B 502, 145 d 15-2 *are*: m taiccthich m cind faelad m diarmata
m findbairr m brenaind m nad froech m hidin m hidchuir m niad chuirp
m lui *a quo* luigni m cornain m taidgc m cein a cais [*sic*] *here the ped. stops.*

The translation in I v 1, referred to in the footnotes, is headed:
A Latin poem containing the Names, Times, and Reign of the much
renowned and noble progeny of O'Hara according [*sic*] the most Authentic
& Warrantable Antiquaries of Ireland from the arival [*sic*] of the Milesians
Anno Mundi 2934 to Charles O'Hara of Leyny Esquire—Lord of the
Country of Leyny; Foreman & Chief Praesid^t. of his Lineage and Kindred
to this present Year One thous^d. seven hundred and fifty Eight—Translated
into Latin by Mr. John O'Gara out of the original Irish *Dán An áil libh
Seanchus Síol cCéin*, 7c Composed by the famous Irish poet Thady Higgins,
rendred into English by Mr. James O'Gara Junior B. A. [not in *Alumni
Dubl.*].

Scriptus per me Rodericus McDermott [= Ruaidhri Mhac Diarmada
on opp. page].

§ 21 A reference to the battle of Crionna, A. D. 248, where Tadhg
gained an award of land from Cormac mhac Airt by his prowess, see
Keat. ii, pp. 288-94.

§ 22 *C. Gailengach*; cf. Gen. 4. The first -*a*- is short: *Gailiong*:
uraigheall [sic leg.], 3 B 14, 91; cf. ZfcP 15, 96.

§ 25 I have not been able to locate *Magh Marr*, nor do I know
which *M. Tuireadh* is referred to, that in Cong, Co. Mayo, or E. of L. Arrow,
Co. Sligo. *Sliabh Muire* may be Slievemurry, Ballymoe, Co. Galway.

§ 26 *L. Laoigh*, in Burrishoole, Co. Mayo? See L. Laig, Hogan.

§ 37 *Taichleach* is the older form, see Gen., above, but I have retained the form with -*lt*- in the text as it is required by the metre in *l.* 149.

§ 58 *Tomaltach*, the -*m*- is not lenited in this name and is doubled in early MSS, e. g. LL 42 dy.

§ 64 Conn was slain by the Scots in 1581, in the skirmish referred to in Introd. p. xxviii. See preliminary note to **30**.

33

Addressed to a weapon belonging to one Aodh Óg, son of Aodh. O'Grady (Cat. 54) supposed him to be a Magennis of Iveigh, probably relying on the ref. to *Clann Eachach* in § 17, but there the poet may be likening the weapon to one of those rewards celebrated in ancient legend, and *codhnach cl. hE.* may refer to Aodh mhac Duach of Imtheacht na Tromdháimhe (Oss. v), although from him a shield, not a blade, was demanded.

§ 4 'black . . . door,' cf. **13** § 17 n.

§ 5 *mionn súla s.* is a very old traditional phr. Similarly *li súla* Wi.; *a ingealt súla sochnidhe* (to Cormac Ó Heaghra) 3 B 14, 52; cf. TBC 5417. Some such phr. may be recalled in *donnéici súil sochuide* (spectaculum facti sumus, etc.) Wb 9 a 4.

§ 8 Read: droichbhliadhna

§ 10 Read: ionnfuar,

§ 18 The first line should probably be rendered: when one shall have sought thee (i. e. if any shall be so importunate as to seek thee), cf. **18** § 11.

34

This difficult piece, although ascribed to Tadhg Dall in the only copy I know, is evidently not by him. It is addressed to O'Carroll, Maol Ruana(dh) son of Seaán son of Maol Ruana(dh); the Maol R. O'Carroll who † 1532, and was succeeded by his son Fer gan ainm is the only member of the family with this pedigree in O'Clery's Genealogies. This wealthy and powerful chief was connected by marriage with the Fitzgeralds, the Burkes and the Butlers, and his obituaries in FM, AU agree with this poem in their references to his hospitable customs and generosity to men of art and learning. See also Gleeson's *History of the Ely-O'Carroll Territory*, p. 25. His grandfather Maol Ruana(dh) may be the chief addressed by Tadhg Óg, YBL 28)a 31 (Quiggin, *Prolegomena* 16).

The piece is very corruptly transmitted, apparently with some interpolated matter, and many passages are hopelessly obscure. Further, the MS is torn and illegible in several places, so that the gaps in the translation are of necessity frequent and wide.

§ 14 *An Cruadhchosach* also appears in D. Ó Bruadair i p. 98, where the editor, perhaps rightly, takes *Léanaigh* as a place-name.

§ 20 This tale seems cognate with the anecdote of foolish Jack in Kennedy's *Legendary Fictions of the Irish Celts* (1891), pp. 37-8.

§ 21 *Port an Phúdair*; a place-name? Hardly a ref. to the court of pie powder.

§ 22 Read: *nGrúdainn*; the *Grúda* is identified with the river Groody in Limerick by Father MacErlean, D. Ó Bruadair i p. 75.

§ 24 *Crosán*; this appears to have been the term for the minstrel who declaimed pieces in this style, see ZfcP 12, 290-1 and RC 28, 318 and cf. D. O'Br. ii p. 90.

§ 25 I have not been able to trace the source of this story about Walter Map, nor do I know where or when the proverbial saying about 'greasing the fat pig' originated; Professor O'Rahilly writes to me that it "seems to be in most languages ... Cf. for Irish, Morris, No. 1013; Gael. Journ. 1896, 104; 1906, 154. In English I note 'Greaze a fat sowe in the tayle' in J. Clarke's *Adagia Anglo-Latina* (1639), p. 220. Manx has: *Slaa sahll er t-yn muck roauyr.* Welsh: *Iro tin hwch a bloneg* and *Iro'r hwch dew a bloneg.* I have seen it also in Spanish, French and German."

It may be worth noting that although Morris gives "Bringing coals to Newcastle" as the English analogue of this saying, 'greasing the fat pig' is usually applied not to a useless, unnecessary proceeding generally, but specially to a possibly useful one, the bestowal of gifts where they are not required, in the hope of obtaining present or future favor thereby. This is the application in the story above.

'Carew,' for *mac an ch.* cf. *An carrúnach .i. Piotur carrun* [slain in the rebellion of James Eustace] FM 1580. I do not know what Carew is referred to above, but apparently one of some standing. Sir Peter Carew, whose heir was the *Piotur* of FM, did not arrive in Ireland till 1567-8, when he found the barony of Idrone, which the Carews claimed, in the possession of the Kavanaghs.

§ 28 *Muintear T.*, see App. C, 3 Cú Choigcriche.

§ 37 For the story referred to here see Ir. Monthly 1921, 27.
Dele foot-note to line 239.

35

Although I have printed this piece in four-lined stanzas, the division is not metrically justified, and a paragraph arrangement would have been better, as each line has not only the same end-rime, but the same stressed vowel alternation throughout, viz:

$$\genfrac{}{}{0pt}{}{e^{(a)}}{o} \quad \bar{a} \ \breve{\imath} \cup \breve{\imath} \cup \breve{\imath} \cup \bar{a}$$

The first stress is usually *ea* or *a*, but in lines 12, 14, 26, 28, 32, 34, 39, we have *o*; in lines 2, 16, 30, 41, *io*, where the *o* may be the essential

sound, as for instance in some pronunciations of *iomdha* today. In 9
ghabháil is perhaps to be sounded as one syllable, with *ā*; in that case
we should have *o* here also; but in line 21 *gabháil* must be dissyllabic.
The second stress falls in most cases on a syllable not naturally stressed
in ordinary speech, e. g. in lines 3, 4, 18 etc. it falls on an *ἰarmbéarla*.
The final stress, moreover, may be on the last syllable of a word of two
or more syllables. Naturally short *a* followed by a double consonant,
broad or slender is equivalent to *ā*; thus *Seadin* apparently rimes with
rann, ceall, badhbh, ainm. Note also *aird* : *faill* : *Flann* in § 1. I leave
to others the question as to whether these rimes represent a local dialect
or a literary convention. It is obvious at any rate that the style in which
the piece is composed is one which has been cultivated for a considerable
period.

　　　The chief addressed was father of the celebrated *Fiachaidh Ó Broin*
'Feagh O'Byrne' of Glenmalure (*Gleann Maoil Ughra*) Co. Wicklow, 'the
fierbrand of the mountaines between Dublin and Wexford.' Aodh Ó Broin
died in 1579. See O'Grady's notes on the family, Cat. 499 ff.

　　　I am indebted to Professor T. F. O'Rahilly for solving some of the
difficulties of this piece, but most of it remains obscure to me.　·

　　　§ 1　*Flann*, cf. *Ridgeway Essays* 346 § 37. The fourth line seems
corrupt; it apparently contains a reference to *Carn Uí Néid*, near Mizen
Head, Co. Cork, and *haoil* should perhaps be emended to *hAoile = Oileach.*
Possibly we should read *Néidmhagh Cairn* 'the *Néd*-plain of Carn' a kind
of slang form of the old placename; cf. *a dtéidchrot meann* § 8. This of
course is merely a dubious conjecture.

　　　§ 2　Here *leath* may be imperat. sg. 2, and *dá* may stand for *do*
'thy.' As this reading improves the sense I have followed it in the translation. The reading *dá* is required for the rime, so possibly this is a
dialectical pronunciation of *do*, cf. line 17, where I have adopted in the
translation the conjectural reading *sleagh do bhíodh*; here again the rime
requires *dá*.

　　　'woodbine,' see 9 § 2 n.

　　　In fourth line read: *féineachtrann* ('banded foreigners').

　　　§ 3　*eas . . . eang* 'a stoat under a line of griffins on the embroidery
of banners' (?).

　　　§ 4　'gauntlet,' Prof. O'R. points out that the true reading is: 's bolard
or: 's molard; *molárd* or *malárd* 'gauntlet' is found in 17th cent. texts.
　　　each díola is used of a saddle-horse or charger, contrasted with
e. iomchair 'pack-horse;' e. g. *an t-each díola nach díol damh . 'san
t-each iomchair gan iomchar* (sic leg.) Tribes of Ireland p. 48. The
literal meaning of the term is not clear; is it an old rendering of *cheval
de prix*?

　　　díon may = *dian* 'swift,' but I have no parallel.

　　　§ 5　See note on § 2. Prof. O'Rahilly points out to me that we
should read: réThuireann "the allusion being to the spear of the 'King

of Persia' secured by the Sons of Tuireann [in Oidhe Cloinne Tuireann Atlantis iv]. The prefixed ré- I suppose stands for réidh-, though there is a possibility of its being a variant of ri- (see Gadelica i 276-7)."

§ 6 'therefrom,' lit. 'through (because of) thee.'

§ 7 'from those who;' read: on account of the number which In the third line the metre requires: 'so

§ 8 Read: A seasoned vigorous throng under him a dteidchrot meann = dtéadaibh meannchrot; cf. 25 § 18 n.

§§ 9-10 seem to refer to games and needlework; as the text is very uncertain I do not attempt a translation.

§ 10 Read: Seantráill and perhaps: ag géaradh crann. As Prof. O'R. points out, the transposition: is beart dá fighe don taoighe, etc. would improve the second line metrically; but if the text is right is don to be pronounced dán? See note on § 2.

§ 11 The ā rime is missing after an tan, unless we are to lengthen the vowel of as. We might read tann but this would raise two difficulties; the preceding syllable would be incorrect, and there is no other instance in the piece of a syllable between ā and i here.

36

This piece relates to five members of the Irish nobility who were absent from Ireland at the time of its composition. We need not take the statement that they were all in London in a narrow literal sense. Some may have been at Oxford, or other educational establishments, in accordance with Cecil's plan for putting 'gentlemen's sons to school in England' (CSPI 1562 p. 188). As we have no collateral evidence for the date of the poem beyond the ascription to Tadhg Dall (which would place it, roughly, between 1560 and 1591), it is not easy to identify the individuals unmistakeably. Dounchadh Ó Conchobhair can hardly be other than D. son of Cathal (14) nephew and successor of Donnell of 15. He went to England in 1588 to present his case to the authorities there, but the poem must refer to an earlier visit, as he is not called Ó Conchobhair. He was probably educated in England, like his uncle Eóghan (CSPI 1369, 408), although his name is not recorded in Alumni Oxonienses. See O'Grady 355. He died in 1609 and was succeeded by his brother Donnell, who had been 'bred up in the wars of France' (Wood-Martin's Hist. of Sligo ii 10). Donnchadh Ó Briain is probably D. Óg son of Conchobhar, afterwards fourth earl of Thomond, who was brought up at the English court. Irial Ó Fearghail may be the Iriel O'Farrell [Boy] who was 'a suitor in England' about the captainship of his kindred in 1589 (CSPI 1588-9 pp. 102 119, 280 etc.; Pat. Rolls. Eliz. 257). Pádraicín Plunket must surely be the "Patrick Plunket, baron of Dunsany in Ireland," who "was sent to Oxford to obtain logicals and philosophicals," and was renowned among the learned in fifteen hundred eighty and four;" see Stanihurst's Descr. Hibern. c. 7; Wood's Athenae Oxonienses (Bliss) 505-6. Brian Mhág

Eochagán I take to be he who slew his brother Rossa in 1580, and was subsequently a refugee on the continent (FM; CSPI 1588, 484; 1589, 153 etc.; Pat. Rolls Eliz. 1587).

It would be idle to pretend to identify the three of § 15; the names of the first two suggest Burkes.

§ 7 For *Lundain* (with hard *d*) beside *Lunnainn* cf. MacNeill's Irish Ogham Inscriptions 22 (PRIA 1909, xxvii C 15).

37

There is an anonymous copy in H 4. 14, flyleaf. It omits §§ 4, 5, 8.

38

O'Curry describes this poem as being "on a pretended friar." The ascription to Tadhg Dall is doubtful, as there was no earl in Sligo in his day. The metre is an imitation of *rannaigheacht bheag*, the rimes being *bruilingeacht* or *amus*.

§ 7 'rent?' I am not sure of the meaning of *brollach* here.

§ 9 Read: prevented it from being sold.

39

The description of feminine beauty in this *aisling* is curiously traditional, some of the comparisons recall the opening paragraphs of *Togal Bruidne Da Derga*, RC 22, pp. 14-15.

§ 3 *dearca* etc., cf. *batir glasithir buga na di súil* YBL 91 a 22 (= BrDD § 2); *cosmail fri buga a suili* (of Cormac mac Airt) Ir. Texte iii 186; "like bluebells were his eyes," Stokes, who cites the gloss *bugha .i. luibh ghorm glas* 'a blue-gray herb' from BB 261a marg. sup. See Tor. Gr. Gr., Gloss. s. *bugh*.

§ 5 For *fras néamhann* also cf. Br. DD § 2; Ir. Texte iii 186. For *ós* see *Dánta P. Feiritéir*, Dinneen, p. 70; Marstr., *Bidrag* p. 125; but the two couches should refer to the lips themselves; *parluinge* is evidently gen. of a corruption of Mid. Ir. *partaing, batir dergithir partaing na beoil* YBL 91 a 23 (= Br. DD § 2); *dar let ba dual partaingi a bhél* Ir. Texte iii 186. See Wi. and Ériu 3, 96 § 5. Stokes explained the word as founded on Lat. *parthicus (pellis)* 'leather dyed of a scarlet red, prepared by the Parthians.' Ir. T. iii 222. Cf. ITS i 52.

§ 6 'with long hands,' *glac leabhar* is attrib. gp., see Introd. p. lxix.

§ 8 'formed the vest;' this is wrong; I do not understand *ionair*, it seems to be *ar* 'tillage,' with the pref. *in-* 'fit for, worth,' but I am not sure how this can be worked into the content.

§ 9 'noble-looking,' *deaghaighthe* is gen. of *deagh aghaidh* 'noble countenance.'

§ 14 Read: re hanmain

§ 15 A reference to the tale *Echtra Conảla*, see *The Voyage of Bran* p. 144 ff. and Best 106.

§ 17 A reference to the tale *Imram Brain maic Febail*, see Meyer's ed. *The Voyage of Bran.*

§ 18 Though *naonbhar* may be an old neuter we should here read: *naonbhair*. The number given in *Imram Brain* (p. 17) is *tri nónbuir*.

§ 20 *S. Midhir*, west of Ardagh, Co. Longford; as *Mag Sainb* is a name of *Mag nAoi* in Roscommon, *Dún S.* may be an alias of *Sioth Cruachan*, the Fairy-mound of Croghan, Boyle. Cf. Sián Clárach 114. *S. Abhartaigh?* Cf. Dún Aberte, Onom. *Abhartach* was one of the Tuatha Dé leaders, see Ériu 8, 44.

§ 21 *Eamhain*, see **5** § 9 n.; mansion of *A.*, i. e. *Brugh na Bóinne.*

§ 22 *gan ... orom* 'what would thwart me (*budh éigin orom*) is, not to be a sojourner in her land, were it possible (?).'

This piece is probably referred to in the poem beginning *An tú táinig go Tadhg Dall?* see App. D, infra.

40

§ 7 'flocks,' a punning reference to the homonym *cuach* 'cuckoo' (the bird of summer) and 'ringlet of hair;' cf. *Dánta Grádha* pp. 1-2.

§ 10 *Aodh*, this line may be corrupt; *Sliabh Aighe meic Úghaine* was a name for *Sliabh na mBan (bhFionn)* = *Siodh na mB. bhF.* 'Slievenaman' NE of Clonmel, see Acall. 5003 (SG ii 222).

§ 11 Cf. Gadelica i 280.

§ 12 Perhaps a reference to the Sick-bed of Cú Chulainn.

§ 13 I do not know the story referred to here.

§ 14 I am not sure of the precise reference.

§ 15 See **39** § 17 n.

§ 17 See **39** § 15 n.

§ 20 *S. na gCuan?* cf. Loch Cuan.

§ 21 The reading of the second line is doubtful.

S. Truim may be the mound on the left bank of the Boyne, or it may be used here of *S. Midhir* in Longford (**39** § 20). See Onom.

41

This is addressed to the Calvach, the only son of Donnell O'Conor Sligo and Mór. See above, p. 249, and Introd. p. xxix.

§ 14 'S. Murray,' the descendants of *Muireadhach Muilleathan*, k. of Connacht, who † 701. See LgC pp. x, 107-8, and ZfcP 8, 292. 32.

42

Apparently an appeal to the leaders of the *Clann Domhnaill Gallóglach*.

§ 1 'Plain of Mar,' here *Magh Marr* may be Mar in Scotland, or the place referred to in **32** § 25.

43

The special interest of these badly preserved stanzas is that they connect the manuscript remains of Tadhg Dall with the living tradition of the present day. No traditions, so far as I can ascertain, are to be found about Tadhg in his native county, but his memory still lives in the Irish-speaking parts of Co. Donegal, and these stanzas occur in an anecdote of him taken down by Professor Edmund Curtis from the narration of Seán Ruadh Mac a' Bháird and Domhnall Ó Baoighill, of Classy, near Doochary, in the summer of 1916. The anecdote was published by Professor Curtis in An Crann, Nodlaic 1916; and with his permission I reprint it here, together with an anonymous MS version of some of the other lines. A slightly fuller version of the whole story has been published by Feargus Mac Róigh in *Oidhche Áirnéil* (Sr. Bhaile Dúin Dealgan 1924). Amongst the metrical portions can be recognized portions of the stanzas printed on p. 284-5 below.

Seal fada bliadhanta ó šoin bhí Tadhg Ó hUigín thiar i gConnachtaibh agus Niall Mac a Bháird i dTír Chonaill . Bhí Ó Domhnaill Dhúin na nGall pósta ar nighean d'Ó Crochuir Sligeach. Lá amháin casadh Ó Domhnaill agus Ó Crochuir ar a cheile agus chuir siad geall mór eadar Niall agus Tadhg[1] a fiachail ceacú ab fearr a dhéanfadh rannai. Chaith siad cruinn ceacú rachadh Niall siar fad le Tadhg no Tadhg a theacht aniar chuig Niall, agus thuit sé ar Thadhg a theacht aniar. Tharluigh nuair a thainic sé go rabh mac óg ag bean Mhac a Bháird, agus rinneadh cáirdeas Críost do Thadhg. Baisteadh Adhamh ar an ghasúr óg. D'fan Tadhg seal laethe ag Niall Mac a Bháird, agus d'imigh abhaile ar ais gan rann ar bith a dheánamh. Bliadhanta 'na dhéigh sin casadh Ó Domhnaill agus Ó Crochuir ar a cheile aríst, agus chuir siad na geallta as a nuadh ar ais. Thainic Tadhg aniar annsin go dí teach Néill Mhac a Bháird.

[1] Tadhg was O'Conor Sligo's poet, according to the tradition in Gweebarra (An Crann p. 17; *Oidhche A.* p. 21).

Nuair a thainic an oidhche chóirigh bean Néill leabaidh ag taobh na teineadh
do Thadg agus chuir sí an bheirt gasúr (an mac ba śine agus Adhamh)
'na luighe aige, fear acú ar gach taobh dó. I gcionn tamaill d'iarr fear
de na gasraí :— Leig liom an t-éadach, adeir sé.

    Tá do cheart agat dó, arsan gasúr eile.

    Roinnigidh eadaraibh féin e, arsa Tadhg, tá misc a lár eadaraibh.

    Bhí sgian ag an ghasúr ba śine, agus rois sé an t-éadach ó bhun go
bárr léithe. Tharraing gach fear acú a leath air agus d'fág Tadhg maol
tárnocht a lár. Annsin chuir bean Mhac A Bháird fallainn Néill ar
Thadhg le n-a choinneal te. Ghlac Tadhg fearg mhór agus thoisigh sé ar
rannuigheacht :

> Goidé 'tchím eadar mé agus léas
>   ach dhá chúpla dhéag 'na luighe ar bán ;
> agus śílim féin gur leór an tocht
>   do chluinn bhoicht Néill Ach Bháird.

> Cóirigh faoim agus tharam
>   is ísiol a clumh is ní hárd
> 'sis fada a bhí sin 'na bréid
>   an fallainn seo Néill Ac[h] Bháird.

Nior labhair Niall leis seo, agus dubhairt Tadhg aríst :

> [1] Clann Ach a Bháird,
> cúl lom corrach gan coirníneach,
> báthadh orthä ach gan Ádhamh orthú,
> is mairg a tarluigh eatorrú

Deir Niall annsin :

> Cha né sin, ar sé, ach —
>   Clann a' Bháird,
>   cúl trom dlaoitheach na gcoirníneach,
>   mar bualadh deilbh ar a dan ;
>   no mar Tadhg a cheanglochaí ar Uigín
>   bhíos a tarraingt orrainn gach aonlá
>   ag gabhail na triobloide.

Deir Tadhg annsin :

> Glas seilc agus síor ar an tslagaire,
> sin fear do bheir geall do gach glagaire. [2]

Deir Mac a' Bháird annsin :

> Is geur bearradh do d[h]eimhse,
> agus ar do ghoile níl cuimse ;
> is duine roimsceach thú os cionn beinnse,
> is mór do cíleamh do bhiadh na bainnse.

---

[1] This is evidently a version of **43** ll. 1-4.

[2] Cf. p. 284 infra. This line may be rendered : there is the man
who excels every babbler, i. e. the biggest babbler of all.

Deir Tadhg annsin (bhí Niall ruadh):

> [1] Dheánfaidh me rann don raduire
> ruadh riabhach nach ridire;
> sladuidhe ar dhual duid bréaguighcacht.

Annsin dubhairt Mac a' Bháird:

> Budh è d'athair féin fear siubhalta reatha
> mar ghadhar a tafaint a ndéigh na sealg;
> Anti-Chríost tíre Bhanbha,
> is mairg a chunuailfeadh a theanga dó;
> diabhal dall bhios da lion.hadh ar lic Ifrinn [2]
> a séid tú [3] a Dhaill Uí Uigin.

> [4] Is tú an finghineach fealltach, fealltach finghineach,
> sginnideach sgathmhar, sgathmhar sginnideach;
> léisineach garanach gránna,
> lom ladhrach leicineach.

Tachtadh Tadhg annsin, agus ní rabh sé ábalta ní ba n.ó a rádh. Phreab sé 'na seasamh, d'fág an áit, agus bhi an bhuaidh le Niall.

---

[1] Cf. the stanzas below.
[2] Cf. 43, concluding lines.
[3] This may be the correct version, 'inspired, incited, thee.' It should be noted that *a séad tú* is not "a very old phrase frequent in the Ms literature," meaning "you resemble," an explanation credited to the present writer in *Oidhche Airneáil* p. 69 (cf. the ed. in An Crann p. 18 note 6). The word *séad* is very old, and frequent in literature with the meaning 'a like, a similitude': *ní fuar a ssét acht Maire* 'I have not found her like save Mary,' Broccán's Hymn, *l.* 98. Such a construction as *a séad tú* with the meaning 'you are its like' would not be absolutely impossible in early Middle Irish verse, but it is extremely doubtful that it could be used here.
[4] Cf. the stanzas below, ll. 9-12.

RIA 23 L 32, p. 36, no heading.

Do-dheanfuinn rann don raduire
ruadh ariamh nach ruidire;
breaguire baoith nach bárd an braduire,
sladuire bídh ar bord an pricuire.

Dubhairt me nár ghreann don ghlioguire;   5
truduire é fuair geall gach glaguire;
fear do chló sméimh gach sgriobuire,
gluguire mór gan chéill an clabuire.

MS. Readings: 3 báird.
4 *possibly* pricuire.

Sgidíneach sgártha sgathmhar sginideach,
fiomínach fán fághalta an feidineach 10
gortíneach gann gan ghreann an goiruideach;
leisíneach lom lothartha leithcionach.

An chrónbhruisg ghránna dána danardha dian,
gan órd crábhadh, gan tráth gan phaidir gan bhia;
seóil tar sáile is gárrtha mallacht na ndiaigh, 15
brútar, báitear, gearthar, trasgarthar iad.

---

9 gh *cancelled after* sgathmhar   12 lothartha: cf. locharthi *Burdúin Bheaga* § 164   13 dána] *danna* MS   14 pháidir   13-16 *do not seem to belong to the preceding stanzas, although not separated from them in* MS.

44

After Vol. i had been printed off I found that I had overlooked an excellent copy of this piece, in a good 17th cent. script, pasted down inside the cover at end of II 5. 32 (H⁴). There is no heading. It is obviously the original of G, as can be seen from its variants (given below) from our printed text, and the note appended to G by O'Curry, suggesting that he had transcribed it from a MS "Pasted down on the inside of the cover at the end" of a MS in "Archbishop Tenison's library . . . London, May 4th, 1855". H⁴, we learn from the Abbot-Gwynn Cat. p. 265, was purchased at the sale of Archbishop Tenison's library in 1861. Tenison's MS collection was as old as 1695 (ib. p. xvi n.).

(I have noted in squ. brackets concordances with G omitted above and a few further varr. from H² H³).

Varr. from H⁴: 1 tha.; thoigh   4 siolánach   5-8 *om.*   9-12 *added after* 48 *with a direction to insert the stanza after* § 5   9 t. dhiom sbudh doiligh sin   11 nochar bfoláir   12 is mór   14 ata an tamhgar   16 sas peaca dh.   17 a bía.   18 cidh bé; a ta.   22 chethairnn   23 fer dámo lór b. da bh.   24 nochar; nó   28 leigemh [léig7 H² leigfe H³] uaim   31 sé sa [*sic* H² H³] mhan   33 c. an ch. fer [*sic* G]   34 ghluaiseas leó [*sic* G]; sgio(d)al [sgio:al G]   35 cheire   36 nochar [*sic* G]; casnach [*sic* G]   40 an í. [*sic* G]   41 man g. nachar bhfiu frigh   42 tainig le [*sic* G]   43 gan ghné ngl.   44 drocharadh ar feachain   45 guidhim an righ [*sic* G]   46 ó sé a mbas [*sic* G]   47 bidh nach buan [*sic* G] a marthuin   48 marbhthar [*sic* G]

Thus we can distinguish three traditions: HO'R, H² H³, and H⁴ G. In the case of each pair the first was obviously the source of the second, so we have in fact only to consider three MSS, of which the latest, II (Introd. p. xciii 67), is the only one that connects the piece with the tradition of Tadhg's maltreatment (Introd. p. xv ff.). The others are both of the

17th century, but I cannot tell which is the earlier. II⁴, which is anonymous, presents on the whole the most correct text, as far as it goes.

O'Grady gives a spirited rendering, Cat. 440, but his text is bad, and his emendations seldom confirmed by better copies.

II contains an English transl. by O'Donovan, and O'R includes one by Peter O'Connell, which I give here, as it is worth preserving. I follow the MS. exactly in spelling etc., but I run on the lines, to save space, and add the number of each stanza. The original is IIO'R.

A Satyr composed by blind Thady O Higgin on a Band of the O Haras — for which they deprived him of his Tongue

1 A Host of Six that came to my House — Of whom I will relate — : Scarce of Milk I on the morrow, From the Thirst of the Six Starvelings.

2 Long theretofore — According to opinion — That not a bit of beefy Food Got into the Limbs — of the trio or two aforesᵈ —.

3 It happed to me — Whence sprung the ill — to take them from Death to Life — To drink my Milk was behove ful — From the great thirst of the dry Bread —.

4 My Loss — & what they deserve — Between which I am dilemmaed¹ To hide these verses is hard for me And it's Sin for me to make them. —

5 Better not to hide the Satyr — whoe'er deserves dispraise As I satyrised the Host of Six It's unfit not to relate it.

6 The first man we saw of the Band the best dressed (was) a Fellow whose full worth was a Groat to him who was not baned by Drink or Play.

7 The second Man as I found him Who came in front of the Tribe A lean man who lost his Marrow I'll not pass him unrecounted.

---

¹ O'D. (?) has underlined the last three words in pencil. and pencilled in marg.: this is wrong [sic] translated. In O'D.'s transl. the line is misrendered: misery dwells amongst them. This would be fairly accurate for some copies, but not for HO'R. O'D.'s transl. of the previous line "want on me, and compulsion on them," is more accurate than that of P. O'C., who possibly confuses 'deserve' and 'require' in this case.

8 The attire of the third Scoundrel—An old Dart & a gapped untempered Axe He—! & his Battle-axe in Fight! Ah me—! the fighting Suit—!

9 The habiliment of the 4th man—who marched with them full of Skitting—Four Darts crosswise on his Rump which never chipped a Target—

10 At the foot of the other four comes the fifth wretchling[1]—! with a short Shirt, not worth a Groat I think his Mantle was not better—

11 A Warrior-fellow not worth a Flesh worm—who was at the foot of the five—A rawboned Man—Unclean of face a bad warrant he for Battle—

12 I pray God who shed his Blood,—As it's their decay—to remain living That State being barely to exist
May the Host of Six not be } killed—.
                            } murdered—.

---

[1] There is a small horizontal stroke across the -in-; possibly the writer intended to delete the second syllable.

§ 1 'vagabonds,' cf. P. O'C.'s tr. He has in his Dict. "*sealánach* a hangman, a villain, a rascal." Cf. Dinneen.

§ 3 *turarán*, cf. Aisl. MeicConGl. p. 199.; read with H⁴ G: is mór 'great is the thirst (caused by) dry bread.'

§ 8 'makings' (?); I have taken *bunaidh* as pl. of *bunadh* 'foundation'. Possibly we should read (as in § 11) *munadh* 'pattern,' see ZfcP 1, 434; *don monadh sin* 'according to that pattern (?)' Ir. Gr. Tr., Decl. § 58 (cf. 31 § 33 n.). We should then read *culadh* in next line (cf. perhaps Ir. Gr., Decl. p. 54. 5; exx. 348, 360). O'Gr., whose text has *bhunadh : chulaidh*, renders: "himself and his ancient family axe."

§ 11 'transparent;' O'Gr., reading *go ngné ngloin*, renders the line: "attenuated varlet of a glassen species." Cf. P. O'C. The more likely reading is *gan ghné ngl.* 'uncleanly of hue.'

§ 12 'since ... living;' the rendering from H⁴ G is: 'since it is their death for them to be living—even though they cannot permanently survive—.'

ADDITIONAL POEMS

The two following pieces were accidentally omitted from the first volume, and are added here with translation and notes.

45

UAIMH PÁDRAIG

1   S . . . cht na bpeacthach Uaimh Pádraig,
     beag na sáraidh Uaimh Letha;
     port glanta anma ó phianaibh,
     glanRóimh iarthair in bhetha.

2   Do-chual (?) go roibhi treimsi   5
     ardesbuc Innsi hEalga,
     mac Calp[ru]inn co gcruas gcrabhaidh,
     san uaimh far lamhaidh demhna.

3   Bheith a n-uaimh chu[mh]aing cloichi
     nír motha ar grádh Íosa   10

    . . . .

MS.: Advocates' Lib. LXIV 23ª.

MS. Readings: 1 uaim 2 saraidh uaim 3 anma o fp. 4 iarthar
read: for lámhaibh?   10 ar gra *after this line a line is left blank; the remaining legible words* on the page are:

      Glor Muire . . . a mic
      . . . ie hucht b(ái)s an uain oirdhric
      . . . eilbh Dhe ni dealph cosm*uil*
      m(a)s e ar lenb in lenbsuin

but these evidently belong to a different piece.

46

LEABA PHÁDRAIG

1 Teach leagha leaba Phádraig
san inis ghuirm ghlanfádbhuig
an aolchloch chorcra chuinsigh
caomthach ochta an éarloimhsin.

2 Do bhí Pádraig Phuirt Manaidh
i bhfad innti ag anamhain,
cois míonchalaidh na srealbh seang,
ag síorchabhair fear nÉireann.

3 Rug an bás, mar do bhí i ndán,
ó chrích Fódla na n-uarán
liaigh cabhartha Cláir Criomhthain,
fáidh adhartha dh'Éireannchaibh.

4 Foireann luingi ar lot an chinn,
nó tréad do bhiadh gan buaichill,
Gaoidhil i ndiaidh a ndeighfir,
liaigh gach aoinfir d'fóiridhin.

5 Fágbhais éarlamh Insi Cuinn
mar buachail othair againn
ar ngéag bhuadha, ar gcraobh chomhdha,
maor na huamha allmhardha.

6 . . . cách ré ndul dáibh
go hUaimh Pádraig an phríomhfáidh,
fan lia saor cneasbháinte cuir
gan taom d'easláinte d'anmain.

7 Do-ghéabha gach lot [li]bh féin
ón bhuachaill othair ainnséin,
luit nuadha cneasfoirfe cáigh
cneasaighthi uadha d'éanláimh

5

10

15

20

25

MS.: Advocate's Lib. LXIV 28ª.

MS. Readings: 1 fp.   2 gu. glan fotbuig   5 íp. manaigh   6 a bf.
10 f. na bfu.   14 bia gan buachall   23-24 *text doubtful*   25 ? lot . . bhfe

E. Knott, Tadhg Dall Ó Huiginn.

19

8 . . . . . dá éis soin
  cuirthear leis an lucht álaidh   30
  san uaimh seada chaoilligh chuir
  leaba gach aoinfir othair.

9 . . . . . teach leagha (?) an leabaidh
  bíodh slán cháigh gur chuireadair
  i n-uaimh éarluimh an einigh   35
  éanghuin nach fuair fóiridhin.

10 Dlighidh gach duine ar domhan
   d'éis a geneadh do chneasughadh
   san uaimh fádbháin ghéagaigh glain
   fágbháil a n-éadaigh othair.   40

11 Tarla linn don leath amuigh,
   don taobh eile don uamhaidh,
   d'fothragadh cháich ó' geneadhaibh,
   lochthobar bláith bordsleamhain.

12 Créacht dá duilghi ní dheachaidh   45
   fan linn bhfairsing bhfoirleathain,
   an tsreabh lionnbhán tiormghlan te
   nach tiobhradh iomlán uaithe.

13 . . . adhbha bhus soillsi soin
   beith 'na huaimh dorcha diamhair;   50
   ní bhfuair neach adhbha dob fearr
   an teach i dtarla Tailgeann.

38 cnedh

45

PATRICK'S CAVE

1 . . . of sinners is the Cave of Patrick, it almost excels the Cave of Letha; a haven to cleanse the soul from torment, bright Rome of the west of the world.

2 I have heard (?) that the high bishop of the Isle of Elg, Calporn's son severe in piety, was for a while in the cave in the hands of demons.

3 Being in a narrow stone cave he noticed not for love of Jesus . . .

46

PATRICK'S BED

1   Patrick's bed — the crimson ... (?) limed stone — is the house of a healer; in the blue isle of bright fertile sods is the bosom comrade (?) of that patron.

2   Patrick of the haven of *Monadh* tarried there a long while, by the smooth shore of slender streams, ever succouring the men of Ireland.

3   Death, as was destined, took from the cool-springed land of *Fódla* the healer who aided *Criomhthan's* Plain; the adored prophet of the Irish people.

4   The crew of a ship when the head has been destroyed (?), or a flock without a shepherd, are the Gaels without their champion, the healer who could cure all.

5   The patron of Conn's Isle hath left us as an attendant to the sick our precious scion, our guarding branch, the steward of the fearsome cavern.

6   ... each one when going to the Cave of the primate Patrick, by the noble stone, white and dry of surface, without any disease remaining (?).

7   From the sick attendant then each hurt of yours (?) — the fresh, skin-perished (?) hurts of all — will be simultaneously healed.

8   After that he places the wounded ..., in the long ... cavern the bed of each sick man.

9   ... the bed, let all be challenged (to show) that they placed in the cave of the generous patron one wound which did not find relief.

10   Each one after his wounds have been healed is obliged to leave his raiment of sickness in the clean, branching, white-floored cave.

11   Without, on the far side of the cave, is a pool to wash all from their wounds, a shining smooth-banked lake-spring.

12 No wound, however grievous, was ever dipped neath the wide, spreading pool, the bright-pooled, dry, clear, warm, stream that it would not bring out of it hale.

13 ... the most lightsome abode, to be in the dark, gloomy cave; none ever found a better dwelling (than) the house in which Tailgeann tarried.

NOTES

45

For transcriptions of this fragment I am indebted to the late Dr. E. C. Quiggin and Professor W. J. Watson. It appears to relate to the Cave or Purgatory, while 46 is concerned mainly with Patrick's Bed. For the mediaeval legends and beliefs about the cave known as The Purgatory of Patrick, on the island of Loch Derg, Tirhugh, Co. Donegal, see the Rev. St. J. D. Seymour's *St. Patrick's Purgatory* (Dundalk 1918), Florence MacCarthy's *Three Dramas of Calderon*, and Pinkerton's history of the cave, Ulster Journal of Archaeology iv-v. Further reff. will be found in Seymour.

§ 1 'the Cave of Letha,' ? some famous resort of Christian pilgrims must be meant. The next line suggests a reference to the catacombs.
'Rome,' cf. in same MS the initial line *Loch Derg athRoimh* (sic leg.? or *ainR*. cf. II 4. 4, p. 86) *na hEirind, Prolegomena* 53.

§ 2 'Isle of Elg,' *Inis Ealga* was an old name of Ireland, Keat. ch. i. Cf. 26 § 13.
'in the hands,' translating the reading suggested in footnote.

46

For a transcript of this piece I am also indebted to the kindness of Professor Watson. It is one of a group of poems on the Loch Derg cave, apparently in commemoration of a pilgrimage thereto by the composers, viz Tadhg Dall, Fearghal Óg Ó Huiginn, Fearghal Óg Mhac an Bhaird, Aonghus son of Aodh Ruadh Ó Huiginn (see App. C), and another whose name is missing in the Edinburgh MS. Cf. II 4. 4, 86-7 (= 24 L 28, 332-4), where apparently two or three poems on the subject are jumbled together. It is not clear that the ascription to Aonghus Ó Dálaigh (Abbott-Gwynn Cat p. 170) belongs to any of them.

The cheerful tone of Tadhg Dall's poem is in remarkable contrast to the lugubrious verses ascribed to Donnchadh Mór, Gael. Journ iv 190 (another ed. Timthire vi 2, p. 40).

§ 1 *Leaba Ph.*, the piece seems principally concerned with the 'circle or cell' known as Patrick's Bed; "Towards the narrowest part of the island are six circles, or cells, or saint's beds, for penance. These are mansions (for so they are termed) dedicated to some of the famous Irish saints. They are of stone and round . . ." (from a seventeenth cent. description quoted U. J. A. v 71. The saints' names are given as: Collumkille, Katherine, Patrick, Avogh, Moloisse and Brendan, cf. Seymour p. 90).

'crimson . . . stone,' I take the third line to follow the first in sense. 'comrade;' I am not sure of the meaning here.

§ 3 'adored prophet,' *adhartha* might be gen. of *adhradh* 'following, adhering to' (20 § 6), but I take *fáidh a.* to be modelled on *dia adhartha*, see TTebe 2590 etc., Contribb.

§ 6 'primate;' for *priomhfáidh* here and in 7 § 16 cf. *primfaid Arda Macha .i. in Coltunach in Xo qui*[*evit*] C iii 1, 44 b 2 (A. D. 1399; cf. Reeves ed. of Colton's Visitation).

§ 11 Judging by the poem in H 4. 4, 86, this refers to Loch Derg itself.

§ 13 Tailgeann, an old name for Patrick, see Trip. p. 34.

ABBREVIATIONS [1]

Acall.	= Acallam na Senórach, ed. Stokes.
ALC	= Annals of Loch Cé, ed. Hennessy.
Alex.	= The Irish History of Alexander, ed. Meyer, Ir. Texte ii pt. 2.
A. R.	= Beatha Aodha Ruaidh Ui Dhomhnuill, ed. Murphy.
Arch.	= Archiv für Celtische Lexikographie, ed. Stokes and Meyer.
Best, Bibliog.	= Bibliography of Irish philology and printed Irish Literature, 1913.
Betha CC.	= Beatha Coluim Chille, ed. G. Schoepperle and A. Kelleher.
Bidrag	= Bidrag til det Norske sprogs Historie i Irland av C. J. S. Marstrander.
Bk.	= Book of O'Conor Don (see vol. i p. xciv). The poems are sometimes referred to by the numbers in the Index published in Ériu 8, 81 ff.
Caithr. Congail	= ITS vol. v.
Celt. Rev.	= The Celtic Review, ed. MacKinnon and Carmichael.
Cog.	= Wars of the Gael and Gall, ed. Todd.
Contribb.	= Meyer's Contributions to Irish Lexicography.
Cormac Y	= Meyer's ed. of Cormac's Glossary, Anecd. from Ir. MSS. iv.
CRR	= Cath Ruis na Ríg, ed. Hogan.

[1] For MSS. see vol. i p. lxxxix ff.

CSPI	=	Calendar of State papers, Ireland.
D. Ó Br(uadair)	=	The poems of D. Ó B., ed. MacErlean.
Fél.	=	Félire Oengusa, ed. Stokes.
FM	=	Annals of the Four Masters, ed. ODonovan.
Gen. Reg. et SS.	=	Genealogiae Regum et Sanctorum Hiberniae, ed. Walsh, Maynooth Record Society.
GF	=	historical poems of Gofraidh Fionn Ó Dálaigh, Irish Monthly 1919.
Hogan	=	Onom.
Iar Connaught	=	O'Flaherty's description of West or Il-Iar Connaught, ed. Hardiman.
Ir. Deeds	=	Irish deeds published in Trans. Royal Irish Academy xv.
Ir. Gr. Tr.	=	Irish Grammatical Tracts, Suppl. to Ériu 8 ff.
Ir. Monthly	=	The Irish Monthly.
Ir. T(exte)	=	Irische Texte ed. Windisch and Stokes.
ITS	=	Irish Texts' Society.
Keat., Keat. Hist.	=	Keating's Forus Feasa ar Éirinn, ed. Comyn and Dinneen.
Keat. Poems	=	Dánta ... Seathrúin Céitinn, ed. MacErlean.
KM Miscell.	=	Miscellany presented to Kuno Meyer, 1913, ed. Bergin and Marstrander.
Lec.	=	Book of Lecan, MS in Royal Irish Academy.
LgC.	=	Leabhar na gCeart (The Book of Rights) ed. O'Donovan.
LL	=	RIA facsimile of the Book of Leinster.
MacCarthy	=	RIA Todd Lectures Series III.
MacFirbis	=	RIA copy of MacFirbis's Genealogies.
Marco Polo	=	The Gaelic abridgement of the Book of Ser M. P., ZfcP I.
Met(r). Dinds.	=	The Metrical Dindshenchas, ed. Gwynn.
Ml.	=	Milan Glosses, Thesaurus palaeohibernicus i.
O'Dav.	=	O'Davoren's Glossary, Archiv. f. Celt. Lex. ii.
O'Gr., Cat.	=	Catalogue of Irish Mss. in the British Museum by S. H. O'Grady (see Preface to vol. i).
Ó Heódhusa T. C.	=	An Teagasg Críostaidhe by Bonaventura Ó H., sec. ed.
Onom.	=	Hogan's Onomasticon Goedelicum.
Prolegomena	=	Pr. to the study of the Later Irish Bards, by E. C. Quiggin, Proc. British Academy vol. v (1911).
Ridgeway Essays	=	Essays ... presented to W. Ridgeway ...,' Cambridge 1913.
SG	=	S. H. O'Grady's Silva Gadelica.
Thes.	=	Thesaurus paleohibernicus, Stokes and Strachan.
Unpubl. Ir. Poems	=	editions by Bergin, Studies 1918 ff.
Wb.	=	Wurzburg Glosses, Thes. palcohib. i.
Wi.	=	glossary to Ir. Texte i.
ZfcP	=	Zeitschrift für celtische Philologie.

APPENDIX

A

The following documents were transcribed by me in August 1919 from the originals in the Public Record Office, Dublin. Cf. Wood-Martin's *Hist. of Sligo* i App. C. As a general rule I have left compendia unextended: invariably so in cases of doubt. I have not added punctuation marks. To mark an unextended contraction, answering to a bar over the last letter of the word in the original, I occasionally use (.).

I

MATHGHAMHAIN Ó HUIGINN

Exchequer Inquisition, Sligo, 12 Eliz. (Cf. Wood-M. 395).

Inquisitio capta apud villam de Sligo in com. Sligo xxvii^e die Julii Anno Domini 1590 et regni Serenissime Domine nostre Elizabethe Dei Gratia Anglie Francie Hibernieque Regine Fidei Defendoris xxxii° coram Johanne Crofton amigero Generali Escheatore dicteque Regine regni sui Hibernie predicte virtute officii sui per sacramentum proborum et legalium hominum comitatus Sligo predicti quorum nomina subsequuntur

    William Tathe de Bononeddan

    Melaghlyn McDonogh de Colony

    Thadeus O Hara de Tullaghhea

    Hugh McDonogh de Castleloghdargan

    Dermote McCranny de Ballyadderdaowen

    Caher McBrehowen de Kyllmacdullan

    Shane Oge O Hara de Ballyara

    Owen O Hara de Ballyara

    Teg McOwen de [L?]arras (cf. Teig McOwen de Lerras, Wood.-M. App. C, Inq. 9)

    Shane mc Ffarginaynme O Conor de Scardan (Fiants Eliz.. 5848)

    Alexander McRoyry (?) de Dromnegrangy

Hugh Boy McMoriertagh de Kynlaghty

Tadeus Boy McTomultagh de Gortyn(earn)ay (cf. Wood.-M., Inq. 9)

Mulmurry McDonell de Rosl . . e (cf. Wood.-M., Inq. 9)

Innys (?) McNemy de Killeny (see last ref. and Irish Poets etc. § 40).

QUI JURATI dicunt super sacra. su. quod Matheus O Higyn de Dougharane in isto comitatu Sligo diem claudebat extremum ix die Januarii 1585 et regni Domine nostre Elizabethe Regine xxvii° Item dicunt pronominati juratores super sacra. su. quod predictus Matheus O Higyn die quo obiit fuit seitus in dominico suo ut de feodo de villa villata sive hamlet vocat. Dougherane in Baronia sive teritoria de Leyny ac de quatuor quarteriis terre omnis generis cum suis pertinentiis ac etiam de duabus aliis quarteriis omnis generis cum suis pertinentiis vocat. Leghbally-moylagh que quid. vi quarterie terre subdita sunt oneribus patrie et igitur valuantur per annum ultra repriss. xl^s curentis monete Anglie Ac dicunt quod predictus Matheus O Hygyn tenuit villam et terras predict. de Domina nostra Regina in capite sed per que . . . penitus ignorant Item dicunt pronominati juratores super sacra. su. quod Tadeus vulgariter dictus Teg Dall O Higyn est proximus et legitimus heres predicti Mathei qui nunc est etatis quadragintorum annorum et maritatus

                                    In testimonium etc.

II

TADHG DALL Ó HUIGINN, TADHG ÓG Ó HUIGINN

Exchequer Inquisition, Sligo, 14 Eliz. (Cf. Wood-Martin i 390).

INQUISICO INDENTATA CAPTA apud villam de Ballymoate in com. Sligo xii° die januarii anno Dni. 1593 Annoque Regni Serenissime Domine nostre Elizabethe Dei gratia Anglie Francie Hybernie Regine Fidei Defendoris . . . xxxuito coram Ricardo Boyle gen. deputat. Ch. Kenney armigeri General. Eschaetor ac ffeodarii dicte Domine Regine in ac per totum hoc Regnum suum Hibernie predictum (?) tam infra (?) libertates quam extra virtute officii sui per sacra. proborum et legalium hominum comitatus Sligo predicti quorum nomina subsequuntur viz

Richardū Lennan gen.

Thadeū mc Tirlaghe Carraghe
(cf. Wood-M. 395, Inq. 11)

William O Harte gen.

Dermiciū O Dowde gen.

Nicholaū Caddle gen.

Connor O Cloan (?) gen. (cf.
Connels OClovan, Wood-M.
395) [1]

Manus Keoghe gen. (Keoghe
Wood-M., cf. ib. pp. 388, 390,
395)

Moriciū Keoghe gen.

Brianū mc Swyne gen.

Dermicū mc Molronye gen.

M[anus OBeolan Wood-M.] gen.

Moriortaghe mc Donogh gen.

Walteiū Walsh gen.

Cahill mc Tumultaghe gen.

Cahill Oge mc Cahill Duffe gen.

Alexander [Mc Swyne, Wood-M.]

(On the back of the document was written: D ... libat. manu ...
Cormock M'Dermot xxix die (?) novembris 1594).

QUI JURATI DICUNT SUPER sacram. su. quod Thadeus
alias Teage Dall O Higgen nuper de Cowlrecoyll in predict. com.
Sligo gen. diem suum clausit extremum apud Cowlrecoyle predict.
ultimo die Martii Anno Dom. 1591 et quod tempore mortis sue
predicte fuit quieta sesitus in dominico suo ut de feodo de et
in duabus quarteriis terre cum pertinentiis vocat. Carrownecashell
et Carrownecromtampla in com. predicto quomodo jacent vastat.
et incult. et nihill valent per annum ultra repriss. sed si cult.
et habitat. forent tunc val. per annum xiii^s iiii^d currente monete
Hibernie ITEM JURATORES predicti super sacram. su. dicunt
quod predictus Thadeus tempore mortis sue predicte fuit similiter
sesitus in dominico suo ut de feodo de et in septem aliis quarteriis
terre cum pertinentiis in com. predict. viz duo quarterie terre
vocat. Leighballycowlrecoyl Carrow Clownegounaghe Carrow
Clownbarrie Carrow Kynekillynbane et Leghballykyldallyhe in
com. predicto et premissa tenuit de Domina nostra per servicium
militar. viz per quadrigesimam partem unius feodi militis quando
scutagium currit in dicto Regno Hibernie ut de castro sive manerio
suo de Ballymoat in com. predict. et ... valent per annum ultra

---

[1] Wood-M. omits N. Caddle and C. O Cloan; instead he has: Jas.
OCrean, Rorie Ballagh McCahillelly, Ohelim [*leg.* Phelim] OConnor, Tady
McOwen. These four names may have been illegible to me.

repriss. nihillum eo quod jacent vast. et incult. sed si habitat.
essent tunc valerent per annum xxvi^s viii^d curr. monete Hibernie
et ulterius (?) juratores predicti super sacra. su. dicunt quod
Thadeus Oge mc Teage O Higgen est fillius legittimus et proximus(?)
heres predicti Thadei Dall O Higgen et fuit de (?) etate novem
annorum tempore obitus patris sui predicti et non maritatus

In testimonium etc.

III ·

TADHG DALL Ó HUIGINN, TADHG ÓG Ó HUIGINN

Exch. Inqu., Ballymote, Co. Sligo, June 1610 (apparently part of general
inquiry into the tenure of lands in Galway, Mayo, Roscommon and Sligo).

Tadeus Cecus O Higgin vulgariter vocat. Teige Dall O
Higgen nuper de Coolracoile in com. predict. gen. diem su.
claudebat extremum octavo die Junii anno Dni. 1595 Preterea
dicunt jur. predict. super sacra. su. predict. quod predictus Tadeus
Cecus O Higgen tempore vite sue et die quo obiit fuit seitus
in dominico suo ut de feodo de et in quindecim quarter. terre
cum *pertinentiis* in com. predict. que quidem *pr*emiss. terr. tenentur
de Domine Regine in capite et qu. val. inter se per annum
ultra repriss. viii^s monete Angl. Dicunt ulterius (?) jurator. predict.
super sacra. su. predict. quod Tadeus Oge O Higgen est verus
proximus et legittimus filius et heres antedicti Tadei Ceci O
Higgin qui erat tempore mortis dicti patris sui duodecim annos
natus et non maritatus Postremo dicunt jur. predict. super sacra.
su. predict. quod predict. Tadeus Oge O Higgen intranit iu
*pr*emiss. terr. et earum (?) . . . (?) percepit atque levavit neque
vero jurator constabat quod predict. Tadeus Oge O Higgin vel
ullus progenitorum suorum obtinuit vel obtinuerunt libertat. reg.
intrandi in dict. *pr*emiss. vel aliquid inde (?) per ull.

In testimonium etc.

IV

TADHG DALL Ó HUIGINN

Chancery Inqu., Sligo, James I 20[1] (perhaps a copy or translation; no seals attached, as there are in the case of the preceding documents).

An Inquisition taken at Sleigoe within the countie of Sleigoe the thirtith day of June in the yeare of Our Lord God One thousand six hundred and seaventeene, and in the yeare of His Mats. Raigne of England Ffraunce and Ireland the fifteenth and of Scotland the fifteth, before us, Thomas Browne Esquire and Owen McDermot gent., by vertue of the comission to us directed under the broade seale of his kingdome of this realm of Ireland bearing date the eighteenth day of March in the fowerteenth yeare of his Mats. raigne of Englande Ffraunce and Ireland and of Scotland the fifteth by the oathes of good and lawful men of the county aforesaide, whose names followeth viz

1 Teige Oge O Higgen of Cowlerecile gen.
2 Brian mc Teige .iagh O Hart of Fformoile
3 Murtogh O Connor of Gortnageilley
4 Thomas Reynolls of Grange
5 Rowry McSwine of Grangebegg
6 Deirmot O Dowde of Ballymoghorny
7 Brian McDonnogh of Cabragh
8 Carbery McDonnogh of Cortliane
9 Moylrawna McDonnogh of Bricklew
10 Connor Oge McManus of Annagh
11 Caghell Oge mc Caghell Duffe of Radownie
12 Dowaltagh O Bennaghan of Clonlorge
13 Ffarrall McDonnogh of Ramollin
14 Owen Duffe McTomoltee of Gort . . .
15 Rowrie O Harra of Ballaghboy
16 Art O Harra of the same.

Which jurors do finde and say by vertue of their oath that one William mc Corcashell and Owen of [sic] Hara of Castlecarragh were attainted of murdering one Teige Dall O Higgen his wife

---

[1] There is a short abstract of this Inquisition in O'Reilly's MS RIA 24 D 4, p. 44. Cf. the earlier Inqu. on the O'Haras, Wood-Martin 397-8 (partly cited infra p. 302).

and childe in the yeare one thousand five hundred nintee and one or therabouts and at the time of their death were seized in their demeisne as of fee of the quarter of land of Carrowcorragh and of the quarter of land of Sessigarrey in the said countie with their appertinences and are of the yearely value of one shilling star.

Wee finde likewise that one Tomoltagh O Hara,[1] late of Gorte ... in the said Countie was killed in actuall rebellion Anno Dni. 1590, or theraboutes by one Walter Welsh (?) then under-sherriffe of the said countie and at his death time was seized in the demeanes as of fee of the quarter of land of Gort ... with the appertinences as in right of tanistrie of the yearely value of sixpence star.

Wee finde likewise that Brian O Hara, Art O Hara and Donnel O Hara were likewise attainted of the foresaid murder the yeare of God one thousand five hundred nintee and one and that the father, grandfather and other auncestors to the said Brian, Art and Donnell were rightful possessors and inheritors of the quarter of land of Sessigarrie with the appertinences in the said co. And that the saide William mc Corcashell, Tomoltagh and Owen at the time of their severall deathes were seized in their demesnes as of fee of the quarter of land of Sessigarrie aforesaid and is of the yearely value of sixpence. And that one Phelim (?) O Hara yonger brother to the said William O Hara by whole bloud do ... and possesse the saide quarter of lande of Gort ... mone in his demesnes as of fee as descended to him by inheritance from his auncestors and that the foresaid William and Owen were coheirs in the same

In witness etc.

V.

The following rough abstracts of further inquisitions were not originally intended for publication in this form, but the destruction of records justifies the printing of them as they stand. The originals were in Latin.

I

TUATHAL Ó HUIGINN, RUAIDHRÍ (?) Ó HUIGINN

At an inquisition held at Ballinafad, Co. Sligo, before Robert Parke and William Berne, to enquire into the estate of Twohill

---

[1] Cf. Wood-Martin p. 397, Inq. 14.

O Higgin, formerly of Carrigwane, the jury swore that Twohill
O Higgin died on the 15th of August 1625 (*decimo quinto die
Augusti A. D. milesimo sexentesimo vicesimo quinto*), and was then
in possession of the land of Scartaleabin in same county; that
R(oger?[1]) Higgin was his son and nearest heir, then aged
16 (?) years and unmarried; that Maria ny Higgin was *uxor
ultima* of the said Twohill and was at the time of this enquiry
in plena vita sua.

2

EÓGHAN (or UAITHNE?) Ó HUIGINN
Exchequ. Inqu., Galway[2]

At an inquisition held in Tuam, Co. Galway in the 3rd year
of James I, before Nicholas Kenney arm., General Escheator,
October 20, the jurors, being Eugenius Higin, Johannes Kyrevane,
Pierce Kyrevane etc.[3], found that Owinus, otherwise Owen O
Higgin, formerly of Ballymoselly, and Edmundus Dorroghe McCragh
of Cell . . . aue in Co. Galway took up arms against the Queen
on March 7 of the 40th year of Elizabeth's reign, and were
slain in battle at Moerowrke (?) along with a certain MacWilliam
(*una cum quodam vocat. M' William*) in Munster[4] on March 8 of
same year, and were at the time of their death *sesiti in dominico
suo ut de feodo de quinta parte unius quart. terr. cum pertinentiis
in vill.* et camp. de Creige et Cell . . aue.

3

UILLIAM Ó HUIGINN, GIOLLA COLUIM Ó HUIGINN
Exch. Inqu., Sligo, Charles I, 22

William O Higgin of Moyntagh, par. of Ackonrie, bar. of
Lynie, Co. Sligo, generosus, died last day of February 1621,
possessed of the quarter of land de Carrowb . . ee, in same par.,

---

[1] Cf. Roger Higgin, of Scartlagh, par. of Achonry, bar. of Leyney,
in 1641, DS.

[2] Cf. The official précis printed infra, p. 302.

[3] I only noted the names given above.

[4] along . . . M'William: this was omitted from my first note of this
inqu. and added after a second reading, with an indication to insert it after
Moerowrke. I am doubtful whether I read the line correctly.

bar. and co., and the quarter of Monacranagh, and seven (?) quarters of land with appurtenances ... Liss .. higgin[1] in same, and Gillacolome O Hyggin *est legittimus fillius et proximus heres antedicti Will. et tempore mortis patris sui fuit de plena etate et maritatus.*

VI

The following are from the draft précis of Inquisitions made under the direction of the Record Commissioners by T. Litton, F. L. Kelly and J. Conroy, and still fortunately preserved in the Office.

I

OWINUS ALS OWEN O'HIGGIN EDMUNDUS DORROGHE MCKATH[2]

Inq:° capt^a apud villam de Twem 20° Octobr. anno regni regis Jacobi 3 coram Nicholao Kenny, per Michaelem Carmick deputatū p̄ sacramēt proborū qui dicunt quod Owinus als Owen O'Higgin et Edmundus Dorroghe McKagh 7° Marcii anno regni Regine Elizabeth 40°, intraverunt in actual rebellionem, et in aperto campo pugnand interfecti fuerunt apud locum vocat Monerowrte in provinc̄ Momonie 8 Martii anno p̄dic̄. Et quod seiti fuerunt de feodo in vill et campis de Creice et Collhane (¹/₃ qr).

2

Exchequer Inquisition, Draft Précis vol. 15, Sligo, Eliz. p. 25.

The original of this, the Exchequer Inquisition of 1593 on the six O'Haras, I did not see. In transcribing the précis I have omitted portions dealing with other lands and families; there are several distinct enquiries on this document. It has already been printed by Wood-Martin, *Hist. of Sligo* i 397-8, but I give this part here for the sake of completeness. Wood-Martin's transcript appears to have been made from the original as he gives the names of the Jurors, which are omitted from the précis.

Inq:° capta apud villam de Ballymoate 12° Januarii 1593, coram Richardo Boyle p̄ sacrā probor qui dicunt ... quod Owinus als Owen Mc Edmond O'Harie, Arthurus als Arte O'Harie mc Phelim, Donaldus O'Harie mc Phelim, Brianus O'Harie mc Phelim et Willis (*sic*) mc Carcashell fuerunt p̄ cursū comunis

---

[1] Cf. Lisshiggin in Achonry, Leyney bar., held by James Lynch jr. in 1641, DS.

[2] Cf. The abstract of the original given above, p. 301.

legis Hib*er*nie alte p̄dicionis attinct, et tempore eor*um* attincture
fuerunt insimull seitī de feodo de ¹/₂ qr et ¹/₃ semi qr in villa
et campis de Cashillcormick.

3

Ó HUIGINN, LANDS OF

Exchequer Inquisition, Sligo, James I (Draft precis Vol. 15, Sligo p. 20).

Inq:° capī apud villā de Sligoe 11° Septembris 1610 coram
Nichō Brady p̄ sacramenī probor qui dicunt quod Shane Oge
O'Harra als O'Harra Reoge diem suum claudebat extremū
19° Julii 1596, seiī ut de feodo de castr et vill de Bally Harra
Reoghe¹ vulgariter Ballinaffenoge una cū 4 qr ad dicī castr et
vill spectañ quiquidem sic nominantur viz Carrowen Roo, Carrowen
Toiryn, Carroañalt Duff et Carro Rath Scanlan—quod p̄dic
Shane fuit similiter seiī de 1 qr vōc Carrowreogh, de 1 qr vōc
Carro Toalocoshen, de 1 qr vocaī Carro Toarentostran, de 1 qr
Croghonan, de 1 qr vōc Clonlawchoole, de ¹/₂ qr vōc Lecarro-
coshenbeg, de ¹/₂ qr Leaghcarronagapoll, de ¹/₂ qr Clonyn Iharra,
de ¹/₂ qr Clonyngan, de ¹/₂ qr Lecarro Idreale, de 3 qr de
Ogham vul vōc Carro Cashelleville, Carro Kenle et Carrowentobber
—Quod Ffelym mc Curcastle O'Hara clamat qr Carro Roo et
¹/₂ qr Carroannalt Duff—quod p̄d Shane fuit seiī de capital
reddiī exeunī de qualibet qr, 6 qr stirpiū O'Higgin quando fuit
manuraī sive occupaī viz ex 4 qr de Doohurne et 2 qr de Moalagh
—quod Shane O'Harra est filius et heres antedicī Shane, et erat
tempore morī patris sui etaī unius añ—quod p̄miss tenentur
de Rege p̄ servitiū militare

B

The following note is from Professor Eóin MacNéill.

Ua hUicing is one of the surnames of a list of families called collec-
tively Fir Sceindi in a detached paragraph, Lecan 458 b, part of a genealogical miscellany. . . . The paragraph is:

Do Fearaib Scei*n*di annso .i. Mag Riabaich a taiseach ocus O Gormgaili
ocus O Caemocan ocus O Muirrthaili ocus O Fichthillich ocus O M*u*roici
ocus O hUicing ocus Mac Mailin ocus Mac Oisin ocus O Lonan ocus O Corra
ocus Mac Danair ocus Mac Mairtin ocus O Dondgaili ocus O Crechnua ocus

¹ Cf. Wood-M. ii 158.

O Drucan ocus O Dudacan ocus O Beandan ocus O Bethrachan ocus Mac Domnaill ocus Mac Landacan ocus Mac Gilli Maine ocus O Timanaich ocus O Birn ocus O Mail Phail ocus O Loacan ocus O Duib Abrad ocus O Dobran ocus Mac Cuind ocus Mac Gilli Glacaich ocus Mag Scalbuidi cona comaicsib.

There is no contextual connexion with what precedes and follows. See Hogan's Onomasticon s. v. Fir Scéne, where the references may lead to more light. Notwithstanding the location there given, viz. Loch Cé, the evidence of AU regarding such of the foregoing surnames as can be located thereby points to the district Dungannon—Armagh as the habitat of Fir Sceindi, and of their chief Mac Riabaig, whose surname ("MacGreevy") is still found in parts of Ulster.

AU 1107: Ui Cremthainn (of Monaghan and Fermanagh) killed Cathusach Ua Tuammain, king of Ui Briúin ar Chaill, and Eogan Mac MaicRiabaig was killed in revenge.

AU 1120: Ragnall Mac MaicRiabaig defeated Ui Echach (of Airgialla) in the plain of Cell Mór Ua Nialláin = Cell Mór (Maige) Enir, 3 miles E. of Armagh. In 1127 the Airthir killed Ragnall in a house in Trian Saxan in Armagh.

AU 1219: Gilla na Naem Ua Gormgaile, priest of Ráith Luraig = Maghera, died. In 1229 and 1234 died two priors of Inis Mac nErin, surnamed Ua Gormgaile.

AU 1540: Gráinne, daughter of Ua hUiginn (chief of his name), died. She was wife of Ó Dobailén (chief of his name) a lord in Tyrone [cf. App. C].

AU 1470: Sons of Ua Néill killed in the house of Ua Corra in Tobran, somewhere in Tyrone.

AU 1281: Mac Mairtin helps Aed Buide Ua Néill to win the battle of Disert Dá Crich against Domnall Ua Domnaill (in Dungannon barony).

AU 1291: Brian Ua Néill made king of Tyrone by Mac Mairtin and Mac Eoin.

AU 1107: Mael Patraic Ua Drucan made head of the school (fer léigind) of Armagh.

Ua Donngaile: the seat of this family was Baile Ui Donngaile, now Castlecaulfield near Dungannon.

Possibly the Fiants etc. would help to locate some of the other families in the list.

Mag Imchláir was in this district, and that suggests that the list of families under Fir Sceindi may have belonged to the ancient tribe called Fo.hairt Imch'áir.

Mac Danair supplies a curious parallel to Ua hUicing.

The only indication of date for the list is that AU names Mac Riabaig by his surname only, thereby indicating him as a chief, in 1107, 1120, and 1127, not earlier or later.

C

UÍ UIGINN

950-1650

This list[1] of members of the bardic kindred of Ó Huiginn is compiled chiefly from the following sources:

Annals (FM, ALC, AU, Clonmacnois, Connacht; when the date alone is given the ref. is to FM).

BK. = O'Conor Don MS. catalogued in Ériu 8, 78 ff. The poems are referred to by the numbers in the Index of first lines in that catalogue.

CSPI = Calendars of State Papers, Ireland (indexes).

DS = the list of Irish landholders in 1641 returned by the Down Survey.

Fiants = the Fiants of Elizabeth in the XVIIIth Rep. of the Deputy Keeper of the Public Records in Ireland.

Gen. = The genealogical table printed at the beginning of vol. 1.

Inquisitions at one time preserved in the Office of Public Records in the Four Courts (App. A).

MacF = Annals of Irel. 1443-1468 transl. by D. Mac Fir Bhisigh for Ware 1666 = Miscell Ir. Arch. Soc. i 198 ff.

Magauran MS. = MS Description of, by Joseph O'Longan, in RIA.

MS. Catalogues, viz O'Grady's Cat. of Ir. MSS. in the British Museum; Abbot — Gwynn Cat. of TCD Ir. MSS. and catalogues published in Ériu, ZfcP, Prolegomena.

Papal Reg. = Calendar of Papal Registers (Papal Letters).

Patent Rolls James I, Calendar.

RIA MS. catalogues by O'Curry, O'Longan etc.

The arrangement is in the alphabetical order of the christian names. Names of different individuals are distinguished by numbers (the numbering is chronological in intention, but I cannot claim to have been invariably accurate, in the absence of sufficient evidence of floruit; in some cases I am doubtful whether a number of references should or should not be assigned to a single individual). It is of course not claimed that this list is exhaustive, or that all the persons named were of the poetic branch.

Aindilis, Gen. 13.

? Antoin, Anthony Higgin of Dublin, gent., prdnd. Pat. 1 Jas. I xcix p. 36.

1 Aodh, father of 1 Maghnus.

2 „ , father of 3 Niall.

3 „ , Odo Ohuigind, a cleric, Papal. Reg. 1429, -31, -41, -47, -48.

---

[1] See also additions infra, p. 356.

4   Aodh, son of Brian s. o. Fearghal Ruadh, † 1487.
5   „ ,   Gen. B 25.
6   „ ,   s. o. Glaisne: *mac hÍ Uiginn .i. Aodh mac Glaisne soi re dán mortuus est* ALC 1529.   Ann. Conn.
7   „ ,   s. o. Domhnall Cam (see Gen. B 26 ff.).
8   „ ,   'Hugh O Higgin of Demginerick,' prdnd. Fiants 5112 (1587); 'Hugh O Higen of Dangenerick Co. Galway,' 5682 (1591).   Cf. p. 335ᵇ 40.
10   „ ,   Hugh O Higgin of Sligo, husbandman, prdnd. Pat. 1 Jas. I vii p. 20.

Aodh Ruadh, see 2 Aonghus, and Síle.

1   Aonghus, s. o. Maghnus; 'Ængus mc Magnusa O-huiginn was murthered by the sonns of Amhly oge O-Kennedy.' MacF. 1449.
2   „ ,   son of Aodh Ruadh, author of poem on Patrick's Purgatory, Prolegomena 53; scribe of and signatory to a deed between the Burkes and the Barretts, Hy Fiachr. 460; TCD F 4. 13, 74a ff.   Probably = the Enys (Eneas, Engus) O'Higgin (Huigin) employed in negotiations with the Burkes in 1596, CSPI 1596 pp. 8, 10, 522; Enys O Higgene (of Belleek, Co. Mayo?), prdnd. Fiants 5607 (1591); and Eneas Higgins of Ballaghdally to whom lands in Tirawley were granted, Pat. 16 Jas. I p. 347.
3   „ ,   Eneas O Higen, husb., of Keologelieghe (= Caol...? Co. Mayo), prdnd. Fiants 5799 (1592-3).
4   „ ,   Eneas Higgins; proprietor in 1641 of Derenislee, Brogher and Buncrannagh in Achonry par., Leyney bar., Sligo, DS; O'Hart's list of forfeiting propp. in *Ir. Landed Gentry* p. 303.
    See also 2, 3 Írial and Írial Óg.

Augustine, Father Augustine Higgin slain at the relief of Sligo, Oct. 1645, Meehan's *Confed. of Kilk.* 118; Hardiman's *Hist. of Galway* 123.

? Barrdhubh, Barrub ni Yhugynd of Elphin diocese, licensed to wed Thady Macegayn (= Tadhg Mhac Aodhagáin?), Papal Reg. 1442.

? Branane, Shane mac Branane alias Higgen, prdnd. Fiants 5682 (1591).

1 Brian, Gen. A 23 (cf. AU 1489) perh. father of 1 Cairbre
and 1 Eóghan. *Brian mac Ferguil Ruaid .h. Uiginn
cend a fine fen 7 oide Erennach 7 Albanach [oide sgol
Ereann 7 Alban lé dán* FM] *mortuus est dia Dardain
Mandail 7 sepultus est i nAth Lethan* Ann. Conn. 1476.
FM. Here may be noted the *n. l.* Baile Briain Uí
Uiginn FM iv 912, probably = Ballymunterhiggin,
(Pat. Rolls Jas. 1 541^b), about a mile S. of Bally-
shannon. Higginstown is also found as a tl. name
in Meath, Westmeath, Longford, Kilkenny and
Tipperary. Cf. remarks on *Baile Breatnach* in place
names, in C. O'Rahilly's *Ireland and Wales* 82-3.

2 „ , see Giolla Pádraig.

3 „ , see 2 Domhnall, and cf. 1 Tomás.

4 „ , Gen. B 27.

?5 „ , Bernard Ohuyghin, resigns bishopric of Elphin, Papal
Reg. 1561, p. 49; O'Rorke's *Hist. of Sligo* i 276-7;
Ware's Bishops, ed. Harris I 633.

6 „ , Brian O Higan of Kilbeg, Westmeath, prdnd. Fiants
1602 (1570).

7 „ , Brian O Higin of Cloincashell (Roscommon), prdnd.
Fiants 4588 (1584).

8 „ , Brian O Higgin of Moytaugh (Sligo), prdnd. Fiants
5026 (1587).

9 „ , Brian O Higgen of Kilclony (*Ceall Chluaine*, see
6 Domhnall; TD 12 § 6 n., and note: *Dá mbeith
h'uaimh . . . i cCill Chluaine do chinidh* in elegy on
13 Brian, I v 1, 39 = Gael. Journ. 1905, 832), Co.
Galway, gent., prdnd., Fiants 5447 (1590); Brian
O'Higgin of Kilclowna, gent., prnd. Pat. 1 Jas. I vi
p. 19; grant of lands in Dunmore bar. to Thomas,
Bryan and Donnell O'H., Pat. 16 Jas. I p. 370.

10 „ , Brian O Higen of Tullye (Co. Sligo), prdnd. Fiants
5434 (1590).

11 „ , Brian O'Higgin of Sligo, husbandman, prdnd. Pat. 1
James I vii p. 20.

12 „ , Brian O'Higgen of Ballindowne (Sligo), kerne, prdnd.
Pat. 1 James I vii p. 21.

13   Brian,   Brian Ó Huiginn, *cléireach corónach*, † in Dublin 1715.
A Sligo man, see his elegy by Seán Ó Gara, Gaelic
Journ. 1905, 832 ff.; see also 1907, 426, and 9 Brian
supra. It is worth noting that the wellknown codex
called the O'Gara MS., compiled by a Sligo man
(O'Grady, Cat. 340), was, according to a note on
f. 6a 'bound by Bryan Higgins of the citty of Dublin,
gent, in the month of October 1715.' Here 'bound
by' probably means 'bound to the order of.' For
a later Brian, chemist and physician, see O'Rorke's
Hist. of Sligo ii 506.

Brian Dorcha, poem by A iv 3, 618; perhaps the father of
4 Fearghal Óg and 2 Tomás, and identical with
Brien Dorrogh O'Higgen, kerne, of Teaghteamplae
(angl. Templehouse), Sligo, prdnd. Pat. 1 James I vii
p. 23.

1   Brian Óg, Gen. B. 28; *Brian Occ mac Briain mic Domhnaill
Chaim Uí Uiccinn d'ecc* FM 1505.

2   „   „ , Briane Oge O'Higgin de Curryvane, acted as juror
in Chancery Inquiss., August 1588, Wood-Martin's
Hist. of Sligo i 381-2. Possibly identical with next.

3   „   „ , Brien Oge O Higen of Garrignan, Sligo, prdnd.
Fiants 5796 (1592-3). Cf. preceding.

1   Cairbre, s. o. of 1 (?) Brian. *Cairpre mac Briain ui Uiccinn
oide lé dán d'ecc i n-iarthar Midhe* FM 1505 =
Cairbri mac Briain hI Uiginn dh'ec do bhiodhg ALC.

2   „   , Carbere m' Cocoggerie O Hugin (Co. Mayo), prdnd.
Fiants 5076 (1587). Cf. 7 Ruaidhrí.

3   „   , Cairbre s. o. Seaán, see 7 Ruaidhrí.

Cairbre Dubh, see 7 Ruaidhrí.

Cathal s. o. Raghnall, Gen. 16.

Cian, poem by, Bk. No. 253; possibly = Kian O Higgen of
Sligoe, prdnd. Fiants 5815 (1593).

1   Conchobhar, Gen. 9.

2   „   , s. o. Ruaidhrí Óg: *Indsoigid la Mac Gosdelbaig ...
7 ingen Ferguil Oic .h. Uiginn .i. Elec do marbad
doib .i. u.vor Conchobuir .h. Uiginn meic Ruaidri
Oic fer Machaire na nOilech ina baile fen go*

donuighe Ann. Conn. 1471. For location of M. na nOilech see Onom. s. caisel na heilidhe.

3 Conchobhar, C. s. o. Éanna †1587: *Concobar mac Enna Uí Uigin d'eg; saoi re dan an Concobar sin, ocus a adnacad a caisill na heilidi ar Machaire na n-ailech* ALC ad ann. Possibly = C. mhac mheic Í Uiginn, mentioned TD **25** §§ 15, 30, 31.

4   „   , Connor Higgin, held Kilkeereelly in Kilmanaghan par., Kilcoursey bar., King's Co., in 1641, DS.

Conn Crosach, see Pilib Bocht.

1 Cormac, Gen. 4.

2   „   , *Cormac mac Domnaill mic Briain I Uiginn do marbadh go timpeisdech d'énurchur* [*sic leg.*] *do śoighid lá Clainn Fheoruis* ALC 1499.

3   „   , fl. c. 1580, author of Bk. No. 110. Probably identical with 4 or 5.

4   „   , Cormock O Higgin (Belleek, or neighbourhood, Co. Mayo), prdnd. Fiants 5058 (1587).

5   „   , s. o. Giolla Coluim, fl. c. 1600; see O'Grady, Cat. 348 = (?) Cormuck O'Higgin of Dwacharny (i. e. Doheran, Achonry par., Co. Sligo), rymer, prdnd. Pat. 1 James I vii p. 24; Cormac (and William) O'Higgin claimed land in Leyney bar., Chancery Inquis. on Cormac O'Hara's lands, James I 34.

6   „   , Cormac O'Higgin of Lishiggen, lands in Co. Sligo granted to, Pat. 14 James I lviii p. 321.

7   „   , Cormock O Higgen of Magherie Quirk, Co. Westmeath, prdnd. Fiants 6506 (1601). See O'Rahilly's Irish Poets etc. § 59.

8   „   , Cormacus Higons, priest, sister's son to Terentius Coghlanus (J. V. D. Protho-notarius, & Vicarius Apostolicus Cluanensis), † at Rattin, Co. Westmeath, see Harris's *Arctomastix* (1633) pp. 46 ff., 51; Meehan's *Confed. of Kilkenny* p. 48.

?1 Cormac Óg, author of Bk. No. 42 (= App. D infra)?

2   „   „, s. o. 13 Brian, see Gael. Journ. 1905, 832 (I v 1, 40).

Cormac Ruadh, *Cormac .R. Ó Huiginn*, religious poems by, YBL 400a ff. = *Dán Dé* 38 ff.

Cormac Uaine, fl. c. 1600? *Olc an toisg da tháinig sinn . a Chormaic Uaine Uí Uiginn; feacha leat an sochar sin . dom chrochadh leat a Laighnibh* Bk. No. 269. See O'Rahilly's Irish Poets etc. § 46.

1   Cú Choigcriche, s. o. Fearghal Ruadh † 1463 AU.

2   „   „   , father of 2 Cairbre.

? 3   „   „   , Cowhegery O Higyn of the Gortine, King's Co., prdnd. Fiants 3344 (1578). Here there may be confusion between the anglicised spellings of Ó Huiginn and the name which is now anglicised O'Hagan; cf. Gogherie [i. e. Gofraidh], Rorie and Edm. O Hegan of Lehinch, Coghigorie O Hegan of Gortin, Toole, Dennys, Connor, Thomas, Owen reogh and Donell O Hegan, of same, Owen m'Toole O Hegan, of Lehinch, Ferrall O Hegan of Killellan Fiants 6488 (1601). These belonged to the barony of Kilcoursey "commonly called Mounterhagan [= Muintear Thadhgáin TD 34. 172] or the Fox's country in the King's Co." (Fiants 6381).

4   „   „   „   , Cucoggery O'Higgin, got lands on trust from Turlogh O'Brien of Dough, Co. Clare, Frost's *Hist. of Clare* p. 303.

5   „   „   , Cowhigry O Higen, of Cullkell (apparently in Ossory; cf. Cúl Coll or Coil, Onom.), prdnd. Fiants 6551 (1601).

Cú Chonnacht, Cowconnaght O'Higgen, kerne, of Teaghtemplae (angl. Templehouse; see Bruodinus, *Propugn.* p. 1040), Sligo, prdnd. Pat. 1 James I vii p. 23 (*bis*; two individuals?).

1   Diarmaid, Ho Uigeinn [*sic*], writing by, in Bk. of Hy Maine 120 [= 63]a 2.

2   „   „   , poem by, A v 2, 2 b.

3   „   „   , Dermot O Higgen of Breaklone (Co. Roscommon?), kera, prdnd. Fiants 4647 (1585).

4   „   „   , Dermot O'Higgin of Downycoffie, labourer, prdnd. Pat. 1 James I vii p. 22.

Doighre Ó Huigind, scribe of part of Magauran MS., c. 1350.

1 Domhnall,   s. o. 1 (?) Tadhg Óg, poem by, see Proleg. 50.

2   „   , s. o. Brian: *Domnall mac Briain hI Uiginn .i. oide sgol Erenn re dán, dh'ec* 1502 ALC Ann. Conn. = *Domhnall Ua Huiccinn oide sccol Ereann lé dán d'écc iar dtocht ó turus San Sém* FM 1501. Cf. O'Grady, Cat. 370, Abbott-Gwynn Cat. 316, and see 1 Tomás.

3   „   , D. s. o. Giolla na Naomh s. o. Maol Seachlainn na nUirsgéal, *Uaigneach sin a Chinn Choradh* attributed to, A iv 3, 704. Possibly = 4.

4   „   , father of 1 Ruaidhrí.

5   „   , Donnell O Higgin of Downbally (Galway?), prdnd. Fiants 5532 (1590).

6   „   , Donyll O'Higgin of Killclona, gen., a party to the Composition of Connacht, 1585, as regards Dunmore bar., Co. Galway. Cf. 10 Domhnall, 2 D. Óg and 9 Brian.

7   „   , s. o. Tomultach? Donnel mac Tomolta (between two individuals of the Ó Huiginn kindred) of Illan Ballenycolle (Co. Galway), prdnd. Fiants 5617 (1591).

8   „   , s. o. Tomás, fl. c. 1570, poem by, 23 F 16.

9   „   , Daniel O'Higgin of Knocks, the town, lands and 2 qurs of Levallineknock granted to, Pat. 16 James I p. 347.

10   „   , s. o. Maol Muire, Donnell O'Higin McMoilmorie gent., of Kilclony, prdnd Pat. 1 James I vi p. 19.

11   „   , Domhnall O Higgin, a franciscan friar in Louvain with Aodh MacAingil; ref. to in letter written by Donnchadh Ó Maonaigh from Antwerp, May 1610, Rev. P. Walsh's *Gleanings from Irish MSS* p. 54.

12   „   , Daniel O Higgin of Belamentan, King's Co., † 1637, Leinster Inquisitions.

13   „   , executed at Limerick in 1651: "Dominus *Daniel Ó Huiginn*, Doctor Medicinæ, vir sapiens, & pius, ibidem [Limerici] eôdem annô su[s]pendio necatur . . . An. 1651." Bruodinus, *Propugn.* p. 706. See Bagwell's *Irel. u. the Stuarts* ii 274.

Domhnall Cam, Gen. B 26. *O Huiginn .i. Domnall Cam, saoi re din ocus re foghluim dh'ec* 1529 ALC; Ann. Conn.

Domhnall Caoch, poem by, 23 L 17, 123ᵃ. Cf. 8 Irial.

1 Domhnall Óg, s. o. Aodh s. o. Domhnall Cam; fl. 1580, 3 B 14. Possibly same as following:

2   „ , Donell Oge O Higgen of Kilclony, gent., prdnd. Fiants 5447 (1590); cf. 6 Domhnall, probably identical with D. Óg Ó Huiginn who wrote out the 1602 NT Acts — Rev. *"do reir oghuim 7 chirt na Gaoidhilge"* (see O'D.'s Preface).

3   „ , Donnell Oge O'Higgen of Achonry, husband-man, prdnd. Pat. 1 James I vii p. 24.

1 Donnchadh, *Donchadh .h. hUiginn sai senchaidh mortuus est* 1364 ALC, Ann. Conn.

2   „ , Donogh O Higgen of Balledowne, (Sligo) prdnd. Fiants 5597 (1591).

3   „ , Donogh O Higine, of the Gurtine; Donogh O Higgin of the Gurtin (King's Co.?), prdnd. Fiants 6699, 6780 (1602-3).

Donnchadh Caoch, fl. c. 1590; poem by recorded, Ériu 6, 128.

Éanna, see 3 Conchobhar and 2 Ruaidhrí.

? Éamonn, Edmund O Higane of Clonemelle, prdnd. Fiants 2068 (1571-2).

Edward, Edwd. Higgin, proprietor of Curraghboy etc. in Kil-coursey bar., King's Co., in 1641, DS.

Elec, see 2 Conchobhar.

1 Eóghan, s. o. Brian, *oide Connacht re din* † 1510 AU.

2   „ , Owen O Higen, kern, of Lysnamnannay, Co. Ros-common, prdnd. Fiants 4074 (1582).

3   „ , Owen O Higine, of. Co. Westmeath, name cancelled in prdn. list Fiants 6121 (1597); cf. CSPI 1597, p. 12.

?4   „ , Owinus, otherwise Owen O Higgin, formerly of Ballymoselly, slain in action against the queen's forces, March. 8, 1598, Exch. Inq., Tuam, Oct. 1606, see App. A v § 2. Possibly Owinus = Uaithne.

5   „ , Eugenius Higin, a juror on above Inq.

6   „ , Owen O Higgine, of Ballimore (Co. Westmeath), prdnd. Fiants 6450 (1600).

7   „   , s. o. Tuathal, Owen m'Towell O Higgan of Ballimore,
        Co. Westmeath, prdnd. Fiants 6450 (1600); cf. next.

8 Eóghan, Owen O Higgin m'Toole of Higgins[town?], King's
        Co., prdnd. Fiants 6488 (1601); cf. preceding.

9   „   , Owen O'Higgin of Lishekeavy (probably = Liskeevy,
        Dunmore Bar., Tuam, Co. Galway), prdnd. Pat. 1
        James I vii p. 19.

10 „   , Owen O'Higgin (of Achonry, Co. Sligo), harper,
        prdnd. Pat. 1 James I vii p. 24.

11 „   , father of 9 Maol Muire.

An tEpscop Ua Huiccinn .i. epscop Maighe Eo na Saxan
        † 1478 FM.

1 Fear Dorcha, s. o. Uilliam, Fardorogh m'Wm. O Huigin (Co.
        Mayo), prdnd. Fiants 5075 (1587).

2   „   „   , grant from the king to Ferdorogh O Higgin
        of Carrownacrossa (Co. Mayo) of the tl. and
        qr. of same, Pat. 15 James I p. 347; possibly
        identical with 1 and 3.

3   „   „   , fl. c. 1630, poems by in A v 2; identical with
        1 and 2?

1 Fearghal, father of 4 Niall.

2   „   , Farrill O Higgen (of Balledowne, Co. Sligo), prdnd.
        Fiants 5597 (1591).

3   „   , Farriell O Higen of Behagh (Galway), prdnd.
        Fiants 5800 (1592-3).

4   „   , Farrell O Higgin (King's Co. or Westmeath), prdnd.
        Fiants 6512 (1601).

1 Fearghal Óg, father of 1 Seaán. Cf. next.

2   „   „ , fa. o. Elec, q. v. Cf. preceding.

3   „   „ , contemporary with Tadhg Dall? author of
        poem on Patrick's Purgatory, see Proleg. 53;
        Mackinnon 104.

4   „   „ , s. o. Brian Dorcha, fl. c. 1645; poems by in
        C iv 1; stanzas on, B iv 1, 126ª.

Fearghal Ruadh, Gen. A 22; Proleg. 49; Studies 1924, 87.

Feircheirtne (or Feirchert), *Feircheirtne mac Uiginn mic Giolla na
        naomh Uí Uigind ceann fine sleachta Giolla na naem
        Uí Uigind d'éc* FM 1419 (Feirchert AU, ALC);
        fa. o. 2 Lochlainn?

Flaithbheartach, Bard Boirne Gen. 5, O'Cl. I have not succeeded
in locating Boireann Baile an Dúin.

Flannagán, Gen. 7.

. 1 Giolla Coluim, Gen. 20.

2   „   „   , s. o. Maol Muire s. o. Brian Óg † 1587 ALC;
      fa. o. 5 Cormac?

3   ,,   ..   , Gille Cullam O Higgin of Moytaugh (Sligo),
      prdnd. Fiants 5026 (1587).

4   ..   „   , Gilla Colome O Hyggin s. o. William O Higgin
      of Moynthagh, Achonry par., Leyney, Co.
      Sligo, see App. A v § 3.

An Giolla Glas, s. o. O Huiginn † 1472 FM. Ann. Conn. Plummer's
     Ir. Litanies p. xiv.

1 Giolla Íosa, Gen. B 30.

2   „   „ , fa. o. 6 Niall.

1 Giolla na Naomh, † 1349 ALC, Ann. Conn. *saoi le dán* FM.
      in file gribdha, glan foclach is coitchinne do
      bi i cerdib na filidhechta i nErinn AU;
      poems by in Magauran MS.

2   ,,   ,,   ..   , s. o. Tadhg Óg, Gen. B 23.

3   ..   ..   ..   , *Ó Huiginn .i. Giolla na Naomh mac Ruaidhri*
      Móir d'écc 1473 FM. Ann. Conn.

4   ..   ..   „   , s. o. Maol [S]eachluinn [na nUirsgéal]
      † 1475 FM. Ann. Conn.

5   ..   ..   ..   , husb. of Fionnghuala dau. o. Mág Raith
      1531 Au.

6   ,, ...   , Gillernewe O Higen, of Owles, Co. Mayo,
      prdnd. Fiants 4351 (1584).

7   ..   ..   ..   , s. o. Irial † 1588 ALC.

8   ..   ..   ..   , Gillenewf O'Higgin of Dwacharny, rymer,
      prdnd. Pat. 1 James I vii p. 24. Cf. 9.

9   ..   ..   ..   , Gillernew O Higgen of Lishiggen, lands
      in Sligo granted to, Pat. 14 James I p. 321;
      probably identical with 8 and with

10   ..   .. Gillernew Higgins, proprietor of lands in
      Achonry par., Leyney, Co. Sligo, in 1641,
      DS; Hart, *Irish Lan led Gentry* p. 303.

Giolla Pádraig, s o. Brian s. o. Maol Seachluinn † 1485 FM.
     Ann. Conn. *Giolla Pattraice Ua Huiccinn mac*

Briain mic Maoil Echlainn, fer tighe aoidhedh coilchinn do thrénaibh 7 do truaghaibh d'éc. FM.

Glaisne, fa. o. 6 Aodh.

1 Gofraidh; Gen. 12.

?2 „ , Goghery O Hegyn of the Gortine, King's Co., prdnd. Fiants 3344 (1578); possibly not an Ó Huiginn, see under 3 Cú Choigcriche.

Gráinne, Grany ny Higgen of Graungemore, Co. Sligo, widow, prdnd. Fiants 5805 (1593). In such records 'ny' may stand for wife or daughter, cf. App. A, v § 1.

Gráinne Óg, dau. of Ó Huiginn, wife of Feidhlim Ó Doibhilen, AU 1540 (the Ó D. family was seated in Corran bar., Co. Sligo, Top. Poems; *Fagurtach .h. Dobhailen, ri in Chorainn quievit* Ann. Conn. 1248).

Iollann, Ullyne O'Higgen, of Rathlie (probably = *Ráith Laogh* 'Rathlee, Easkey par., Tireragh bar., Co. Sligo,' Onom.) kerne, prdnd. Pat. 1 James I vii p. 22. For the spelling cf. Ulline Mc Ellay, surgeon, ib. p. 23 (for *Iollann Mac an Leagha?*), and Uline O Mulconry, O'Rahilly, Irish Poets etc. § 17.

Íomhar an tSléibhe, Gen. 8.

1 Irial, fa. o. 7 Giolla na Naomh.

2 „ , fl. c. 1585, poem by 3 B 14; cf. ZfcP 2, 340. Identical with I. s. o. Aonghus, ib.? Cf. 3.

3 „ , s. o. Aonghus; Iryell m'Anis O Higen of Lysalvye (= Lissalway, Castlereagh bar.. Co. Roscommon?), prdnd. Fiants 4777 (1585), Cf. Í Óg.

4 „ , Iriell O Higgyn of the Clonyn (Co Sligo?), prdnd. Fiants 5606 (1591).

5 „ , Eriel O'Higgin, made Dean of Elphin by James I, Pat. 4 James I xx p. 98.

6 „ , Iriell O Higin of Kilnenynim (Westmeath?), chirurgeon, prdnd. Fiants 6533 (1601).

7 „ , Irill O'Higgin of Baskan (Baskin, Westmeath?), horseman, prdnd. Pat. 2 James I xxxvi p. 44.

8 „ , Irriel mc Donnell Keogh O'Higgin (of Achonry), harper, prdnd. Pat. 1 James I vii p. 24, cf. p. 151b 8.

9 „ , Irriell Mc Moelrony O'Higgin (of Achonry), friar, prdnd. Pat. 1 James I vii p. 24.

10 Irial, Iriell () Higgin, holding land in Westmeath, Inqu. Charles I, Sept. 1636.

Írial Óg, s. o. Aonghus, Eriell oge m'Genise () Higen, Co. Roscommon, prdnd. Fiants 4240 (1583).· Cf. 3 Irial.

1 Lochlainn, Gen. 14.

2 ,, , s. o. Firceirtne † 1464.

3 ,, , Laghlen () Higen, prdnd. Fiants 4027 (1582).

4 ,, , Loghlan () Higgen, of Balledowne, Co. Sligo, prdnd. Fiants 5597 (1591).

1 Maghnus, s. o. Aodh † 1405 FM, ALC., Ann. Conn. Cf. 1 Aonghus.

2 ,, , s. o. Giolla na Naomh, Gen. B 24.

Maghnus Óg, s. o. Aodh, fl. c. 1580, poems by, 3 B 14.

1 Maol Muire, s. o. Tadhg Óg, oide Ereann le dán † 1488 FM sáoi re dán ALC, Ann. Conn.

2 ,, ,, , s. o. Cairbre, religious poem by, 23 D 14, 112.

3 ,, ,, , s. o. Brian Óg, Gen. B 29, fa. o. 2 Tadhg Óg, q. v. Cf. next.

4 ,, ,, , fl. c. 1580, poems by, 3 B 14. Cf. preceding.

5 ,, ,, , s. o. Mathghamhain, archbp. of Tuam; brother of Tadhg Dall, see Introd., vol. I p. xvi.

6 ,, ,, , fl. c. 1600, poem by, 24 P 9, 205. Cf. 9.

7 ,, ,, , fa. o. 10 Domhnall?

8 ,, ,, , Mulmorie O'Higgin of Partris (Mayo), prdnd. Pat. 2 James I xl p. 45.

9 ,, ,, , s. o. Eóghan, fl. c. 1645, poems by A v 2, C iv 1. Cf. 6.

Maol Muire Ciotach, Moylemore ketagh () Higin, of Illan Ballenycoile (Co. Galway), prdnd. Fiants 5617 (1591).

Maol Ruanadh, fa. o. 9 Írial.

1 Maol Seachluinn, see Giolla Pádraig.

2 ,, ,, , Maoil Eachluinn () Huiginn of Ceall Lughain, poems by, c. 1640, C iv 1. Melaughlin O'Higgin, surrenders Killowan, Co. Galway, for regrant, Pat. 15 James I p. 357.

Maol Seachluinn na nUirsgéal, fl. c. 1440, poems by Bk. etc. Louth Arch. Journ. 1921.

Marcus, Marcus Higgin, proprietor in 1641 of Ballanamancor, Killmanaghan par., Kilcoursey bar., King's Co., DS.

Matha, *saoi re dán 7 re daonnacht* † 1337 FM, ALC, Ann. Conn. = Mathew, Ann. Clonmacnois.

1 Mathghamhain, fl. c. 1350, Magauran MS.

2   „   , s. o. Maol Muire, Gen. B 30; s. o. Ó Huiginn, Bk. No. 267, O'Gr., Cat. 380; fa. o. Tadhg Dall, vol. i p. xiv; App. A 1. Cf. TD 13 § 9 n., and Tomultach Óg.

3   „   , poem by A v 2, 53ᵃ; cf. 2ᵇ.

? Mathghamhain Maol, s. o. Ruaidhrí, Maghan moell m'Rorye O Hygan, of Balletample, Co. Clare, prdnd. Fiants 5848 (1593-4). An unusual spelling, but elsewhere in this Fiant y is used for i in stressed syll., e. g., Lehynch. It can hardly be for Ó Hógáin, which is represented by Ioggayne a few lines previous.

Mathghamhain Ruadh, † 1441. *O Huiginn, Mathghamhain Ruadh saoi fir dhána do écc* FM.

Murchadh, Gen. 17.

? Murchadh Dubh, Morrogh duff O Hygane, cottier, of Moidrome, Co. Westmeath, prdnd. Fiants 6550 (1601).

1 Niall, Gen. 18.

2   „   . † 1340, *Niall Ua Huigind saoi fir dhána do bháthadh* FM; poems by in Magauran MS?

3   „   , s. o. Aodh, slays the deputy, Sir John Stanley, with a satire, 1414 FM. Ann. Conn.

4   „   , s. o. Fearghal † 1461 FM. 'Niall fitz Feargal oge O-huiginn,' MacF.

5   „   , Nyall O Higgen of Clonoughill, Sligo, prdnd. Fiants 5805 (1593).

6   „   , Neeile mc Gilliffe (misreading of Gillisse = Giolla Íosa?) O'Higgen of Skardane (Sligo), rymer, prdnd. Pat. 1 James I vii p. 24.

Niall Mór, plundered by some of the Burkes 1400 ALC. Ann. Conn.

Niall Óg, † 1461 FM. MacF.

Peadar, Father Peter O Higgin, Dominican Prior at Naas † 1641. Heyne's *Irish Dominicans* (1902) p. 50.

Pilib Bocht, s. o. Conn Crosach, *brathair Minur de Obseruancia, nech is mó is ferr duanaire diadhachta san aimsir deigheanaigh* † 1487 AU, author of *Tuar feirge foighide Dé*, the first thing to be printed in Irish (1571); see Best's *Bibliography* p. 198.

1 Pól, s. o. 3 Tadhg Óg, proprietor in 1641 of Ballincurry, Moylagh and Doughorne, in Achonry par.; Moylaga, Carrowreagh, Drumbane, Clunnegunnagh, Kinkelly, Clonberry, Coolerekyle and Dunrus, in par. of Kilmacteige, with wood and bog of Letteebrony and Coyledallee, Co. Sligo, DS. Married Cecilia Jordan, see cit. from *Anat. Exam.* under 3 Tadhg Óg.

2 „ , Paul Higgins, lecturer in Irish in Trinity College, Dublin, under Narcissus Marsh, in 1688; stanza on in *Sgéalaidhe Oirghiall* p. 119, *Seanfocla Uladh* p. 310.

1 Raghnall, Gen. 15.

2 „ , † 1325 FM, poems by in Magauran MS.

Roiberd, Gen. 11.

1 Ruaidhrí, s. o. Domhnall, fl. c. 1560, poem by, Bk. No. 286.

2 „ , s. o. Éanna, of Roscommon, † 1581 ALC; cf. 1590 (ii 510).

3 „ , fa. o. Mathghamhain Maol.

4 „ , Rorie O Higgin (of King's Co.) prdnd. Fiants 6512 (1601).

5 „ , Roderick O Higgin of Partris (Mayo), prdnd. Pat. 2 James I xl p. 45.

6 „ , Roger Higgin, proprietor in 1641 of Scartlagh, Achonry par., Leyney, Co. Sligo, DS. Cf. App. A v § 1.

7 „ , s. o. Cairbre s. o. Seaán, i. e. Ó Huiginn an Tearmoinn (cf. ALC 1582, ii 454, and 7 Tadhg), scribe of RIA 24 P 33 (see KM Miscell. 53) in 1680, and sometime owner of 24 P 9. In a note in the latter he describes himself as Ruaidhrí Ó Huiginn s. o. Cairbre s. o. Seaán s. o. Cairbre (.i. Ó Huiginn) s. o. Cú Choigcríche s. o. Cairbre Dubh.

Ruaidhrí Mór, fa. o. 3 Giolla na Naomh.

Ruaidhrí Óg, Ruairy oge O-huigginn *tollitur de medio* MacF. 1450. See 2 Conchobhar.

Ruaidhrí Ruadh, † 1425 *saoi fir dhána* FM, AU, poems by, see Ériu 4, 188; Proleg. 49.

an sagart Ua Huiginn (var.: an s. Mac Uiginn), a noble elder who was priest in the neighborhood of Carnaun, Kilrush par., Co. Clare, ZfcP 10, 20. Undateable.

1 Seaán, s. o. Fearghal Óg, *priomhsaoi Ereann lé dán* † 1490 FM.

2 „ , s. o. Ruaidhrí, poem by, H 4. 4, 141; cf. next.

3 „ , s. o. Ruaidhrí Óg, fl. c. 1580, poem by, see ZfcP 2, 343; Abbott-Gwynn Cat. p. 50 (in Index to latter, p. 435, read Seaán m. Ruaidhrí). Probably identical with preceding.

4 „ , Shane O Higgin (Co. Mayo?), prdnd. Fiants 5058 (1587). Probably = 5.

5 „ , Sheane O Higgene (Co. Mayo), prdnd. Fiants 5607 (1591). Cf. 4.

6 „ , Shane O Higen, of the Boagh, prdnd. Fiants 5685 (1591). Probably = 7.

7 „ , Shane O Higgen, of Behagh, Co. Galway, prdnd. Fiants 5682 (1591). Cf. 6.

8? „ , Shana mac Branane alias Higgen, prdnd. Fiants 5682 (1591).

9 „ , Shane O Higgen, of Rahlackane (= Ráith Leacáin in Tirawley bar., Co. Mayo; for final syll. cf. O'Rahilly, Irish Poets, etc. § 39 n. 2), prdnd. Fiants 5740 (1592).

10 „ , Shan O Higen, of Trinagh (probably = Treanagh, Tirawley, Co. Mayo, cf. 4 Tomas), husbandman, prdnd. Fiants 5798 (1592-3).

11 „ , Shane O Higgen, of Ballindoin (Sligo), prdnd. Fiants 5805 (1593); Shane O Higgen, of Ballyndowne (Sligo), prdnd. Fiants 5815 (1593); Shane O'Higin, of Ballindowne, husbandman, prdnd. Pat. 1 James I vii p. 21.

12 „ , Shane O Higgin, of Ballyhaly (Co. Clare), yeoman, prdnd. Fiants 6615 (1602).

13 „ , Shane O'Higgin, of Killeny (Queen's Co.), kerne, prdnd. Pat. 1 James I vii p. 22.

14 „ , John O'Higgin, of Partris (Co. Mayo), prdnd. Pat. 2 James I xl p. 45.

15 Seaán, John Higgins, amongst the garrison of Sligo captured
           by the Parliamentary forces, Oct. 1645.

16   „   , Seaán Ó Huiginn an Tearmoinn, see 7 Ruaidhrí.

17   „   , John Iliggin, son and heir of 5 Tadhg, Westmeath
           Inqq., Car. I 91.

1 Seaán Ruadh, John Roe O Higin, of the Nele (Co. Galway),
           husbandman, prdnd. Fiants 4691 (1585).

2   „   „   , John Roe O Higkin, of Conigy (Co. Galway),
           prdnd. Fiants 5519 (1590).

Sile inghean Aodha Ruaidh (?), Sily ny Higen ny Hue Ro of
           Ballinduff, Co. Galway, prdnd.
           Fiants 5800 (1592-3). 'Hue Ro'
           may have been her husband,
           see note on Gráinne.

*Stiofán, Stephen Higgins, propr. of in 1641 Cluonbroen and
           Moyvane in Morhor (Murher) par., Iraghticonnor bar.,
           Co. Kerry, DS. Here Higgins is probably an anglicised
           form of some name other than Ó Huiginn. Professor
           O'Rahilly informs me that he heard Ó Hídeacáin =
           Higgins in Ring, Co. Waterford.

1 Tadhg, *saoi i ndán* † 1315 FM; *sai chotchend cech ceirdi da
           mbenand re filidecht* Ann. Conn., ALC; poems by in
           Magauran MS.? = 1 Tadhg Mór?

2   „   , s. o. Giolla Coluim, Gen. 21; † 1391 *ollamh derseccaighte*
           [*dingbala* v. l., Ann. Conn., ALC] *i ndán* 7 *i ndaonnacht*
           FM, ALC, Ann. Conn.; Magauran MS.? I have taken
           him and Tadhg Mór, O'Clery Gen. B 21, as identical;
           wrongly? See 2 Tadhg Mór.

3   „   , Thaddeus O'Higgin, of the Trinitarian house of Adare,
           one of those recorded in the Book of Adare as
           having "laid down their lives in distant lands for
           the redemption of their fellowman," see Meehan's
           Franciscan Monasteries (6ᵗʰ ed.) p. 258 (p. 302 of
           5ᵗʰ ed.).

4   „   , a priest, † 1515 FM.

5   „   , Teig O Higgin, of Kilbegg (Co. Westmeath), freeholder,
           prdnd. Fiants 6507 (1601); Inqq. Kildare, Jas. I
           No. 37, 1618; Car. I 29, 78; Teig Higgen, of Kilbeg,
           Co. Westmeath, † 1633, Westmeath Inqq. Car. I 91.

6 Tadhg, Teige O Higgen, of Magherie Quirk (= Machaire
        Cuirc), Co. Westmeath, prdnd. Fiants 6506 (1601).

7   „   , Teige O Higgen, of the Tarmen, Co. Mayo (cf.
        7 Ruaidhrí), prdnd. Fiants 6567 (1601).

8   „   , of Coolavin, Co. Sligo, mentioned in a (17th cent.?)
        poem (23 L 7 etc.). See Hyde's *Literary Hist.* 521,
        where he is, I think wrongly, identified with
        Tadhg Dall.

Tadhg Bacach, Teig backagh O Higgen, of Downeballagh, Co.
        Galway, husbandman, prdnd. Fiants 5075 (1587).

Tadhg Bán, Thadeus bane O'Higen, labourer, of Rathmolin.
        prdnd. Pat. 1 James I vii p. 23.

Tadhg Crosach, Teig crossagh O Higgen, of Cloinnegrosse (Co.
        Mayo?), prdnd. Fiants 5458 (1590).

Tadhg Dall, † 1591; Introd., p. 1 ff.

  1 Tadhg Mór, Gen. 19; O'Grady, Cat. 487; Ir. Monthly 1920,
        163; 1921, 288; cf. 1 Tadhg, and next,

  2   „   „ , Tadhg Mór Ó Huigeng, author of poem des-
        cribing how Brian Mág Samhradháin was burnt
        in a house by his enemies, Magauran MS. This
        seems to refer to Brian Breaghach who was slain
        in his own house in 1298 ALC, Ann. Conn.
        Cf. 2 Tadhg.

  1 Tadhg Óg, s. o. Tadhg s. o. Giolla Coluim, *priomhoide aosa*
        dána Ereann 7 *Alban* FM *sáí re dan ocus cend*
        sgoile Erenn na aimsir fein ALC *primode Erenn*
        7 *Alpan* Ann. Conn. † 1448 in Cill Chonnla (see
        12 § 6 n.) and was buried in Mainistir Átha
        Leathain FM. MacF.; Gen. B 22; cf. 1 Maol
        Muire, and 1 Domhnall.

  2   „   „ , s. o. 3 Maol Muire, see Gen. 30; poem by to
        Cian, fa. of Cormac O'Hara of TD 29 etc., 3 B 14.
        Possibly identical with Teige O Higan m'Moyl-
        more, of Tulanydala (Co. Galway), prdnd. Fiants
        4798 (1585).

  3   „   „ , s. o. Tadhg Dall; see Introd. pp. xv (App. A II),
        xxxii; Teige Oge mc Teige Daile O'Higgin of
        Dwacharny, rymer, prdnd. Pat. 1 James I vii p. 24;
        grant to Teige O'Higgen of Coolerecoile, Leyney

bar.: the town and lands of Dougharne[1]; Carch-
fruihe or Carownebrinny or Carowknock, 1 qr.;
Carowkeele, 1 qr., near Doogharne; Carrowletrim,
1 qr.; Carowmoolagha or Poolruhan, 1 qr.; Moy-
lagha otherwise Clogher, 1 qr.; the town, lands
and qr. of Carowreagh, in or near Dogharne;
Lecarrow-Tworiny, 1 qr.; Lecarrowkillinny, $\frac{1}{2}$ qr.;
the town, lands and qr. of Ballincurry otherwise
Dromantample[1], and of Caroweashell, 1 qr.; Coil-
daloy, 1 qr.; Kincoilenalavan, 1 qr.; the town,
lands and qr. of Coolerecoill. of Carowentracky,
of Cloonegownagh, of Litterbrone and of Cloon-
varry. Pat. 14 James I lviii p. 321. Identical
with Teige O'Higgen, sheriff of Sligo, 1634
(Wood-Martin, *Sligo and the Enniskilleners*, App. D,
p. 173). According to the author of *Anatomicum
Examen* (Prague 1671; cf. note in O'Grady,
Cat. 388) Tadhg Óg married Fionnghuala, dau.
of An Cosnamhach Mac Bruaideadha (bro. of the
celebrated Tadhg Mac Dáire), by whom he had
issue; Pól, who married Cecilia Jordan, and two
daughters, the elder of whom, Maria, married
Terence MacDonogh (Toirdhealbhach Mac Donnchadha, see Gael. Journ. 1905, Sept. p. 10; Oct.
p. 23; 1907, 426; *Dánfhocail* § 198 n.; Wood-
Martin, *Hist. of Sligo* ii 109), and the younger,
Matilda, married Seaán Ó Heaghra. The same
authority refers also to Tadhg [Óg] as sheriff
and justice of the peace:

Thadeus Ô Higgin, de Kulracheil, comitatus
de Sligo toties Capitaneus (vulgò schirriff) &
pacis Iusticiarius, in uxorem habuit *Phinolam
Bruodinam Constantini* de *Balliogan* filiam. Horum
filius *Paulus* in uxorem accepit *Caeciliam Iordanam*,

---

[1] In an Inq. taken at Sligo, Ap. 1607, the jury are said to have stated
that they "heard that the six quarters of land of Dowchoine [= Dougharne,
etc. > Doheran?], and the quarter of land of Dromeentemple in the barony
of Leyne with their appurtenances did anciently belong to the nunery [of
Killcrenat]." Wood-Martin, *Hist. of Sligo* ii 299.

perillustris Domini *mac Iordan* filiam. filia vero
primogenita *Maria Higgin* dicta, nupsit nobilissimo
viro, Domino Therentio Mag Donoghu, iunior
autem filia *Mathilda* dicta, nupsit perillustri
Domino *Ioanni de Hara*, potenti quondam in
illa patria Dynastae[1]. *Anal. Exam.* p. 133. See
also Wood-Martin, *Hist. of Sligo* ii pp. 158, 162,
163y-164.

? Tadhg Ruadh, in 23 C 21 (c. 1816) a very ill-written *crosántacht*,
Tugam aghaidh ar Maol Mhórdha, is headed
Tadhg mc D*air*e & Tadhg Ruadh higin cct.

Toirdhealbhach, Terence O Higgin, of Killemyn (Co. Westmeath?),
shot, prdnd. Fiants 6550 (1601).

1 Tomás, s. o. Domhnall s. o. Brian s. o. Fearghal Ruadh *oide fer
nErenn ocus nAlban re dán* † 1536 ALC. Cf. 2 Domhnall.

2   „   , fa. of 8 Domhnall. Cf. preceding.

3   „   , Tho. O Higgan, of Kilclony (Co. Galway), prdnd. Fiants
5447 (1590). Grant by the king of lands in Dunmore
bar., Co. Galway, to Thomas O'Higgin and others,
Pat. 16 James I p. 370, see 9 Brian.

4   „   , Tho. O Higgen, of Tryenagh (Co. Mayo), prdnd.
Fiants 5798 (1592-3).

5   „   , Tho. O Hyggine, of (?), prdnd. Fiants 6495 (1601).

6   „   , s. o. Brían Dorcha, fl. c. 1640, poems by, C iv 1;
stanzas on, B iv 1, 126[a].

Tomás Ruadh, fl. c. 1630, poem by, A v 2.

1 Tomultach, Gen. 6.

2   „   , Tomultagh O Hygin, of Killelynyane, Co. Mayo,
prdnd. Fiants 4667 (1585) = T. Óg? Cf.
7 Domhnall.

Tomultach Óg, s. o. Mathghamhain, witness to agreements between Burkes and Barretts in 1584, Hy Fiachrach
460, 461 (TCD F 4. 13). Cf. 2 Tomultach. In
a Sligo Inquisition of 1607 the jury are said
to have stated "that there was a certain writing
concerning the nunery (of Killcrenat) burned by

---

[1] Cf. Inter Nobiles familias hujus Comitatûs de *Sligo*, sequentes Iucent:
Ô Conori, *Ô Hara*, *Ô Gara*, *Ô Duda*, *mac Donogh*. Comites *Faaffe*,
mac Jordan, *Ô Higgin* &c. Bruodinus, *Propugn.* p. 1040.

one Tomoltagh Oge O'Higgin," Wood-Martin, *Hist. of Sligo* ii 299.

1 Tuathal, successor of 1 Tadhg Óg in the chair of poetry, 1448 AU (*ollomnughadh < ollamh* 'poet'?); *O Huigind .i. Tuathal priomhoide aosa dána Ereann do ég do ghalar obann* 1450 FM; cf. YBL 402 b; Abbott-Gwynn Cat. 97.

2   „   , s. o. Tadhg, Gen. A 25; cf. Proleg. 49 and Thole O Huggin of Mageoghegan's country, in Kildare Rental, 1562, Kilk. Arch. J. 2 S. iv 128.

3   „   , see 7, 8 Eóghan.

4   „   , Towhill O Higgen, of Kilclony, Co. Galway (see 9 Brian), gentleman, prdnd. Fiants 5447 (1590).

5   „   , Twoholl O'Higgin of Dwacharny, rymer, prdnd. Pat. 1 James I vii p. 24; author of poems in 3 B 14?

6   „   , Tohell O'Higin, of the Killin in Galway Co., husbandman, prdnd. Pat. 1 James I xxi p. 28.

7   „   , Twohill O'Higgin of Garriguane, land in Sligo (including Scartleah) granted to, Pat. 14 James I lviii p. 321; probably = Twohill O Higgin of Carrigwane and Scartaleahin, Co. Sligo, who † 1625, Sligo Inquisitions 1629; cf. App. A v § 1.

1 (?) Tuileagna, Tully Higgin, of the Dorow, King's Co., prdnd. Fiants 6780 (1602-3).

2 (?)   „   , Tully Higgin de Gurtin, mentioned King's Co. Inqu. Car. I 48. For the form cf. Tully Conry = Tuileagna Ó Maoil Chonaire ZfcP 8, 181. Tully may be based on the fanciful latinisation Tullius (Tullius O Mulconry, Fiants 5617).

1 Uiginn, Gen. 3; mythical?

2   „   , Gen. 10; *a quo* the surname; see Introd. pp. xx-xxi.

3   „   , see Feircheirtne.

1 Uilliam, † 1378 AU; Magauran MS.

2   „   , fa. o. Fear Dorcha.

3   „   , William O Higgen. of Moytaugh (Co. Sligo), prdnd. Fiants 5026 (1587); cf. Wille O Higgin of Moyntaghe juror in Exch. Inqu., Ballymote, 1593, Wood-Martin's *Hist. of Sligo* i 395; † 1621, see App. A v § 3.

4 Uilliam, Wm. O Higgen, of Clonerin, Co. Mayo, prdnd. Fiants
5452 (1590).

5   ,,   (?), Wm. O Higen of Tullye (Co. Sligo?), prdnd. Fiants
5434 (1590).

6   ,,   , Will. O'Higgin of Dwacharny, rymer, prdnd. Pat. 1
James I vii p. 24.

7   ,,   , Will O Higgen of Lishiggen, grant to, Pat. 14 James I
p. 321 (including qr. of Killmolover otherwise Lishiggin
or Taghcloihe; the latter is elsewhere on this p. spelt
Teaghcloyhae). Cf. under 5 Cormac.

8   ,,   , Wm. Higgin, proprietor in 1641 of Tubber, Killmanaghan par., Kilcoursey bar., King's Co., DS.

Uilliam Óg, slain 1401 ALC. Ann. Conn.

Uilliam Ruadh, Wm. Roe O Higgen, of the Park (Co. Galway),
prdnd. Fiants 5682 (1591).

D

The following *aisling* seems to refer to TD 39. I have not met a second copy.

1   An tú táinig go Tadhg Dall,
a thaidhbhse táinig chugam?
mun tú é is rochosmhuil ribh,
a ghné íochobhsaidh faoilidh.

2   Taidhbhse mná oile i n-amhra   5
do-chí Tadhg mhac Mathghamhna,
mar taoi, a inghean chruithgheal chorr,
le gcuirthear imneadh orom.

3   An bhean tarbhás do Thadhg Dhall,
a ghnúis ríogh na rosg romhall,   10
dob ionann gnáth dhí agus duid,
dá thráth nó t[h]rí acht go dtánuig.

MS: Book of O'Conor Don 401 b.
    Heading: cormac óg .cc. (*by the scribe, but a later hand has added*
briain oig mc conmide *after* cormac)
MS Readings: 9 a bh.   10 roscc

4   Beag nách cosmhuil riomsa is ribh,
     tuigse, a Thaidhg, athadh d'aimsir,
     an inghean níor chrádh cuimse,   15
     lán d'imneadh is d'athtuirse.

5   I ndiaidh ar imdhigh air féin
     léd chruth sneachtuighe soilléir,
     taidhbhse Taidhg, a chnú chroidhe,
     más tú is mairg do meallfaidhe.   20

6   Ní chluinfeam, ní chuala sinn—
     acht taidhbhse Taidhg Í Uiginn—
     do mhac samhla riamh roimhe
     go dtarla d'iath Úghoine.

7   Iongnadh leam ar neach fa nimh   25
     dar dhealbh Dia dona daoinibh—
     aingeal Dé munab duine—
     do ghné, a ainnear foltbhuidhe.

8   Do-chluinfinn fa chlár Bhanbha
     dá mbeith bean do bharamhla,   30
     a sduaigh roigheal chéibhfionn chlaon,
     i n-oirear Éirionn d'éantaobh.

9   Abair riom do rún folaigh,
     a ghnúis faoilidh éagsamhail—
     beanfa dhíne ar naidhm anois—   35
     ainm na tíre asar thriallois.

10   Innis damh 'na dTír fa Thuinn
     do bhí tú ria dteacht chuguinn,
     a chneas mhín ar méin lile,
     aréir, nó i dTír Thairngire?   40

11   Nó innis damh, a rosg mhall,
     Tuatha dealbhdha Dé Danann—
     cia an sídh i mbí do bhunadh,
     nó an í an tír 'sa dtángabhar?

---

14 tuigsi th. ath⁻   17 imgidh   24 iugoine   35 snaidm   40 na
44 an ni; asa ttangabhair

12 Nó a Síothbhrugh Sainbh, nó a Síth Truim
táinig sibh, nó a Síth Sioghmhuill—
bheith gan fios ní féidir linn—
nó a lios éigin i nÉirinn?   45

13 Nó dámadh thusa thú féin,
a ghnúis séaghanta soilléir,
a ghruaidh ghairthe ar ghné na subh,   50
gan mé dot' aithne is iongnudh.

14 Ós imtheacht duit 'na dheaghaidh,
truagh an chuairt do chuireabhair;
triall do thógbháil mo thuirse,   55
a fial ógnáir áluinnse!

15 Cosmhail riot ar n-imtheacht uaim
gur tríot tánuig an chéaduair
mealladh Taidhg, a fial Íosaidh;
mairg do thriall san turussain.   60

16 Mairg do lean led' dhraoitheacht dhíom,
mairg duit do mhéadaigh m'imsníomh;
mairg, a bhean, do mhear meise,
mairg do gheabh im ghoireise.

17 Má tá nách tusa, a thaobh slim,   65
tánuig go Tadhg Ó Huiginn,
a throightheach saor chneasda chorr,
bhar dteasda araon is iononn.

AN

GLOSSARIAL INDEX

The poems are referred to by number and number of stanza.
For further reff. see Notes.

Ábhacht 3,5. adhbhacht 41,2.
abaidh, abaigh 1,46; 16,12.
abháin = amháin 22,10.
abhra 2,57. —donn 1,26; 23,22.
—dubh 1,17; 2,29; 18,14. —dhonn
2,36. —dhubh 3,50; 27,41.
-acla 9,48.
-aclaidh 4,42.
adhbhann 23,7.
adbhar 19,15; 23,9; 29,19.
ág = óg 2,29; 24,19. ág- 16,39; 39,11.
aghaidh 11,12; 24,29; 39,9.
agraim 24,5.
aigmhéil 3,27; 36,9; this may also
be the correct reading in 24,10
aighmhéil as a separate word is
not well established. *aigmhéile* :
Braidsléibhe Ir. Monthly 1921, 68.
aigéan 13,16; 15,30.
áilghean 16,11; 41,9.
airc leithimil 16,6.
airdhe 20,6; 21,41.
aireachas, oireachas 1,5; 3,28; 20,43.
áirghe 16,11. (Cf. *Midach na mo-
cháirgi* Ir. Texte iii 246. In npr.
moichérghi (-óirghi) may originally
have meant 'early spancelling'?)
(d')áiridhe 16,21.
airleagadh 13,35.
aiteacht 23,7.
aithearrach 27,10.
aithris 13,33.
aithrisim 27,29.
am, mun, aimsin 8,9.
amach, ó x amach 7,9; 8,9.

amlach 28,8.
anáir = onóir 14,29.
anghlonnach 4.23.
anuallach 2,31.
aoighe 22 a,12; 24,18.
aon- (éan-) 1,1; 7,26; 17,57; 31,16;
32,77. d'éanláimh 2,31. fear (lucht)
aouuaire 16,25; 17,18; 39,22.
aos ealadhna 8,16. a. fuinn 11,15.
a. gráidh (grádha) 2,36; 8,12.
athadh 20,16. athadh, *gen.*, 4,9.
athadhnadh 1,22.
athaidh, athaigh, *acc.*, 1,42; 36,1;
41,15; 3,2; 13,48; 24,2. athaidh,
gen., 39,10. Cf. 4,9.
athmhaoin 18,37.
athraighim 15,3.

báigh 2,7,24; 10,17; 26,17,19; 30,13.
bandragún 1,20.
baránta 16,7.
barr 1,20.
bárraim 17,64.
beanaim 3,40; 28,12. Cf. *Síol Uidhir
. . . nír bhean riu nach rabhadar,
a Aodh, ar gach beainn dot bhrot*
F 16,7 § 10. In each of these
cases *beanaim re* could mean
'befall'. b. le 'concern' 24,18.
b. re 'meddle with' 13,7.
beann 7,10.
beirim as 11,23. b. go bun 13,30.
Cf. 32,1.
biasd 4.33.
biasduidhe 4,20.

bioth, tre bh. síor 13,39; 15,18; 25,31.
bithin, do bh. 15,8.
bodhang 16,49.
bog 1,19; 33,12; 38,4; 44,8.
bolard 35,4.
branán 2,7; 25,6.
branar 13,38.
braon, braon- 'humid; verdant' 1,3;
  7,29; 17,7,18.
braonach 1,17; 9,44; 32,26.
-bras 6,18.
brat 1,7; 11,20.   b. is tanoide a
  thilleadh (prov.) 23,8.
breath 15,38. do bhreith 15,16; 24,32.
-brios 6,18.
bró(in) 10,18; 11,30; 16,26.
brollach 38,7.
bruidhean 29,5.
buabhall 4,32.
buaidh 1,22; 13,13.   buadha (attrib.)
  14,13; 41,17.
buain 18,34.
bugha 39,3.
bun, ar b. 19,19.
bunadh, do bh. 21,8.   App. D, 11.
bunaidh (?) 44,8.

cagadh 1,16.
cagail 16,12.
caillim = coillim 18,5.
caithim 15,12.
car 11,23.
cára = córe 'peace' 25,40.
carbh 11,9.
cás 7,15.
cathardha 2,24.
céadáir 2,29; 18,10.
cean see cion.
ceann i gceann 1,5; 21,4.
ceanntrom 4,35; 15,6.
ceas naoidhean 20,27.
céidfear, an 1,20.
céile comhloinn 10,4.   c. cuil 1,56.
cinéal (better ceinéal, Ir. Gr. Tr.,
  Decl. 77) 3,17; 9,48; 16,35; 32,68.
ciodh 15,28; 28,30.
cion 19,10. gp. 1,45; 4,11; 21,6.

(os) cionn 11,20.
clampar 22,2.
cleamhnaoi 2,9.
cleathmhongach 2,23.
cleithleabhar 2,1; 7,47.
cliath 10,10.
cliatbach 16,50; 20,25.
clúmh 1,5.
cneas 1,13; 9,24.
cnú 28,20.
cnuaisdiugh 11,17.
cogthach 19,16.
coicéad 1,51.
cóir 7,7; 24.1.
combáidh 2,7; 16,11.
comhanta 16,48.
comhar 3,2.
comharthaighim 2,56; cf. Ar Finghin
  mach [sic] meic Donnchaidh . na
  coillte do chomhorthaigh, ni tar-
  gaidh a siodh ó sin . fa ríor ar
  n-argain Finghin 23 H 8, 45 a.
comhnámha 2,9 (: Welsh kyfnofant,
  RC 41, 213 ?).
comhraidhneach, comhraighneach
  21,29; 17.32.
commórt(h)as 2,5; 25,38.
concha(i)r 11,16; cf. conchar ic sreith
  riag rig LL 33 a 38; cland Duind
  Desa andso 7 na cerda do bi
  aco . . . Fer Glas fri conchora
  Lec. 458 a.
cougal 29,31.
congháireach 4,34.
connailbhe 2,7.
cor 3,17.
corcradh 11,20.
corr 1,6,25; 18,5.
corthar 11,16.
craobha ciúil 14,7.
craoithe see crú.
creachthóir 4,29.
críoch 3,37.
cróbhuaile 4,22.
cro(i)s 9,20; 24,11,43.
crosaim 22 a,19.
crosán 34,24.

téigleach 7,37.
téiglidhe 13,1.
teisbéanadh 15,28.
tibhre 13,8.
tilim, tileadh 10,11; 14,34.
tiomargadh 2,38.
tiomna? 33,7.
tnúthach 1,45.
tógbhaim 18,30; 20,33. t. idir 1,1.
  togbhaim 18,16.
togha 25,32.
toinighthe 9,;.
toirbhirim 6,7.
toireamhain 1,50.

-tónn 7,28.
treimhse 1,21.
tuilleamh 14,23.
tuillmheadh 13,33.
túr 21,;1.
turarán 44,3.
turbhaidh 2,40.

uaill 18,2.
uaithbhéalda 4,33.
uille 14,17,18.
um 3,54.
urra see orra.

PERSONAL NAMES

The references are not exhaustive in each case.

Ádhamh 7,34; 13,18.
Áighmhionóin, Agamemuon 26,33.
Aodh mhac Úghoine? 40,10.
Aodh Athlamhain 26,14,16.
Aoibheall 21,19-35; 27,29.
Aonghus 35,5; 39,21; cf. 39,7.
Art 1,8; 19,9.
Art s. o. Nia Corb 32,29.
Art Aoinfear 34,30,31.
Artúr(?) 8,41.
Artúr, Cing A., 40,9.

Páidricín = Pádraicín 36,14.
Balor 24,5.
Béac mhac Flaithgheasa 32,39-40.
Bearchán 6,17; 9,52.
Bháitéar Máb 34 l. 146.
Bile 32,4.
Blod s. o. Cas, hence síol (m)Bloid, i. e. the Dalcassians 29,13.
Bran mhac Feabhail 39,17-19; 40,15.
Bréanuinn s. o. Nad Fraoich 32,33-4.
Breas s. o. Ealatha 4,9,10.
Breóghon, an ancestor of the Gaels, 25,38; 32,4.
Brian Bóromha 14,29; 21,19-35; B. Bóroimhe 1,16; 21,24; 40,11; = Brian
    21,20; 25,34; 32,9.
Búrc:
    Bháitéar 19,15 (cf. Uáitéar).

Éamonn s. o. Tomás 17,42.
Éamonn s. o. MacUilliam 18 *pass.*, cf. 19.
Éamonn Albanach 17,11.
Mac Uilliam Búrc 17,56; 25,12.
Maoilir s. o. Uáitéar 21 *pass.* (1,5,36-38).
Oiluéarus s. o. Seaán 17,49,50; 20,6.
Riocard s. o. Éamonn 17,43.
Riocard Mór 17,27.
Riocard Óg s. o. Riocard 22a *pass.* (1,2,8,58).
Risdeard 17,28-36.
Risdeard s. o. Oiluéarus s. o. Seaán 20 *pass.* (6,8,9).
Seaán s. o. Oiluéarus s. o. Seaán 17 *pass.* (50,58).
Seaán Mór s. o. Riocard 17,48.
Sile wife of Risdeard 20,56.
Siobhán mo. of Riocard Óg 22a,58.
Tomás s. o. Éamonn 17,42.
Uáitéar s. o. MacUilliam 21,10,36-38 (cf. Bháitéar).
Uilliam, ancestor of the kin, 17,22,51.
Uilliam 22 (1,19,20); cf. 23.
Uilliam, Sior U., 17,37.
Uilliam Óg 17,38.

Cairbre 26,4; ciú C., i. e. Gaels, 16,62.
Cas (clann, síol, fuil etc. of) 3,3,6,12; 17,50; 21,32; 32,16.
Cathaoir, clann Ch. i. e. the Leinstermen, from C. Mór, 16,1.
Ceann Faoladh 32,36-7.
Cearmaid 4,13, C. Mirbhéal 28,14.
Ceasair, a pre-Milesian princess, 3,31.
Cian s. o. Oilill Ólum 32,14,17.
Cobhthach (clann, clár etc. Cobhthaigh i. e. Irishmen, Ireland) 1,11,42; 4,26;
     7,2; 10,3,13; 24,2, etc.
Colla (clann, síol etc. C.) 2,9; 9 *pass.*; 11,11; 13,18.
Colla Dá Chríoch 9,50.
Colla Uais 24,38.
Colla, na C., 11,39; cf. 10,41.
Colu(i)m 27,31,35.
Conaire, C. Mór, 26,11; 31,36; 40,14.
Conall, C. Gulban s. o. Niall Naoighiallach, 23,19; 26,6, clann, síol etc.
     Conaill means especially the O'Donnells of Donegal: 3,2,3; 4,14;
     26,12,21,49 etc.; but is also used in a more general meaning to include
     other kindreds descended from the same ancestor: 2,11-12 etc.
Conall Criomhthann s. o. Niall Naoighiallach 26,3.
Conall Cruachna 2,22-37.
Conchobhar, síol etc. Conchobhair means esp. the O'Conors of Sligo: 15,6,47,49;
     in 16,1 it seems to mean Connachtmen; in 8,26, it seems to mean
     the men of Ireland in general, or possibly of east Ulster. clár C.
     is used of Ulster, or rather Tír Eóghain, 7,42; more vaguely 5,3.

Conmhaol s. o. Éibhear 32$_{,8,9}$.

Conn, C. Céadchathach, 2$_{,23-37}$; 14$_{,25}$; 18$_{,27-8}$; síol etc. Cuinn is used generally of the men of Ireland, or the Irish nobility: 3$_{,43}$; 10$_{,20}$; 33$_{,9}$ etc.; ráth, lios etc. C., of Ireland: 1$_{,11}$; 9$_{,1}$; 19$_{,11}$ etc.; Banbha Cuinn 14$_{,25}$, Teamhair C. 17$_{,45}$; bean Ch.; i. e. Ireland 6$_{,11}$. C. Céadchathach 1$_{,42}$; 3$_{,4}$; 8$_{,12}$.

Connla, clár etc. C., i. e. Ireland 6$_{,15}$; 14$_{.33}$; in 10$_{,25}$ it may mean the land of the Oirghialla. See 6$_{,15}$ n., 10$_{,25}$ n.

Connla s. o. Tadhg 32$_{,22}$.

Connla Ruadh s. o. Conn Céadchathach 39$_{,15,16}$; 40$_{,17}$.

Conuing s. o. Faobhar 4$_{,6,7}$.

Corc 3$_{,5,51}$; 5$_{,10}$; 14$_{,27}$; 18$_{,11}$.

Cormac, C. mhac Airt, 14$_{,26}$; clár Cor(b)maic, i. e. Ireland 2$_{,21}$; 12$_{,12}$; 14$_{,8}$.

Cormac s. o. Oilill Ólum 32$_{,14,16}$.

Cormac Gaileangach 32$_{,22,24,25}$.

Craoidhe, crú C. i. e. the Maguires 10$_{,14}$.

Criomhthan, clann etc. Criomhthain 7$_{,18}$; 12$_{,2}$. I am not sure if the meaning is restricted to any particular kindred in these instances. clár C., i. e. Ireland, 46$_{,3}$.

Criomhthann, crú Criomhthainn? 33$_{,13}$.

Cruadhchosach, an 34$_{,11}$.

Cú Chulainn 6$_{,16}$; 34$_{,12}$; 40$_{,12}$; Cú an chleasraidh 6$_{,7,10}$.

Dálach, clann etc. Dálaigh i. e. the O'Donnells, 2$_{,10,12}$; 3$_{,22,53}$; 27$_{,25,26}$.

Dá Thí, clár D., Teagh D. i. e. Ireland, Tara, 25$_{,26}$; 28$_{,19}$. Possibly from Da Thí or Na Thí (Nath Í) s. o. Fiachra (see RIA Dict. fasc. i), but it seems to be from the older mythology, like Tailte.

Déadsolus s. o. Sádarn = Dædalus s. o. Saturn 20$_{,15,17,24}$.

Deala (gen.) s. o. mac Lóigh 4$_{,8}$.

Deichtine, mo. of Cú Chulainn 40$_{,12}$.

Deirgtheine, síol D , 31$_{,56}$.

Diarmaid s. o. Fionnbharr 32$_{,35}$.

Dochartach, eponym of the O'Dohertys, 28$_{,23}$; one of the kin, 2$_{,12}$.

Donnchadh s. o. Brian Bóromha 21$_{,21,24}$ ff.

Eachaidh fa. o. Niall Naoighiallach, gen. Eachach 1$_{,15}$.

Eachaidh (Eochu), E. Doimléan, see Notes, ii pp. 226-7; gen. Eachaidh 9$_{,8,9,18,19}$; Eachach 9$_{,42,46,53}$; Eochaidh 24$_{,8}$. Eath-, varr.

Eaghra, eponym of the O'Haras, 32$_{,11}$; ciobhuing E. 30$_{,13}$. See Ó He.

Ealcmha(i)r, brugh Ealcmhair 6$_{,2}$.

Éanna s. o. Niall Naoighiallach 26$_{,4}$. See also 6$_{,11}$ n.

Earcoil = Hercules 13$_{,31,39}$; Earcal 13$_{,52}$; gen. Earcoil 13$_{,35,37}$.

Éibhear s. o. Míl anc. of the southern Gaels, 18$_{,25}$; common in síol etc. Éibhir 16$_{,6}$ etc. É. Fionn 21$_{,28}$; 32$_{,1}$.

Éircamhón s. o. Míl anc. of the northern Gaels, 18$_{,25}$; common in síol etc. Éireamhó(i)n 10$_{,22}$; 16$_{,6}$; gort. É., i. e. Ireland, 30$_{,9}$.

Eisibéal mo. of Ó Cearbhaill 34$_{,10}$.

Oilill s. o. Maghnus 32,$_{60}$.

Onóra, wi. of Oilill, grandmother of Cormac, 30.$_{5}$.

Ruaidhrí 32,$_{59}$.

Seaán s. o. Uilliam 32,$_{61}$.

Seaán Buidhe s. o. Tadhg 32,$_{55}$.

Seaán Mór 32,$_{52}$.

Tadhg s. o. Cian 32,$_{63}$.

Tadhg s. o. Fearghal 32,$_{54}$.

Tailteach (Taichleach) s. o. Muircheartach 32,$_{45}$.

Tomaltach s. o. Seaán 32,$_{56}$.

Uilliam 32,$_{61}$.

Úna, wife of Cian, mo. of Cormac, 29,$_{13}$; 30,$_{23}$; 32,$_{79}$.

Ó Huiginn, Conchobhar, 25,$_{15,30}$.

Ó Léanaigh Mhóir(?), an Cruadhchosach, 34 *l.* 74.

Ó Máille, Mathghamhain, 40,$_{13}$.

Ó Mao(i)l Doraidh 17,$_{30}$.

Ó Néill:

Auna, wife of Toirdhealbhach Ó N., 8,$_{40}$.

Conn s. o. Conn 26,$_{51}$.

Domhuall s. o. Muircheartach 3,$_{29,34}$.

Seaán 6 *pass.* ($_{11,12,13}$); dau. of, 5,$_{4}$.

Toirdhealbhach s. o. Niall 7-8 *pass.* (7,$_{19,29,52}$; 8,$_{3,24,36}$). Anna, wife of, 8,$_{43}$.

Ó Ruairc, Brian s. o. Brian, 16 *pass.* ($_{11,32,43,57}$). See Ó Conchobhair.

Odhar, *gen.* Uidhir, ancestor of Mág Uidhir; cíú, fuil etc. U., i. e. the Maguire kindred, 10,$_{2,16}$ etc.

Oilill, in fonn O., 3,$_{15}$, see Note.

Oilill Ólum s. o. Eóghan Mór, *gen.* Oilill 32,$_{10,65}$; *dat.* Oilill 32,$_{12,17}$ etc.; 34 *l.* 188.

Pádraig 7,$_{16}$; 45,$_{1}$; 46,$_{1,2,6}$.

Parthalón, -án 28,$_{5-6,7}$.

Pluingcéad, Pádraicín 36,$_{10,12,14}$.

Poimp, Pompey 18,$_{17-19}$.

Risdeard 36,$_{15}$.

Ruadhán [of Lothra] 28,$_{42}$.

Ruarc, eponym. of Ó Ruairc; síol Ruairc, 16,$_{28,57}$.

Rudhroighe 36,$_{15}$.

Rudhroighe, in Clanna R., i. e. the royal line of Ulster, 7,$_{33}$.

Sadhbh, wife of Oilill Ólum, from whom his descendants, and the Munstermen generally are termed síol etc. Sadhbha, 3,$_{11}$; 29,$_{36}$.

Saorghus s. o. Béac 32,$_{40,41}$.

Séadna 27,$_{33}$.

Séadna, síol S., i. e. the Maguires, 10,$_{8}$.

Séarlas, Charlemagne; síol etc. Séarlais, i. e. the Burkes, 17,$_{13,14,19}$; 23,$_{19}$.
Séasar, Séasäir, Caesar, 24,$_{21,31}$ (*leg.* -air?); Séasair, *nom.* 18,$_{19}$; 24,$_{35}$. *gen.*
    18,$_{17}$; 24,$_{27}$; Seasáir, *nom.* 24,$_{34}$, cf. 17,$_{56}$.
Seisgnéan s. o. Laoi 32,$_{28}$.
Sioghmhall, Síoth Sioghmhuill, 13,$_{15}$. Cf. Ériu 9, 8. 99.
Solamh, S. mhac Dáibhidh, Solomon s. o. David, 2,$_{44,45,48}$.
Sreang 2,$_{16}$.
Suibhne, in clann etc. S., i. e. the MacSweenys, 26,$_{18,41}$ etc.

Tadhg s. o. Brian Bóromha 21,$_{21,26}$.
Tadhg s. o. Cathal, see Ó Ceallaigh.
Tadhg s. o. Cian 32,$_{20}$.
Táilgeann 46,$_{13}$.
Tailte, common in Teach etc. Tailte, i. e. Ireland, 26,$_3$ etc. Cf. Place-
    names.
Tailteach (Taichleach) s. o. Ceann Faoladh 32,$_{37,38}$.
Tailteach (Taichleach) s. o. Muircheartach 32,$_{45}$.
Tál 3,$_1$; 21,$_{25}$.
Toirdhealbhach s. o. Marcas (T. Mhac Marcais?) 42,$_3$.
Toirdhealbhach s. o. Tadhg s. o. Brian Bóromha 21,$_{32,33}$.
Tuathal, T. Teachtmhar, 1,$_{51}$, also in Teach Tuathail, i. e. Tara, Ireland, 10,$_{19}$.
Tuireann 35,$_5$, see Note.

Uilliam 36,$_{13}$.
Uilliam 17,$_{22,51}$; probably William FitzAdelm is meant.
Úghoine, in iath etc. Ú., i. e. Ireland, 4 $_{16}$; 16,$_{18}$ etc. I have also noted
    Iúghoine.
Úna, mo. of Conn Céadchathach, hence clár, etc., Ú., i. e. Ireland, 16,$_{18}$.

PLACE AND POPULATION NAMES

Note:—fanciful names, such as Clár Cuinn, Clann Éibhir, etc., are usually noted in the Index of Personal Names (Conn, Éibhear). The reff. are not exhaustive in each case. For identifications see also Notes and Translation.

Abha Ó gCearnaigh 34 *l.* 156.
Afraig, Africa, 1,$_{19}$.
Áine 31,$_{34}$.
Alba, *gen.* Alban, 24,$_4$; 41,$_4$. with attenuating suff. 24,$_2$, *dat.* Albain 24,$_3$.
Albanach 24,$_2$.
Almha 27,$_{4,7,8}$, etc.; *gen.* Almhan 3,$_{21}$; 27,$_{1,6}$; Almhoine S,$_4$; 27,$_{12}$; crioch
    Almhan, i. e. Meath, the Pale, 16,$_{28}$.
Annla 7,$_{50}$; cath A. 17,$_{29}$.
Aolmhagh, *gen.* -mhoighe, 16,$_{16}$; -mhuigh 33,$_{14}$.
Ára, see Caol Árann.
Ard Uladh, bar. of Ards, Co. Down, 8,$_{34}$; 17,$_{14}$.

Áth Buidhe 34 *l.* 90.
Áth Conaill 13,[19].
Áth na Ríogh 17,[40].
Áth Truim 17,[27].

Baile Lithbhir, Lifford, 11,[40]. See Leithbhear.
Banbha, a poetical name for Ireland, 1,[7]; 4,[20]; 24,[5] etc.
Banna, the river Bann, 9,[35]; 17,[34].
Baoi 24.[40].
Baoill, *gen.* -e, the Boyle r., Co. Roscommon, 16,[82]; 32,[26]; = Búill, q. v.
Beanna Bághoine (Bóghoine) 4,[43]; 27,[42].
Beanna Boirche 3,[18].
Beanna Bladhma 31,[42].
Beann Éadair 17,[47]; 24,[36]; 34,[22].
Beannchor, Bangor, Co. Down, 7,[21]; 17,[29]; cf. 14,[10].
Bearnas, Barnasmore, Donegal, 1,[53]; 3,[24]; 13,[20]; 17,[50]; 26,[30], etc.
Bealta 10,[15]; 28,[32].
Biorra, the Birr river, King's Co., 16,[20].
Bóinn, *gen.* -e, the Boyne, 8,[34]; 9,[35]; 13,[20]; 16,[69]; 26,[19]; fig. for Ireland,
    1,[41]; 21,[24] etc.; in this use frequently B. Breagh, 2,[55]; 7,[1]; 24,[34]
    etc.; críoch Bhóinne, 16,[57] may be used definitely of Meath, the Pale,
    or figuratively of Ireland generally.
Bóroimhe (Bóromha) 22a,[51], common in epithets, 3,[30]; 8,[26]; 18,[4]; 30,[1] etc.
    When used in ref. to a chief of a southern family, B. near Killaloe
    is probably intended, see Ériu 8, 71. Otherwise the ref. is vague.
    In 17,[36] bruach B. denotes Munster.
Breagh, only occurs here in this form, which is *gen.*, as a name for Ireland,
    . *pass.* See note on 1,[2].
Breaghmhach 19,[14], rendered 'Bregia's plain,' perhaps wrongly; it is probably
    used of the Pale, see Bregmag in Onom.
Bréifne 14,[20]; 16,[50], see 16,[13] n.
Bréifneach, a native of Bréifne; one of the O'Rorkes, 13,[17]; 16,[32].
Brugh Aonghuis 35,[5]; 39,[21].
Brugh Bóinne 6,[2].
Brugh Ealcmhair 6,[2].
Bruidhean Lir 11,[15].
Buanaid 22a,[52].
Búill 16,[53]; 22a,[51], see Baoill.
Bun Duibhe 22a,[54].
Búrcach, a Burke; *np.* 17,[17]; *gp.* 17,[38,55]; 25,[11]; as *adj.* 22a,[15].

Cabhán, an, 38,[9].
Cairbre 15,[51]; 16,[50]; 41,[14].
Caiseal 5,[10]; 14,[27]; 17,[14]; 24,[42]; 30,[14]; 34 *l.* 112.
Calgach 17,[27].
Calraighe 3,[23]; 14,[1].
Caol Árann 17,[14]; the North Sound, Galway Bay, ?

Carraig Fearghosa 26,$_{46}$.

Casán 34 *l.* 29, the Cashen r., Kerry.

Cathair Chröoinn 4,$_{13}$; 28,$_{15}$.

Ceall Chluaine 12,$_{6}$.

Ceanannas 17,$_{45}$.

Ceann Coradh 21,$_{29}$; 22a,$_{47}$.

Ceann Tire 24,$_{6}$.

Ceara 14,$_{22}$; 20,$_{51}$.

Ciarraighe Luachra 34 *l.* 29.

Ceinéal (Clann, Síol etc.) Conaill, the O'Donnell kindred, 2,$_{8}$; 4,$_{37}$; 26,$_{18}$, etc.

Clann Bhaoisgne, the kindred of Fionn s. o. Cumhall, 27,$_{8}$.

Clann Charthaigh 32,$_{15}$

Clann Chonchobhair 16,$_{54}$.

Clann Chonchobhair Chianachta 32,$_{23}$ (see Top. Poems p. 21).

Clann Chubháin 14,$_{22}$.

Clann Ghoisdealbhaigh 14,$_{22}$.

Clann Domhnaill 16,$_{55}$; 24,$_{17}$.

Clann Fearghasa ('the MagRannells and O Ferralls of Leitrim and Long-ford,' Onom.) 16,$_{52}$.

Clann Israhél 9,$_{3}$.

Clann Mheic an Bhaird 43.

Clann Róigh 28,$_{19}$.

Clann Rosa 26,$_{46}$.

Clann Uilliam, the Mayo Burkes, 14,$_{20}$; 22a,$_{16,18}$.

Clár Crot 31,$_{17}$.

Clár na gCuradh 10,$_{32}$; 17,$_{46}$; 34 *l.* 49; apparently a poetical name for Ireland.

Clár (Fiadh, Magh, Tulach etc.) na bhFionn (*or* na dTri bhF.), a poetical name for Ireland, see Introd. p. lvii-lviii, 4,$_{25,45}$; 7,$_{2,8,17}$; 8,$_{5}$;- 9,$_{3}$; 18,$_{5,8}$; 32,$_{20}$. Teamhair na bhF. 24,$_{14}$.

Cliú, *gen.* Cliach, 34,$_{5}$, *acc.* Cliaich 16,$_{70}$, Cliaigh 21,$_{22}$. *dat.* Cliaigh 9,$_{55}$.

Cluain 7,$_{14}$.

Cnoc Breagh 15,$_{48}$; 20,$_{53}$; 22a,$_{22}$.

Cnoc Midhe 21,$_{37}$; cf. 16,$_{63}$.

Cnodhbha *gen.*, Clár C. 18,$_{17}$; 22a,$_{17}$.

Cnuca 34,$_{25}$.

Codhal 9,$_{40}$; 19,$_{19}$.

Cóigeadh Ól nEagmhocht 2,$_{3}$.

Coirrsliabh 4,$_{39}$; 17,$_{68}$.

Collán, in W. Clare, see Onom., 32,$_{63}$.

Colt 16,$_{25}$.

Conallach, one of the O'Donnell kindred, 2,$_{56}$; 3,$_{11}$; 16,$_{49}$.

Conga (Cunga) 17,$_{34}$; 20,$_{49}$

Connacht, oilltrian C., 9,$_{34}$, min C. 18,$_{32}$, righe, clár, magh, etc. C., 2,$_{4,27}$; 13,$_{50}$, etc.; ar C. 2,$_{55}$, *dat.* Connachtaibh 12,$_{6}$; 13,$_{18}$; 17,$_{39}$, etc. (see MacNeill, Population Groups §§ 4, 41, Proc. RIA xxix C 4).

Connachtach, a native of Connacht, *npl.* 2,$_{6,26}$; 17,$_{31}$; *gp.* 21,$_{2}$; as *adj.*, *dsf.* 13,$_{51}$.

Corann, críoch Coruinn, 13,21.

Corannach, a native of Corann, *npl.* 16,50.

Craobh, an Ch., 8,1,5.

Craobhruadh 13,21; 26,46, this placename may be preserved in the name of Creeveroe tl., Armagh; in the second instance it is evidently used symbolically.

Craoi, *gen.* of Cró 'fold;' common in poetical names for Ireland, as C. Chobhthaigh 10,13. C. Theamhrach 21,35, etc.

Cruacha, *gen.* Cruachan or Cruachna, *dat.*, *acc.* Cruachain, Croghan, Co. Roscommon, the ancient seat of the kings of Connacht. Sometimes used figuratively for Connacht, or in a wider application, for Ireland; *nom.* 2,54; *acc.* 19,13; *gen.* 2,1; 3,39; 16,22. The *nom.* Cruachain 5,9 is not rimed.

Cruachán Lighean 4,5,8, etc.

Cuan Dor, Glandore, 31,35.

Cunga see Conga.

Dearc? *gen.* Deirce, 29,37.

Dearg, *gen.* Deirge, 8,35; 25,8.

Deirgiort 22a,54. Cf. Loch Deirgceirt.

Dochartach, one of the O'Doherty kindred, 2,12.

Doire, Derry, 7,13; 17,36.

Doladh 34 *l.* 51.

Drobhaois 8,34.

Druim Caoin 11,17.

Druim Feabhail 4,18.

Druim Lighean 4,1 ff.

Dubh, *acc.* Duibh, *gen.* Duibhe, the r. Duff, Sligo-Leitrim, 14,14; 15,50; 16,46; 19,13; 30,18.

Duibhlinn 3,23.

Dún Breagh 13,18; probably a name for Tara.

Dún Dealgan 6,5; 26,46.

Dún Durlais 4,44. See Durlas.

Dún Geanuinn 6,16.

Dún Iomgháin 5,4. See Iomghán.

Dún Mhic Pádraiccín 34 *l.* 155, DownmacPatrick, near Kinsale?

Dún na nGall 1,50; 3,10.

Dún oide an Ioldánuigh (?) 40,21.

Dún Oiligh 28,26.

Dún Sainbh 39,20.

Dún Sámhnoidhe 36,11.

Dún Uisnigh 6,7.

Durlas 6,3, Durlaistreibh 5,8, ráth Durlais 20,54. See Dún D.

Eacoill 17,57, rinn Eacla 22a,54.

Eachtgha, Aughty, 14,23; 19,13.

Eadáil, Eadáill (Iodáill) 15,17, *gen.* -e, 24,19.

Ealga, clár E., Inis E., i. e. Ireland, 26,13; 45,2.

Eamhain, in Ulster, 14,17; fig. 10,9, etc., 32,11.

Eamhain, E. Abhlach, 5,9; 6,1; 17,51; 39,21.

Eanghuile 17,40.

Eas Caoille 25.1.

Eas Dá Éagann 1,50. Cf. 8,33.

Eas Ruaidh 17,35; 22,22.

Easbáin, acc. 24,20; gen. 4,12, etc.

Éile, the O'Carroll territory, K.'s Co. — Tipperary, 34,13, Crioch É. 34,35, i nÉilibh 34,18. Éileach, a native of the territory, 34,17.

Eine, clár E., 41,3, a plain near L. Melvin, see Mag Ene, Onom.

Éire, nom. 10,7; 12,1; acc. 10,11; 17,11; gen. 9,49; 17,44; dat. 17,18.

Éireannach, an Irishman, gen. 7,4; npl. 16,17; dp. 7,18; 12,2; as adj., gsm. 16,42.

Éirne, the Erne r. or lake, 9,35; 14,23, fig. 10,13 etc.

Eithne, often used symbolically, fear E. 1,45, clár E. 9,20, see Note; in 16,53, 17,49 it seems to be the r. Inny, Westmeath.

Eóghanach, one of the kindred of Eóghan (q. v.); esp. one of the O'Neill family, 7,2; 8,20; 26,19 etc.

Eóraip, gen. Eórpa, 9,2; 13,52; 24,21 etc.

Fainn, gen. Foinne, 2,41.

Fál, a poetical name for Ireland, pass. (14,16 etc. fiadh Fáil 4,12, magh F. 4,24, flaith F. 18,28, etc.) See Introd. p. lvii.

Fánaid, dat. 27,4; 28,32; gen. Fánad 4,42; 27,13.

Fathan, gen. Faithne, 28,37.

Féil, the Feale r., Kerry, 34 l. 29.

Fiachrach, a native of Tireragh (< Tir Fiachrach) bar., Co. Sligo, npl. 16,50.

Finn, see Clár na bhFionn.

Fionn r., Co. Donegal, nom. 9,35; dat. 8,33; gen. 16 41.

Fir Bolg 17,6.

Fódla, a poetical name for Ireland, 10,8; 16,47, etc.

Foinne, see Fainn.

Forbhar 22a,53, a place or river probably in east or north-east Clare: do gabh som (sc. Toirdhelbhach Ó Briain) righe Tuadhmuman o Luachar go Bladhma 7 o Léim Conculaind go Forbor, 7 o Medhraide go Bealach Abhrat ZfcP 10, 8 n. 2.

Forghas, the r. Fergus, Clare, 3,3; 21,32; 32,16.

Formaol, Fermoyle in Cork or Kerry, 3,7.

Frainge, gen. na F-e, 17,10.

Frangcach, adj., 17,11.

Fréamhainn, Frewin, Westmeath; generally in fig. use (Introd. p. lix), acc. 1,45; dat. 7,20; gen. 1,52; 24,41; 30 7.

Gabhra, gen., 12,3, Gort G. 10,9; 13,12.

Gabhrán, magh Gabhráin, 19,5, location doubtful.

Gaileanga, gen. Gailiong, 32,30,39.

Gaileangaigh 14,22.

Gáilian, Gort G., i. e. Leinster, 27,3.

Gáille 30,26.

Gaillimh, *gen.* Gaillmhe, Galway, 22 a,11.

Gáirighe 3,35; 16,21; 31,59.

Gall, a foreigner, an Englishman, *gs.* Goill 17,67; *npl.* Goill 16,28; 17,12; Gaill 34 *l.* 150; *gp.* Gall 9,5 etc.; *dp.* Gallaibh 16,3.

Gaoidh al, an Irishman, 17,67; *gs.* 7,52; 17,67; *npl.* 1,55; *gp.* 1,18; 10,38. etc.

Gaoidhealach, Irish, *gsm.* 16,51.

Garmna 21,43.

Goill, see Gall.

Goisdealbhaigh 14,22.

Gréag, *gen.*, seóid Gh. 'the treasures of the Greeks' 13,41, damhradh G. 18,21, milidh na nG. 20,15; common in Gaoidhil G. 25,7 etc., see Introd. p. lix, and 17,10 n.

Gréagach, a Greek, *npl.* 13,24; 18,24; 26,36; of the Fitzgeralds 17,11; as *adj.* 13,31; 17,10 etc.

Gréig, Greece, *acc.* fan nG. 13,25; *dat.* 17,12.

Grúda, *acc.* fán nGrúdainn (*sic leg.*), 34 *l.* 128.

Í Mhaine 16,52. Cf. Síol M.

Iarmhumha 34 *l.* 31.

Iarusaléim 17,25.

Íle 16,55; 24,6,14.

Inbhear Dá Éagann 8,33. Cf. 1,50.

Inis Cé 25,15.

Inis Ceithleann 11,1,7.

Inis Ealga 45,2.

Inis Eóghain, *gen.* Inse hE., 4.42.

Inis Fáil, Innisfail, i. e. Ireland, 20,9; 25,10 etc.

Iomghán 3,48, etc. See Dún I.

Iorrus Domhnann 22 a,52.

Laighin, Leinstermen, Leinster, *gen.* Laighean 5,10; 16,26; 27,40 etc., *voc.* Laighne 27,34, *dat.* Laighnibh 17,39; 21,3.

Laighneach, a Leinsterman, *dp.* 17.38, *gp.* 27,37.

Leamhnach (?) 34,20.

Leath Cathail 17,13.

Leath Cuinn 9,51; 17,31,32,38. *Is é Leth Cuind hÚ Neill in descirt 7 h. Neill in tuascirt. 7 teora Connachta 7 Airgialla 7c.* LL 333 b 6; cf. ZfcP 8, 319. 13.

Leath Mogha, i. e. the southern half of Ireland, Munster, 14,26; 29,2 etc.

Leithbhear, Lifford, 5,1 etc.

Liag, *gen.*, 11,13. See Note, and add: possibly Sliabh L., 'Slieveleague' Co. Donegal, is meant.

Liathdruim, *gen.* -droma, 2,9; 9,1 etc.

Lie see Liag.

Life 17,39.

Lighean see Druim L.

Line 3,49.

Lios Gréine 6,1.

Loch Cé 19,14; 25,10.

Loch Con 22,22.

Loch Cuan 17,29.

Loch Deirgceirt 40,16.   Cf. Deirgiort.

Loch nEachaidh 17,39.

Loch Éirne 11,32; 16,53.

Loch Feabhail 1,50; 28,32.

Loch Gile 41,11.

Loch Laoigh 32,26.

Loch Measg 17,46.

Loch Oirbsean 22a,57; 32,26.

Loch Raoibh 25,13.

Loch Riach 19,14.

Loch Ribh mhic Muireadha 34 l. 155.

Loch Seimhdidhe 22a,52.

Loch Uachtair 16,53.

Lochlann, *gen.*, 4,9; 21,22.

Lonndáin 17,24; *gen.* 41,4; *dat.* Lunnuinn 17,43; 36,3, Lundain 36,7,13.

Luighne 32,38, na trí L. 16,50; 32,21, ar Luighnibh 32,47; *gen.* 14,17; 29,12; 32,32 etc.

Luighneach, *adj. gp.*? possibly a *gen.* of Luighne, 32,49.

Luimneach 17,13,15; 16,11 etc.

Lunnainn, Lundain see Lonndain.

Macha, *gen.*, fig. of Ulster, or east U., 4,28; 7,16 etc.

Magh an Scáil 2,31.

Magh Breagh 26,3.

Magh Ceóil 16,61.   Unidentified.

Magh Dreimhne 34,28.   Modreeny, Lr. Ormond, Co. Tipperary, Onom.

Magh Léana 2,22.

Magh Luirg 27,15.

Magh Máil 17,39.

Magh Maistean 31,61.

Magh Marr 32,25; in 42,1 Mar in Scotland may be intended.

Magh Meann 25,21.

Magh Monaidh 24,9,32 etc.; the Mounth in Scotland? but cf. Monadh.

Magh Rath 9,42, cf. 10,44.

Magh Sléacht, *gen.* Moighe S-a, 16,13.

Magh Tuireadh 17,46; 32,25.

Máigh, the Maigue r. Limerick, *dat.* 3,1; 32,28; *gen.* Máighe 16,69.

Maighean, *gen.*, 9,39. probably preserved in Donaghmoyne (Domnach Maigne) Farney, Co. Monaghan; see Onom. s. magen.

Málainn, *dat.*, 28,32.

Manann, *gen.*, Man, Isle of M.? 17,[47], from the exploit referred to the
   ep. *griobh M.* may be applied to Richard's descendant, 22a,[16].
Manchach, a man of Fermanagh; Manchaigh, *gen*, 10,[13]; *npl.* 16,[53] etc.;
   dat. Manchachaibh 9,[42]; as *adj.* 10,[3]; 12,[4].
Maonmhagh, in Galway 3,[31].
Midhe 34 *l.* 172; 16,[20]; 17,[45] etc.; see Cnoc M.
Modharn, *gen.* Modhuirne, the Mourne r., Tyrone, 26,[24,45]; fig. 2,[6]; 8,[19];
   9,[38].
Moir see Muir.
Monadh, *gen.* Monaidh, in ref. to the O'Neills, 8,[28]; 26,[31]; cf. 46,[2], probably
   in Co. Down, see M. Ulad in Onom.
Muadh the r. Moy, Co. Mayo; *dat.* Muaidh 2,[44]; 4,[39]; 13.[20] etc.; *gen.*
   Muaidhe 20,[11]; 34,[8].
Mucroimhe 22a,[2].
Muir Meann 40,[11].
Muintear Thadhgáin 34 *l.* 172.
Mumha, Munster, *gen.* Mumhan, 3,[8]; 21,[20]; *dat.* Mumhain 3,[9].
Múr Té 1,[6,8] n.
Murbhach 2,[37]; 3,[20]; 14,[13]; 20,[10].

Nás 5,[10]; 16,[26].

Oileach 2,[39]; 28,[1] etc.; see Introd. pp. lviii-lix.
Oirghialla 9,[28], *gen.* Oirghiall 4,[39]; 9,[6] etc.; *dat.* 9,[10,26] etc.; see 9,[10] n.
Oirghiallach a native of Oriel, one of the Oirghialla, 9,[37,45]; as *adj.*, *dsf.*
   9,[22].
Ól nÉagmhocht see Cóigeadh Ó.

Port an Púdair? 34,[21].
Port Manaidh 46,[2] (cf. Monadh).

Raghallach, an O'Reilly, *npl.*, 16,[53].
Raoileann, *gen.*, 8,[3].
Ráth Eochuill 40,[21].
Ráth Maoláin 27,[5].
Ráth Oiligh 28,[1,11].
Ráth Truim 32,[10]; 40,[12].
Róimh, Rome, *nom.*, 24,[23,25]; *dat.* 24,[24]; *voc.* 24,[27]; *acc.* 24,[31]; *gen.* 24,[30].
Rómhán, a Roman, *gp.* 17,[56].
Ros Guill 17,[30].
Ruarcach, one of the O'Rorke kindred, *npl.*, 16,[53].

Saxa (Sagsa), Saxon, English, Saxon-land, England; *gen.* Saxan 16,[7,44];
   17,[11,24]; *dat.* Saxoibh 17,[10], Saxain (England) 17,[12].
Seaghais 17,[36]. See Met. Dinds iv 44.
Síodh (Síoth) Ábhartaigh 39,[20].
Síodh Ban bhFionn 40,[10].

Síodh Bóinne 40,[20.]

Síodh Buidhbh 11,[18.]

Síodh Easa Ruaidh 40,[21.]

Síodh Midhir 39,[20.]

Síodh na gCuan 40,[20.]

Síodh Sioghmhuill 13,[15.]

Síodh Truim 11,[29]; 22a,[5×]; 40,[21]; 41,[1.]

Síol Airt 8,[21.]

Síol mBaoighill 2,[12.]

Síol gCearbhuill 32,[23.]

Síol gColla 9 *pass.*

Síol Gallchubhair 2,[12.]

Síol Maine 9,[42.] Cf. Í M.

Síol Mathghamhna 9,[42.]

Síol Muireadhaigh, the leading Roscommon kindreds, 41,[14.]

Síol Rosa 3,[1.]

Sionann 41,[5]; *dat.*, *acc.* -ainn 17,[34]; 22a,[53]; *gen.* Sionna 22,[22.]

Siúr, Súr, the Suir; *dat.* Siúir 17,[34], Súir 17,[33]; *gen.* Siúire 17,[33.] For
    broad initial cf. Ir. Texte iii 80 § 55 [II], RC 36, 262 § 8.

Sliabh Gamh 25,[24.]

Sliabh Muire 17,[40]; 32,[25.]

Sliabh Riabhach (?) 34,[18.]

Sligeach, Sligo, *acc.*, 38,[10]; 41,[5]; *gen.* Sligigh 1,[51]; 15,[7,48] etc., Sligighe
    2,[22]; 14,[6,20]; 41,[11] etc.

Srúbh Breagh (?) 8,[34.]

Srúbh Broin 4,[39]; cf. 8,[34] varr.

Srúbh Iorrais 17,[33]

Sruth Orthanáin, the Jordan, 17,[23.]

Suca, the Suck, 15,[13.]

Súir see Siúr.

Tail(l)te, *gen.* -tean, *acc.*, *dat.* -tin, Telton, Roscommon, 2,[30,54]; 30,[4];
    Teltown in Meath 6,[1]; 16,[23.] Tuatha Tailtean 9,[36], stands for the
    Gaels; cf. Tailte in Pers.names.

Teach Oiligh 28,[40.]

Teach an Túir, i. e. Tara, 9,[48.] Probably from *na trí Finn*, see Introd. p. lvii.

Teach na bhFionn, i. e. Tara, Ireland; see Clár na bhF.

Teach Truim 4,[35]; 25,[9.]

Tealach na bhFionn, see Clár na bhF.

Teamhair, Tara, 5,[9]; *gen.* Teamhrach 4,[41]; 21,[32]; Teamhra 2,[11]; 21,[17];
    dat. Teamhraigh 9,[32.] T. Breagh 17,[46.] T. Midhe 22a,[52], T. Truim
    8,[22]; for T. na bhFionn see Clár na bhF.

Tír Chonaill, Tirconnell, Donegal, 2,[1]; 27,[14] etc.

Torach, *acc.* Toraigh 17,[30]; *gen.* Toruighe 27,[15]; cf. 8,[34] varr. Usually
    Torry I., Donegal, but in our instances it seems to be a river-name,
    and in the verse *Ó Thoraigh co Cliodhna* ... *do thimchil aoinbhen*
    Erinn (Cog. 138) some place within or on the coastline seems meant.
    Cf. Toragh tl. in Mevagh, Kilmacrenan, Donegal.

INDEX OF FIRST LINES OF POEMS

Reference is to pages. Unless (ii) is prefixed vol. i is indicated.

ADDENDA AND CORRIGENDA

Note:—In reckoning the lines on a page the heading is ignored.

Volume One

Ó Huiginn Pedigree (constructed): omit (?) after 33 Pól (see 1 Pól in Appendix C, vol. ii p. 318).

p. xiii: there is a copy (possibly from O'Clery's source) of this pedigree in H 3. 18, 816.

p. xiii, n. 1: *Duinech*aid is a doubtful form; in a pedigree of Ó Maoil Mhuaidh by Gofraidh Mhac an Bhaird in C iv 1, 169, the name Duinechair (undeclinable) appears. Add.: *is ar slíocht Cairbre* (s. o. Niall N. G.) *atá Ó Flanagáin Thuath Ratha agus Ó Huiginn* (sic leg.) Keat. iv 58.

p. xiv, par. 3: See Wood-Martin, *Hist. of Sligo* i 394.

p. xiv, n. 3: See Appendix A.

p. xv, lines 12, 17: Read: nintee.

p. xvi: To references to TD in official documents of the 17th. cent. add the following (which I owe to Professor T. F. O'Rahilly): "Grant to Sir Theobald Dillon, Knt., of two-thirds of the fines for intrusions and alienations of the lands of" various parties in Co. Sligo, including those of "Teige Dalle O'Higgin, late of Coolerecoile, gent." 4th March, 11 James I., Pat. Rolls Jas. I, p. 277a.

p. xvi, n. 2: O'Grady was doubtless following O'Reilly, *Ir. Writers* p. clxx.

p. xvii, line 9: I inadvertently omitted to mention that Father Paul Walsh was my authority for the date of Ó Heódhusa's death. See Irish Ecclesiastical Record 1923, 221.

p. xviii, n. 3: Cf. also Maeil Echlainn, Ir. Gr. Tr., Decl. ex. 621.

p. xix, line 20: For: birth read : death (see next).

p. xx, line 1: The phrasing is elliptical, and corresponds to: *Máire inghen T. D. Uí U.* [*d'écc*] *do bhreith* [*leinbh*] etc., i. e. 'death of Mary, daughter of T. D. Ó H. in childbed.' Cf. *M. inghen Uí Ch. . . . do écc* (with addit. *do bhreith linibh*) FM 1396, note o; similarly 1395.

p. xx, line 25: Add.: The source of O'Clery's gloss. (cited in Bidrag) may be: *ucing .i. cablach ut est ucing la Sesur for muir* H 3.18, 79. 3 = Trans. Phil. Soc. 1859, 206.

p. xxii, n. 2: See 12 Seaán in Appendix C.

p. xxv, line 4: Professor O'Rahilly and Professor Watson have pointed out to me that I altogether missed the point of the quatrain, which is in effect a version of 'all is not gold that glitters.'

p. xxv, line 33: Read: AUDM.

p. xxviii, line 22 } : Read: Múrtha (see vol. ii p. 251).
p. xxix, line 24 }

p. xxxi: The date of 17 is uncertain; see vol. ii p. 255.

p. xxxi, line 22: See O'Rorke's *Hist. of Sligo* ii 505.

p. xxxii, line 19: Dele: possibly a (see Appendix C, under 1 Pól).

p. xxxii, lines 23-5: See Appendix C, under 2 Pól.

p. xxxii, n. 2: The ordinary meaning of *tionnsgnaim*, 'I begin,' will do here, or we might render it 'undertake.' Cf. *a gcuinne chriche maithe do thecht ar an duillechanso chum gloire De, 7 lesa anmann gach druinge dar thionsgnas é* O'Molloy's *Lucerna Fidelium* 13.

p. xxxvii, n.: See also CSPI, Carew 1575-88 p. xxiv n.

p. xxxviii, n. 1: Another paper of great interest and containing matter supplementary to the others mentioned is Professor W. J. Watson's Classic Gaelic Poetry . . . in Scotland, Trans. Gaelic Soc. of Inverness xxix.

p. xxxix, line 5: The elegy has since been edited and translated by Professor Bergin, Studies 1924, 85 ff.

p. xl, line 11 ff.: Cf. SG 336-7.

p. xliii, line 4 ff.: The poem has been edited and translated by Rev. L. MacKenna, Louth Arch. Journal 1921.

p. xlv, lines 1-2: Read: attributed by Father MacErlean to Flann

p. xlvi, line 9: It may be that battle-rolls were regularly included in panegyrics (when the material was available), but only preserved in the chief's own poem-book. We sometimes find them in family collections.

p. lv, line 21: Read: requisites of poetry

p. lvi, line 19: Read: *caor*

p. lvii, line 4: *fiadh fuinidh*, an early instance is: *firflaith fer funid* (of Tuathal Techtmar) LL 296 a 4 = SG 361.

p. lviii, line 32: As to Breagh see 1 § 2 n., vol. ii p. 188.

p. lix, line 23: Read: § 10.

p. lxiii, line z: Dele: the superior 1.

p. lxviii, line 33: The term 'acc. of respect' is of course historically incorrect, as in O. Ir. the noun in such sentences is in the nom.; but cf. the use of the gen., p. lxix, line 9.

p. lxx: Add references to the infixed prons.: -d- 1. 38; -m- 12. 7, 38; 14. 146.

p. lxxi, line 13: Add: deid 22 a 79.

p. lxxii, line 22: The connection of fa with O. Ir. imm was also suggested by Quiggin, see *Dialect of Donegal* § 314.

p. lxxvi, line 11: Cf. -pir 35. 10.

p. lxxviii, line 31: Cf. -éibert 35. 3.

p. lxxxii, line z: See also 22 a § 5 n.

p. lxxxiii, n. 2: Read: abs. 3 rd pl.

p. lxxxiv, line 10: Read: lamh

p. lxxxiv, n. 1: Read: *dhréachtaibh* : *léamhaid*

p. lxxxviii, line 23: For 42 read: 43

p. lxxxviii, line 21: The superior 2 at the end of the line is to be transferred to Óglachas in the line following.

p. lxxxix, line 10: Since the publication of vol. i I have learned that the original of 3 B 14 is still in the possession of the O'Hara family.

p. xcii, line 4: Read: 1685,

p. xciii, line 7: Dele 5

p. xciv, line 9: For sent. read: cent.

p. xcvii, line 13: For surname read: father's name (In the case of the 3rd century king, Cormac mhac Airt, we cannot of course correctly speak of a 'christian' name.).

p. ci, lines 21-2: Read: begins almost in every case with a vowel, and when it begins with a consonant the *do-* or *ad-* will cause, etc.

p. ciii, line 2: Read: the sound of *t*;

Text of the Poems

(See also vol. i p. cviii).

No. 1, line 98: Here: dá n-éaduinn is a possible reading (Bergin).

No. 3, line 193: Read: Bréigneóchaidh

No. 4, line 15: The gen. moighe should not cause lenition, and probably f. f. is the correct reading. Cf. 7. 83; 10. 9.

No. 4, line 170: Read: mBóghoine (see 27 § 42 n.).

No. 6, line 43: Read: bean Chuinn i ngaisdibh grádha (?) (Bergin).

No. 6, line 47: Read: tóir ó áth gur th. (?) (Bergin).

No. 6, line 71: Read: d'éis cean (Bergin).

No. 8, line 3: Read: buig

No. 8, line 149: Read: dháibh

No. 9, line 190: (Con) Chonnacht; the lenition of the C is historically irregular, but it is so common even in good MSS. that I have generalized it in the text. See varr.

No. 11, line 71: Read: lamh

No. 11, line 150: Read: ré ;

No. 11, line 151: Read: aithle,

No. 12, line 8: Read: an éigse

No. 12, line 10: Read: féachfaidh

No. 13, line 69: Dele comma.

No. 15, line 117: Read: éan

No. 16, heading, Read: MÚRTHA.

No. 16, line 34: Probably fa governs acc. here, and we should then read: fan droing bhf. bhf.

No. 16, lines 42, 44: Read: áirgheadha áilgheana (see Notes).

No. 17: There are also copies in II 4. 19, 117 and II 5. 10, 121. See Abbott-
    Gwynn Cat. p. 150.
No. 17, line 114: Read: Cuan,
No. 17, line 161: Read: lamh
No. 20, line   4: Read: radhocar
No. 20, lines 241-4: are in Ed. XLIV 12a (remainder missing). They are
    followed by 25, q. v.
No. 21, line   48: Read: nách éadfaidhir (?)
No. 21, line 115: Eclipsis would be better here (as in 123).
No. 21, line 153: Read: lamh
No. 22, line   26: Read: seirbhísi
No. 22, line   35: Read: luchta (?)
No. 22a, line 30: fuarais may be retained, as there is alliteration in any case.
No. 22a, line 198: Read: anallód,
No. 24: Probably some lines are omitted between lines 114-115.
No. 26, line   12: Read: Tailltean
No. 26, line   80: Read: a gcáir 'sgach (?) (Bergin).
No. 26, lines 129-30: Read: thionól : Aighmhionón (?)
No. 26, line 138: Read: do bhí
No. 27, line   95: Read: do-ionnmaoid
No. 29, lines 106, 108: Read: neoch; eoch (Bergin).
No. 31, line 122: oirichill mun a. is a better reading.
No. 32, line 269: Read: Taibhcóchaidh
No. 32, line 280: Read: athghlantair
No. 33, line   31: Read: droichbhliadhna
No. 33, line   38: Read: ionniuar.
No. 34, line 128: Read: nGrúdainn
No. 34, line 239: Dele footnote.
No. 35, line   7: Read: Seáin
No. 35, line   17: Read: réThuireann (see Notes).
No. 37, line   14: Read: och (: folt).
No. 38, line   28: Read: h'afán.
No. 39, line   9: Read: gruaidh daithgheal (Bergin).
No. 39, line   53: Read: h'anmain
No. 39, line   69: Read: naonbhair
No. 39, line   91: Read: in gach
No. 43, line   1: Better: Clanna an Bhaird
No. 44, line 24 varr.: Read: ná G
No. 44, line   48: Read: slógh
No. 44: For further vair. see Notes.

Volume Two

p. 21, line 34: whetting (?); see Glossarial Index.
p. 23, line 2: Read: *Bóghaine* (?); see 27 § 42 n.
p. 41, line 12: Read: The third of U.
p. 60, line 24: Read: rejected — and

p. 61, line 3: Dele comma.

p. 93, line 2: Read: eldest, even if his fellow(-claimant) excel him (i. e. seniority decides here).

p. 103, line 6: Read: about to proclaim

p. 107, lines 13-14: For about . . . thee, read: which makes us timid towards thee,

p. 109, line 1: Read: He sees far off

p. 113, line 15: Read: Fanad

p. 115, line 8: Read: undulating

p. 130, line 8: Read: *Gáiliain.*

p. 136, line 6: Read: green-

p. 142, line 23: Read: would not be profitable

p. 175, line 24: formed the vest; this is a doubtful rendering, see Notes.

p. 177, lines 9-10: See Notes.

p. 190, line 17: Read: BethaCCille. For *tugann t. dá hinntinn* see also under *inntinn* in Glossarial Index.

p. 201, line 23: Read: P. O'C.

p. 205, line 20: Read: the text

p. 207, line 20: Read: old tale

p. 208, line 12: Read: we should

p. 208, line 31: Dele § 49; the Note belongs to § 48.

p. 210, line 39: Read: as there both

p. 211, line 23: Read: Walsh s. v. (i. e. the Lat.-Ir.-Engl. Glossary begun by the Very Rev. Francis Walsh, and completed by Tadhg Ó Neachtain; see Abbott-Gwynn Cat. p. 304).

p. 215, lines 18-20: should follow line 14, the Note belongs to § 6.

p. 217, line 35: For *prios* < Engl. press see Quiggin, *Dialect of Donegal* § 97. It may be an old borrowing.

p. 222, line 41: For *firminte* (nom.) see Glossarial Index.

p. 224, line 16: Dele parenthese.

p. 228, line 6: Mr. J. Delargy refers me to copies of this tract in the Clannaboy MS. and elsewhere.

p. 232, line w: The use of *cruthaighim* with *comhairle* is at least as old as the 12th cent., see TBC 1356; and I erred in assuming a confusion with *crúdh c.* in the ex. cited from 24 P 5.

p. 258, line 12: Read: *Cuairsgi*

p. 260, line 22: Read: it was

p. 261, line 27: Read: had been

p. 265, line 7: Read: merely

p. 265, line 23: Read: *dhraoithibh*

p. 267, line 35: Read: p. 273

p. 269, line 36: Read: and the masc.

p. 280, line 5: Read: suggest

p. 281, line 22: Add after this: § 9 Professor O'Rahilly informs me that this refers to a still unpublished tale, entitled *Céilidhe na hIosgaide.*

p. 2S4, line 32 : Read : Do dheanfuinn
p. 2S5, line 25 : Read : siolánach [sic G].
p. 291, § 1 : comrade ; for *caomthach* cf. *ina choimlebaid 7 ina chaemtach*
      YBL 63ᵇ 36.
p. 293, line 24 : Read : celtische

To Appendix C

p. 305.

(For all but a few of the following additions
and corrections to Appendix C I am indebted
to Professor T. F. O'Rahilly. In referring to the
Cal. of Pat. Rolls Jas. 1 I occasionally cite merely
page and col., as: 335ᵇ.)
Aodh: add. 11 Aodh, Hugh O'Higgin of Kilcomoin.
      Pat. Jas. 1 p. 335ᵇ.
1 Brian, possibly author of poem on David Roche,
      Bk. of Fermoy 117ᵇ 2 (Todd's Cat. p. 49).

p. 307.

As to the n. l. Higginstown, etc., note also the
tl. names : Higginstown, in Killkenny, Longford,
Meath (2), Westmeath (3; Higginston, Inqu. Westmeath, Carol 1 no. 78) and Tipperary. "A parcel
of land near the town of Higgins in bar. of
Roscommon." Pat. Jas. 1 p. 341ᵃ. Cf. further
Castlehiggins, Tipperary (if not modern): Huggins-
town, Killkenny, and Ballyhigeen, Cork.
      9 Brian, cf. add. to 3 Tomás, below.
      12 „ , cf. 9ᵃ Maol Muire, below.

p. 308.

Cairbre, probably another than those mentioned
      above was the subject of the following
      stanzas :

Maghnus .h. Dom*hnaill* .cc.

An oiread oile ar airde
   ar Chairbre mac Ui Uiginn
air chaoile[agu]s ar chuirre
   truagh, a Mhuire, n*ach* ccuirionn.

O n*ach* bhfaghuinn croch ré a cen[n]ach
   [i]san chrichsi 'nair hoileadh Conn
suidh, a Lochluinn, os tú ais airde
   go ccrochuinn riot Cairbre Corr.   H 4. 4, 166.

Here may be noted that a stanza of the satirical composition in Bk. (see Ériu 8, 81 n.) is addressed to: *a mhic Uí Uiginn ó Thuaim.*

Add: 2 Cathal, s. o. Niall (?), Cale mcNevill O'Higane (Donegal or Sligo), prdnd. Pat. 7 Jas. 1 xix p. 151[a].

Add: 2 Cian, grant to Kean O'Higgin of Tybohin (= Tibohine, bar. Frenchpark, Co. Roscommon? cf. under Ruaidhrí, below), gent., Pat. 15 Jas. 1 v p. 333.

p. 310. 3 Cú Choigcriche, these names from Kilcoursey may belong to members of the O Huiginn kindred, see below, add. to 12 Domhnall and 2 Tuileagna.

Add: 6 Cú Choigcriche, grant of land in Dunmore bar., Co. Galway to Cowchegry O'Higgin of Clounebare, Pat. Jas. 1 p. 443[b].

Add: (?) Dailtín (pet-name?), Daltine mcTheige O'Higine (Donegal or Sligo), prdnd. Pat. 7 Jas. 1 xix p. 152.

Add: Domecowne O Higen of Kellbeg (Galway?), prdnd. Fiants 5449. This might stand for Donn Cuan, but that is an unlikely name; possibly < D . . . mac Eoghain.

6 Domhnall, cf. add. to 3 Tomás, below.

p. 311. 12 Domhnall add.: grant of part of Bealanamentan and other lands, including part of Tobber (cf. 8 Uilliam) to Daniel bro. of Tully Higgen (see add. to 2 Tuileagna, below, and cf. p. 310 above), Pat. Jas. 1 p. 563[a].

p. 312. Add: Eochaidh, grant of lands in Dunmore bar., Co. Galway, to Oghy O'Higgin of Elan, Pat. Jas. 1 p. 443[a].

Add: 12 Eóghan, Owen O'Higgen, prdnd. Pat. 7 Jas. 1 xix p. 151.

13 .. , grant to Owen O'Higgin Fitzpatrick of Killinlieh (Co. Sligo), gent., Pat. 15 Jas. 1 viii p. 334.

p. 313.   4 Fearghal Óg, the stanzas referred to are printed
                          below under add. to 6 Tomás.

p. 314.   Add :   5 Giolla Coluim, grant of land in Dunmore
                          bar., Co. Galway, to Gillecollum
                          O'Higgin of Tobber Roe, Pat.
                          Jas. 1 p. 443^b.

           Add :   Giolla Críost, Gillchrist O'Higgine of Tyrone,
                          prdnd. Pat. 6 Jas. 1 cii p. 136.

                   An Giolla Glas, add: MS. written by, see
                          Plummer's *Irish Litanies* (HBS
                          1925) p. xiv n. 2.

                   Giolla na Naomh, Gillernewe O Higen (of Co.
                          Sligo), Fiants 4290 (= 7, 8
                          or 9 ?), and Gillernewe O'Hig-
                          gine, prdnd. Pat. 7 Jas. 1 xix
                          p. 152.

p. 315.   Gráinne: in such records etc.; Professòr O'Rahilly
                          thinks that it is too early for the meaning
                          'wife,' and points out that in each case
                          the woman's own surname may have
                          been Ó Huiginn. Cf. under 2 Con-
                          chobhar.

           Add :   2 Gráinne, grant of land in Dunmore bar.,
                          Co. Galway, to Grany ny Higgin of
                          Claisseganie, Pat. Jas. 1 p. 443^a.

                   Írial, cf. Irrill O'Higgine, Pat. Jas. 1 p. 151^b;
                          pardon to "Bryan O'Flyn, county of Ros-
                          common, convicted for robbing Irriel
                          O'Higgin," Pat. Jas. 1, p. 546-7.

p. 316.   Maol Muire, add: M. s. o. Brian; Mulmurrie
                          McBrian O'Higgine, prdnd. Pat. 7
                          Jas. 1 xix p. 151.

                   2 Maol Seachluinn, add: Melaughlin O'Hugen of
                          Killoam (Co. Galway), Pat. Jas. 1 p. 18^b;
                          grant to Melaghlin O'Higgin of Killowan,
                          in Galway Co., gent.: $^1/_a$ cartron of Killo-
                          wan in said bar. (*viz.* bar. of Teaquin),
                          Pat. Jas. 1 p. 414^b.

p. 317.   2 Mathghamhain, cf. Abbot-Gwynn Cat. p. 48. 8.

Add : Muircheartach, grant of part of Ballinekelly,
Kilcoursey bar. K.'s Co. to Mur-
tagh Higgen, Pat. Jas. 1 p. 563ª.

Add : 7 Niall, Neale O'Higgine (Donegal or Sligo),
prdnd. Pat. 7 Jas. 1 xix p. 151ª. Cf.
also under 2 Cathal, above.

p. 318. Ruaidhrí, probably the earliest on the list should
have been Ruaidhrí Ó Huiginn of Lios
Aedháin in Ciarraighe Airtigh (equated
by Hogan with Lissian, Co. Roscommon,
in bar. of Frenchpark, cf. under 2 Cian,
above), in whose house part of the
Liber Flavus Fergusiorum was written;
see Lib. Fl. i 23ʳᵒa, and Gwynn's description, Proc. RIA xxvi C 2 pp. 15, 24.

p. 319. an sagart Mac Uiginn; cf. the surname Mac
Quiggin, Fiants Eliz. 5523, 6616, 6713,
6724 (Co. Down); later also Quiggin, etc.

p. 320. Add : Seaán Óg, Shane oge O'Higgine, of Tyrone, prdnd.
Pat. 6 Jas. 1 cii p. 136.

Stíofán, add : cf. Ó hAoilleacháin in Fr. Woulfe's
Sloinnte Gaedheal is Gall.

5 Tadhg, add: grant to Teige O'Higgen: Kilbegg
in bar. of Moycashell, Co. Westmeath,
Pat. Jas. 1 p. 481ª (previously surrendered by him, p. 464ª).

p. 321. Add : 9 „ , Thadeus Higgin, schoolmaster in Connacht c. 1608, tutor of Hugo Wardeus,
a student at Salamanca, from Tiriga
(< *Tír Aodha* 'Tirhugh'?), Arch. Hib.
ii 29 (possibly = 8 Tadhg). Cf. also
Theige O'Higgine (Donegal or Sligo),
prdnd. Pat. 7 Jas. 1 xix p. 151ª; Thadeus
O'Higgin of Coolcovally, Co. Sligo, 1616,
Pat. Jas. 1 p. 589ᵇ. See also Dailtín,
above.

p. 323. 3 Tomás, cf. joint grant of lands in Dunmore
bar., Co. Galway, to Thomas O'Higgin
of Kilclunie, Brian O'Higgin of Imlaghlie

and Donnell O'Higgin of Bannaghir
Pat. Jas. 1 p. 443ª.

6 Tomás, the stanzas referred to are:

Ni he Tómás O Huiginn
   maith thuigim ar a dhántaibh
daoi dhúir n-oigeadh nemhglan
   acht Ferghal Og a bhráthair.

A bprós 7 a mhiodarracht [sic]
   da gcuireadh ar Ferghal dólás
adeir an t-aois ealadhan   .
   go bhfuil anollamh (?) Tómás
                        B iv 1, 126ª

some lines are obscure and apparently corrupt.

Add: 7 Tomás, Thomas O'Higgin O. P., hanged by
     Cromwellians (at Clonmel?) 1651,
     Murphy, *Our Martyrs* p. 337-8.

p. 324.   4 Tuathal, add: grant of part o estate (in
     Killclouny) of "Towhill O'Higgen (of
     same), slain in rebellion," Pat. Jas. 1
     p. 81ª (1606); grant of castle and
     part of lands of Towthill O'Higgin (in
     Killcloyne), slain in rebellion, ib. 179ᵇ.

6   . ,, , cf. grant of land in Dunmore bar.,
     Co. Galway, to Tuohill O'Higgin of
     Cullencleigh, Pat. Jas. 1 p. 443ª.

2 Tuileagna, Professor O'Rahilly suggests that
     Tully < Tuathal here. Cf. grant
     of Gurtyn etc., Kilcoursey bar.,
     King's Co., to Tully Higgen (= Toole
     p. 310. 10 above), Pat. Jas. 1 p. 563ª.

Add: Uaithne (?), Oney O'Higgen (Donegal or Sligo),
     prdnd. Pat. 7 Jas. 1 xix p. 151. Cf.
     4 Eóghan for another possible in-
     stance of Uaithne.

p. 325.   8 Uilliam, for Tubber, cf. add. to 12 Domhnall.

Printed by Karras, Kröber & Nietschmann, Halle-an-Saale (Germany).

IRISH TEXTS SOCIETY,

—◦— ···◦||◦··· —◦—

OFFICERS, 1922.

PRESIDENT:

PROFESSOR DOUGLAS HYDE, D.Litt., LL.D., M.R.I.A.

Joint { Miss ELEANOR HULL.   } c/o National Bank,
Honorary Secretaries { T. D. FITZGERALD, B.A. }   Charing Cross,
Honorary Treasurer—T. A ENGLAND, I.L.D. }   London, S.W. 1.

VICE-PRESIDENTS:

THE RIGHT HON. LORD CASTLETOWN, K.P., C.M.G.
THE MOST REV. DR. O'DONNELL, D.D.
THE RIGHT REV. THOMAS J. SHAHAN, D.D.

EXECUTIVE COUNCIL:

Chairman—ROBIN FLOWER, B.A.

MRS. M. M. BANKS.	M. J. FITZGERALD.
J. BUCKLEY, M.R.I.A.	A. M. FREEMAN.
J. S. CRONE, M.D., J.P., M.R.I.A.	THE REV. T. O'SULLIVAN.

Distributors—SIMPKIN, MARSHALL, HAMILTON, KENT & Co., 4 Stationers' Hall Court, London, E.C. 4.

CONSULTATIVE COMMITTEE:

DR. J. BAUDIS.	DR. CARL MARSTRANDER.
PROFESSOR OSBORN BERGIN, PH.D.	PROF. TADHG Ó DONNCHADHA.
REV. P. S. DINNEEN, M.A., D.LITT.	J. G. O'KEEFFE.
PROFESSOR G. DOTTIN.	PROF. TOMÁS O'MAÍLLE, M.A., PH.D.
PROFESSOR HENRI GAIDOZ.	PROF. T. F. O'RAHILLY, M.A., M.R.I.A.
PROFESSOR EDWARD GWYNN, F.T.C.D.	DR. HOLGER PEDERSEN.
PROF. DOUGLAS HYDE, LL.D., M.R.I.A.	PROF. F. N. ROBINSON.
J. H. LLOYD, M.R.I.A.	PROF. DR. L. RUDOLF THURNEYSEN
PROFESSOR J. LOTH.	PROFESSOR J. VENDRYES.
PROF. JOHN MACNEILL, D LITT.	

N.B.—New Address: c/o National Bank Ltd., Charing Cross, London, S.W I.

THE IRISH TEXTS SOCIETY *was established in* 1898 *for the purpose of publishing texts in the Irish language, accompanied by such introductions, English translations, glossaries, and notes as may be deemed desirable.*

The Annual Subscription (from 1st *January,* 1922*),*is* 21/-*(American subscribers,* $5), *payable on* 1st *January, on payment of which members will be entitled to receive, post free, the current volume. There is no entrance fee.*

NOTE.—Regular members, whose subscriptions have been paid up to date, may, however, fill up gaps in their sets of back volumes at 12/6 *per volume.*

The payment of a single sum of £12 12s. 0d. *(colonial or foreign members* £13 0s. 0d.; *American members* 65 dollars*), entitles to life membership. Life members will receive one copy of each volume issued subsequently to the receipt of this sum by the Society.*

Vols. I., II. III. and XIV. are now out of print and others are rapidly becoming scarce. The ordinary sale price to non-members through Messrs. Simpkin, Marshall & Co, is 25/- *per volume (post free).*

The Council makes a strong appeal to all interested in the preservation and publication of Irish Manuscripts to join the Society and to contribute to its funds, and especially to the Editorial Fund, which has been established for the remuneration of Editors for their arduous work.

NOTE Change of Address.

All communications should be addressed to the Hon. Secretary, Irish Texts Society, c/o National Bank Ltd., Charing Cross, London, S.W.1.

* See Subscriptions, infra pp. 4, 8.

FATHER DINNEEN'S IRISH-ENGLISH DICTIONARY.

The Council is anxiously pressing on the new edition of its Irish-English Dictionary, a work of the most urgent importance at the present moment. In view of the new developments, it is imperative that it should be published at once. The Council has engaged Father Dinneen to make the new work a far fuller and more useful book than the first Dictionary of eighteen years ago. The compilation of the work is complete, and only lack of funds prevents its immediate publication.

Large funds are urgently needed for this national object. The Society will be glad to receive either Donations or Loans. All the loans provided for the first Dictionary, amounting to over £500, were repaid shortly after publication. A yet larger amount is now required, in addition to what the Society has in hand. The Society looks to the Irish people at home and abroad to enable it to carry this undertaking through.

Contributions should be sent to T. D. FitzGerald, B.A., Hon. Secretary, or to T. A. England LL.D., Hon. Treasurer, Irish Texts Society, c/o National Bank Ltd., Charing Cross, London, S.W. 1.

To the Hon. Secretary, Irish Texts Society,

  c o National Bank Ltd.,

    Charing Cross, London, S.W. 1.

I enclose herewith $\left\{\begin{array}{l}\textit{Postal Order}\\ \textit{Money Order}\\ \textit{Cheque}\end{array}\right\}$ for £ : :

being my $\left\{\begin{array}{l}\textit{donation}\\ \textit{loan (repayable)}\end{array}\right\}$ to the IRISH TEXTS SOCIETY

for the production of their new edition of Father Dinneen's

Irish-English Dictionary.

Signed...
    Please add designation, Mr, Mrs., &c.

Address

Date

FORM OF APPLICATION.

·——

I shall be glad to have my name added to the List of Members of the
IRISH TEXTS SOCIETY, and I enclose the sum of

being {

First Annual Subscription

Life Membership Subscription } for Volumes No.

Donation

Name

Address

Date

To Hon. Secretary, Irish Texts Society,
c/o National Bank Ltd.,
Charing Cross, London, S.W. 1.

IRISH TEXTS SOCIETY.

————◄◆►————

THE Twenty-third Annual Meeting of the Irish Texts Society
was held on 28th January, 1922, in the library of the Irish
Literary Society, London, W.C.1.

Mr. R. Flower, Chairman of the Executive Council, presided.

The Minutes of the last Annual Meeting, held on 22nd January,
1921, were taken as read. The Honorary Secretary read the

TWENTY-THIRD ANNUAL REPORT.

The Council has to report that at the close of the year 1921
the Poems of Tadhg Dall O h-Uiggin (in two volumes) already
announced for the years 1920 and 1921 are still in the hands of
the printers. The printing has been delayed owing to the
pressure on the editor, Miss Eleanor Knott, of private business
which could not be neglected. But before the end of the
year 1921, proofs of 240 pages of Part I. of Tadhg Dall had been
passed and it is hoped that this volume will not now be much
further delayed. Part II. should follow at a very short interval ;
the printing of this volume should be a much more rapid process
owing to the fact that all the text and other matter in Irish will
appear in the first part, the second containing the translation,
notes and other subsidiary matter.

The Poems of the O Neills of Clannaboy, edited by Professor
Tadhg O Donnchadha, are still under revision, as the work is
one of much difficulty. This publication, in two volumes, was in-
tended for the years 1922 and 1923, but the Council has decided
to proceed during the present year with the printing of "The
Pursuit of Gruaidh Grian-Sholus," a prose romance of the
Cuchulainn cycle, edited from a unique copy in a 17th century
MS. in Trinity College, Dublin, by Miss Cecile O Rahilly, M.A.

The publication of the above-mentioned works will bring the
number of the Society's volumes up to twenty-six, including the
larger and smaller Irish-English dictionaries edited by the Rev.
P. S. Dinneen, M.A., D.Litt.

The printing of the new and revised edition of the larger
dictionary has not yet been undertaken owing to the inadequate
response to the widely distributed appeals for donations in aid
of the project. No help has hitherto been received from any
national organisation in Ireland.

4

The amounts received during 1921 were : Donations £56 1s.0d., Loans £123 13s. 6d., bringing the total Donations to £219 0s. 0d. and total Loans to £780 10s. 6d. It is hoped that one of the results of the changed conditions in Ireland may be that this project shall receive some worthy measure of support especially as regards donations, and that more Irishmen and women will see their way to support the work of the Society generally by becoming members during the present year and by purchasing the volumes already published. The increase in the amount of the subscription from 12/6 to 21/-, which was decided upon at the last annual meeting came into force on the 1st January, 1922. (For the other rates see rules 9 and 12).

The Council did not recommend this increase without careful consideration of the financial condition of the Society and no time shall be lost in reducing the subscription again, as soon as the costs of paper, printing and binding and the number of regularly paying members warrant an alteration. In this connection, it may be pointed out that, should the volume for the year in which a member joins be not ready, he may, at his option, have one of the earlier volumes of the series or may await the publication of the volume for the year in which he joins. For subsequent years, members are expected and are indeed required by the rules of the Society to pay the annual subscription in January and to take the current volume. The records show that despite constant reminders and the circulation of the usual notices several members of long standing pay their subscriptions at rare intervals, and have consequently many gaps in their sets of the Society's publications. It is proposed to alter the wording of Rule 13 to read "Members whose subscriptions are in arrear shall not have the right of voting at the Annual General Meeting of the Society."

Volume 14 (for 1912) "an Irish Astronomical Tract" is now out of print, as are also Volumes 1, 2 and 3, but Volume 3a (Revised Edition of O Rahilly's Poems, 1909) is still available. The stock of certain other volumes is running low.

The Council gratefully acknowledge the receipt of the sum of £300 0s. 0d., being an instalment of a legacy of £500 0s. 0d. from the estate of the late Mr. P. O Kinealy a generous friend of the Society.*

Forty-seven new ordinary members and three new life members joined the Society during the year 1921. Eight ordinary members became life members. There have been five resignations and two deaths have been reported. There are now about four hundred members including forty-two life members.

---

* The total amount of this legacy has now been paid over to the Society by the Trustees.

On the proposal of Dr. Crone, seconded by Mr. James Buckley, M.R.I.A., the report was adopted.

The financial statement and balance sheet presented by Dr. England were adopted on the proposal of Dr. Crone, seconded by the Rev. T. O'Sullivan.

To fill a vacancy it was resolved, on the proposal of Dr. Crone, seconded by the Rev. T. O Sullivan, that the name of Mr. James Buckley, M.R.I.A., be added to the Council.

The re-election of the outgoing members of the Council, Mr. Robin Flower, Mr. M. J. FitzGerald and the Rev. T. O Sullivan, was carried on the proposal of Mrs. Banks, seconded by Dr. England.

The re-election of Professor Douglas Hyde as President of the Society, of Miss Eleanor Hull and Mr. T. D. FitzGerald as Joint Honorary Secretaries, and of Dr. England as Hon. Treasurer, was carried unanimously on the proposal of Mr. James Buckley, seconded by Mrs. Banks.

The Council received with much regret the resignation of Mr. Charlton B. Walker upon the occasion of his going abroad, and a resolution thanking Mr. Walker for his valuable services and advice to the Council was passed on the proposal of the Rev. T. O Sullivan, seconded by Mr. T. D. FitzGerald.

A hearty vote of thanks was accorded to Mr. R. W. Farrell, F.L.A.A., for auditing the accounts, and his appointment as auditor for 1922 was confirmed.

IRISH TEXTS SOCIETY.

FINANCIAL STATEMENT, 1921.

INCOME AND EXPENDITURE ACCOUNT FOR YEAR 1921.

EXPENDITURE.	£	s.	d.	RECEIPTS.	£	s.	d
By Editorial Fees:—				By Subscriptions, Ordinary	336	8	10
Dictionary	80	0	0	„ Life Members,	64	10	0
.. Printing and Binding...	145	10	7	„ Donations to Editorial			
.. Rent, Insurance, Sun-				Fund	8	18	0
dries	11	12	6	,. Interest on Investments	37	7	5
„Salary, Postage & Stationery	57	12	3	,, Advertisements in Annual			
				Report	6	0	0
				„ Sales of Smaller Diction-			
				y 1920	200	16	3
				.. New Dictionary Fund:—			
				Loans 1921 ...	123	13	6
				Donations 1921 ...	56	1	0
				„ Legacy	300	0	0
				„ Postage for Irish Folk			
				Song Society ...		14	7
Balance	839	14	3				
	1134	9	7		1134	9	7

BALANCE SHEET.

LIABILITIES	£	s	d.	ASSETS.	£	s.	d.
Dictionary Fund Loans to				Investments—			
31 12/1921	780	10	6	£300 War Loan at 92¾ ...	278	5	0
Income Tax...	11	8	0	£250 C.N. Rly. Stk. at 73 ...	182	10	
Printing of Work in hand ...	171	10	0	Sales of Smaller Dictionary			
Distribution of Volumes ...	3	2	0	(estimate)	200	0	0
Postage due to secretary ...	2	5	0	Value of Stock of Volumes			
				(Estimate at Cost) ...	1100	0	0
				Advertisements in Annual			
				Report—Outstanding ...	2	15	0
				Cash—			
				On Deposit	400	0	0
				Current A c. at Bank	995	11	2
Balance	2195	5	8	Cash in hand	5	0	0
	3164	1	2		3164	1	2

T. A. ENGLAND, Hon. Treasurer.

The undersigned, having had access to all the Books and Accounts of the Society, and having examined the foregoing statements and verified them with the Books, Deeds and Documents, etc., relating thereto, now signs the same as found to be correct.

ROBERT W. FARRELL, F.L.A.A.,
Certified Accountant.

13th February, 1922.

GENERAL RULES.

────── ·• ──────

OBJECTS.

1.—The Society is instituted for the purpose of promoting the publication of Texts in the Irish Language, accompanied by such Introductions, English Translations, Glossaries and Notes as may be deemed desirable.

CONSTITUTION.

2.—The Society shall consist of a President, Vice-Presidents, an Executive Council, a Consultative Committee and Ordinary and Life Members.

OFFICERS.

3.—The Officers of the Society shall be the President, the Honorary Secretaries and the Honorary Treasurer.

EXECUTIVE COUNCIL.

4.—The entire management of the Society shall be entrusted to the Executive Council, consisting of the Officers of the Society and not more than ten other Members, to whom the Executive Council may add by co-optation not more than two members, who shall retire annually.

5.—All property of the Society shall be vested in the Executive Council, and shall be disposed of as they shall direct by a two-thirds majority.

6.—Three Members of the Executive Council shall retire each year by rotation at the Annual General Meeting, but shall be eligible for re-election, the Members to retire being selected according to seniority of election, or, in case of equality, by lot. The Council shall have power to co-opt Members to fill up casual vacancies occurring throughout the year. Any Member of Council who is absent from five consecutive Ordinary Meetings of the Council to which he (or she) has been duly summoned, shall be considered as having vacated his (or her) place on the Council.

CONSULTATIVE COMMITTEE.

7.—The Consultative Committee, or individual Members thereof, shall give advice, when consulted by the Executive Council, on questions relating to the Publications of the Society, but shall not be responsible for the management of the business of the Society.

MEMBERS.

8.—Members may be elected either at the Annual General Meeting, r from time to time, by the Executive Council.

Subscription.

9.—The Subscription for each Member of the Society shall (from 1st January, 1922,) be £1 1s. 0d. per annum (American subscribers, $5), entitling the Member to one copy (post free) of the volume published by the Society for the year, and giving the right to vote on all questions submitted to the General Meetings of the Society. Regular members, whose subscriptions have been paid up to date, may, however, fill up gaps in their sets of back volumes at 12/6 per volume. The payment of a single sum of £12 12s. 0d. (Colonial or foreign members £13 0s. 0d., American members 65 dollars) entitles to life membership. Life members will receive one copy of each volume issued subsequently to the receipt of this sum by the Society.

10.—Subscriptions shall be payable in advance on the 1st January in each year.

11.—Members whose Subscriptions for the year have not been paid are not entitled to any volume published by the Society for that year, and any Member whose Subscription for the current year remains unpaid, and who receives and retains any publication for the year, shall be held liable for the payment of the full published price of such publication.

12.—The Publications of the Society shall not be sold to persons other than Members, except at the advanced price of 25/- (from 1st January, 1922).

13.—Members whose Subscriptions are in arrear shall not have the right of voting at the Annual General Meeting of the Society.

14.—Members wishing to resign must give notice in writing to the Honorary Secretary, before the end of the year, of their intention to do so : otherwise they will be liable for their subscriptions for the ensuing year.

Editorial Fund.

15.—A fund shall be opened for the remuneration of Editors for their work in preparing Texts for publication. All subscriptions and donations to this fund shall be purely voluntary, and shall not be applicable to other purposes of the Society.

Annual General Meeting.

16.—A General Meeting shall be held each year in the month of January, or as soon after as the Executive Council shall determine, when the Council shall submit their Report and the Accounts of the Society for the preceding year, and when vacant seats on the Council shall be filled up, and the ordinary business of a General Meeting transacted.

Audit.

17.—The Accounts of the Society shall be audited each year by auditors appointed at the preceding General Meeting.

Changes in these Rules.

18.—With the notice summoning the General Meeting, the Executive Council shall give notice of any change proposed by them in these Rules. Ordinary Members proposing any change in the Rules must give notice thereof in writing to the Honorary Secretary seven clear days before the date of the Annual General Meeting.

LIST OF IRISH
TEXTS SOCIETY'S PUBLICATIONS.

(Out of print).

(1.) Ꝼɪoᴌᴌᴀ ᴀɴ Ꝼɪuᵹᴀ. [The Lad of the Ferule].
Eᴀᴄᴛᴘᴀ Cᴌoᵯɴe Ꝛɪᵹ ɴᴀ ħ-ɪoᵯᴀɪᵳe [Adventures of the
Children of the King of Norway].
Edited by
PROFESSOR DOUGLAS HYDE, D.Litt., LL.D.

(Out of print).

(2.) Ꝼᴌeᴅ Ƀᴘɪcᴘeɴᴅ [The Feast of Bricriu].
(From Leabhar na h-Uidhre).
Edited by GEORGE HENDERSON, M.A., Ph.D.

(Out of print.) See (Volume 3a) New Edition.

(3.) Ɗᴀɴᴛᴀ Ꝃoᵳᴀᵹᴀɪɴ uɪ Ꝛᴀᴄᴀɪᴌᴌe [The Poems of Egan
O'Rahilly].
Edited, chiefly from Mss. in Maynooth College, by
REV. P. S. DINNEEN, M.A., D.Litt

(Volume for 1909.) (See No. 3.)

(3A.) New Edition of the Poems of Egan O'Rahilly.
Revised by PROFESSOR Ꞇᴀᵭᵹ ó Ɗoɴɴᴄᴀᵭᴀ and
REV. P. S. DINNEEN, M.A., D.Litt.

10

(*Volume for* 1901.)

(4.) Ⲣⲟⲣⲁⲣ Ⲫⲉⲁⲣⲁ ⲁⲣ Ⲉⲓⲣⲓⲛⲛ [History of Ireland]. By
GEOFFREY KEATING. Part I. (See Vols. 8,
9, 15).
Edited by DAVID COMYN, ESQ., M.R.I.A.

___

(*Volume for* 1902.)

(5.) Ⲥⲁⲓⲧⲣⲉⲓⲙ Ⲥⲟⲛⲅⲁⲓⲗ Ⲥⲗⲁⲓⲣⲓⲛⲅⲛⲓⲅ (The Martial Career
of Conghal Clairinghneach. .
Edited by The
VERY REV. PROFESSOR P.M. MacSWEENEY, M.A

___

(*Volume for* 1903.)

(6.) Virgil's Æneid, the Irish Version, from the Book
of Ballymote.
Edited by REV. GEORGE CALDER, B.D., D.Litt.

___

(*Volume for* 1904.)

(7.) Ⲇⲩⲁⲛⲁⲓⲣⲉ Ⲫⲓⲛⲛ. The Poem Book of Finn. [Ossianic
Poems].
Edited by PROFESSOR JOHN MacNEILL, D.Litt.

___

(*Volume for* 1905.)

(8.) Ⲣⲟⲣⲁⲣ Ⲫⲉⲁⲣⲁ ⲁⲣ Ⲉⲓⲣⲓⲛⲛ [History of Ireland]. By
GEOFFREY KEATING. Part II.
Edited by REV. P. S. DINNEEN, M.A., D.Litt.
(See Vols. 4, 9, and 15).

___

(*Volume for* 1906.)

(9.) Ⲣⲟⲣⲁⲣ Ⲫⲉⲁⲣⲁ ⲁⲣ Ⲉⲓⲣⲓⲛⲛ [History of Ireland]. By
GEOFFREY KEATING. Part III.
Edited by REV. P. S. DINNEEN, M.A., D.Litt.
(See Vols. 4, 8, and 15).

___

(*Volume for* 1907.)

(10.) Two Arthurian Romances [Ⲉⲁⲉⲧⲣⲁ Ⲙⲁⲥⲁⲟⲓⲙ ⲁⲛ
ⲓⲟⲗⲁⲓⲣ ⲁⲅⲩⲣ Ⲉⲁⲉⲧⲣⲁ ⲁⲛ Ⲙⲁⲇⲣⲁ Ⲙⲁⲟⲓⲗ.] Adventures
of the Eagle Boy and Crop Eared Dog
Edited by
PROFESSOR R. A. S. MacALISTER, M.A., D.Litt.

11

(Volume for 1908.)

(11.) Poems of David O'Bruadair.　(Part I.)

Edited by REV. J. MacERLEAN, S.J.

(See Vols. 13, 18).

Volume for 1909—*see 3a supra).*

(Volume for 1910.)

(12.) Buile Suibhne Geilt, A Middle-Irish Romance.

Edited by J. G. O'KEEFFE.

(Volume for 1911.)

(13.) Poems of David O'Bruadair.　(Part II.)

Edited by REV. J. MacERLEAN, S.J.

(See Vols. 11, 18).

(Volume for 1912—*Out of Print).*

[(14.　An Irish Astronomical Tract, based on a Mediæval Latin version of a work by Messahalah.

Edited by MAURA POWER M.A]

N.B.—Volume 14 is out of print.

(Volume for 1913.)

(15.) Foраг Реага аг Éinn　[History of Ireland].　By GEOFFREY KEATING. Part IV. Containing the Genealogies and Synchronisms and an index including the elucidation of place names and annotations to Parts I., II., III.　(See Vols. 4, 8, 9 *supra.*)

Compiled and Edited by REV. P. S. DINNEEN. M.A.

(Volume for 1914.)

(16.) Life of St. Declan of Ardmore and Life of St. Mochuda of Lismore.

Edited by REV. PROFESSOR P. POWER, M.R.I.A.

(*Volume for* 1915).

(17.) Poems of Turlogh O'Carolan and additional Poems.

Edited by
PROFESSOR TOMÁS O'MÁILLE, M.A., Ph D.

(*Volume for* 1916.)

(18.) Poems of David O'Bruadair; (Part III.)

Edited by REV. J. MacERLEAN, S.J.
(See Vols. 11, 13).

(*Volume for* 1917).

(19.) ᵹᴀ́ḃᴀℓᴄᴀṗ Ṡeṗℓᴜıṗ ṁóıṗ [The Wars of Charlemagne].

Edited by
PROF DOUGLAS HYDE, D.Litt., LL.D., M.R.I.A.

(*Volume for* 1918).

(20.) ıoṁᴀṗḃᴀ́ᵹ nᴀ ḃᶠıℓeᴀ́ḋ [The Contention of the Bards]. (Part I.)

Edited by REV. LAMBERT McKENNA, S.J., M.A.

(*Volume for* 1919).

(21.) ıoṁᴀṗḃᴀ́ᵹ nᴀ ḃᶠıℓeᴀ́ḋ (Part II.)

Edited by REV. LAMBERT McKENNA, S.J., M.A.

(*Volumes for* 1920 *and* 1921).

(22 & 23.) Poems of Cᴀ́ḋᵹ Ḋᴀℓℓ O ṅℓıᵹınn (in 2 vols.)

Edited by MISS ELEANOR KNOTT (*in the press, see p.* 3).

(*Volume for* 1922).

(24.) The Pursuit of ᵹṗᴜᴀıḋ ᵹṗᴜᴀn-ṗoℓᴜṗ.

Edited from a MS. in Trinity College, Dublin, by MISS CECILE O'RAHILLY, M.A. (*in the press, see p.* 3).

The Society's Larger Irish-English Dictionary, edited by Rev. P. S. Dinneen, M.A., is now out of print. *See Report.* The Smaller Irish-English Dictionary, by the same author, can be had of all booksellers, price 4/- net.

ImTheStory.com

Personalized Classic Books in many genre's

Unique gift for kids, partners, friends, colleagues

Customize:

- Character Names
- Upload your own front/back cover images (optional)
- Inscribe a personal message/dedication on the inside page (optional)

Customize many titles Including
- Alice in Wonderland
- Romeo and Juliet
- The Wizard of Oz
- A Christmas Carol
- Dracula
- Dr. Jekyll & Mr. Hyde
- And more...

CPSIA information can be obtained at www.ICGtesting.com
Printed in the USA
BVOW04s2229040514

352422BV00013BA/367/P